Scottish Planning Appeals

Scottish Planning Appeals

Decisions on Law and Procedure

By

ERIC YOUNG, M.A., LL.B.,
Reader in Law, University of Strathclyde

W. GREEN/SWEET & MAXWELL
EDINBURGH
1991

First Published in 1991 by
W. Green & Son Ltd.

© 1991 W. Green & Son Ltd.

British Library Cataloguing in Publication Data
Young, Eric *1941–*
Scottish planning appeals.
1. Scotland. Environment planning. Law
344.110645

ISBN 0 414 00931 2

Typeset by
LBJ Enterprises Ltd., Tadley.
Printed in Great Britain by
Butler & Tanner Ltd, Frome and London

PREFACE

The notes of which this book is made up seek to extract points of legal and procedural interest from decisions on appeals under the town and country planning legislation made by the Secretary of State for Scotland or persons appointed for the purpose of determining appeals (*i.e.* reporters of the Scottish Office Inquiry Reporters Unit). In recent years the great majority of appeals have been determined by reporters.

The decision on a planning appeal will often turn on the application of perceived principles of good planning to the facts of the particular case but elements of law, procedure and policy will sometimes be relevant. Though one cannot speak of precedent in connection with planning appeals, it may well be useful to consider previous appeal decisons as indicating the views of those who have to make the decisions, the Secretary of State and his reporters, on matters of law and procedure. Some of the decisions noted here provide examples of the application of established principles of law to particular facts. In other cases, where the particular matter has not yet come before the courts, the point in issue may be worthy of serious consideration; at the very least a previous decision is a "material consideration."

The points highlighted in this book are drawn from the whole range of appeals which may be made under the town and country planning legislation and include appeals against the refusal or conditional grant of planning permission, appeals against enforcement notices, listed building appeals, waste land appeals and advertisement appeals. The decision letters (identified by their Scottish Office reference numbers) and, where appropriate, the inquiry reports on appeals are available for reference at the National Library of Scotland and can also be obtained from The Planning Exchange. The Scottish Planning Appeal Decisions (SPADs) service, available from The Planning Exchange, comprises monthly reports containing summaries of all Scottish appeal decisions indexed by year, a telephone inquiry service, and provision of copies of decision letters.

It is intended that this book be used in conjunction with a planning law textbook and therefore each section contains a reference to the appropriate part of *Scottish Planning Law and Procedure*, by E. Young and J. Rowan-Robinson (Hodge, 1985).

Eric Young

CONTENTS

TABLE OF CASES

ix

TABLE OF STATUTES

TABLE OF STATUTORY INSTRUMENTS

ABBREVIATIONS

1972 Act — The Town and Country Planning (Scotland) Act 1972.

DCPN — Development Control Policy Note.

DoE — Department of the Environment.

DHS — Department of Health for Scotland.

EUC — Established use certificate.

GDO — The Town and Country Planning (General Development) (Scotland) Order 1975 or The Town and Country Planning (General Development) (Scotland) Order 1981, as appropriate.

SDD — Scottish Development Department.

SEPD — Scottish Economic Planning Department.

UCO — The Town and Country Planning (Use Classes) (Scotland) Order 1973.

SECTION 1

ADMINISTRATION

This short section is made up of summaries of appeal decisions concerned with administrative matters. Appeal number 1.1 involves the question of how the situation is to be resolved when copies of a plan accompanying a planning application have been lost. Numbers 1.2 to 1.4 raise the question of personal bar in planning law. Personal bar in a planning context is dealt with at some length in Chapter 2 of Young and Rowan-Robinson, *Scottish Planning Law and Procedure.*

Appeal 1.5 raises the question whether an appeal is rendered incompetent by the fact that the appellant's option to purchase the land in question has expired. In appeal number 1.6 the Secretary of State decided that the re-siting of a proposed development would require a fresh planning application. In appeal 1.7 the reporter concluded that where there had been a deemed refusal of planning permission, grounds of appeal were not required.

A dispute as to whether the applicant owned all the land which was the subject of the application was said by the reporter in appeal 1.8 to be a legal matter which would perhaps have to be settled by the courts in due course. Appeals numbers 1.9 to 1.12 raise the question of who is an "aggrieved person" for the purposes of a planning appeal. Appeals 1.13 and 1.14 are concerned with "call in" by regional planning authorities.

1

APPEAL DECISIONS

1.1 Extrinsic evidence

Copies of a plan accompanying an application made in 1949 had been lost. The planning authority had to rely on extrinsic evidence in support of their contention that the permission applied only to a limited area which excluded the appeal site. The reporter was persuaded that such evidence could be accepted in a case like this. He referred to *Miller-Mead* v. *Minister of Housing and Local Government* [1963] 2 Q.B. 196, and *Slough Estates* v. *Slough Borough Council* [1971] A.C. 967. These cases established that it would be in order to have regard to evidence from people who had seen a lost plan and to build up a case on a balance of probabilities. (Ref. P/ENA/SA/56, February 3, 1986.)

1.2 Domestic garages—finish—personal bar

Enforcement notices had been served in respect of the finish of two domestic garages. In terms of the planning permission, the garages were to be recessed behind the building lines of the houses and the pilasters to be finished in granite. They were finished in synthetic stone. There was doubt about what information or assurances (if any) had passed at meetings between the appellants and one of the authority's officers but the reporter concluded that there was no firm evidence of the officer's acquiescing in the use of the materials employed, and no personal bar could be established against the authority. The synthetic material was to be replaced by natural granite. (Refs. P/PPA/GA/116; P/ENA/GA/39, January 14, 1982.)

1.3 Personal bar—applicability

The appellant alleged in this case that the planning authority were personally barred from taking enforcement action against him. On the basis of the court cases cited by both sides, it appeared to the reporter that personal bar could arise where a council official, acting with the authority of his council, provided a specific statement to an applicant in response to a specific request; and always taking account of fairness both to the applicant and to other affected persons.

In this case an enforcement notice related to activities at a sand pit. The Director of Planning had in a report to the authority relating in part to the issue of a waste disposal licence mentioned "backfilling of waste materials" but the report contained a clear caveat as to the scope of the advice. The advice related to future intentions whereas the enforcement notice related to existing activities at the site. In addition the enforcement notice related to existing activities not covered by the proposed waste disposal licence. Bearing in mind the caveat in the report to the authority, the reporter considered that neither the limited matter there referred to nor the proposed large scale tipping corresponded to the breaches of planning control. Further, the advice seemed to be incorrect and it would have been grossly unfair to nearby residents to accept it as binding on the planning authority and their enforcement notice. The reporter therefore found that the advice did not relate to the matters which were the subject of the enforcement notice and that the planning authority were not personally barred by their actions from pursuing the present enforcement action. (Ref. P/ENA/FC/19, March 24, 1987.)

1.4 Enforcement notice—personal bar—authority's discretionary power

The appellant was served with an enforcement notice in respect of the parking of a commercial vehicle within the curtilage of his house. He argued that no action had been taken in respect of the parking of taxis, of mobile shops and of other commercial vehicles parked within driveways in the district. He claimed that the planning authority were biased in taking action in his case while others escaped. The reporter said that it was not to be expected that the authority would take action against every breach of control. The power to take action was a discretionary one. (Ref. P/ENA/LA/62, October 4, 1983.)

1.5 Option to purchase expired—competency of appeal

At a public inquiry into an appeal against a refusal of planning permission, it emerged that the appellant's option to purchase a shop property had expired. The reporter considered whether the appeal had been rendered incompetent by the expiry of the option. He noted that the correct certification procedures had been followed at the time of the planning application. Since there was a possibility that the appellants might still acquire the property if the appeal was successful it was, he thought, competent for the appeal to be determined. (Ref. P/PPA/GA/86, December 12, 1980.)

1.6 Appeal—amendment—mast—location—height

In the course of an appeal against the refusal of planning permission for a microwave radio station and mast the appellant sought to relocate the station and reduce the height of the proposed mast. The Secretary of State agreed that the appeal could proceed on the basis of the original application subject to amendment of the height of the mast. He denied the request to re-site the station as this constituted a material change of the original application. A change of location would require a fresh application to the planning authority. (Refs. P/PPA/LD/77; P/PPA/FB/158, February 4, 1986.)

1.7 Appeal—grounds required—deemed refusal of a planning permission

This was an appeal against the failure of the planning authority to issue a decision within the prescribed period on an application for outline permission.

At the opening of the inquiry the planning authority moved that the appeal be dismissed without the hearing of evidence because no grounds of appeal had been submitted as required by the Town and Country Planning (General Development) (Scotland) Order 1981. The appeal depended on a legal fiction that the application had been refused. All that the appellants had said was that there had been a failure to determine their application and that did not provide a basis for proceeding to a public inquiry. It was the case that the Scottish Development Department had ruled that the appeal was sufficiently constituted but that had not meant that grounds of appeal were not required to follow. The appellants had flouted the intentions of Parliament. In support of this motion the planning authority referred to the following cases: *London and Clydeside Estates Ltd.* v. *Aberdeen District Council*, 1980 S.L.T. 81; *Howard* v. *Secretary of State for the Environment* [1974] 2 W.L.R. 459; and *Brayhead (Ascot) Ltd.* v. *Berkshire County Council* [1964] 2 W.L.R. 507. It was usually the local authorities who had failed to act as required, but the same principles were applicable to the appellants in the present case. These cases showed that grounds of appeal could have been submitted at any time subsequent to the lodging of the appeal.

For the appellants it was submitted that the motion was without foundation. Where an application had not been determined in the prescribed period or in such extended period as might be agreed on, the provisions of section 33 of the 1972 Act were applied as if planning permission had been refused. By the GDO the planning authority were required to state reasons for refusal of planning permission or imposition of conditions on a grant of planning permission. Where a planning authority had failed to state reasons for a refusal of a planning permission, a proper ground of appeal was that there had been a failure to give reasons and the position was precisely the same where there had been a failure to determine an application. Where no reasons for refusal of planning permission were available the appellant need do no more and perhaps could do no more than say that the application had not been determined.

The reporter ruled that the inquiry should proceed for the reason that common sense suggested that grounds of appeal were a direct response to reasons for refusal of planning permission or imposition of conditions on a grant of planning permission, as the case might be. It was implicit in a deemed refusal of planning permission that there were no reasons available to the applicant and so the only logical ground of appeal was that used in the present case, *i.e.* that the planning authority had not made its decision known within the statutory period. (Ref. P/PPA/GA/132, November 29, 1982.)

1.8 Planning application—ownership of land—not a question for reporter

The planning authority denied the appellant's claim that he owned all of the land which was the subject of the application. The reporter said that this was a legal matter which would perhaps have to be settled in court in due course. In the event of the reporter sustaining the appeal, the matter would become of critical importance. It was not, however, a matter for the reporter to decide. (Ref. P/PPA/CC/182, June 27, 1988.)

1.9 Appeal procedure—whether person "aggrieved" by decision—authority not prepared to sell site—bank office

This was an appeal against a refusal of planning permission for the creation of a bank office. Where an applicant for planning permission is "aggrieved" by such a decision he is entitled to appeal to the Secretary of State (1972 Act, section 33(1)). Here the Secretary of State considered whether the bank had a right to appeal. Even if they had been granted planning permission, they would not have been able to implement the permission since the planning authority, as owners of the site, had made clear that they were not prepared to sell the site for the bank's purposes. In these circumstances the applicants could not be regarded as being "aggrieved" by the planning authority's refusal of planning permission; and appeal under section 33(1) of the 1972 Act was therefore inappropriate. (Ref. P/PPA/ST/29, April 21, 1980.)

1.10 Appeal procedure—"aggrieved person"—legal interest in site

The planning authority submitted that since the appellants' lease only entitled them to possession of 2,500 square yards, which formed only part of the 2 acre appeal site, it could not be said that they were "aggrieved" by the decision of the planning authority and that they therefore had no title to appeal against a refusal of planning permission. The decision letter stated that: "The Secretary of State would not accept a submission of this type unless he were satisfied that the appellant had no legal interest in the result of the original planning application." (Ref. P/PPA/LR/636, September 29, 1977.)

1.11 Appeal—"aggrieved person"
Application was made for outline planning permission to erect a function room with bar and lounge facilities. The Secretary of State considered the appellant's statutory right of appeal and was satisfied that in the event that planning permission was granted, the appellant's interest in the appeal site was not one which would enable him to operate the desired planning permission without the landlords' consent. The district council, as owners of the site, had confirmed that they were not prepared to dispose of the ground for the purposes of the proposed development. In these circumstances the Secretary of State held that the applicant for planning permission could not be regarded as being "aggrieved" by the planning authority's refusal of planning permission and that therefore an appeal under section 33(1) of the 1972 Act to the Secretary of State was inappropriate. He therefore dismissed the appeal. (Ref. P/PPA/SL/84, April 3, 1980.)

1.12 Appeal—"aggrieved person"
The planning authority cast doubt upon whether an appellant who was appealing against a refusal of planning permission was an "aggrieved person" in the sense of section 33(1) of the 1972 Act. His failure to provide details of his lease cast doubt upon his legal standing and his right to pursue an appeal. The Secretary of State's decision letter stated that if the planning authority doubted the appellant's interest in the appeal site, they had had ample opportunity to raise the matter and the Secretary of State rejected the implication that it was incumbent upon an appellant to produce at the inquiry details of his lease. (Refs. P/PPA/ST/1; P/ENA/MHW/3, April 7, 1977.)

1.13 "Call in" by region—building of architectural or historic interest—station building
The regional planning authority "called in" an application for planning permission to redevelop a station. In support of this

decision the regional planning authority submitted that the structure plan contained policies for the protection of the region's heritage. The consultative draft of a review of the structure plan contained a list of buildings considered to be of regional significance. This list included the station. The regional planing authority conceded that "call in" could not be justified in terms of section 179(1)(*a*) of the Local Government (Scotland) Act 1973 (that the proposed development does not conform to a structure plan approved by the Secretary of State) but argued that the 1973 Act did not preclude a reference to a draft policy in support of their contention that the application raised a new planning issue of general significance to the district of the regional planning authority in terms of section 179(1)(*b*) of the 1973 Act. It was on that ground that the "call in" was made.

The district council argued that the heritage policies in the draft review would, if approved, enable the regional planning authority to duplicate the role of the Secretary of State in matters concerning the protection of the heritage. The district council also rejected the proposition that the station was a building of regional significance.

The Secretary of State considered that the provisions of the 1972 Act, which enabled buildings of special architectural or historic interest to be listed, and the related provisions for control by the district planning authority or the Secretary of State of works affecting such buildings were the appropriate means of safeguarding such buildings. The Secretary of State therefore took the view that the proposed issue did not raise a new planning issue of general significance to the district of the regional planning authority. (Ref. P/RCA, June 28, 1984.)

1.14 "Call in" by regional planning authority—structure plan policies—revisal

This was an appeal by the district planning authority against the "call in" by the regional planning authority of an application for development comprising a superstore and sports centre, together with car parking and a petrol filling station. The regional council contended that the proposed development represented a significant departure from the approved structure plan. The district planning authority argued that the proposal accorded with revised but not yet approved structure plan policies. The regional planning authority contended that the Secretary of State should not base his decision on policies he had not yet approved.

The Secretary of State concluded that the regional planning authority were entitled to "call in" the application as contrary to the approved structure plan, even though, as here, the regional planning authority had approved policies superseding those in the structure plan. The appeal was therefore dismissed. (Ref. P/RCA, March 30, 1987.)

SECTION 2

DEVELOPMENT—OPERATIONS

See generally Young and Rowan-Robinson, *Scottish Planning Law and Procedure*, pp. 118–125.

"Development" was described by Lord Wilberforce in the course of a speech in the House of Lords (*Coleshill and District Investment Co. Ltd.* v. *Minister of Housing and Local Government* [1969] 1 W.L.R. 746) as "a key word in the planners' vocabulary." The reason for the importance of the term "development" in planning law is that the system of regulatory planning revolves around the meaning of this word. If, for example, particular proposals do not involve development, as defined in the Town and Country Planning (Scotland) Act 1972, planning permission is not required for the carrying out of those proposals. If, on the other hand, particular proposals do involve "development," planning permission will almost always be required.

In terms of section 19(1) of the 1972 Act, "development" is defined (subject to certain limitations) as "the carrying out of building, engineering, mining or other operations in, on, over or under land or the making of any material change in the use of any buildings or other land." Although the same activity may well involve both "operations" and a "material change in the use" of land, the general scheme of the planning legislation is to distinguish between the concepts of, on the one hand, "operations" and, on the other hand, "material change in the use" of land: "operations" comprise activities which result in some physical alteration of land, an alteration which has some degree of permanence in relation to the land, whereas "use," in contrast, refers to activities done in or on land but which do not interfere with the physical characteristics of the land. This section is concerned with the "operations" limb of the statutory definition: material change in the use of buildings or other land is the subject of the next section.

Operations

In some circumstances different descriptions might well be applied to the same operation; the removal of material from land

9

might, for example, depending on the circumstances, sometimes be described as a building operation, sometimes as an engineering operation and sometimes as a mining operation. The use of one description rather than another is generally of no practical significance so far as the law is concerned. An attempt has, however, been made in this section to divide operations into the different categories. Some works may be too trifling to be regarded as "operations" and may be disregarded for planning purposes.

The word "building" and the phrase "building operations" are widely defined in the 1972 Act. However, the scope of "building operations" is limited to some extent by section 19(2)(*a*) of the 1972 Act, which provides that the "carrying out of works for the maintenance, improvement or other alteration of any building, being works which affect only the interior of the building or which do not materially affect the external appearance of the building" is not to constitute development. The line between works of maintenance, improvement or other alteration of a building (which do not constitute development) and rebuilding works (which will involve development even though the external appearance of the building is not to be altered) can be difficult to draw.

The only specific guidance provided by the 1972 Act as to the meaning of the phrase "engineering operations" is that the term is declared to include the laying out or formation of means of access (whether vehicular or pedestrian) to a road. The 1972 Act does not define "mining operations" but states that the word "minerals" includes "all minerals and substances in or under land of a kind ordinarily worked for removal by underground or surface working."

APPEAL DECISIONS
Building operations

2.1 Building—football ground—planning unit

In an appeal concerning the siting of an open-air market on the car park of a football ground, the ground, with its terracing and grandstands, was held by the Secretary of State to come within the statutory definition of "building." Being part of the same planning unit as the football stadium, the car park had to be treated as part of the building. (Ref. P/ENA/D/1 and 2, October 8, 1976.)

2.2 Building operation—automatic telling machine

Planning permission had been refused for the installation of an automatic telling machine (ATM) at a bank. Section 19(2) of the 1972 Act states:

"The following operations or uses of land shall not be taken for the purposes of this Act to involve development of the land, that is to say—
(*a*) the carrying out of works for the maintenance, improvement or other alteration of any building, being works which affect only the interior of the building or which do not materially affect the external appearance of the building."

It was argued on behalf of the planning authority that whether the proposal was an exception in terms of section 19(2)(*a*) of the Act was a matter of fact and degree. The proposal was clearly a building operation. The proposal would involve the alteration of a window and the installation of a large machine, one third the size of the window, into an opening 1.1 by 0.9 metres in one of a series of symmetrical window openings in the elevation. The machine would be boarded in, with an aluminium facing, and a contrasting matt black finish. The installation would be a noticeable feature and one third of its depth would be an illuminated panel. The night-safe in the building was smaller, not lit, and on a different frontage. Taking into account the position, size, illumination and appearance of the proposed ATM, it was argued that the installation works would be an operation which would materially affect the external appearance of the building. The proposal did not come within the terms of the exception in section 19(2)(*a*): it thus comprised development in terms of the Act and planning permission was necessary.

The appellants stated that though the planning authority submitted that the installation would materially affect the appearance of the building, they had no objection to the proposed appearance. The view of the appellants was that the authority should have considered not just one elevation, but the whole building which already included a night-safe in one of the windows, together with the scale, character and design of the proposal. The scale of the proposal would be small, with the installation in an existing window with the surrounding glass retained. In terms of character, the building had a modern infill-panel design, with the frame components strongly expressed, while the machine itself epitomised "the bank," in a building which was a bank in appearance.

On these criteria, the impact of the proposal would be negligible; it could not be regarded as a material change, and therefore would not be development.

The reporter said that the proposal clearly involved the carrying out of works for the alteration of a building which would not only affect the interior. As regards the effect on the external appearance he took the view that account should be taken of both the appearance of the proposed autoteller and the appearance of the building in which it was proposed to install it. These considerations included scale, location and style.

Though he accepted that the proposed ATM would be a very small proportion of the overall facade of the building, the machine itself would not necessarily appear small when viewed from the street. However, in terms of style, the machine would appear consistent with that of the bank, including its modern and muted materials; this assessment allowed for the appearance of the illuminated panel, which in his view would not be significant in the context of the existing lighting and signs. What he regarded as particularly important was that the proposed ATM would be located in an existing window opening, without alteration to any other feature of the appearance of the building. Taking these factors into account, it was his judgment that in this case the proposed installation would not materially affect the external appearance of the building. (Ref. P/PPA/GA/359, March 16, 1987.)

2.3 Building operation—material effect on appearance

The reporter found that a significant part of shop windows had been obscured by plywood panelling to a depth of about 1 metre. The reporter found this to be an alteration which had materially altered the appearance of the building and therefore was development for which planning permission was required. (Ref. P/ENA/SL/215, December 1, 1986.)

2.4 Building operations—external appearance—whether materially affected

An enforcement notice had been served in respect of work on the renovation of a former smithy. The question arose whether there had been a breach of planning control in connection with the works. The reporter found that the building was dilapidated and in need of substantial repairs. It was, however, still usable as a smithy. The repairs needed were numerous but were not of such a scale as to amount to rebuilding the smithy. In terms of section 19(2)(*a*) of the 1972 Act "the carrying out of works for the maintenance, improvement or other alteration of any building, being works which affect only the interior of the building or which do not materially affect the external appearance of the building" do not involve development. The reporter found that the extensive works did not materially alter the building's external appearance. The building retained its former size and shape, the windows to be installed were similar to the former ones, while the door was in the same position as the original one. The only changes in materials used were in the colour of the roof tiles, the use of brick in rebuilding the chimney-heads and the use of concrete blocks (instead of stone) in rebuilding part of one gable. These were all matters which could normally occur when the accrued dilapidations of an old building were finally tackled in a comprehensive scheme of repair. The application of some form of external rendering or harling to an old stone wall did not amount to work requiring planning permission. Thus, though the works would alter the external appearance, they would not do so materially. (Refs. P/ENA/SP/16; P/WEN/SP/3, April 2, 1985.)

2.5 Building operations—external alterations to flats—abandonment

The appellant was refused planning permission for alterations to flats situated above a public house. On one side, at a fairly high level, ran the main railway line. In the arches below the railway various industrial activities took place. A lorry park adjoined the appeal premises. One of the planning authority's reasons for refusal was that the dwellings would be unsatisfactory on environmental grounds, given the proximity of the lorry park, the railway and premises used for the gutting and packing of fish (one of the uses of the railway arches). Their other reason was that the alterations would be prejudicial to any future improvement of the street in question.

For the appellant it was argued that the appeal premises had been occupied as residential flats until about 1972 and since then had not been used for any other purpose. They were in an area zoned for residential use in the development plan. The proposals barely constituted development under the Town and Country Planning (Scotland) Act 1972. The four original flats were to be reduced to three. The only external alterations were to be the reconstruction of four dormers, removed some years previously, the formation of an extra dormer and the introduction of a mansard type roof.

The planning authority argued that the proposal was development requiring planning permission. It involved the construction of dormers and a mansard roof, all of which were external alterations to the shell of the existing building. As the flats had been declared not to meet the tolerable standard under the housing legislation, their residential use had been abandoned.

The reporter said that the first question was whether the proposals were development. Since they included the construction of dormers and a mansard roof, all of which materially extended beyond the shell of the existing building, they constituted development. They therefore required planning permission. (Ref. P/PPA/GA/246, January 31, 1985.)

2.6　Building operations—effect on external appearance of building

Building work had been carried out on a house. Under the terms of section 19(2) of the Town and Country Planning (Scotland) Act 1972 the reconstruction of the house would not constitute development if the work involved did not materially affect the external appearance of the building. It was agreed at the inquiry that the plans submitted with the application did reflect the appearance of the house both prior to and following reconstruction. The reporter's examination of the plans indicated that the dormer windows were of a different form, that the rear extension was higher and had a longer roof pitch, and that there was a quite different distribution and sizes of windows and doors on the east and west elevations. Although the work had been carried out with much sympathy for the original building, the reporter considered that these alterations in total amounted to a material change in the external appearance of the building and, accordingly, that they amounted to development within the terms of section 19 of the 1972 Act. As the dormer windows had been so enlarged in width and height, they contravened the specifications given in Class I(1)(*d*)(i) of the Town and Country Planning (General Development) (Scotland) Order 1981. In consequence the reconstruction work exceeded the tolerances for permitted development and therefore planning permission was necessary. (Ref. P/PPA/SC/77, March 22, 1982.)

2.7 Building operations—external appearance of building

In this appeal it was held that replacing a sash window of a terraced house with a pivot window had had a material effect on the external appearance of the building in question. (Ref. P/ENA/LA/35, January 12, 1981.)

2.8 Building operations—removal of mullion—shape of window

A central stone mullion had been removed from a window and the two vertical windows thus replaced by a square one. The reporter found that the work had a material effect on the external appearance of the building; it was therefore development. Consequently, an appeal on ground (*b*) of section 85(1) of the 1972 Act, *i.e.* that the matters alleged did not constitute a breach of planning control, failed. (Ref. P/ENA/LB/18, April 22, 1980.)

2.9 Development—balanced flue extract—amenity

A small balanced flue extract was installed on the outer wall of a flat at first floor level. The council explained that the area benefited from a distinctive structural layout, consistency of building materials and scale, with a variety and hue of red sandstone adding to the overall character of the area. The council considered that in this context modern materials could be visually intrusive—*e.g.* the metal of the balanced flue and its projection. The appellant produced photographs of similar flues and of burglar alarms in the area. He was willing to paint the flue to tone with the sandstone.

The reporter understood the council's concern that a multiplicity of such installations would be unsightly, would tend to clutter the front facades of the attractive tenements and that this would detract from the character and appearance of the conservation area. There was no question that burglar alarms were to be seen in great abundance; the brightly coloured boxes were visually intrusive.

However, on the merits of this case, a single engineering operation had taken place. The external flue was approximately one foot square and six inches deep. He thought it reasonably inconspicuous in its setting. In the reporter's view it did not materially affect the appearance of the building and therefore did not constitute "development" as defined in section 19 of the 1972 Act. (Refs. P/PPA/SL/344; P/ENA/SL/212, October 30, 1986.)

2.10 Operations—material change in external appearance—shop front

Enforcement action had been taken in respect of an altered shop front. The Secretary of State agreed with the reporter's view that the altered shop front, which was clad in timber wall-boarding mounted vertically and coloured orange-yellow, was distinctive not only by reason of its colouring but also because of the non-traditional way in which the timber had been used. The framing of the small display window with a low fascia and a high stall riser gave the premises a horizontal visual emphasis which did not accord with the original street frontage. The Secretary of State accepted that the alterations had materially affected the external appearance of the building; they therefore amounted to development. The planning appeal and enforcement appeal made by the appellant were both dismissed. (Refs. P/PPA/SL/70; P/ENA/SL 92 and 93, January 8, 1980.)

2.11 Development—material change in appearance—roller shutters

A shop had metal roller shutters fitted to its five windows and two doors. The reporter considered whether a material change in the external appearance of the building resulted. He concluded that it did. (Refs. P/PPA/SL/75; P/ENA/SL/121, September 13, 1979.)

2.12 Operations—canopies

Each of three windows had been fitted with folding canopies of the pram-hood type. The reporter thought it undeniable that the canopies materially affected the appearance of the building. There had therefore been a breach of planning control. (Ref. P/ENA/TC/62, April 28, 1988.)

2.13 Operations—cottages demolished—rebuilding

Planning permission had been granted for the enlargement and alteration of two single-storey farm cottages. The cottages were later demolished and work commenced for a new house on the site. Planning permission for this cottage was refused. The reporter considered that the planning authority were not justified in refusing permission for a new house when permission had previously been given for a substantially similar scheme. He therefore granted planning permission. (Refs. P/PPA/FB/38; P/ENA/FB/13 and 18, December 3, 1979.)

2.14 Rebuilding—cottages

Planning permission had been sought for the renovation and alteration of a pair of cottages. The reporter said that although the walls of the former houses were still recognisable as such, in the absence of a roof, windows, doors, and even internal floors and fireplaces, the remains constituted little more than a shell of the former houses. They clearly could not be reoccupied or used as a house without extensive rebuilding. For these reasons the reporter considered that the remains of the former cottages could not be considered in their present state to be a house or houses. (Ref. P/PPA/FB/236, September 30, 1987.)

2.15 Development—renovation of old cottage
This was an appeal against a refusal of outline planning permission for renovation of an old cottage. The appellant's planning consultants submitted that under the Town and Country Planning (Scotland) Act 1947 planning permission was not required as, since the building in question had been in use as a dwelling when that Act was passed, planning permission was deemed to have been granted. However, it was noted that a closing order had been served in 1951 since when the use of the building had changed from residential to agricultural storage. Planning permission was therefore required. The reporter was also of the opinion that, such was the poor state of repair of the building, renovation would be tantamount to a new development in open countryside. (Ref. P/PPA/SF/6, February 2, 1979.)

2.16 Former house—rebuilding—residential status lapsed
The walls of a house were still standing. Rehabilitation of the building could not, however, be made without substantial demolition of the existing structure. The reporter considered that the residential status of the existing building had long since lapsed. Renovation would require a substantial rebuilding of the main fabric. Development was therefore involved. (Ref. P/PPA/D/31, February 8, 1978.)

2.17 Development—building operations
An enforcement notice had been served alleging the removal of part of a concrete retaining barrier from a loch. The authority were concerned about the environmental effect of lowering the water level of the loch. The owner alleged that he had only dug away a mass of stones and soil, revealing what would appear to be a sluice gap in the wall. He appealed against the notice on ground (*bb*) of section 85(1)—that the breach of planning control alleged in the notice had not taken place.
The reporter said that consideration had to be given to the question of whether the work at issue was subject to planning control. The definitions of "building" and "building operations" in the 1972 Act included structural alterations of any structure or erection. The reporter considered that the work undertaken

involved partial demolition of the existing retaining barrier and thus was properly described as an alteration to the structure. It therefore fell within the statutory definition. In reaching that view the reporter took account of the small scale of the works and the more substantial extent of their environmental implications. In the light of this he did not consider that the works could be excluded as *de minimis*. (Ref. P/ENA/FA/62, April 5, 1989.)

2.18   Barbed wire on fencing—development
   Three horizontal strands of barbed wire with a roll above had been erected on top of a 3 metre high boundary fence. The appellants argued that planning permission was not required since the effect on the external appearance was too small to be material. The reporter considered the erection of the barbed wire made a material difference to the metal palisade fence at the appeal site. Development was therefore involved. He could not accept that it was so insignificant as to be regarded as *de minimis*. (Refs. P/ENA/SL/234; P/PPA/SL/426, April 28, 1988.)

2.19   Use of outbuildings—domestic use—not development
   Planning permission had been refused for the conversion of existing outbuildings to form part of the house to which they were attached. The outbuildings were presently used for domestic storage. Although the conversion could result in accommodation capable of separate occupancy, it was clear that there was no intention of so using the premises. The intended works would mainly affect the interior of the buildings. Where they would affect the exterior (for example, fitting patio doors where there were at present garage doors), the reporter formed the view that these did not materially affect the external appearance of the building, having regard to the enclosed nature of the courtyard. Section 19(2)(*a*) of the 1972 Act provides that the carrying out of works which affect only the interior of a building or which do not materially affect the external appearance of the building are not to be taken as involving development. The reporter concluded that in terms of section 19(2)(*a*) development was not involved and the application for planning permission had been unnecessary. (Ref. P/PPA/FC/88, April 25, 1988.)

Engineering and mining operations

2.20   Engineering operations—paving of vehicle hardstanding—not "de minimis"
   The owner of a house had paved an area of about 48 square feet beside the apron of his double garage. This paved area,

intended for use as a vehicle hardstanding, covered almost 10 per cent. of the total area of the appeal premises, including the house and garage, and in these circumstances was held not to be *de minimis*. The reporter concluded that in terms of section 19(1) the formation of the hardstanding involved development. (Ref. P/ENA/LA/62, October 4, 1983.)

2.21 Engineering or other operations—importance—path

Steps had been removed from a steep path leading to a house. An enforcement notice required their reinstatement. Appeal was made on the ground that no breach of planning control had occurred. However, the reporter found that the works carried out were either "engineering operations" or "other operations." Whether the operations required planning permission was a matter of fact and degree. Operations involving alterations to a path within the curtilage of a building were not generally significant enough to require the submission of a planning application. However, in this case a large number of steps had been removed or built over, a mature tree had been felled and a path or driveway up to 2.5 metres wide and at least 20 metres long had been constructed. The reporter considered that whether or not a car was driven part way up the path, the operations were significant enough to require planning permission. (Ref. P/ENA/SA/73, April 18, 1988.)

2.22 Engineering operations—garden

It was held that the combination of substantial excavation of land together with the removal of a stone wall amounted to an engineering operation requiring planning permission, even though the land formed part of a garden. (Ref. P/ENA/SC/38, April 7, 1986.)

2.23 Development—war memorial—removal

The Secretary of State concluded that planning permission was not required for the removal of a war memorial in the absence of the necessity for works which could reasonably be described as development for the purposes of the planning legislation. (Ref. P/PPA/FA/102, November 12, 1987.)

2.24 Development—clearing and levelling site—"de minimis"

A site had been cleared and levelled for the stationing of a caravan. These works involved the removal of turf and the laying of a bed of stones. In the reporter's opinion the works were so slight as to come within the description *de minimis*. (Refs. P/PPA/SA/99 and 101; P/ENA/SA/44, July 4, 1985.)

2.25 Engineering operations—garden ground

Planning permission was refused for the formation of a car parking area at the rear of a dwelling. In the reporter's view the scale of the infilling, earth-mounding and stabilisation required was such that the works had to be regarded as engineering operations beyond the scope of activities that were incidental to the usual enjoyment of a dwelling-house. The amount of infilling in some places was likely to amount to a depth of at least 3 metres and to extend some 10 to 13 metres from the wall. This went beyond the usual scale of ground remodelling that might occur for landscaping reasons in the garden of a dwelling-house. Planning permission was required as engineering operations were not included in the types of development within the curtilage of a dwelling-house listed in Part I of Schedule 1 to the Town and Country Planning (General Development) (Scotland) Order 1975. (Refs. P/PPA/LA/132; HGJ/2/LA/19, May 29, 1981.)

2.26 Operations—works not "de minimis"—enforcement

An enforcement notice required householders, the owners of a house on a new housing estate, to reinstate a parking space outside their house. The appellants had asked that the parking space be removed as it was immediately outside their front window. When no action was taken they took matters into their own hands and removed the surface of the parking space, leaving an unsurfaced area of earth. An appeal against the enforcement notice was lodged on ground (*b*) of section 85(1)—that the matters alleged in the enforcement notice did not constitute a breach of planning control. The reporter thought it a question of fact and degree whether the works to remove the tarmac surface should be regarded as *de minimis*. In the reporter's view they could not. These engineering operations involved the removal of the surface from an area reserved for public parking. (Refs. P/ENA/CB/23 and 24, March 3, 1980.)

2.27 Engineering operations—means of access

In a case where a wall had been built, the wall enclosing part of the forecourt of a building and running along a shared access road, the planning authority argued that the building of the wall amounted to the laying out of a means of access. The Secretary of State concluded, however, that though the appellant had, in building the wall, restricted the width of the previous access, since the means of access already existed the work in question could not be described as the laying out of a means of access to a road. (Ref. P/ENA/SA/1, June 28, 1979.)

2.28 Mining operations—engineering operations—removal of soil

The appellants were engaged in removing soil from an area of land. They argued that this was not development; it did not involve "operations" as defined in section 19 of the 1972 Act. To describe the work as a mining operation was unsatisfactory as soil could not be regarded as a mineral. To describe the work as "other operations" would also be inaccurate as it had been said in a case in the House of Lords (*Coleshill and District Investment Co. Ltd.* v. *Minister of Housing and Local Government* [1969] 1 W.L.R. 746, *per* Lord Morris) that such operations had to be viewed in the context of building, engineering or mining operations.

The reporter was satisfied that the removal of soil by mechanical means and its transportation elsewhere as a commercial venture was a surface mining operation for the extraction of soil. It constituted development. The means of soil removal from the site also came within the meaning of an engineering operation and the infilling and covering of waste materials deposited on the site could reasonably be treated as "other operations" required to facilitate the principal mining or engineering operations. The previous use of the land had been agricultural, so that a material change of use had clearly occurred. (Ref. P/ENA/SL/214, July 7, 1987.)

Operations or material change of use

2.29 Development—autoteller at building society office—ancillary use

It was proposed to instal an autoteller machine (ATM) at a building society office. Planning permission and listed building consent were refused. The reporter said that he accepted that in this appeal it could be argued that the proposal amounted either to a building operation or to a change of use. Installation of the autoteller machine would involve the removal of a glazed screen located in a recessed position on the frontage and its replacement with the ATM. The reporter considered that the ATM would not materially affect the external appearance of the building when located in the position involved. The form of the ATM would be consistent with the contemporary design and appearance of the remainder of the frontage. Consequently, the reporter found that within the terms of section 19(2)(*a*) of the 1972 Act there was no material effect on the external appearance of the building. The reporter found no support for the view that the installation of such a machine could be held to represent a change of use. The appeal premises had an established use as an office and the proposal was clearly ancillary to that use. Nor had any objective evidence been presented to suggest that the increase in the overall level of activity of the premises, consequent on the installation of an ATM, would amount to a material intensification of use.

The Secretary of State agreed with the reporter's conclusions. (Refs. P/PPA/GA/344; HGJ/2/GA/16, October 5, 1987.)

SECTION 3

DEVELOPMENT—MATERIAL CHANGE OF USE

See generally Young and Rowan-Robinson, *Scottish Planning Law and Procedure*, pp. 125–166.

As mentioned in the introduction to Section 2, in terms of section 19(1) of the Town and Country Planning (Scotland) Act 1972 "development" includes "the making of any material change in the use of buildings or other land." Questions sometimes arise as to whether particular proposals amount to "operations" or to a material change of use; a number of appeals raising this question are included in this section.

In seeking to achieve a degree of uniformity in the application of the "change of use" limb of the statutory definition in different circumstances there have evolved a number of concepts of which no mention is to be found in the legislation. Several important such concepts including the "planning unit," "abandonment of use," and "ancillary use" are employed in the appeal decisions contained in this section.

The section includes summaries of a number of appeal decisions in which there were raised the questions whether as a matter of fact and degree a "material" change of use had occurred; the issue of identification of the "planning unit," *i.e.* the area of land to be looked at in considering the materiality or otherwise of the particular change of use; the circumstances in which intensification of a use may be sufficiently marked to amount to a material change in the use of land; whether the proper inference to be drawn from the facts is such that a use has to be held to have been abandoned so that even if the new use is the same as the previous one, development is involved; whether, where several activities are carried on upon a single planning unit, it is possible to recognise a single primary use to which the land is put and to which other uses of the land are ancillary or incidental.

Section 19(2)(*f*) of the 1972 Act provides that in the case of buildings or other land "used for a purpose of any class specified in an order made by the Secretary of State under this section, the use thereof for any other purpose of the same class" is not to

23

involve development. The Town and Country Planning (Use
Classes) (Scotland) Order 1989 was made under section 19. This
section also includes summaries of appeal decisions involving the
interpretation and application of the Use Classes Order (UCO).
Appeal decisions involving use for agriculture or forestry and the
deposit of refuse on land are also included, as are two decisions
arising out of applications to determine whether planning permission is required.

APPEAL DECISIONS

Material change of use

3.1 Material change of use—parking of vehicles at house—enforcement

An enforcement notice had been served, alleging the unauthorised use of garden ground as a base for the operation of mobile shops and ice cream vans and the parking of such vehicles at the appellant's house. The reporter accepted that a breach of planning control had occurred. He pointed out that compliance with an enforcement notice did not discharge its continuing effect. (Ref. P/ENA/HE/2, August 28, 1981.)

3.2 Storage of vehicles—curtilage of dwelling-house

Planning permission had been refused for the formation of a vehicular access, erection of a garage and use of garden ground for the storage of three commercial vans. The appellant submitted that all three vans were required in connection with the delivery of newspapers. The nature of the job was such that he and his son had to leave home at 3 and 3.30 a.m. every day. The reporter considered that the number and type of vehicles involved and the hours at which they were generally operated clearly distinguished the appellant's situation from a normal domestic one and that a material charge of use had occurred. (Refs. P/PPA/FA/92; P/ENA/FA/42, May 8, 1986.)

3.3 Material change of use—car parking—scrap cars

The appeal site was allocated in the current development plan for commercial and shopping use. Its authorised use was for car parking. The appellant argued that the current use of the land for the storage of scrap cars, amounted to no more than car parking since any dismantling of vehicles took place elsewhere. The planning authority regarded the current use as a scrap-yard coming within Class VI (iii) (Special Industrial Group B—recovery of metal from scrap, etc.) of the Town and Country Planning (Use Classes) (Scotland) Order 1973. The planning authority regarded the use as incompatible with the surrounding, mainly residential, use. The reporter considered that the current use of the land was materially different from the planning authority's permitted use for car parking. Planning permission was required for the new use. (Ref. P/ENA/FB/19, February 29, 1980.)

3.4 Material change of use—shop—bureau de change

An enforcement notice was served alleging a material change in the use of premises from a shop to an office/bureau de change.

It seemed to the reporter that although a bureau de change could be considered to "sell" one currency for another, it was more realistic to describe the process as one of exchange. For this reason the bureau de change could not be considered to be a shop. In addition, although some work normally effected in a travel agency was carried out in the bureau de change, it was, in comparison with the main function of the bureau de change, so small as to be insignificant. Accordingly, the reporter considered that the change of use which had occurred constituted development for which planning permission was required. (Ref. P/ENA/LA/97, July 27, 1987.)

3.5   Material change of use—"service house"—boarding house

Planning permission was sought for a change in the use of premises from a "service house" to a private hotel. "Service house" was not, said the reporter, a use specified in the Use Classes Order nor in any other planning order, instrument or statute. It appeared that in a service house persons hired the use of rooms for residential occupation and were provided with breakfast facilities in a communal dining room. In granting planning permission for a change of use from boarding house to service house, the planning authority must have considered the uses to be different but, having regard to the nature of the accommodation provided and the facility for obtaining a meal in a room shared by all, the reporter concluded that the property should properly be described as a boarding house or guest house. Boarding houses and guest houses are included within Class X of the Town and Country Planning (Use Classes) (Scotland) Order 1973. So too is a hotel not licensed for the sale of excisable liquor to persons other than residents or to persons other than residents consuming meals on the premises. The reporter therefore concluded that since the present use and the use applied for both fell within the same use class, the proposed change of use did not involve development. (Ref. P/PPA/LB/120, August 29, 1987.)

3.6   Material change of use—unauthorised tipping—ancillary use

An enforcement notice served on the operators of a sandpit alleged several unauthorised developments relating to the reception and disposal of waste materials. The use of a number of skips on the site could be incidental to the authorised activities on the site, sand extraction and coal depot operations. However, a skip hire service offered since 1982, and which had resulted in ten or more skips being held at the site, was not ancillary to either of these activities. The skip hire use was a modern method of collecting waste materials which were either dumped at the site or taken elsewhere. In either event skip hire was unconnected with the sand and coal activities except perhaps that some skips might be used from time to time for these different purposes. It was a separate new activity or, at most, an activity that was incidental to the unauthorised tipping. The burning of waste materials appeared to be ancillary to the tipping operations. It would have been a way of disposing of waste which was not suitable for tipping and which did not have a resale value. Burning rubbish would not normally be ancillary to either the sand extraction or the coal depot use. The reporter found that the skip hire and the burning of waste materials were unauthorised activities. Neither was protected from enforcement action by having commenced before the beginning of 1965. (Ref. P/ENA/FC/19, January 24, 1987.)

3.7 Material change of use—coffee shop—shop for the sale of hot food
Planning permission for a coffee shop was granted subject to the erection of an approved external duct for dispersal of cooking odours in the event of there being any extension in the proposed level of cooking. Within a short time hot filled rolls and soup were being served, the cooking facilities consisting of an electric griddle with a hot plate and a microwave oven. The planning authority received complaints of offensive smells permeating adjoining property. The reporter found that the premises were in use wholly as a shop selling hot food. He was satisfied there had been a material change of use from coffee shop to use as a shop for the sale of hot food. Planning permission was granted for the use of the premises for the sale of hot food subject to a condition that details of the type of cooking equipment to be used should be approved by the planning authority before it was installed. (Ref. P/ENA/SL/189, April 29, 1985.)

3.8 Material change of use—restaurant—refreshment licence
This was an appeal against a determination, made under section 51 of the Town and Country Planning (Scotland) Act 1972, that planning permission would be required for the addition of a refreshment licence to a restaurant. (A refreshment licence rather than a restaurant licence was requested because the former allows children on the premises). A refreshment licence allows drinks to be sold irrespective of whether persons are consuming food. In the evenings the premises could operate virtually as a lounge bar. The reporter considered that the addition of a refreshment licence would be likely to lead to the appeal prem-

ises being used in a way materially different from a restaurant. Planning permission was therefore required. (Ref. P/DEV/1/ SL/2, December 13, 1983.)

3.9   Material change of use—taxi business—control from dwelling

An enforcement notice had been served in respect of the use of part of a house as a taxi office. Appeal was made on ground (*b*) of section 85(1) of the Town and Country Planning (Scotland) Act 1972, *i.e.* that no breach of planning control had occurred. The appellant claimed that the use of the house in connection with the taxi business was confined to the reception of incoming telephone calls from persons requiring private hire. The reporter said that he would accept that use of that sort might be regarded as ancillary to the authorised residential use of the premises if the business had been confined to persons normally resident at the address using their own private car or cars for hire purposes with telephoned bookings being relayed by radio. However, it was clear that the scale of the business was much greater, with the house being used as a base for employed drivers and other persons not normally resident in the house, albeit some of them might be related to the appellant. In the reporter's opinion the scale of the operation was such that the premises had to be regarded as having a dual use, of which the commercial element amounted to a material change of use. (Ref. P/ENA/D/53; November 14, 1983.)

3.10   Material change of use—car repairs

The reporter accepted that from 1947 to 1974 some sort of car servicing and minor repair business had been carried on in the premises. The current use was, however, a specialised paint-spraying and body repair business. This the reporter regarded as an entirely different activity from the previous use. The appeal against the enforcement notice was dismissed. (Ref. P/ENA/ GC/30, November 17, 1983.)

3.11   Material change of use—club—public house—sanctions

A British Legion social club sought planning permission for a change in the use of the premises to public house. The reporter noted that under the provisions of the Licensing (Scotland) Act 1976 a club had sanctions over its members' conduct outwith the premises. However, he granted planning permission for a public house subject to conditions. (Ref. P/PPA/SN/34, October 19, 1982.)

3.12   Material change of use—storage of boats—storage of caravans

The storage of caravans on a site was held to be a mattterially different use from storage of boats on the site, though both were, the applicant argued, used for leisure living accommodation. The appeal was dismissed. (Ref. P/ENA/FC/1, October 28, 1981.)

3.13 Material change of use—car repair—industrial use rights
 An enforcement notice had been served in respect of the allegedly unauthorised use of premises for the repair and mainte- nance of cars. The planning authority acknowledged that the site, part of a former industrial works, had an established industrial use. However, the authority alleged that the present commercial use for car repair involved a material change from the previous use. In the reporter's view no material change of use had occurred. (Ref. P/PPA/TB/10, May 20, 1981.)

3.14 Material change of use—display of vehicles for sale—vacant site
 This was an appeal against an enforcement notice requiring the appellant to remove all vehicles displayed for sale on a vacant site. The reporter was satisfied that a material change in the use of the site had taken place. No evidence had been produced to show that the site had been used prior to 1965. (Refs. P/ENA/ CB/32 and 33, February 18, 1981.)

3.15 Material change of use—abandonment—new house on site of earlier house
 This was an appeal against a refusal of planning permission for a house on the site of a ruined building. The appellant argued that the premises had been in use as a house until 1958. The reporter considered that when, in 1960, the original dwelling had been demolished, the residential use of the site had come to an end. The present state of the property was such that the necessary work could not be described as an alteration of an existing building. (Ref. P/PPA/GD/54, January 12, 1981.)

3.16 Material change of use—garage parking—vehicle repair
 An enforcement notice alleged the unauthorised use of garage premises and a forecourt for the sale and commercial repair of motor vehicles. An appeal was lodged on ground (*b*) of section 85(1) of the 1972 Act—*i.e.* that the matters alleged in the enforcement notice did not constitute a breach of planning control. The appellant submitted that the previous use of the premises had been the garaging, repair and maintenance of mini- buses. The reporter accepted the appellant's evidence that one of the allegedly unauthorised uses, car sales, did not usually take place on the appeal premises. He concluded, however, that the repair activity was being carried on upon the site. On the

evidence available the reporter concluded that the use had changed from domestic garage parking to the preparation of cars for sale. The reporter considered this to be a material change of use requiring planning permission. He considered that permission should not be granted as the appeal premises were close to houses in a well-established residential area. (Ref. P/ENA/ FA/13, August 1, 1980.)

3.17 Material change of use—haulage contractor—vehicle repair

The previous use of the appeal premises had been part use of the site for the business of a haulage contractor and part use for the repair of lorries and agricultural equipment. It was estimated that about 40 per cent. of the time on the site had been devoted to repair purposes. The appellant, the current occupier of the site, did not operate a haulage business but carried out both mechanical and bodywork repairs on cars and agricultural machinery. The reporter concluded that the present use, with repairs taking up 100 per cent. of the time represented a material change for which planning permission was required. (Ref. P/ENA/B/2, December 13, 1979.)

3.18 Material change of use—curtilage of dwelling—parking of lorry

Permission had been refused for the use of land within the curtilage of the appellant's house for the overnight parking of a lorry. The house was situated in a residential area. Further, the appellant had installed a 500 gallon tank for diesel fuel in order to avoid the effects of a strike. He had, however, a depot for servicing and parking a lorry elsewhere and it was his intention only to park his unladen lorry at his house. The reporter considered that as long as the use was continued at the present level, *i.e.* overnight parking of one unladen lorry, it should be permitted for a reasonable period. Permission was granted for two years. (Ref. P/PPA/SS/32, October 30, 1979.)

3.19 Material change of use—restricted hotel licence—full hotel licence

Premises consisting of two houses came to be used as a hotel under a restricted hotel liquor licence. This involved a breach of planning control before 1965. There was a change in 1975 when the premises came to be used under a full hotel certificate. The change in 1975 was held to be a material change of use involving as it did a change from the last authorised use of the premises as two dwelling-houses to a fully licensed hotel. The use as a hotel with a restricted licence was an unauthorised use which could not be resumed without a grant of planning permission. The question whether that unauthorised use and the present use fell within the same use class in the Town and Country Planning (Use Classes) (Scotland) Order 1973 was therefore irrelevant, though the view was expressed that the change was a material one amounting to development within the terms of section 19(1) of the 1972 Act. The Secretary of State dismissed the appeal but granted planning permission for the purposes specified in Class X of the UCO (*i.e.* use as a guest house or hotel not possessing a full hotel certificate). (Ref. P/ENA/SL/96, July 12, 1978.)

3.20 Material change of use—haulage yard—storage of freight containers

A yard possessed established use rights (*i.e.* use rights pre-dating the planning legislation or which have become immune from enforcement action) as a carrier's and haulage yard. It came to be operated as a yard for the storage of freight containers. The new use involved the deployment of mechanical container-lifting gear, the two-tier storage of containers, the use of noisy trucks to move containers onto lorries and the very noisy activity of repairing containers by rivetting and welding. The reporter concluded that the use of the yard as a container depot was a use materially different from the previous use. The Secretary of State agreed. (Ref. P/ENA/SD/2, May 25, 1977.)

3.21 Plant and materials on site—enforcement action—removal required

An enforcement notice required the removal from an area of land of building materials, plant and equipment. The appellant argued that with the exception of some items, the materials were to be used in connection with the erection of a stable. The Secretary of State considered that the plant and equipment exceeded what was necessary for the building of the stable. This, he thought, constituted development requiring planning permission. (Ref. P/ENA/D/38, April 16, 1981.)

3.22 Material change of use—garage—enforcement

Enforcement action was taken against the appellants in respect of their use of a garage at a hotel as a bus garage. An appeal was lodged on ground (*b*) of section 85(1) of the 1972 Act (*i.e.* that the matters alleged in the notice did not constitute a breach of planning control). The Secretary of State took the view that a material change of use had occurred when the appellants came to use the garage for its present purpose. (Ref. P/ENA/SA/1, July 12, 1976.)

3.23 Material change of use—curtilage of house—ice-cream vans—hardstanding

This was an appeal against the refusal of planning permission for laying down a hardstanding for the parking of ice cream vans within the curtilage of a dwelling-house. The reporter considered that the determining issue was whether the proposed use of the hardstanding would cause material harm to the character of the area and whether the change of use involved would increase traffic and kerbside parking to an unacceptable degree. The reporter decided that the parking of ice cream vans would be alien to the residential character of the area. In consequence, the reporter considered that the appeal could be allowed in part only; the use of the hardstanding was to be restricted to domestic vehicles only. (Ref. P/PPA/D/16, January 17, 1977.)

3.24 Material change of use—single family house—house in multiple occupation

An enforcement notice had been served alleging a breach of planning control in that there had been a change from use as a single family dwelling-house to a house in multiple occupation. The appellant argued that the appeal premises had normally been occupied by eight persons who were not blood-related but who were living as a family group; there had, he argued, been no material change of use. The Secretary of State upheld the planning authority's contention that occupation of the appeal premises by eight to ten students as paying guests had substantially altered the character of the appeal premises in such a way as to amount to a material change of use. (Ref. P/ENA/LA/4, January 1, 1977.)

3.25 Material change of use—dwelling-house—bed and breakfast

An enforcement notice alleged that the use of a six-apartment private dwelling-house for bed and breakfast purposes involved a material change of use. The reporter said that on the question of a breach of planning control he considered that the evidence pointed to a material change of use having taken place. Two rooms (one a sitting room/dining room) were clearly devoted to visitor use with any single family occupation thereof having been ousted. A further room was also occasionally involved. Advertising bed and breakfast with evening meal in the local paper for DHSS-funded visitors was not easily reconciled with the use of the house as a single-family dwelling-house. Even with two or three rooms available for visitors at the time of the site inspection, the reporter considered that as a matter of fact and degree, a material change of use had taken place without the required planning permission. He found that the matters alleged in the notice therefore constituted a breach of planning control. (Ref. P/ENA/SR/60, April 18, 1989.)

3.26 Material change of use—market garden—depot for landscape gardening

It was clear that in the autumn of 1973, when premises were purchased by the appellants, they were being used as a nursery and market garden where the growing and selling of plants or the products of plants was the essential part of the business. It was equally clear that such activity had ceased, the predominant use of the site being for the storage of goods and plants brought onto the site to await distribution to contract sites. The current use of the site probably began shortly after the occupation of the site by the appellants in 1973–74, and certainly within a few years of the appellants' entry on the site. Whether the main use should be described as a depot for landscape gardening or as a civil engineering depot was of little importance, said the reporter. The essential point was that the ground was no longer used for the growing and selling of plants and produce, and that its predominant use was as a storage depot for manufactured products such as kerb stones, drainage pipes and manhole covers, for earth-moving vehicles and equipment, and for plants, trees and shrubs brought to the site from elsewhere, and kept until they were required on contract sites. As a matter of fact and degree the reporter considered that this constituted a material change of use and amounted to development. (Refs. P/PPA/SL/429 and 430; P/ENA/SL/226, April 10, 1989.)

3.27 Development—material change of use—"de minimis"

An enforcement notice alleged the use of part of the roadway in front of the appellant's house for parking and storage of damaged vehicles. The enforcement notice was quashed. The Secretary of State would in any case have upheld the appeal on the ground that the matters alleged in the enforcement notice did not constitute a breach of planning control: the change of use was *de minimis* and did not amount to development. (Ref. P/ENA/SL/32, October 18, 1976.)

3.28 Material change of use—multiple occupation of dwelling-house

An enforcement notice alleged unauthorised use of a single family dwelling-house as individual bed sitting rooms without planning permission. The reporter noted that there was no authoritative Scottish case which would serve as a guide as to whether there had been a material change of use in this case but on general planning considerations he was of the opinion that the occupancy now introduced, with eight unrelated tenants occupying separate rooms and sharing cooking, bathing and toilet facilities, differed materially both in fact and degree from the immediately preceding occupancy which he took to be of a residential family character with the addition of one or two lodgers. He concluded that this represented a material change of use in terms of section 19(1) of the Town and Country Planning (Scotland) Act 1972. He expressed the view, however, that the development did not appear (as alleged by the planning authority) to fall within the provision of section 19(3) of the 1972 Act (relating to use as two or more separate dwellings).

Bearing in mind that the evidence available did not include guidance from the Scottish courts, the Secretary of State was disposed to agree with the reporter's conclusion that a breach of planning control under section 19(1) of the 1972 Act had occurred. (Refs. P/ENA/GLW/54, 58–62, October 18, 1976.)

3.29   Material change of use—steel stockholder—haulage contractor
The appeal premises had previously been used for storage for an ironmonger and steel stockholder. The premises were open to the public and lorry deliveries were involved. The premises came to be used for the purpose of a haulage contractor's business. The haulage contractor collected, delivered and sometimes stored household furniture and effects. Almost all the goods stored in the premises belonged to householders in the process of moving house. The reporter noted that there was no claim that the new use had changed the appearance of the premises, nor could he see how the replacement of the former ironmongery and steel stock by household furniture and effects could have any direct effect on the character of the locality. Comparing the nature and scale of the activities now carried on upon the appeal premises with the previous use, the reporter concluded that though there had been a change of use in the appeal premises, the change was not a material one and therefore no planning permission was required. The Secretary of State saw no reason to dissent. (Refs. P/ENA/GA/1; P/ENA/GA/2, March 22, 1977.)

3.30   Established use—successive unauthorised uses
An unauthorised change in the use of premises from single-family house to lodging house began after 1948. That use was unlawful. In 1968 the use of the premises was changed to a

hostel. The question was raised whether the previous use as a guest house or lodging house fell within the same class as a hostel under the Town and Country Planning (Use Classes) (Scotland) Order 1973. However, since the earlier use was unlawful, that question was irrelevant. The change of use to hostel from the unauthorised use as a single-family dwelling-house was a material one. No use begun after 1964 in breach of planning control and for which planning permission had not been subsequently obtained is immune from enforcement action. (Ref. P/PPA/HD/5, January 11, 1978.)

3.31 Material change of use—general retail market

On behalf of the appellants it was submitted that planning permission was not required to use premises as a general retail market because there was an existing planning permission for a cattle market. The Secretary of State considered that use as a cattle market was different from use as a general retail market on a regular basis and that planning permission was required for use as a general retail market. (Refs. P/PPA/SU/32 and 33; P/ENA/SU/9, 10, 11 and 12, August 23, 1979.)

3.32 Established use rights—caravan

A caravan had been sited on a particular site since 1964 or earlier and thus had existing use rights. In 1977 it was moved some 15 feet towards the shore onto land which was probably in different ownership. The reporter considered that the caravan was now stationed on a site materially different from the original site and that planning permission was required for the change of use. (Ref. P/ENA/HG/5, August 27, 1979.)

3.33 Material change of use—hotel—licensed bar

It was proposed to form a licensed bar with cellar at an existing hotel. The planning authority argued that the proposal constituted a material change of use through the provision of a bar open to the public; this would result in increased patronage of the premises, noise, increased parking requirements and increased vehicle movements, with a possible detrimental effect on the amenity of surrounding dwelling-houses. The appellant argued it was not a material change of use.

The reporter said that there was no doubt that the inclusion of a cocktail bar and of a room capable of accommodating 50 persons at functions at which alcohol might be consumed would change the character of the hotel. This would be particularly evident in the non-tourist season when the hotel would be less well-patronised by guests and more by day visitors and members of the public calling in for a drink. This was the appellant's declared intention in order to maintain the viability of the hotel as a year-round facility. Class X of the Town and Country Planning (Use Classes) (Scotland) Order 1973 clarifies the point that it is the sale of excisable liquor to persons other than residents or to persons other than those consuming meals on the premises that is the criterion as to change of use. Planning permission for the public bar was refused. (Ref. P/PPA/SQ/59, September 10, 1979.)

3.34 Material change of use—use for garaging—commercial garage

Premises had been used by the Territorial Army for the garaging of vehicles. They were also used for the inspection of vehicles and, to a limited extent, for maintenance of vehicles. In 1970 the premises were sold to the appellant who used them as a store for animal fodder and as a garage for agricultural equipment and vehicles. Some maintenance was done.

When, however, in 1978 the premises came to be used as a commercial garage, that amounted, the reporter concluded, to a material change of use. Previously work had only been carried out on the relatively few vehicles belonging to the occupant of, and garaged in, the premises. In contrast, he said, a commercial garage had to attract vehicles from various owners. Before 1978 little noise or traffic was generated by the activities at the premises; noise and traffic increased greatly after the premises became a commercial garage. (Ref. P/ENA/HA/7, February 18, 1980.)

3.35 Material change of use—planning unit—established use

Part of a large site came into separate ownership from the rest of the site. The reporter accepted the planning authority's view that the new planning unit had inherited an established use for industrial purposes, a use conferred on it by the previous use of the whole site. (Ref. P/PPA/TB/10, May 20, 1981.)

3.36 Material change of use—use of dining room as office

One room in an upper-floor flat was used jointly as a dining room and for the administration of the appellant's business as a theatrical casting agent. A small desk and filing cabinet and a built-in cupboard were used for the storage of documents. There was also a typewriter and telephone. A small notice on the wall of the common stair gave the name of the agency.

An enforcement notice alleged that a breach of planning control had occurred in that the room was being used as an office without planning permission. The planning authority alleged disturbance caused by callers at the property. The appellant argued that there had been no breach of planning control. He did not employ staff and no clients came to the premises. There were no advertisements apart from the small sign. All business was conducted by telephone.

The reporter was satisfied that provided all the rooms in the appeal premises remained principally in residential use, that no one other than the appellant was engaged in work for the agency at the appeal premises and that no clients called at the premises for professional or business purposes, there was no material change of use. The telephone and postal communications could be regarded as *de minimis*, not affecting the principal use of the property for residential purposes. It had not been adequately demonstrated, the reporter thought, that a material change of use had taken place, either in terms of clients visiting the premises or of any other person coming to work on the premises. He therefore concluded that there had been no breach of planning control. (Ref. P/ENA/SL/139, June 11, 1981.)

3.37 Material change of use—footpath to garden ground

The four appellants in this case owned neighbouring houses, two of which fronted one road while the other two fronted a different road. A tarmac-surfaced footpath connecting the two roads separated the gardens of each pair of houses.

In 1980 the appellants had, in effect, incorporated the footpath into their respective gardens. The fences on either side of the footpath had been removed and replaced by a single fence running along the centre line of the path. At one of the houses the tarmac surface of the path had been removed; at the other three houses gravel had been spread over the tarmac. The result was that the site of the path now had the appearance of forming part of the garden ground or driveway at each of the four houses. A fence separating the two sets of gardens had been extended so as to close off the footpath. Although each appellant owned the ground up to the centre line of the footpath, the titles to each property contained a reservation of a right of access over the path.

The appellants sought permission, retrospectively, to change the use of the footpath to driveway and garden ground. Permission was refused by the planning authority. The authority also served enforcement notices requiring the reinstatement of the path to its former condition and the removal of the fences. These were appeals against the refusal of planning permission and against the enforcement notices.

The appellants submitted that there was no evidence of planning permission ever having been granted for the use of the land as a footpath, that there was no public right of way over the path and that responsibility for its maintenance had not been accepted by the highway authority. They argued that the denial of public passage over the land did not involve development. Discontinuance of a use does not, they said, amount to a change of use. It is, as was said by the Lord Justice-Clerk in *Paul* v. *Ayrshire County Council*, 1964 S.C. 116, merely the first step towards the making of such a change; a change of use only occurs when some new use emerges.

The appellants also put forward the argument that what had taken place in the present case was covered by the provisions of section 19(2)(*d*) of the Town and Country Planning (Scotland) Act 1972. Section 19(2)(*d*) provides that the use of any building or other land within the curtilage of a dwelling-house for any purpose incidental to the enjoyment of the dwelling-house as such does not involve development. The appellants also claimed that title restrictions were not relevant considerations in the making of a planning decision.

The planning authority accepted that the mere discontinuance of a use did not amount to a change of use but argued that that was not the situation here. There had, they argued, been a material change in the use of the land; the use had been changed from footpath to driveway and garden ground. The authority submitted that section 19(2)(*d*) of the 1972 Act was not applicable here. That provision related to the use of land within the curtilage of a dwelling-house. In *Sinclair Lockhart's Trustees* v. *Central Land Board*, 1951 S.C. 258, Lord Mackintosh declared that the curtilage of a house or other building might be said to be the "ground which is used for the comfortable enjoyment" of that house or building. In the present case the appeal site was a footpath available for public use: it could not be said to fall within the curtilage of the houses.

The planning authority stated that even if there was no specific planning permission for the path, it had at the very least been in use for over four years at the time when it was closed. Existing use rights had therefore been established and enforcement action in respect of the path was barred by section 84(3) of the 1972 Act. The authority also claimed that the reservation in the appellant's titles of rights of access over the path destroyed the argueent that passage over the path was a mere privilege which the appellants could withdraw when they pleased.

The reporter considered that there had been a material change in the use of the footpath site. Even if planning permission had not been granted for the path, it was beyond dispute that the path had been in use for more than four years and had acquired existing use rights under section 84(3) of the 1972 Act. Realigning the fence had done more than cause the use of the footpath to cease; it had enclosed the area of the path within the curtilages of the four houses and the land had thereupon been put to a new use.

In the view of the reporter, therefore, a breach of planning control had taken place. The reporter did not consider that planning permission should be granted for the closure of the footpath. All the appeals were therefore dismissed and the enforcement notices were upheld. (Refs. P/PPA/SS/53; P/ENA/SS 27–30, October 12, 1981.)

3.38 Material change of use—enforcement notice—hot food shop

An enforcement notice was served in respect of the part use of a shop as a hot food shop. The shop sold a variety of household convenience goods including cigarettes, confectionery, greeting cards, comics and paperback books, soft drinks and cleaning materials. Pies, filled rolls and soup were offered for sale. Among the fillings available were certain hot items such as sausage and hamburger. The food for sale was prepared in the back shop where there was a domestic cooker, an electric griddle, and a hot water urn. Ventilation was to the rear of the building by means of an extractor fan and there was also a cooker hood and duct leading to the original chimney flue. The display fascia on the shop stated "Tobacconist; Stationery; Greeting Cards."

For the appellants it was stated that the food items referred to were sold between the hours of 12 noon and 2.00pm. The rolls were sold cold but some contained warmed fillings. Warming was carried out by electric heater, with no frying. No cooking smells were noticeable in and around the premises or in any premises nearby and no complaints had been made about cooking smells. The appellants considered that the use did not fall into the classification for planning purposes as a "shop for the sale of hot food."

For the planning authority it was stated that the activities at the appeal premises were considered to involve a part change of use to a shop for the sale of hot food. The authority would not have wished planning permission to be granted for this use as the lack of a ventilation duct allowed cooking odours to escape into the residential properties above. Complaints might arise if there was intensification of cooking or other foods were cooked. The council was not satisfied that adequate ventilation arrangements would be made.

The reporter said that he first had to consider whether the activities carried on at the appeal premises amounted to a material change of use to part use as a shop for the sale of hot food. He said that the sale of food prepared on the premises formed part of the activities at the shop, but was only one of several types of goods on sale. Only part of the food for sale was hot and the sale of such food appeared to take place mainly during a limited period in the middle of the day. The scale of the cooking operation was modest, and the type of cooking carried out did not have the distinctive environmental problems associated with deep frying or pungent food. The premises continued to have the appearance and character of an ordinary retail shop rather than a hot food shop, and did not have external advertisements for the sale of hot food. For these reasons the reporter was not convinced that the hot food component of the activities at the shop was on such a scale or had caused sufficient change in circumstances to amount to a material change of use. There was therefore no breach of planning control. (Ref. P/ENA/SL/161, November 11, 1982.)

3.39 Development—enforcement notice—"four year rule"

An enforcement notice required removal of a fish and chip van from a public car park. An appeal was lodged on grounds (*b*) and (*c*) of section 85(1) of the 1972 Act—that the matters alleged in the notice did not constitute a breach of planning control and that the notice had not been served within four years from the date of the breach. There had been no physical change by building or engineering works. The reporter accepted that the car park was intended to be used for parking and that stationing a fish and chip van was comparable to parking it there. However, it was considerably larger and more conspicuous than most vehicles usually found in a car park. Secondly, in contrast to most other vehicles using the car park, it was likely to remain on site for relatively long periods, even if it were removed every night. Thirdly, and most importantly, the mobile van was likely to attract groups of customers throughout its period of operations. For these reasons the reporter considered that a material change of use had occurred and that the appeal on ground (*b*) therefore failed.

As regards the appeal on section 85(1)(*c*), the expression "other operations" appearing in section 84(3)(*a*) (and referred to in section 85(1)(*c*)) could not be considered in isolation; it needed to be interpreted as describing physical changes akin to those made as a result of building, engineering or mining activities. The activities here could not be included as "other operations." The appeal on ground (*c*) of section 85(1) therefore failed. (Refs. P/EUC/SA/2; P/ENA/SA/41, October 10, 1983.)

3.40 Material change of use—restaurant—discothèque

An enforcement notice alleged a material change of use from use as a public house/restaurant to use as a public house/restaurant/discothèque. An appeal was lodged against the notice on ground (*b*) of section 85(1) of the 1972 Act—*i.e.* that the matters alleged in the notice did not constitute a breach of planning control.

The premises had previously been used as a lounge bar and restaurant. Music was relayed, evidently to give a relaxed background to the service and consumption of food and drink. The advertising laid stress upon the unhurried nature of the restaurant. No reference was made to dancing and all the available evidence showed that only at one function was the dance floor uncovered and used. There was no evidence that on that occasion the music was loud enough to be heard in neighbouring premises.

Immediately after the appellants took over the appeal premises a change of emphasis in the operation became apparent. The enterprise concentrated upon the operation of a discothèque in the semi-basement. Drinks were available there and in a bar above. Late suppers were provided. Loud music was played through fixed equipment. Music and dancing, instead of being incidental to the use of the premises as a restaurant became the main use of the semi-basement and the serving of food became ancillary to the music and dancing. The reporter's reading of the evidence made it clear that there was also an intensification of the use of the premises as a whole.

There was in the reporter's view a material change of use due to the introduction of the discothèque as a principal use together with the use of the public house. As this was done without planning permission, there was a breach of planning control. The appeal was therefore dismissed. (Ref. P/ENA/CC/14, March 30, 1984.)

3.41 Material change of use—retail shop—meat packaging

This was an appeal against a refusal of planning permission for the installation of a refrigeration unit, vehicle parking and an extension at the appellant's premises. Appeal was also lodged against an enforcement notice alleging unauthorised installation of the refrigeration unit.

The site included a single shop unit operating through the front shop as a butcher's shop and general store. The shop was surrounded mainly by houses and lock-up garages. At the back of the shop and visible to passers-by was a large refrigeration unit (12 metres by 2.3 metres). The question whether the access it blocked was a right of way was not within the scope of the planning inquiry. There were objections from the community council and from numerous nearby residents, including a petition with 60 signatures. Most of the complaints related to noise from the refrigeration unit; increase in traffic hazards in the garage court area (used by vans delivering materials to and from the shop premises); congestion; formation of potholes by large delivery vehicles; and general loss of amenity through expansion of the business to the level of a small factory which would be better located in an industrial or commercial area. Other objections included loss of privacy, obnoxious smells from a lock-up garage used for the storage of offal and bones, and the attraction of vermin.

The planning authority's planning officer observed in a report to the planning committee that there was little doubt that there had been a change in emphasis from a shop to a manufacturing and distribution unit with a retail outlet. In his view the use would be better suited to an industrial site. However, he was doubtful whether the current proposals constituted such a marked change in intensity to justify a refusal of planning permission.

The reporter said that he would agree that it would be difficult from available evidence to establish conclusively whether there had been an intensification of the use of the premises amounting to a material change of use requiring planning permission, *i.e.* whether meat production, packaging and distribution had become the predominant use of the premises rather than being ancillary to the retail shop use—but the appellant had admitted he supplied hotels, restaurants and other shops; also that since taking over the premises in 1979 he had more than doubled his staff to a total of 25 including 8 full-time employees in the back-shop alone. It was clear that considerable expansion of the business had taken place and the reporter therefore considered the determining factor in these appeals was whether the proposed development would consolidate such expansion and/or facilitate further expansion to the detriment of the established character and amenity of this residential area. The reporter's conclusion was that it would, and would seriously erode the character and amenity of the area and would be likely to exacerbate problems already encountered in connection with service vehicles. He implied no criticism of the appellant's acumen, only that in this particular location he considered that protection of the existing environment must take priority. Both appeals were therefore dismissed. (Refs. P/PPA/TA/73; P/ENA/TA/9, December 24, 1984.)

3.42 Material change of use—counter-service restaurant—additional hot food take-away facility

Planning permission had been granted for a counter-service restaurant. It was used as a restaurant with additional hot food take-away facilities. The planning authority alleged that the additional use was a breach of planning control.

The appellants argued that a counter-service restaurant was one where food was paid for at the counter before being consumed. At the point of purchase the food belonged to the customer and he or she had a free choice of whether to eat it in the premises or to take it away to eat elsewhere.

The reporter said the question was whether the take-away side of the business involved a material change of use. He found it was inherent in the description "counter-service restaurant" that the customer was entitled to take away duly purchased hot or cold food or refreshments from the premises covered by that description. (Refs. P/PPA/GA/262; P/ENA/GA/55, December 20, 1984.)

3.43 Material change of use—outline application

Two planning applications were refused by the planning authority. The first was an application for the erection of 364 houses on 25 acres of land, the second, which related to the same area of land, was for change of use from industrial and agricultural use to residential use and public open space. Following a public inquiry, the reporter granted planning permission for the change of use but refused the outline application because he was not convinced that the site could accommodate the number of dwellings applied for. The decision, said the report, did not commit either the planning authority or the developer to any particular form or extent of residential development or to any particular balance between open space and housing, but did have the advantage of establishing the planning status of the land. (Refs. P/PPA/GA/176 and 194, December 4, 1984.)

3.44 Material change of use—dwelling—business use

An enforcement notice alleged a material change from use as a dwelling and garden ground to use in connection with a plumbing and heating engineer's business.

The reporter said that on the question of whether there had been a material change of use the salient facts were (a) that the appellants acquired the house with the intention of running the business from it; (b) that until 1984 they had no other premises from which to run the business; (c) that the appellants erected a timber building on the site which was fitted out for the purposes of a plumber's store and was still so used to a certain extent; (d) that the nature of the business was advertised in the window of the dwelling; (e) that the business was administered from the dwelling; (f) that three vehicles used for business as well as private purposes had been kept within the dwelling's curtilage; and (g) that the employees assembled at the dwelling in the morning and returned there in the evening.

Taking these facts together, the reporter had no doubt that the extent of the business use of the house had exceeded the bounds of activities which could reasonably be described as incidental to the normal use of the house. The submission that the commercial use of the house was now minimal and that there was little or no evidence of such use on the day of the site inspection was not a material consideration, since compliance with an enforcement notice did not secure its discharge. The appeal therefore failed. However, because the conduct of a plumber's business might entail response to emergency calls outside business hours, the reporter considered that the appellants would suffer undue hardship if one vehicle suitable for carrying plumber's materials were not allowed to be kept at the premises. (Ref. P/ENA/FB/59, April 25, 1985.)

3.45 Material change of use—lock-ups—light industry/warehousing
Planning permission had been granted for a number of lock-up garages. These came to be used for light industry or warehousing. This was a material change of use requiring planning permission which had not been obtained. (Refs. P/ENA/ST/27 and 28, June 24, 1985.)

3.46 Mobile stall—breach of planning control
A mobile stall had been situated on land. Fish was sold by retail from the stall. The planning authority served an enforcement notice alleging an unauthorised material change of use. The stall was operated on five or six days a week according to the planning authority, on three-and-a-half days according to the appellant. An appeal was lodged on ground (¼b) of section 85(1) of the 1972 Act—that the matters alleged in the notice did not constitute a breach of planning control. The reporter considered that whether for six, five or three-and-a-half days a week, the

regular use of the land for this purpose was a material change of use. A breach of planning control had therefore occurred. (Ref. P/ENA/LC/34, July 29, 1985.)

3.47 Material change of use—commercial vehicles—domestic driveway

The reporter was satisfied that there had been a material change of use of premises in that a domestic garage was used for storage and the driveway for parking commercial vehicles. Delivery vehicles had caused congestion. There was disturbance at night with the arrival and departure of commercial vehicles including a mobile showroom. Parking and unloading of commercial vehicles represented a visual intrusion in the street-scene. The use of the premises also tended to attract an unusual number of visitors, customers or tradesmen calling at the house. The storage, delivery and removal of goods was also likely to cause disturbance. The enforcement notice appeal was dismissed. (Refs. P/ENA/SK/8; P/PPA/SK/64, October 7, 1986.)

3.48 Development—private club—public house

Planning permission was refused for the change of use of a private club to a public house. The appellant claimed that although a different type of licence would be required in order to use the premises as a public house, its use would not be materially different from what it was when it was operated as a private social club.

The reporter considered that although the Town and Country Planning (Use Classes) (Scotland) Order 1973 was silent upon the matter, the view generally held was that a public house was materially different in kind from a private social club because of the differences in the clientele and in the potential effect of the public house on the environs. The public house would serve any member of the public who chose to attend, within the terms of its licence; the private social club would be attended only by its members or by affiliated members or guests, all of whom would have to act within the club's code of conduct. The act of selecting members involved the creation of a narrower and more cohesive social group than would be found in the clientele of a public house. Generally the effect upon the environs of a private social club was likely to be less marked than that of a public house. Accordingly, he believed that what was proposed was a material change of use for which planning permission was required. (Ref. P/PPA/FB/212, November 25, 1986.)

3.49 Material change of use—café—Indian restaurant

This was an appeal against a refusal of planning permission for a change of use from a licensed café to a licensed Indian restaurant. The planning authority refused permission on the grounds of nuisance caused to neighbours as a result of cooking odours and noise and disturbance late at night. The authority considered that the restaurant operation was substantially different in character from a café, with a greater emphasis on larger cooked meals, pronounced lunchtime and mid/late evening use and longer visits by clients likely to come from a wider catchment area by car. The authority also considered that the restaurant use placed greater demands on the ventilation system (which it would be difficult to improve) and that more cars would be attracted to the area, adding to parking difficulties and causing noise in the evenings.

The reporter concluded that use as a licensed Indian restaurant was not a material change from the approved use as a café. He considered that there was a great variety of restaurant and café establishments and it was not possible to define different subcategories on the basis of the characteristics suggested by the planning authority. Planning permission was therefore not required for the change from café to restaurant. (Refs. P/PPA/SD/34; P/ENA/SD/13, January 8, 1987.)

3.50 Material change of use—house in multiple occupation
The reporter agreed with the planning authority that the use of a single dwelling-house for multiple occupation was a use *sui generis*. It amounted to a material change of use in terms of section 19(1) of the 1972 Act and so required planning permission. (Ref. P/ENA/TB/36, August 19, 1987.)

3.51 Material change of use—house in multiple occupation
The reporter said that it could not be assumed that a change of use from a house in multiple occupation to a guest house or hotel was not a material change of use requiring planning permission. (Ref. P/PPA/FA/110, September 3, 1987.)

3.52 Guest house—criteria
The planning authority did not consider premises to be in use as a guest house when a house was used for no more than four weeks in the summer, when not more than two bedrooms were used for paying guests or when accommodation was provided for a maximum of three students. (Ref. P/PPA/LA/506, October 16, 1987.)

3.53 Development—material change of use—shop—"property shop"
This was an appeal against a change of use from a shop to a "property shop." The appellants argued that as the proposed use

would not include legal or insurance services, it could not be described as an estate agency. Indeed, by advertising property for sale by displaying photos, etc., by providing prospective purchasers with schedules and by arranging times for viewing, the appeal proposal would be comparable with a retail shop from which other goods were sold. For these reasons the proposal did not involve development.

The reporter considered that although a potential housebuyer would be able to enter the premises and see, and subsequently take away, photographs and/or details of properties for sale, as the goods to be purchased, *i.e.* the houses or other property, would not be available in the "property shop," this would not be comparable with entering a retail shop where the actual goods could be seen, inspected and taken away after purchase. For these reasons, and taking account of the fact that in the Town and Country Planning (Use Classes) (Scotland) Order 1973 the term "office" (Class II) includes an estate agency whilst the use of premises as a shop is in Class I, he considered that the proposed change of use constituted development for which planning permission was required. (Ref. P/PPA/TC/218, March 9, 1988.)

3.54 Curtilage of dwelling-house—caravan—occupation
A caravan within the curtilage of a dwelling-house was used to provide emergency accommodation for persons sent by the Department of Health and Social Security. It was the planning authority's policy that caravans should not be used as independent dwellings. The reporter agreed with the planning authority that both the appearance and occupation of the caravan affected the amenity of the area. There was a risk of disturbance to neighbours and the residential standard of the area would be lowered. (Refs. P/ENA/CC/20; P/PPA/CC/160, April 6, 1988.)

3.55 Development—material change of use
This was an appeal against a refusal of planning permission for the use of two basement bedrooms and a ground floor lounge for the purposes of a guest house. The whole house comprised a lounge, a kitchen/dining area and five bedrooms.

The reporter considered that the first of the determining issues was whether the appeal proposal represented a material change in the use of the house. He said that a decision as to whether the change of use was material could only be taken by determining whether the character of the existing use of the property would be substantially altered by the proposed change. Factors which had to be taken into account in making this assessment were the size of the property and the proportionate floor space allocated to the proposed use, the impact of the proposed change on the appearance of the property and the neighbourhood, and the difference between the characteristics of the existing and proposed uses.

Excluding stairs, passageways and storage areas, half of the net floor area of the property would be allocated to guest house use. When the proposed guest house area was fully occupied, the number of guests would equal, or if children were allowed to share parents' bedrooms, possibly exceed, the number of family residents. The reporter agreed with the planning authority that the extent of coming and going generated by the use would be greater than that normally associated with a private dwelling-house, as would the demand for parking space in the vicinity. Taking these factors alone, the reporter was satisfied as a matter of fact and degree that the change of use proposed was a material one for which planning permission was required. (Ref. P/PPA/GA/424, January 23, 1989.)

3.56 Material change of use—separate dwelling-houses—planning permission

An established use certificate had been refused for the subdivision of a house into two flats. The reporter found that the property had been built in 1890 as a single dwelling-house but was altered in 1961 or 1962 to form two flats which were occupied from 1962 to 1982 by separate households. The premises had never been used as two separate dwelling-houses. The reporter was of the opinion that where residential use was concerned, the test of separateness was not so much in the form of occupation as in the form of construction and that "separate dwelling-houses" meant dwelling-houses which were physically separate from one another such as to provide security and domestic privacy for each. No material change of use had occurred. Proposed building works would, taken together with the intention of separate occupation, constitute a material change in the use of the premises. Planning permission was refused as there was no special reason for overriding council policy. (Ref. P/EUC/LA/3, July 7, 1987.)

3.57 Material change of use—multiple occupation of dwelling-house

This was an appeal against a determination under section 51 of the 1972 Act that proposed alterations at 58 Bank Street, Irvine and proposals for the future use of 60 Bank Street constituted development for which planning permission was required. Number 58 consisted of the first and attic floors of the property. On the first floor there were four rooms and a bathroom while in the attic there were two rooms and a bathroom. Number 60, on the basement and ground floors, consisted of six rooms, a kitchen and a bathroom. Three of the rooms had an electricity meter and a cooker point.

The planning authority received complaints that Number 58 was being used for DHSS lodgings. The appellant said that it was his intention to refurbish Number 58 as residential accommodation for six individuals in the form of "shared housing" as described in Scottish Housing Handbook Number 7. The downstairs part was later to be put to a similar use. The council determined that the appellant's proposals constituted development for the following reasons:

1. Each individual occupant of Numbers 58 and 60 would live independently rather than communally as a family unit. The factors leading to this conclusion were: (a) there was no communal living area; (b) the installation of separate electric meters and the provision of individual supply points for cookers in each room clearly indicated that all costs were not to be shared; and (c) the draft tenancy agreement set out a clearly defined landlord/tenant relationship in relation to each individual occupier. The council therefore considered that the use of Numbers 58 and 60 would be for multiple paying occupation.

2. As the current use of Numbers 58 and 60 was in each case a single private dwelling-house, the change of use to multiple paying occupation represented a material change of use in terms of section 19(1) of the 1972 Act on the grounds that the change of use involved a change in the nature of occupation and function of the said premises which would have material implications for common services, the amenity of neighbouring properties through increased noise and disturbance, on street parking and on cleansing services.

The appellant said that he intended to provide accommodation similar to mainstream dwellings which would be occupied by a group of people who were usually unrelated. The number of people residing in each dwelling would be no more than the range normally encountered in a single family household. He had originally intended that each room for individual occupation would be provided with a metered electricity supply and a cooker point. The appellant considered that residents might wish to do some cooking in their own rooms. Individual tenants would be responsible for providing their own heating arrangements but there would be an electric storage heater in each lettable room, connected to the landlord's supply so that minimum background heat would be provided during very cold periods and periods of vacancy. The power to kitchens, bathrooms and common areas would be metered through the landlord's supply. After the council issued its determination the appellant said he was pre-pared to have one room used as a living room for occupiers, the electricity meter and cooker control point being removed from that room, and heating being provided through the landlord's supply.

The reporter said that the wording of section 51(1) made it clear that determinations under that section could not be made retrospectively. Although the property at Number 58 was occupied and in its new use at the time of the reporter's visit, he understood that this commenced subsequent to the appellant's application for the determination. On that basis the reporter accepted that the application in respect of both properties was competent.

He said it was clear that the original dwelling had been sub-divided into two flats some considerable time previously. Not-withstanding the length of time they may have lain empty, it seemed to the reporter that this was the use with which the appellant's proposal had to be compared to establish whether a material change of use was involved. In support of the appeal the appellant referred to "shared housing" as described in Scottish Housing Handbook Number 7. While one could have regard to the Handbook, it was merely advisory and did not purport to interpret the planning legislation. The appeal had to be deter-mined as a question of fact and degree and in the reporter's opinion the determining issue was the extent to which the new use could be said to be similar to a normal family use of the flats.

In reaching a view on this matter, the reporter thought that consideration had to be given to the two aspects of the new use which had been correctly identified in the council's two reasons for refusal of the application. First, there was the question of whether the individual occupants would be living independently rather than communally. On the basis of the information avail-able to it at the time of the determination the reporter believed the council to have been correct in deciding that the former would be the case. However, the reporter believed also that the amended arrangements suggested by the appellant were sufficient to overcome this reason. The balance had swung towards com-munal rather than independent living.

The second aspect related to what the council described in its second reason for refusal as "the nature of occupation and function of the said premises." It was established, said the reporter, that one of the factors to be taken into account in considering whether a change of use was material was the possible effect of the development proposal on local amenity. In general terms, planning had no concern with the characteristics of individual people or how they behaved. But the potential environmental impact of a new use was relevant, and the same applied in relation to the intensification of an existing use. In this context, the council had particularly mentioned the effect on common services, on the amenity of neighbouring properties (through increased noise and disturbance), on street parking and on cleansing services. In the reporter's view the council's approach to this matter was correct. The proposed use of the premises was likely to have these effects to an extent materially greater than would be experienced as a result of the use of the flats. There would be a high turnover of occupiers and the individual rooms could conceivably be occupied by couples or even families, although the reporter appreciated that that might not be the appellant's present intention. Nonetheless, it was reasonable to consider the potential impact as the premises might not always be under the appellant's control. In these circumstances the reporter was in no doubt that what was proposed was materially different from what was there before and that development was involved. The appeal was therefore dismissed. (Ref. P/DEV/1/SG/2, March 8, 1989.)

3.58 Material change of use—use subsisting—site of demolished dwelling-house—countryside policy

A house was demolished in 1985 as a dangerous building. Its occupation was thought to have ceased some 30 years previously. The site comprised the mature landscaped grounds of the former house. The only remains of the former house were an ornamental stone fountain and a classical pediment salvaged from a garden "folly."

The planning authority refused outline planning permission for a house on the site because it would be contrary to their policy for development in the countryside. That policy was based on DHS Circular 40/1960 (replaced by SDD Circular 24/1985).

The appellants argued that there were legal precedents for accepting that the discontinuance of a use was not a change of use and that where a sole use was suspended and later resumed, the resumption did not constitute development. It had been assumed that residential use of the site was regarded as being established when planning permission in principle had been granted by the former county council in 1973.

The reporter said that the most important issue was the application of the planning authority's countryside policy. Both the structure plan and the local plan contained a general presumption against new development in the countryside. Such policies were generally directed towards protecting the countryside from proliferation of unnecessary development which would detract from rural amenity, would lead to a loss of agricultural land and would place a disproportionate burden on community services. However, he thought the present proposal was in a different category; the site appeared to have been occupied by a dwelling-house for perhaps a couple of centuries; and although physical occupation might have ceased some 30 years ago, it was clear from the site inspection that no other use had intervened. For that reason he would agree that the site retained existing use rights for a single dwelling-house. Reoccupation of the site would help to restore the previous levels of amenity which had obviously been of a high order. Some contribution would also be made towards widening the range of choice in private housing. There would be no loss of agricultural land. The appeal was sustained. (Ref. P/PPA/CA/34, March 14, 1986.)

3.59   Parking of caravans—material change of use

At the time of the site inspection 31 large residential caravans, 10 touring-type caravans, three transportable chalets/caravans and a number of trailers had been sited on a large industrial area. An enforcement notice was served in respect of the material change of use. An appeal was lodged on, *inter alia*, ground (*bb*) of section 85(1) of the 1972 Act, *i.e.* that the breach of planning control alleged in the notice had not taken place. In respect of ground (*bb*) it seemed to the reporter that the parking of vehicles, including trailers and caravans—whether or not they were occupied—was a material change of use of the ground, and was not an engineering operation. He agreed that by fastening the two halves of transportable chalets together, connecting the chalets and caravans to services, and forming covers round their bases, there was an element of construction work. However, these were relatively minor operations. Also, the chalets could be easily separated into two halves for transportation to another site. For these reasons he considered that as ground previously used for industrial purposes was now occupied by residential transportable chalets a material change of use had occurred. Accordingly, the appeal on ground (*bb*) had to fail. (Ref. P/ENA/SL/250, June 14, 1989.)

Material change of use or operations

3.60 Development—engineering operation—hardstanding

The main question in this appeal was whether the formation and use of a car-parking space in the appellant's front garden came within either limb of the statutory definition of development. On an area of about 85 square feet adjacent to an existing driveway the appellant had laid concrete slabs to create a parking space, access to which was gained from the drive. To facilitate access, the appellant had altered the level of a 3-foot length of concrete boundary slab.

Whether or not particular operations amount to development is a matter of fact and degree. The works that had been carried out in the present case—the laying of 17 concrete slabs and the moving of the boundary slab—were, in the reporter's judgment, so trifling that they could not be said to amount to engineering operations. As regards the "change of use" limb of the definition of "development," the reporter was satisfied that the use of this piece of garden ground as a vehicle hardstanding area was excluded from the statutory definition by section 19(2)(*d*) of the 1972 Act, which provides that the use of any building or other land within the curtilage of a dwelling-house for any purpose incidental to the enjoyment of the dwelling-house as such does not amount to development. (Ref. P/PPA/SL/78, January 30, 1980.)

3.61 Operation or change of use—scrap-yard

The reporter said that the breach of planning control that was alleged, unauthorised use as a scrap-yard, was clearly a change of use rather than an operation. The provisions of section 84(3) (relating to operations) did not apply and the appeal on ground (*c*) of section 85(1) of the 1972 Act—*i.e.* that the works had taken place more than four years previously—therefore failed. The information before the reporter indicated that the change of use occurred after the end of 1964 and immunity from enforcement action had not therefore been achieved. (Ref. P/ENA/W/35, May 5, 1988.)

3.62 Operations—use of fish and chip van

The parking of a fish and chip van in a car park could not be regarded as "other operations" within the meaning of section 19(1) of the 1972 Act. The phrase had to be interpreted as describing physical changes akin to those made as a result of building, engineering or mining works. The activities here could not be regarded as "other operations." (Refs. P/EUC/SA/2; P/ENA/SA/41, October 10, 1983.)

3.63 Operation—material change of use—enforcement
An enforcement notice required the cessation of vehicle storage, repair and vehicle breaking up on an area of land. Appeal was made (*inter alia*) on ground (*c*) of section 85(1) of the 1972 Act, which provides that an enforcement notice relating to operational development must be served within four years of the allegedly unauthorised development. The reporter held that an appeal on this ground was not competent in this case since the enforcement notice did not relate to operational development. The allegedly unauthorised activity was a material change of use, not an operation. (Ref. P/ENA/TC/51, August 13, 1986.)

3.64 Caravan—whether siting a building operation or a material change of use
It was alleged that a caravan had been sited without authority on a superseded stretch of road. The caravan was a large mobile home supported on blocks of wood with no wheels. The appellant suggested that since the caravan had been on the site for more than four years his appeal on ground (*c*) of section 85(1) of the 1972 Act should succeed. Section 85(1)(*c*) relates to breaches of planning control consisting of operations. There had to be considered, therefore, the question of whether the siting of the caravan was an operation or a change of use. The reporter took the view that it might be reasonable to describe the siting of a caravan which had masonry underbuilding and was connected to a full range of services as an operation since to some extent such a caravan would have the appearance and character of a building. The appellant's caravan had no electric connection. It had no wheels but it did not look like a fixed structure and it could be moved relatively easily. The reporter therefore concluded that the siting of the caravan involved a material change of use rather than an operation. The "four year rule" was therefore not applicable. (Ref. P/ENA/SA/72, April 25, 1988.)

3.65 Material change of use—erection of structures—clay-pigeon shooting
An enforcement notice alleged the erection of structures and the making of associated excavations in connection with the carrying on of clay-pigeon shooting. The appellant's claim that the land was used by livestock was outweighed by the evidence of numerous objectors. Clay-pigeon shooting took place on the site

on more than 28 days in any year. The reporter considered that the structures adversely affected the appearance of the area. The firing of cartridges was likely to have a disturbing effect, by reason of noise and potential danger, upon visitors to the nearby countryside. He concluded that it would be wrong to grant planning permission for either the structures or for the use of the site for clay-pigeon shooting. (Ref. P/ENA/SK/11, July 15, 1987.)

Planning unit

3.66 Planning unit—division of garden

The reporter accepted the planning authority's view that the legal separation of a garden into two parts did not constitute the formation of two separate planning units. If this were the case a dwelling-house could be converted into flats or a department store into a row of shops without planning permission being required. (Ref. P/PPA/SK/84, June 8, 1988.)

3.67 Petrol filling station—use for vehicle recovery—planning unit—breach of planning control

An enforcement notice had been served alleging that there had been a breach of planning control by unauthorised change of use from petrol filling station to vehicle recovery centre. The enforcement notice also alleged unauthorised erection of a perimeter fence 2.1 metres high, with strands of barbed wire above. The notice required discontinuance of the use as a vehicle recovery centre and of the use of the forecourt for storage of vehicles and removal of the unauthorised fences. The appellant averred that the alleged activity did not constitute a breach of planning control.

The whole unbuilt-on area of the site was, at the time of the site inspection, occupied by a variety of vehicles. The planning authority considered that the matters alleged were detrimental to the visual amenity of the adjacent residential area. They stated that the lawful use of the site was as a petrol filling station, *i.e.* retail selling, while the lawful use of the remainder of the site was as a garage, *i.e.* general industry.

The appellants argued that the site had been a general garage since the 1930s, establishing the use of the premises as a whole. Petrol was no longer sold but the other uses, vehicle repair, recovery and servicing all fell within the term "garage" and had always been carried on. None of the uses was ancillary to another and none could be allocated to one part of the site. The enforcement notice related to the forecourt, not to the planning unit which it was unreasonable to subdivide. The planning unit was the unit of occupation and the use here was a composite use of a general industrial nature. The petrol filling station was not a discrete planning unit. Nor was it ever the predominant use.

The reporter concluded that there had been a material change of use. A planning permission granted in 1964 to the Regent Oil Company was for buildings on the site on which there already was a petrol filling station. In addition the approved layout and use as a petrol filling station on a busy main road firmly tied the front portion of the central site to petrol sales, with unimpeded circulation for customers' vehicles. The consent related to the whole site and therefore the planning unit was (and remained) the entire site, the authorised use of which was a petrol filling station and a workshop for repair. Such a site was not a general industrial building within the terms of Class IV of the Schedule to the Town and Country Planning (Use Classes) (Scotland) Order 1973. Petrol filling facilities and vehicle repairs on the scale implied by the joint use of the site for these purposes could not be said to be covered by the definition of "industrial buildings" in article 2(2) of the UCO; consequently, the scale of both the petrol filling station and repair activities must have been limited by the nature of the site and building. The scale of activities associated with the current vehicle recovery business, including the number and size of vehicles on the site, was something very different. Development was therefore involved. Planning permission was refused. (Ref. P/ENA/SL/229, March 30, 1988.)

3.68   Planning unit—curtilage of flats—dwelling-house

Planning permission had been refused for the erection of a dwelling-house at the rear of a block of five flats. The appeal site comprised most of the garden at the rear of the flats. The land which had been conveyed to the flat owners was restricted to the solum of the building, the front garden and a narrow strip varying between 2 metres and 4 metres running along the rear of the building.

The application for the dwelling-house was refused as being detrimental to the amenity of the neighbourhood due to the over-development of the site and the loss of mature trees. On behalf of the planning authority it was submitted that a proper consideration of the application required the entire curtilage, the area including the five flats and the garden ground, to be viewed as a whole. The development ratio would be excessive in this area.

The reporter said that although, in granting consent for subdivision into five flats in 1981, the planning authority assumed that the whole curtilage of the property would continue to serve that function for the five flats, no condition to that effect was imposed. The appeal site was retained by the appellants and the purchasers of the flats bought in full knowledge of the position. In the reporter's earlier decision, he proceeded on the basis that the entire curtilage of the existing flatted property remained one planning unit and the reporter considered the small strip of rear garden allocated to the flats to be inadequate. The Court of Session held that he had erred in his approach and he was required to accept that legal separation had been effected and to consider the appeal site as a separate plot.

So regarded, he found that the proposed development would not have an unacceptable impact on the amenity of nearby residents or upon the appearance of the nearby conservation area. (Ref. P/PPA/GA/236, March 25, 1986.)

3.69 Material change of use—planning unit—cellar
In respect of the conversion of the cellar of a public house into a games room, it seemed to the reporter that as (1) the room was not large, particularly when compared with the rest of the public house; (2) neither the existing use as a cellar nor the proposed new use could realistically be expected to operate independently of the rest of the public house; and (3) the room was contained within the existing external walls of the public house so that the cellar of itself could not be considered to be a separate planning unit but had to be thought of as an integral part of the public house, the proposed conversion was not a material change of use of the premises. In terms of the 1972 Act development was not involved. (Ref. P/PPA/SU/138, March 14, 1984.)

3.70 Material change of use—ancillary use—planning unit—bothy
The building which was the subject of the appeal had originally been one of several buildings associated with a large house. The appeal premises had been used as a dairy, a laundry and a one-room gardener's bothy. When the appellant sold the main house and grounds he retained the appeal building which he rehabilitated and used as a studio and guest bed-sitting room. The premises included a kitchen and toilet.

It was held that there had been a breach of planning control. The previous use as a residence for a gardener was ancillary to the use of the main house. The appeal premises had become a main use in their own right when the house to which they were ancillary was sold. That sale did not include the appeal premises and effectively created a new planning unit. (Ref. P/ENA/LC/ 39, May 27, 1987.)

3.71 Material change of use—formation of games room

An enforcement notice was served in respect of an allegedly unauthorised change of use involving the installation of video games machines and a pool table for use as a games room at a general grocery store and off-licence. The games room was located at the rear of the building. It contained one pool table, a juke box and seven video games machines. The games room was reached through the shop and was advertised as being open between 4 p.m. and 9 p.m. on weekdays and 12 noon and 9 p.m. on Saturdays and Sundays.

The reporter found that the appellant's actions had resulted in the creation of a new planning unit within premises which had an established use as a shop. He found that the use as a games room could not be regarded as *de minimis* because of its size, the range of facilities provided and the number of patrons which could be accommodated. He also found that in planning terms it had no functional or other relationship with the primary established use of the building. The development was not in any way ancillary to the shop use but was a commercial entertainment use in its own right.

The space involved was formerly used for the storage of stock and the council's concern to ensure that adequate storage space remained was reasonable. The reporter noted that the appellant might no longer require it for storage, but that fact itself did not provide grounds for the establishment of a new use which had an entirely different character and impact.

The games room was under a neighbour's home and was in close proximity to a number of other flats and houses. The games room would attract an entirely different clientele from a licensed corner shop and could lead to a significant level of coming and going in the evenings which in itself was incompatible with the residential amenity which ought to be available in the centre of this village.

The reporter found no grounds to justify the grant of planning permission. (Ref. P/ENA/HF/53, March 15, 1989.)

Material change of use—intensification

3.72 Material change of use—intensification—use for boats

An enforcement notice required the cessation of the use of land for storage, repair and servicing of boats, the planning authority taking the view that a material change of use had occurred through intensification. The intensification had several elements: the use was located in a specific area; it was associated with the placing of boats on a levelled area unsuitable for small boats and extending to an area where the ground had become severely churned up; it was associated with the maintenance of comparatively large boats; it was mainly concerned with the activities of one firm; maintenance had exceeded periods of 28 days in a year; and the use was seen as an on-going one.

The reporter said that the use and maintenance of boats would always be of special importance on a small island and the presence of small craft moored or drawn-up around the coastline was a traditional feature. Nevertheless, the carrying out of such operations on a larger scale and in a more industrial way would at some stage amount to a material change of use. It was evident that such activities had taken place on the appeal site. (Ref. P/ENA/SA/75, June 7, 1988.)

3.73 Material change of use — intensification — automatic telling machine

Planning permission had been refused for the installation of an automatic telling machine (ATM) at a bank. The reporter considered, *inter alia*, whether the proposal could constitute development as a change of use through intensification. In his opinion, in some circumstances it might be argued that the combination of extending trading from within the bank premises on to the public footpath, the extension from office hours to almost continuous activity, and the extent of additional custom and use generated, would amount to intensification. Clearly the planning implications which stemmed from the installation of an ATM, apart from matters of appearance, related to these characteristics. In this case, however, he agreed with the planning authority that the likely intensification of use of the appeal premises would be quite insufficient to amount to a change of use. (Ref. P/PPA/GA/359, March 16, 1987.)

3.74 Material change of use—intensification of use— Use Classes Order—"leisure centre"

Planning permission had been granted in 1982 for the use of a former cinema as a "leisure centre, pool room, licensed snooker club" and for the ancillary sale of hot food. The appellants now sought to use the licensed snooker hall as a licensed disco; to use an unused balcony area as a new snooker lounge with a 50 per cent. reduction in the number of tables on the premises; to provide an additional bar/lounge in the previously unused upper foyer; and to extend the opening hours. The disco use would give rise to a considerable increase in the number of patrons using the premises. The majority of those customers would arrive and depart at the commencement and termination of the dance sessions rather than in the present more diffuse fashion. Planning permission had been refused by the planning authority for the reason that the change of use would give rise to unacceptable levels of noise and disturbance.

The appellants suggested that the proposal would not involve development. A disco, like a snooker hall, was a place for public entertainment and the whole premises had planning permission as a "leisure centre." The fact that the proposals might lead to the attraction of more customers was irrelevant in this context. The usable space in the building would be increased by a very small amount. The proposed change was so slight as to cast doubt upon whether planning permission was required.

The reporter considered this claim. The description "leisure centre" was not specific, nor was it referred to in the Town and Country Planning (Use Classes) (Scotland) Order 1973. If one adopted the "entertainment" connotation referred to in the presentation of the appellants' case it would embrace at least three of the scheduled use classes—XV, XVI and XVII. After considering all the factors the reporter concluded that the proposed changes would, as a matter of fact and degree, lead to an intensification of the use of the premises as a whole amounting to a maaterial change of use. However, bearing in mind the town centre location of the premises and the predominantly commercial/industrial nature of its surroundings, the reporter concluded that planning permission should be granted. (Ref. P/PPA/TL/182, July 29, 1986.)

3.75 Material change of use—intensification—car sales—car repairs

The first question to be determined was whether the current use of the premises required planning permission. The previous use of the premises was as a garage and workshop for a haulage contractor. The present use was for the refurbishment and repair of cars for sale. Bearing in mind the narrrow confines of the building, the size of the haulage contractor's vehicles and that for most of the time the vehicles would not be left unused in the workshop, yard or street, the reporter's conclusion was that the current use of the premises for cars, their refurbishment and repair for sale, the overflow of vehicles into the street, and the primary emphasis on retailing was, as a matter of fact and degree, an intensification of use of the premises constituting development requiring planning permission. (Ref. P/PPA/TB/108, July 18, 1986.)

3.76 Material change of use—intensification—mobile homes

For the planning authority it was argued that the placing of two caravans on a hotel car park and using them as bedrooms changed the use of the land from ancillary to the hotel to land for use as a hotel. There was on that count a material change of use. There was also a material change of use by intensification in that four new bedrooms had been added to the 12 existing bedrooms within the hotel building.

The appellants argued that the land occupied by the caravans was within the curtilage of the hotel and was therefore part of the hotel use. It was further argued that the caravans were intended and had been in use as "overflow" accommodation for guests. The use of the caravans was the same as the use of the hotel and therefore no material change of use was involved.

In the reporter's view the determining issue was whether, as a matter of fact and degree, there had been a material change of use and therefore a breach of planning control. The mobile homes were very large structures permanently installed with drainage and other services. In the reporter's view the extra accommodation provided by the caravans was significant and amounted to an intensification of the use of the land in that the number of bedrooms was increased from 14 to 18 or possibly even to 20. He was therefore of the opinion that a material change of use had occurred by reason of the intensification of the use of the land. (Ref. P/ENA/W/27, March 20, 1985.)

3.77 Material change of use—1972 Act, section 20(3)—breach of planning control prior to 1965—intensification

An enforcement notice was served in respect of the allegedly material change of use of premises from sign-writer's and vehicle painter's business to use for the preparation and sale of motor cars.

Appeal was lodged on grounds (*b*) and (*d*) of section 85(1) of the 1972 Act (*i.e.* that the matters alleged in the enforcement notice did not constitute a breach of planning control and that the alleged breach of planning control occurred before the beginning of 1965).

The appeal site consisted of a traditional single-storey cottage, now used for meetings with customers, etc., a timber workshop having a floor area of 56 square metres, and associated open land.

It was established to the reporter's satisfaction; (a) that prior to July 1, 1948 (the date of coming into force of the Town and Country Planning (Scotland) Act 1947) until he died in 1961 the then owner of the property operated from the premises as a dealer, mainly involved in the buying and selling of horses, floats, gigs and gypsy caravans; (b) that prior to July 1, 1948 one of the owner's sons used the workshop and part of the yard in connection with his sign-writing and vehicle painting business; (c) that part of the yard and drying green were used for parking personal vehicles and as access to the cottage which was occupied as a dwelling-house by the owner and his family; (d) on occasions vehicles were available for sale at the property; (e) the sign-writing and vehicle painting business and occasional sale of vehicles continued until about 1975 when the previous owner's son retired; (f) the property was sold to the appellant in 1983 following the son's death.

The appellant referred to section 20(3) of the 1972 Act which relates to land which on the appointed day (July 1, 1948) was normally used for one purpose and was also used on occasions, whether at regular intervals or not, for another purpose. Provided that land was used for that other purpose on at least one similar occasion between the appointed day and the beginning of 1969, planning permission was not required in respect of the use of the land for that other purpose on similar occasions. It was also argued that on July 1, 1948 there was an established use of the property for retailing motor and horse-drawn vehicles. That being so, the enforcement notice should be quashed as there had been no material change of use.

Alternatively, the appellant argued that ground (*d*) of section 85(1) of the 1972 Act applied—the breach of planning control, if any, occurred before the beginning of 1965.

The planning authority argued that section 20(3) was not applicable in as much that on the appointed day the site was used for more than one purpose. Even if one did attempt to apply the subsection it would only mean that the appellant would be entitled to make occasional use of the site for car sales. In fact he used all of the land for that purpose on a full-time basis. Here there was a clear and material intensification of use compared with the previous level of retailing which was *de minimis* and incidental to the main use of the workshop and part of the yard for vehicle painting and sign-writing. In their view any sales of vehicles in the past must have been on a very small scale, for it never came to the attention of the planning authority, whereas the present use was challenged almost as soon as it commenced in April 1983.

The reporter said that in examining the legal arguments, he agreed that section 20(3) was not applicable to the current appeal

as, on July 1, 1948, the site was in mixed use for three purposes—
a dwelling-house, a business for the sale and purchase of horses,
floats, gigs and gypsy caravans, and for sign-writing and vehicle
painting. Even accepting that the occasional sale of motor
vehicles occurred prior to the appointed day, section 20(3) would
only allow continuance of that occasional use, not its expansion
to become the dominant full-time use of the site. The use of the
workshop and original yard was, in the reporter's opinion, a light
industrial use as defined in article 2(2) of the Town and Country
Planning (Use Classes) (Scotland) Order 1973. It would follow
that any light industrial use of that workshop and yard area
would not involve development requiring planning permission.

However, the use and character of the appeal site had changed
to use for the sale of second-hand cars and, incidental thereto,
the use of the workshop for the checking and valeting of those
cars before their sale. It had also been extended to the former
drying green—in all, nearly the whole unbuilt-on area of the site.
It was primarily a retail use. It could be argued that this was not
too different from its pre-war and pre-1965 use of the purchase
and sale of wheeled vehicles, together with light industrial use in
the workshop, but the reporter considered that what had
occurred was, by fact and degree, a material intensification of use
since 1983 which required the submission of an application for
planning permission. The enforcement notice was therefore
upheld. (Ref. P/ENA/ST/26, December 21, 1984.)

3.78 Material change of use—intensification—guest house

Planning permission had been refused for the change of use
from a private guest house to a hotel on the grounds that (1) the
intensification of the use of the premises, and in particular their
licensing, would result in vehicular and pedestrian noise in a rural
community, especially late at night; and (2) the unsuitability of a
semi-detached house for this intensity of use.

Other houses were in close proximity. The occupier of the
other of the pair of semi-detached houses said that in their sitting
room and bedroom, which adjoined the dining room/lounge of
the appeal premises, noise could already be heard. Bar lunches
were already being advertised and the business advertised as a
licensed hotel. The planning authority considered that the provision of meals and refreshments could become the predominant
use if the hotel use were to be approved. The effect on car and
pedestrian movements between the proposed hotel, the layby
opposite and the proposed car park nearby would result in
increased noise and activity, to the detriment of nearby residents.

The appellant argued that the proposed change was only a minor one with a very small bar proposed.

The reporter said that the change of use would take the premises out of Class X of the Town and Country Planning (Use Classes) (Scotland) Order 1973 and the planning authority would have no control over any expansion of the bar activity within the premises. In the reporter's view the premises were acceptable for a guest house but the increased scale of activity associated with full hotel status would detract from residential amenity. (Ref. P/PPA/SR/62, January 24, 1985.)

3.79 Material change of use—licensed clubrooms

Planning permission was refused for the change of use of clubrooms belonging to a football club to licensed clubrooms. The planning authority considered that the change of use was a material one and that planning permission was necessary. This view was supported by the inclusion of licensed premises in article 17 of the Town and Country Planning (General Development) (Scotland) Order 1975, specifying development requiring advertisement under section 23 of the Town and Country Planning (Scotland) Act 1972. A change from use by a football club to use mainly by a social club would be more intensive than that originally proposed, amounting to a material change of use. It was also suggested that there could be no change of use from what was merely a permitted use not yet in operation. In the particular circumstances of this case the proposed change was from non-use to licensed use, which had to amount to a material change of use.

As regards the argument that planning permission was needed, the reporter said that it would appear that this could be justified on the grounds of intensification of use as argued by the planning authority. (Ref. P/PPA/GB/38, April 16, 1981.)

Material change of use—abandonment

3.80 Material change of use—abandonment—cabin

A site accommodated a dilapidated wooden cabin in unkempt garden ground. The reporter had no doubt that any residential use rights which may have attached to the timber cabin had long since been abandoned. (Ref. P/PPA/SG/129, March 28, 1988.)

3.81 Material change of use—abandonment—cottage

The cottage which was the subject of this appeal was in a state of considerable disrepair; its roof had virtually disappeared, one chimney had collapsed, the timberwork was in poor condition and trees and bushes had established themselves within its walls. According to the appellants the cottage was last used as a dwelling in 1946. The planning authority determined, under section 51 of the 1972 Act, that rehabilitation of the cottage as proposed by the appellants would amount to development.

The first question to be considered was whether the appellants' proposals were excluded from the scope of development by section 19(2)(*a*) of the 1972 Act, which provides, *inter alia*, that works for the maintenance, improvement or alteration of a building are not development if the external appearance of the building is not materially affected. The Secretary of State accepted the reporter's view that the extent of the work proposed was such that it would result in a material change in the external appearance of the building, whether that was taken to be the appearance of the building before it fell into disrepair or its appearance in its present ruinous state. That being so, it was considered that the proposals did not come within the terms of section 19(2)(*a*) of the 1972 Act.

Did the appellants' proposal to use the cottage for residential purposes amount to development as a material change in the use of the property? Mere discontinuance of a use of land will not, as Lord Grant made clear in *Paul* v. *Ayrshire County Council*, 1964 S.C. 116, amount in itself to a material change in the use of that land; if, however, the proper inference to be drawn from the facts of any case is that a particular use of the land has been abandoned rather than merely suspended, then the resumption of that use may amount to a material change of use (as a change from non-use to a positive use). In *Hartley* v. *Minister of Housing and Local Government* [1969] 2 Q.B. 46, Lord Denning declared: "Abandonment depends on the circumstances. If the land has remained unused for a considerable time, in such circumstances that a reasonable man might conclude that the previous use had been abandoned, then the tribunal may hold it to have been abandoned."

In the present appeal the reporter considered that it would not be "appropriate or accurate to describe the use of the cottage as having been suspended after such a long intervening period. The present situation might better be described as a non-use or as derelict land." The long period of non-use together with the uninhabitable state of the building led the Secretary of State to accept that the residential use had been abandoned. Quite apart, therefore, from the development constituted by the proposed renovation operations, the resumption of residential use would, said the decision letter, amount to development as a material change in the use of the property. (Refs. P/PPA/CC/43; P/DEV/1/CC/1, February 15, 1980.)

3.82   Abandonment of use—reversion to lawful use

These were appeals against (a) a refusal of planning permission for a change of use from licensed club to offices; and (b) a determination under section 51 of the 1972 Act that such a change of use would constitute development.

The appeal premises were in use from 1947 to about 1966 as offices. Thereafter, though planning permission was never sought or obtained, they were used as a licensed club. The question was raised as to whether the previous use of the premises as offices could be said to have been abandoned as a result of the unauthorised change to club use. The appellants contended that in the event of an enforcement notice being served in respect of the use of the premises as a club, the resumption of the prior use of the premises as offices would not, having regard to section 20(9) of the 1972 Act, require planning permission.

Section 20(9) of the 1972 Act provides that where an enforcement notice has been served in respect of any development of land, planning permission is not required for the use of that land for the purpose for which it could lawfully have been used if the unauthorised development had not been carried out. A "lawful use" for this purpose is, it seems, one begun with the benefit of a valid planning permission or, alternatively, begun before July 1, 1948 and not since abandoned or replaced by another use.

The reporter took the view that as no enforcement notice had been served, section 20(9) was not relevant. He considered, however, that he could not ignore the clear fact that a change having been made from office to club use, the previous use no longer subsisted and had been replaced by another use. He was therefore of the opinion that the office use had been abandoned and that the planning authority were therefore right in determining that the proposal to revert to office use would be a material change of use.

The reporter decided, however, to grant planning permission for office use. Such a change would be likely, in his view, to improve the amenity of the street. He also considered it undesirable that the premises should be left with no lawful use. (Refs. P/PPA/LA/183; P/DEV/1/LA/2, April 30, 1982.)

3.83   Material change of use—abandonment—residential use

This was an appeal against a refusal of planning permission for a house on the site of a ruined building. The appellant stated that the premises had been in use as a house until 20 years previously. The reporter considered that when, in 1960, the original dwelling had been demolished, the residential use of the site had come to an end. (Ref. P/PPA/GD/54, January 12, 1981.)

3.84 Material change of use—abandonment—houses

Application was made to renovate and extend premises described as cottages. The reporter considered that the first question was whether the remains of the former semi-detached cottages could be regarded as a house or houses. Although the walls of the former houses were still recognisable as such, in the absence of a roof, windows and doors and even interior floors and fireplaces, the remains constituted little more than a shell. The houses clearly could not be re-occupied without extensive rebuilding. For this reason the reporter considered that the remains of the former "houses" could not in their present state be considered to be a house or houses. (Ref. P/PPA/FB/236, September 30, 1987.)

3.85 Abandonment—ancillary use—condition

This was an appeal against a refusal of planning permission for alterations to form a dwelling-house. The appeal premises adjoined a large shed used for the appellant's metal recovery business. The ground floor of the appeal premises had become part of the shed while the upper floor, reached by an external stair, had been in residential use. The appellant said that he required to live on the site to be able to provide increased supervision in the light of vandalism and break-ins. The appellant said that he had ascertained that the appeal premises were in residential use in association with the then industrial activity on the site in the early 1950s, but the planning authority's researches indicated that the premises were last rated for residential purposes in 1949.

The reporter said the first determining issue was whether the proposal involved a material change of use which required planning permission. He said that the building was last rated for residential use in the late 1940s, that this use might have persisted into the 1950s and that no other use, apart from that associated with the remainder of the site, had intervened. He therefore considered that there was no evidence of the former residential use being abandoned and that the building had an established residential use which was incidental and ancillary to the established use of the site for industrial purposes. In these circumstances there was no requirement to obtain planning permission for a change of use. The only aspects requiring planning permission were the proposed alterations. The reporter did not consider it appropriate to apply any occupancy condition to the house because no change of use requiring planning permission was involved and because the house was clearly incidental to the industrial use of the planning unit. (Ref. P/PPA/SU/177, August 30, 1985.)

3.86   Material change of use—tipping on land—abandonment

Application was made to the planning authority under section 51 of the 1972 Act for a determination whether tipping on land would involve development. The appellant's proposals involved the deposit on an 18 acre site of waste material and soil.

The land had been used as a tip by the British Transport Commission at the date of coming into force of the Town and Country Planning (Scotland) Act 1947. That use continued until 1967 and the parties agreed that no tipping had taken place for at least 13 years. While the decision of the House of Lords in *Pioneer Aggregates (UK) Ltd.* v. *Secretary of State for the Environment* [1985] A.C. 132 rejected the possibility of abandonment of a grant of planning permission, Lord Scarman excepted from the argument the class of uses which had existing use rights and lent his support to the view that where an existing use had been deliberately ended, resumption of that use after a number of years was a material change of use. The use for tipping here was held to have been abandoned. (Ref. P/DEV/1/LC/2, June 12, 1985.)

3.87   Material change of use—renovation of cottage

This was an appeal against a refusal of planning permission for renovation of an old cottage. The appellant's planning consultants submitted that under the Town and Country Planning (Scotland) Act 1947, planning permission was not required since the building in question had been in use as a dwelling when the Act was passed; planning permission was therefore deemed to have been granted. However, it was noted that a closing order had been served in respect of the house in 1951. Since that date the use of the building had been changed to agricultural storage. Planning permission was therefore required. (Ref. P/PPA/SF/6, February 2, 1979.)

3.88   Material change of use—abandonment—store—dwelling-house

This was an appeal against a refusal of planning permission for the renovation of an existing store to form a dwelling-house. The appellant argued that the site and its surroundings had a history of residential use and that the restoration did not therefore involve development. However, the reporter accepted the planning authority's view that the residential use of the site had been abandoned. The proposal was therefore for a new house in the countryside, contrary to the planning authority's policy. (Ref. P/PPA/FB/46, February 7, 1980.)

3.89 Material change of use—abandonment—former smithy

An enforcement notice had been served in respect of the renovation of a derelict building and the enforcement notice required the removal of all new construction. The authority claimed that the use of the building, as a smithy, had come to an end in 1976 with the retiral of the previous owner. The use had not, the reporter held, been abandoned. Referring to *Fyson* v. *Buckinghamshire County Council* [1958] 1 W.L.R. 634, the use had continued, if only sporadically. This was enough to dispel the notion of abandonment. The building was dilapidated and in need of substantial repairs but was still usable as a smithy. The fact that the owner had at one time intended to convert the building into a dwelling (but had been refused planning permission) did not, the reporter thought, amount to abandonment. The forge had been removed when rehabilitation work had begun and the reporter accepted that it was stored elsewhere for safekeeping. (Ref. P/ENA/SP/16; April 2, 1984.)

3.90 Material change of use—abandonment of use—fire-damaged building

A two-storey house had been severely damaged by a fire in 1976. All that remained were the outer walls. However, the shell of the building had all the hallmarks of a dwelling-house form. The reporter had no doubt that the house could have been reconstructed after the fire and there had now been three planning proposals to secure the reinstatement of the premises as a dwelling-house. In the circumstances the reporter considered that the use of the building as a dwelling-house had not been abandoned but only suspended pending reconstruction. The intention to use the building as a dwelling-house had not been given up. (Ref. P/PPA/LC/135, April 27, 1987.)

3.91 Material change of use—abandonment of use—dwelling-house

An enforcement notice had been served in respect of the storage of scrap and building materials on the site of a former house. The appellant indicated that part of the building had been lived in until 1946 and that the other part was lived in until some later date. Since 1981, when he acquired the building, he had stored materials on the site with the intention of using them to renovate the building and to return it to residential use. He alleged that no breach of planning control had occurred as planning permission was not necessary. The planning authority argued that the residential use of the property had long since been abandoned. The reporter agreed. (Ref. P/ENA/TC/57, July 20, 1987.)

3.92 Material change of use—multiple occupation—abandonment
Planning permission had been refused for a change of use from a single dwelling-house to use for multiple occupation. The reporter considered two of the determining issues to be whether the previous use of the property was such that its use for multiple occupation (1) was established before the end of 1964, and (2) had continued without material interruption since that time.

On the first issue the evidence submitted by the appellants was of little substance. However, the planning authority and the agents for the objectors accepted that according to the valuation rolls—which were virtually the only evidence available to the reporter—the appeal premises were identified as service flats for the period 1962 to 1978. This, according to a letter from the office of the Regional Assessor, indicated a form of multiple occupancy. In the absence of contrary evidence the reporter therefore had to accept that the use for multiple occupancy purposes was established before the end of 1964. On the second period, the letter from the Regional Assessor's office showed that his records extended the period of service flats until 1985. For the period 1986 to 1987 the premises were entered in the valuation roll as "apartment house." The letter explained that this phrase meant a different type of multiple occupancy. There was therefore only a gap of about one year in the period 1962–1986 when the valuation roll described the property as a house. However, (1) the appellant had purchased the property in 1985; (2) a purchaser of property should be allowed a reasonable time in which to decide exactly what to do with the property, especially when it was in poor repair; (3) the property required substantial repairs and it was difficult to provide accommodation for multiple occupation when repairs were going on; and (4) the description "house" seemed to have been included in the period when the appellant and his family lived in part of the house. The reporter considered that this period was too short to justify a finding that use for multiple occupation had been abandoned. The reporter therefore concluded that the use of the property for multiple occupation was immune from enforcement action, that the proposed use of the property did not amount to development and that there was no need for planning permission. (Ref. P/PPA/TB/131, November 9, 1987.)

Primary and ancillary uses

3.93 Development—business from home—taxi business
An enforcement notice alleged partial use of a dwelling in a housing estate for the organisation and running of a taxi-hiring business. It was also alleged that a caravan in the rear garden was used in connection with the taxi business. The reporter found that the operation of the taxi hire business involved activities that went far beyond what could be regarded as incidental to the enjoyment and normal use of a dwelling, notably the coming and going of taxis at unsocial hours; vehicles and drivers waiting during periods of inactivity between trips; clients coming to the premises to wait for taxis; and the sound of two-way radios. It appeared from letters of complaint that all of these activities had occurred at or outside the appeal site, and had a serious adverse effect on the amenity of local residents. The reporter was therefore satisfied that a material change of use had occurred and that a continuation of the taxi business at the appeal site would have a harmful effect on the amenity of local residents. (Ref. P/ENA/SM/18, July 6, 1987.)

3.94 Material change of use—paying guests—number
The appellant provided accommodation on a temporary basis for young people. The appellant said that he would be willing to restrict the number of paying guests in his home to four and the number of rooms in use by paying guests to two. The planning authority accepted that if this were done they would not consider that there was a material change in the use of the premises. In the authority's view the use of only two rooms in the appellant's house by paying guests would be incidental to the use as a single dwelling-house, whereas the use of three or more rooms by paying guests would constitute multiple occupancy. The reporter considered that as regards these premises this approach was both fair and practical. (Ref. P/ENA/TB/37, August 10, 1987.)

3.95 Material change of use—ancillary use—works canteen
This was an appeal against the refusal of planning permission to extend the "welfare" use of the appellant's works canteen in

order to hold works functions. Social functions would take place on up to 20 times in the year. The appellants contended that the use of the canteen for social events was ancillary to the canteen function and did not therefore require planning permission. The reporter considered that the appeal hinged largely on the definition of "works canteen" and doubted whether that description included use as a licensed club, as was proposed. The Secretary of State accepted the main part of the reporter's recommendation but because of the difficulties of definition he granted planning permission subject to a condition as to the hours during which the premises could be used for social functions. (Ref. P/PPA/SL/71, December 3, 1980.)

3.96 Material change of use—ancillary use—warehouse—garage—enforcement notice

An enforcement notice was served in respect of an allegedly unauthorised change in the use of a warehouse. Previously the premises had been used as a fruit and vegetable warehouse with facilities for the garaging, repair and maintenance of the occupier's vehicles. They were now being used simply for the repair and maintenance of vehicles. It was held that a material change of use had occurred. (Ref. P/ENA/FB/10, February 28, 1979.)

3.97 Material change of use—coal storage depot—coach depot

This was an appeal against an enforcement notice served by the planning authority in respect of the use of land as a coach depot. Planning permission had been granted in 1965 for development of the site as a coal storage depot and in 1972 permission had been granted for the erection of a garage building to accommodate coal and haulage trucks.

The nature of the uses involved in the appeal were, the reporter considered, materially different. Although the site had previously been used for the garaging of vehicles, it was the storage of coal rather than the garage use which was then the principal use of the site. The present main use of the site was for the parking, storage and maintenance of coaches. Whether or not the vehicles used before and after the change of use were equally large or were built on the same type of chassis, the two uses were different in kind. The reporter added that such increase in traffic activity as had occurred at the site was not sufficient to amount to a material change of use by intensification. (Ref. P/ENA/SK/3, October 12, 1981.)

3.98 Material change of use—ancillary use—"de minimis"

An enforcement notice had been served in respect of the storage use of premises situated in the green belt. The premises formed part of a stable block on an estate and had, since 1985, been used for the storage and distribution of dairy products. The reporter accepted that the appeal premises might previously have been used for storage but it appeared that the previous use must have been ancillary to the use of the estate or to one of the houses in the stable block. By contrast, the present use was independent of the use of the rest of the estate or of any of the houses. Development had therefore taken place. The reporter was, however, satisfied that the scale of the business was very small. It had no effect on amenity and there was no risk of a bigger operation developing. (Refs. P/PPA/SC/159; P/ENA/SC/50, May 9, 1987.)

3.99 Material change of use—restaurant—take-away facility—whether ancillary use

The reporter stated that it had been normal planning practice to make a distinction between an "eating-in" restaurant and take-away facilities because of the very significant planning differences between them, the main differences being the duration and frequency of customer visits, which had implications for traffic generation, parking and amenity; and a greater tendency for some people consuming take-away food to linger in the vicinity of the shop, sometimes creating disturbance and litter. The reporter considered that take-away food sales would only be incidental to a restaurant if they were so small as to be insignificant. The appellants argued that the take-away facility should be a recognised component of a fast food restaurant. The reporter considered that here the take-away facility would be a significant element involving a materially different use from a restaurant. Planning permission was therefore required. (Ref. P/PPA/GA/376, February 2, 1987.)

3.100 Material change of use—haulage use—disturbance

As regards vehicles visiting the site of a vegetable packing concern, the reporter considered that provided they were directly associated with the produce packing business, including their being used for bringing new materials to the premises and taking away any finished products, they were an ancillary part of the operation.

If, however, vehicles were used to bring other goods, such as steel plate, timber or even fruit and vegetables, to the site for

onward transmission to another destination without being processed in any way on the site, the reporter said he would consider
that to constitute the use of the site as a haulage contractor's
yard. Such a use was not an industrial use in terms of the Town
and Country Planning (Use Classes) (Scotland) Order 1973. For
that reason such a use constituted development for which planning permission was required. Furthermore, in view of the
disturbance and annoyance which this use had caused to nearby
householders, the reporter found it an unacceptable use for
which planning permission should not be granted. (Ref. P/ENA/
TB/31, September 1, 1986.)

3.101 Material change of use—ancillary use—coffee bar—opening hours
   This appeal related to the opening hours of a coffee bar inside
a bingo club. The coffee bar had 15 seats. The capacity of the
bingo club was 500.
   The planning authority refused planning permission on the
ground that an extension of the opening hours of the coffee bar
would result in its no longer being ancillary to the bingo club
since the coffee bar would be open daily before bingo was
licensed to begin. The reporter agreed that with the extended
opening hours the coffee bar use would no longer be ancillary to
the main use. By opening for two hours daily before bingo was
licensed to begin, the appellants would clearly be providing a
separate service, even if technically restricted to members of the
club.
   However, on the merits of the case the reporter granted
permission for the extended hours of opening. (Ref. P/PPA/
FB/193, March 29, 1986.)

3.102 Material change of use—ancillary use—car park—builder's yard
   Planning permission had been refused for the change of use of
a former National Coal Board car park to a builder's yard.
   The reporter said that the appellant's approach to the question
appeared to be that where an established or authorised main use
of a site ceased, the constituent elements could be taken over and
used independently by another operator. This contradicted the
concept of such elements being ancillary or incidental to the main
use and would allow a minor use (*e.g.* an office or a store) to
become a main use in its own right. As these incidental uses
could change legitimately from day to day under the umbrella of
the main use, the concept immediately raised the question of
what were the actual constituent uses of the particular parts of
the land that might be taken over by a particular user. For the

appellant it was argued that they would be the uses existing at the date the colliery use ceased. In the present case that would be storage of scrap equipment, a trade union office hut and car parking.

Both sides were agreed that a new planning unit had been formed and the reporter's own view was that the use of that unit other than for an activity related to the production of coal would almost inevitably be a material change of use. The activities carried on by the appellant were unrelated to the production of coal and were in important respects quite different from the use of the site by the National Coal Board.

The Secretary of State agreed with the reporter that in order to show no material change of use had taken place it was necessary to look at the primary use of a site rather than to look at uses which were ancillary to that primary purpose. The Secretary of State's view was that a material change of use had occurred here. (Refs. P/PPA/LC/102; P/ENA/LC/31, September 24, 1985.)

3.103 Car park—change of use—garden area

Planning permission had been refused for the use as a car park of an area of garden ground formerly used by the residents of four upper flats.

The reporter considered the determining issue to be whether the appeal site had been separated from the flats. Where there was a drying green and area of ground in use by the occupiers of the flats he would have considered the area to be within the curtilage of the flats. But the ancillary use had now been severed by the change of ownership of the drying green and garden to another. In his view the present owners of the flats had no rights to the use of the land. (Ref. P/PPA/GA/285, September 10, 1985.)

3.104 Material change of use—ancillary use—enforcement—"four year rule"

A number of haulage lorries, a bulldozer and sometimes cars were parked in the curtilage of a dwelling-house. A certain amount of maintenance activity also took place. An enforcement notice was served in respect of these uses. The reporter said he was satisfied that the uses could not be regarded as incidental to the primary use of the appeal site as a dwelling. Even if the uses had subsisted for more than four years, the "four year rule," limiting the service of an enforcement notice to four years after development began, did not apply to changes of use. The uses would only have been immune from enforcement action if they had begun before the beginning of 1965. The reporter therefore concluded that the uses in question amounted to material changes of use requiring planning permission. (Ref. P/ENA/SL/187, August 19, 1985.)

3.105 Material change of use—whether ancillary use—carry-out hot food shop

An enforcement notice alleged the unauthorised operation of a carry-out facility from a restaurant. An appeal was lodged on ground (*b*) of section 85(1) of the 1972 Act—that the matters alleged in the notice did not constitute a breach of planning control. The appellants argued that the appeal premises had been granted planning permission for a restaurant several years previously. It was regarded as a matter of common sense that the provision of a hot food carry-out facility did not constitute a material change of use from the provision of a restaurant. Every Chinese restaurant in the area provided carry-out sales.

The reporter raised the question whether the take-away facility could be regarded as an ancillary activity, incidental to the main restaurant use. It was, however, clear that the scale of the carry-out facilities constituted a material change of use from a restaurant because of the volume and frequency of extra business it attracted and the distinctively different pattern of collecting and consuming food. The take-away facility could not be regarded as being dependent on the restaurant—the premises now had a dual use. The appeal on ground (*b*) therefore failed. (Ref. P/ENA/SP/18, May 30, 1985.)

3.106 Material change of use—whether ancillary use—amusement machines

Enforcement action was taken in respect of what was described as part change of use of a shop to amusement arcade. The enforcement notice required the appellant to remove all amusement machines from his grocer's shop. At the time the matter was drawn to the planning authority's attention there were seven machines in the shop. At the time of the appeal visit there were five. The appellant argued that the machines did not constitute a breach of planning control in that their use was ancillary to the main use of the premises as a shop. Approximately 75 per cent. of the shop's floor space was devoted to grocery storage and sales, while the other 25 per cent. was occupied by the machines. The primary use was the sale of groceries while the amusement machines provided an ancillary activity for shoppers. While the income from the machines amounted to about 6 per cent. of the total income of the shop premises, it amounted to 20 per cent. of total profits. The planning authority argued that the range of goods offered for sale in the shop was very limited. In their view up to two machines might be regarded as ancillary to the main use.

The reporter said that in his view while one or two machines might be installed in a fairly large, busy shop for the convenience of customers, the need for up to seven machines in a small corner shop suggested that a disproportionately high number of customers were making very extensive use of them. In all the circumstances—the smallness of the shop, the number of machines and the space they took up, the character of the use made of them and the vital contribution they made to the income of the shop—the reporter considered that the machines could not be regarded as an insignificant or as an ancillary use. A material change of use had therefore taken place.

The fact that the appellant had also appealed on the ground that the steps required by the enforcement notice exceeded what was necessary to remedy any breach of control, obliged the reporter to consider the number of machines that might be ancillary to a shop as small as this one and selling such a limited range of goods. He considered that the installation of even one machine would have a significant effect on the character of use of the premises. The breach of planning control would not therefore be completely remedied until all the machines were removed. (Ref. P/ENA/SL/188, May 28, 1985.)

3.107 Material change of use—ancillary use—haulage use—agriculture

The appellant submitted that his haulage operations were ancillary to the agricultural use of his land. The definition of "agriculture" in section 275 of the Town and Country Planning (Scotland) Act 1972 includes "dairy farming, the breeding and keeping of livestock . . . the use of land as grazing land, meadow land . . . [and] market gardens." It makes no reference to haulage operations. For the appellant's operations to be regarded as ancillary to agriculture, the reporter believed that the operations would require to be ancillary to the agricultural uses on the appellant's farm. Clearly they were not. The stock movements associated with the haulage business were generated on other farms quite unrelated to this unit, involving transport to and from markets and abattoirs.

The appellant claimed alternatively that the haulage business was an agricultural business because the steading might be used for the overnight storage of animals. This, the reporter thought, strained the definition of agriculture. Even if no lorries were stored overnight on the steading, the animals' short stay on the site could not credibly be regarded as "the keeping of livestock" or the use of the land as grazing land. (Ref. P/PPA/SD/25, September 10, 1984.)

3.108 Ancillary use—refreshment licence

The planning authority had taken the view that a refreshment licence was ancillary to a café use and did not require any additional planning permission.

The reporter felt obliged to record his opinion in connection with the refreshment licence that the planning authority might well have erred in considering that the grant of a refreshment licence was merely ancillary to the use of the premises as a café. A refreshment licence permitted the holder to "sell by retail or supply alcoholic liquor for consumption on the premises when food and non-alcoholic beverages are also on sale." It seemed to the reporter to be a material change in use to move from an unlicensed café/restaurant to a café/restaurant licensed to sell drink to people who were not necessarily also having a meal in the premises. This was not, however, a factor in the present decision and he made the point solely to discourage the use of the decision letter in support of the view taken by the planning authority. (Ref. P/PPA/SD/23, January 24, 1984.)

3.109 Material change of use—ancillary use

A room off a fish and chip shop was used for a pool table and two non-prize amusement machines. The planning authority served an enforcement notice in respect of this use. An appeal was lodged on ground (*b*) of section 85(1) of the 1972 Act—that the matters alleged in the enforcement notice did not constitute a breach of planning control. It was alleged for the appellant that the pool table and machines were ancillary to the main use as a fish and chip shop.

The reporter could see no dependent relationship between the playing of games and the cooking and sale of food. Moreover, as the two rooms in which these different activities took place had their own external doors, there was no reason why they should not operate independently of one another. Finally, the games room took up about one third of the whole premises. For these reasons it was not ancillary to the main use; it was development, for which planning permission was required. (Ref. P/ENA/CB/45, July 7, 1983.)

3.110 Material change of use—house—taxi business—ancillary use

The reporter said that no part of the appeal premises—a dwelling-house—was set aside for use in connection with the appellant's taxi business. The use in connection with the taxi business amounted to the use of the telephone and a properly licensed radio receiver/transmitter for which the reporter saw no external aerial. In the reporter's opinion the business use was ancillary to the authorised use of the premises as a dwelling-house and therefore did not constitute a material change of use. (Ref. P/ENA/FB/43, July 6, 1983.)

3.111 Material change of use—ancillary use—shop—amusement machines

A number of amusement machines were situated in a shop. The reporter said that in view of the minimal separation of the amusement machine area from the retail area of the shop, the planning unit was the whole shop. The main question was therefore whether the operation of the machines was ancillary to the use of the premises as a newsagent's and general store. In the cases cited (*Brazil* (*Concrete*) *Ltd.* v. *Amersham R.D.C.* (1967) 18 P. & C.R. 396; *Alexandra Transport Company Ltd.* v. *Secretary of State for Scotland*, 1974 S.L.T. 81; and *Jones* v. *Secretary of State for the Environment* (1974) 28 P. & C.R. 362) and in any other example of ancillary use the reporter could remember, the ancillary use had derived in some way from the main use—for example, the sale or other disposal of by-products or the sale on a small scale to others of some product manufactured by the seller for his own use. In this case the retail use and the amusement centre use were entirely different. Since the profits from the machines were kept by the appellant's son, it seemed to the reporter that in spite of the fact that separate accounts were not kept, it was in fact a separate business run by the appellant's son for his own benefit and making only a small contribution to the turnover of the appellant's business. A breach of planning control had therefore occurred. (Ref. P/ENA/CB/37, May 9, 1983.)

3.112 Material change of use—contractor's yard—repair garage

These related appeals were concerned with the use of a site for the purpose of the repair of motor vehicles. The planning authority had· served an enforcement notice alleging that an unauthorised change in the use of the land had occurred in that the premises had previously been used as lock-up garages. The appellant's main contention was that the change did not amount to "development" as defined in the planning legislation. No material change in the use of the premises had occurred; the site had previously been used as a haulage contractor's yard and vehicles belonging to the contractor had been repaired at the premises. It was submitted that the appellant had simply increased the level of repair activity.

In support of his argument the appellant cited the decision in *Lewis* v. *Secretary of State for the Environment* (1971) 23 P. & C.R. 125. In that case it was held that the Secretary of State had erred in treating as material a change in the use of premises from use for the repair of vehicles belonging to a single company to use for the repair of vehicles belonging to the public at large. The use throughout had, in the court's view, remained the same. Lord Widgery C.J. said: "[I]t is not my understanding of the law that, if the activity is exactly the same throughout the relevant period, a material change of use can occur merely because of a change in the identity of the person carrying out that activity."

The reporter concluded that the *Lewis* decision had to be distinguished in the circumstances of this particular appeal. Here the previous use of the site was primarily for the purpose of the parking of lorries. Although servicing of and running repairs on these vehicles had been carried out on the site, these activities were merely ancillary to the storage use. All major repairs were carried out at a repair garage. The present main use of the premises was use as a vehicle repairing garage. The primary use of the site had therefore changed in a material fashion. (Refs. P/PPA/ST/32; P/ENA/ST/21, October 14, 1981.)

3.113 Material change of use—ancillary use—shop to bakery

An enforcement notice alleged the unauthorised use of a shop as a bakery. The planning authority argued (a) that the premises could be used as a baker's shop; (b) that confectionery could be baked there, provided that such bakery was ancillary to the primary use of the premises as a shop; and (c) that goods baked on the premises could be distributed from the shop to other premises, provided that the sale of such products was effected on a retail basis. However, the planning authority considered that as 60 per cent. of the confectionery baked on the premises was sold to other establishments on a wholesale basis, the baking of goods on the premises was no longer ancillary to the accepted use as a baker's shop and that for that reason a material .change of use had occurred.

The appellants denied any material change of use. The primary purpose of the premises was still that of a baker's shop. They argued that the destination of the confectionery baked on the premises was of no relevance in assessing whether a material change of use had occurred.

The reporter took the view that the main issue was whether the sale and supply of confectionery baked on the premises to restaurants on a commercial and wholesale basis had so changed the character of the premises as to constitute a material change of use. In his opinion it was insufficient to claim that as some of the uses to which the premises were put were not ancillary to the main use of the premises as a shop, a material change of use had occurred. It was necessary to show that the character of the premises or the effect of their use upon the locality had changed materially. He concluded that the extended use of the premises had not materially increased traffic, smells, noise or working hours. Nor did it appear to have materially changed the appearance of the premises and it was unlikely to have changed the floor area in the premises used for different purposes—the main front room was still a retail baker's shop. The reporter therefore considered that there had been no material change of use and therefore no breach of planning control. (Ref. P/ENA/ LA/36, June 11, 1981.)

3.114 Material change of use—ancillary use—hot food take-away

This was an appeal against a refusal of planning permission for the use of a restaurant for the sale of hot food to take away, and against an enforcement notice requiring the cessation of the unauthorised sale of take-away food.

An appeal was lodged against the enforcement notice on, *inter alia*, ground (*b*) of section 85(1) of the Town and Country Planning (Scotland) Act 1972—that the matters alleged in the notice did not constitute a breach of planning control. The appellant argued that had it not been for a condition on the original planning permission for the restaurant—that "there shall be no sales of take-away food from the restaurant"—the use for the sale of hot food, being ancillary to the use as a restaurant, would not have amounted to development requiring planning permission.

The reporter was far from convinced that a hot food take-away service of this nature could be regarded as ancillary to a restaurant to the extent that planning permission was not required. Questions of fact and degree would arise here, but in the general case it seemed to him that for one activity or use to be classed as ancillary to another and so be deemed to fall within the same use class as the principal use, that use had to be dependent on the principal use. One example would be an office attached to a factory and required for management and clerical staff, records and files, etc. In the present case he would regard the restaurant use and the proposed use for the sale of hot food to take away as being mutually exclusive; it could even be said that one worked to the disadvantage of the other, apart from the convenience of being able to share food preparation facilities. In planning terms each of these uses was a separate use. Planning permission would therefore be required for the sale of hot food to take away, quite apart from the terms of the condition attached to the original permission. (Refs. P/PPA/FC/36; P/ENA/FC/10, September 4, 1981.)

3.115 Material change of use—ancillary use—bed and breakfast—fancy goods

The appellant sought permission to use two bedrooms in a house for bed and breakfast purposes and also sought permission to sell fancy goods in the premises. The planning authority imposed a condition to the effect that the "total scale of commercial use should be incidental to the use of the property as a dwelling-house and to this end fancy goods shall only be sold to paying guests making use of the bed and breakfast facility."

On this condition the Secretary of State's letter declared that it was also considered that, if, as the appellant claimed, the commercial use was to be incidental to the use of the property as a dwelling-house and was to consist only of selling fancy goods to the bed and breakfast guests and the provision of a book-keeping service for the appellant's son only, planning permission was not required and it was not necessary to make it the subject of a planning condition in the form proposed by the planning authority. However, if the commercial use ever became of a scale that was not purely incidental to the use of the house as a dwelling-house it would be necessary for the appellant to obtain planning permission separately for this. The Secretary of State therefore amended the condition to read: "Only two bedrooms shall be allocated for bed and breakfast." (Ref. P/PPA/TC/50, August 3, 1979.)

3.116 Material change of use—ancillary use

The reporter found that a farm byre had been used for occasional joinery work associated with the farm between 1963 and 1969. In 1969 a joinery firm entered into a lease with the owner of the farm to use the byre for a commercial joinery business. At that date the byre ceased to be used for a purpose ancillary to the farm use and a material change of use occurred. (Refs. P/EUC/LR/8; P/ENA/LR/75, August 25, 1976.)

3.117 Ancillary use—stacking of pallets

The Secretary of State held that the stacking of pallets in the forecourt of a dairy was simply storage as it was ancillary to the use of the premises as a dairy. It did not therefore involve development. (Ref. P/ENA/SC/8, December 15, 1978.)

3.118 Material change of use—ancillary use—amusement machines

An enforcement notice had been served requiring discontinuance of the use of premises as an amusement arcade together with the removal of all machines. The front part of the premises was taken up by a shop, a room behind that had been used as a café, and behind that a third room had been used for amusement machines. The café use had ceased and the middle room now contained six amusement machines. The reporter said that it was now common for such machines to be installed in various sorts of premises catering for leisure activities, but usually in small numbers which did not prejudice the main use of the premises and which could readily be recognised as being ancillary to that use. The precise number of machines which could be regarded as "ancillary" depended, in the reporter's view, on the circumstances of each case. He would not have ruled out as many as six machines provided they could be located so that there was no undue interference with the main use or the patrons thereof.

The reporter considered that on these criteria six machines located in the back room of the appeal premises could be regarded as being ancillary to the previous main use as a shop/café. However, the café use had been terminated and the machines were now associated with the shop only. The reporter was not convinced that the amusement machines could be regarded as a use ancillary to shop use. A small retail shop seemed to him to be a use which was materially different in character from the type of leisure-related main use already described including use as a shop/café. For this reason the reporter found that the six amusement machines installed in the middle room constituted a material change of use for which planning permission was required but had not been obtained. (Ref. P/ENA/GE/5, November 29, 1982.)

3.119 Material change of use—ancillary use—reception area for flat letting

This was an appeal against a refusal of planning permission for the change of use of a room in a house in multiple occupation to use as a reception area for flat-letting. It was argued for the appellant that the use of the room as an office was ancillary to the residential character of the building. The Secretary of State took the view that such a use could not be ancillary to the residential use of that property because it was intended to use the office for the administration and control of other properties which were part of the business. (Ref. P/PPA/SL/56, June 19, 1979.)

Use of curtilage of dwelling-house

3.120 Incidental to enjoyment of dwelling-house—caravan
A caravan was sited permanently at the rear of a house. The caravan measured 9 metres by 3 metres. It was not connected to mains water or sewerage. It would be used, the appellant said, only at holiday periods and only by the appellant's relatives. The appellant argued that the use of the caravan was for a purpose incidental to the enjoyment of the dwelling-house as such and so, under section 19(2)(*d*) of the Town and Country Planning (Scotland) Act 1972, did not constitute development. The planning authority stated that the size, permanent siting and location of the caravan amounted to development both as a material change of use and as the carrying out of an operation on land. The siting of the caravan was not excepted by section 19(2)(*d*) and planning permission was necessary. There was no evidence of the caravan being let on a commercial basis.

The Secretary of State took the view that a caravan of the mobile home type such as that in this case was too large and too comprehensively equipped for its use to be regarded as incidental to the enjoyment of the dwelling-house. The caravan was capable of permanent and largely independent occupation and was therefore to be regarded as falling within the category of a separate dwelling requiring planning permission. (Ref. P/ENA/HA/4, October 17, 1978.)

3.121 Material change of use—incidental use—taxi
It was argued for the appellant that in terms of section 19(2)(*d*) of the 1972 Act there was no breach of planning control in using the driveway of his private house for parking a commercial vehicle, namely a black hackney taxi. Section 19(2)(*d*) of the 1972 Act provides that the use of any buildings or other land within the curtilage of a dwelling-house for any purpose incidental to the enjoyment of the dwelling-house as such does not involve development. The Secretary of State agreed with his reporter's conclusion that the parking of the taxi was not incidental to the enjoyment of the dwelling-house as such. (Ref. P/ENA/LA/20, June 26, 1979.)

3.122 Material change of use—parking commercial vehicle—section 19(2)(*d*)

The decision letter in this appeal stated that it was considered that the regular garaging or parking of a commercial vehicle within the curtilage of a dwelling-house could not be regarded as incidental to the enjoyment of the dwelling-house as such in terms of section 19(2)(*d*) of the 1972 Act (section 19(2)(*d*) provides that the use of any buildings or other land within the curtilage of a dwelling-house for any purpose incidental to the enjoyment of the dwelling-house as such is not to be taken to involve development). The view was also expressed that the change from use as a driveway incidental to the enjoyment of a dwelling-house to use for the regular parking of an ice cream van was a material change of use for which planning permission was required. (Ref. P/ENA/LA/15, October 12, 1978.)

3.123 Material change of use—car repairs at dwelling-house

An enforcement notice alleged that the appeal site, within the curtilage of a dwelling-house, was being used for the commercial repair of vehicles. The reporter noted that there was a clear dispute between the parties as to the nature, frequency and scale of the alleged repair and maintenance activity. The appellants averred that all the operations were related to the repair and maintenance of their own and a few friends' vehicles. The planning authority asserted that the activity went far beyond the level of domestic use and was no longer incidental to the enjoyment of the dwelling-house. The boundary between these levels of intensity of activity was, said the reporter, always difficult to establish with certainty and hence to judge whether planning permission was required. In this appeal the reporter considered that the combination of evidence from the planning authority's surveys and the information collected by neighbours indicated that repair of vehicles was not only a regular activity but included the more complex and intrusive operations of body repair and paint spraying. He regarded the intensity of use and the operations involved as going beyond what would normally be relevant for a domestic garage in a residential neighbourhood. The reporter concluded that a material change of use from a domestic garage to a commercial use had taken place. (Ref. P/ENA/ST/55, April 11, 1989.)

3.124 Incidental to enjoyment of dwelling-house—car parking

An enforcement notice was served in respect of the use of the front garden of a house as a car parking area. The determining issue was seen to be the nature and scale of the activity. It was accepted that for the comfortable enjoyment of a house, a car at the side of the house or on ample open ground at the front of the house would normally be a use incidental to the enjoyment of the house but where a car was accommodated in such a small piece of ground, such as the appeal site, that it occupied a substantial part of the house's amenity ground, the view was taken that the parking of a car was not merely not incidental to the enjoyment of the house but amounted to a substantial change in the manner in which an important part (the ornamental ground) of the dwelling-house as a whole was being used. The appeal was dismissed. (Ref. P/ENA/LA/11, July 5, 1978.)

3.125 Material change of use—car repair

An enforcement notice had been served in respect of the unauthorised storage and repair of motor vehicles at a house. Prior to 1965 the use was not carried on to such an extent that the appellant could be said to be making a commercial use of the premises. He was, in effect, indulging in a spare-time activity which, though a source of gain, was nevertheless incidental to the use of the dwelling-house in which he resided. The car repair and storage was, in terms of section $19(2)(d)$, incidental to the enjoyment of the dwelling-house as such. At that time, therefore, the activity did not involve a breach of planning control. The reporter considered, however, that the position changed when the appellant ceased to live in the house in question; the use of property for storing and repairing cars with a view to commercial gain on the part of someone not resident on the premises could not be said to be incidental to the residential use of the premises. The Secretary of State agreed and held that the breach had not occurred before the beginning of 1965 (with the result that the use was not established). (Ref. P/ENA/FA/7, April 19, 1979.)

3.126 Development—chalet in garden—not incidental to use of dwelling-house

Planning permission had been refused for the siting, in a garden attached to a dwelling-house, of a chalet or caravan. The reporter considered that the first issue to be addressed was whether the chalet constituted development. He said:

"Whether the appeal subject should be described as a caravan or as a structure/chalet/caravan, as it is large enough to include a living room, three separate bedrooms, a kitchen and a water closet, as it is provided with running water and mains electricity, and as it is connected to a sewer, it can clearly be considered to be a separate dwelling-unit, the occupants of which could live independently of [the appellant's] main dwelling-house. Such a use of the appeal subject cannot be considered to be incidental to the enjoyment as such of [the appellant's] own dwelling-house even if the occupation of the unit is restricted to [the appellant's] own family or to relatives on four occasions each year. For these reasons I am satisfied that the appeal subject is not excluded from the requirements of the Act and that planning permission for it is required." (Ref. P/PPA/D/78, February 18, 1981.)

3.127 Material change of use—not incidental to use of dwelling-house

A pre-fabricated hut in the garden of a dwelling-house was used in connection with a funeral business. At the time of the site inspection there were three trestles inside the hut and two coffins.

The reporter said that the building was not required for a purpose incidental to the enjoyment of a dwelling-house as such but was used in furtherance of a business which was carried on within the house. It was a business which involved comings and goings of people on foot or with vehicles. According to neighbouring residents black bags believed to contain bodies of the dead and coffins had been seen being carried into and out of the hut. While some neighbours had given support to the erection and present use of the hut, others objected to this use in a residential area; they also suggested that the hut lacked some of the facilities required for such a business and lacked the discreet privacy and dignity that was needed.

The reporter concluded that this was a use which could not be conducted unobtrusively on the site and was bound to give offence to reasonably-minded people. The use was incompatible with adjacent residential uses. (Ref. P/PPA/SP/65, February 14, 1984.)

3.128 Material change of use—business vehicle—parking at dwelling-house

The appellant claimed that planning permission was not required for parking a business vehicle in his domestic lock up, claiming, in terms of section 19(2)(d) of the 1972 Act, that the use of any buildings or land within the curtilage of a dwelling-house for any purpose incidental to the enjoyment of the dwelling-house as such did not involve development.

The reporter said that the broad principle to be applied was whether the parking of the business vehicle was ancillary to the domestic enjoyment of the dwelling-house and was unlikely to disturb the reasonable enjoyment of nearby houses. If the appellant's van was simply to be kept in the garage overnight, the reporter said that he would find it to be reasonable in the setting. However, the appellant ran a 24-hour window repair service and could be called out in emergencies as often as two or three times per week. There had been complaints from neighbours about late night disturbance from the diesel engine as the van started up and drove up the lane. The reporter therefore found that the parking of the vehicle was not reasonably ancillary to the appellant's domestic use of the property. (Ref. P/ENA/SD/11, November 26, 1984.)

3.129 Material change of use—whether ancillary to dwelling-house— vehicle compound

The appellant's hobby was the restoration of vintage and veteran military vehicles. He proposed to use a piece of detached garden ground for siting the vehicles.

In the reporter's opinion the use for this purpose of 180 square metres of ground was not a use incidental to the enjoyment of a dwelling-house. It was a type of use not defined in the Town and Country Planning (Use Classes) (Scotland) Order 1973 and therefore had to be treated as *sui generis*. In the reporter's view what was proposed was a storage compound and the described use, scale and number of items to be stored, together with the recognised need to screen and limit the number of vehicles so stored, did require planning permission, whether or not it was a use carried out in the course of a business or a hobby. The hobby of vehicle restoration would inevitably necessitate mechanical operations and create noise of varying degrees of intensity. The appeal was dismissed. (Ref. P/PPA/TC/157, May 29, 1985.)

3.130 Caravans—curtilage of dwelling-house—"four year rule"

An enforcement notice was served in respect of two large caravans in the curtilage of a private house. The reporter agreed that permitted development rights only extended to a single caravan required for a purpose "incidental to the enjoyment of a dwelling-house as such" (1972 Act, section 19(2)(*d*)). The present case concerned two large residential-type caravans, in effect mobile homes. The caravans were connected to all services— water, electricity and drainage. The reporter took the view that they were residential units in their own right. A material change of use, as distinct from operations, had occurred. The planning authority were correct in arguing that the "four year rule" referred to in section 84(3) of the 1972 Act did not apply to changes of use other than a change to a single dwelling-house. The reporter regarded the caravans on the appeal site as having been transformed into permanent dwelling-houses; a caravan was not a "building" but in his view remained a caravan and the land on which it was stationed became a caravan site as defined in section 275(1) of the 1972 Act. Section 84(3) of the Act did not therefore apply and the appeal failed. (Refs. P/ENA/ST/27 and 28, June 24, 1985.)

3.131 Curtilage of dwelling-house—use for parking vans

The appeal subjects were in a residential area. An enforcement notice was served alleging the unauthorised formation of a vehicular access, the erection of a garage and use of the garden ground for the storage and/or parking of vehicles used for commercial purposes.

The planning authority argued that none of the three uses was incidental to the use of the dwelling. They alleged that the appellant was using the curtilage of the dwelling-house to store three 25cwt. or 35cwt. commercial vehicles. This in the council's view had reduced residential amenity through noise in the early hours of the morning and had caused damage to the roadside verge outside the house. Several complaints had been made by neighbours alleging disturbance at night and the vehicles' presence detracted from the appearance of the appeal property.

Upholding the enforcement notice, the reporter said that the prevailing position was different from the normal domestic situation. Planning permission for the garage was granted subject to a condition that it be not used for commercial vehicles. (Refs. P/PPA/FA/92; P/ENA/FA/42, May 8, 1986.)

3.132 Material change of use—curtilage—1972 Act, section 19(2)(*d*)

An enforcement notice was served in respect of the storage of vehicle bodies and components on land surrounding a dwelling-house. Part of the 1.3 acre site around the house was in cultivation.

The planning authority claimed that the storage of car bodies fell within the definition of "development," and referred in particular to section 19(3)(*b*) which provides that in defined circumstances the deposit of refuse on land involves a material change of use. The authority also argued that the appellant could not take advantage of the provisions of section 19(2)(*d*)—that the use of any buildings or other land within the curtilage of a dwelling-house for any purpose incidental to the enjoyment of the dwelling-house as such does not involve development. The authority argued that the ground on which car bodies were stored could not be regarded as part of the curtilage of the house, taking the word "curtilage" as meaning "ground which is used for the comfortable enjoyment of a house or other building" and "serving the purpose of the house or building in some necessary or reasonably useful way." (See *Sinclair-Lockharts' Trustees* v. *Central Land Board*, 1951 S.C. 258; 1951 S.L.T. 121.)

The appellant said there might be up to four roadworthy vehicles on the site and "donor" vehicles from which parts were taken to renovate still other cars. There was no desire to retain the "donor" vehicles on site. No commercial transactions took place, something which differentiated the site from a conventional scrap-yard. The "donor" vehicles were not refuse or waste materials; they were fully roadworthy when brought to the site and once stripped were taken to a scrap-yard. On the issue whether their presence was incidental to the use of a dwelling-house the appellant emphasised the need for his family to have efficient roadworthy vehicles to enable them to travel to work. In addition his eldest son's hobby was stock car racing.

The reporter said that it was clear that "development" was involved because, while he accepted that the vehicles were roadworthy when they first arrived at the site, they soon thereafter ceased to be so, and at some stage they fell into the category of "waste materials," the deposit of which on land constituted a material change of use (1972 Act, section 19(3)(*b*)). Certainly, the three car bodies which were present at the date of the inspection fell into this category.

As regards section 19(2)(*d*) it was in the reporter's view unrealistic to speak of the "curtilage" of the appellant's house extending any further eastwards than a small fence which separated an attractive garden from the grassed area on which the cars stood. The reporter accepted that the appellant made use of most of the 1.3 acre site but this was a very extensive area when related to the modestly-sized house in one corner of the site. The reporter concluded that the appellant could not claim the exemption from the need to obtain planning permission which might have been obtained had the three car bodies been sited, for example, in his driveway. In any event, the reporter could not be persuaded that the storage of vehicle bodies and their component parts could be considered to represent a purpose which was incidental to the enjoyment of the dwelling-house. (Ref. P/ENA/SR/47, June 22, 1987.)

3.133 Caravan siting—curtilage of dwelling-house

It was alleged that the curtilage of a dwelling-house was being unlawfully used as a site for two caravans. The reporter pointed out that section 19(2)(*d*) of the Town and Country Planning (Scotland) Act 1972 specifically excludes from the definition of "development" "the use of any buildings or other land within the curtilage of a dwelling-house for any purpose incidental to the enjoyment of the dwelling-house as such." Whether or not a particular use is "incidental to the enjoyment" of a dwelling-house was, said the reporter, generally a question of fact and degree. Whereas the storage of a touring caravan within a dwelling-house's curtilage or the use of a caravan as additional sleeping accommodation by persons who also made substantial use of the house was not considered to constitute development, the siting of completely self-contained accommodation for occupation by separate and independent family units was a different matter. In the reporter's view the caravans which were the subject of this appeal were clearly not used for purposes incidental to the use of the house.

It was alleged that the caravans were now exempt from enforcement action as they had been on the site for more than four years. That ground of exemption applies to buildings. Here, although both caravans were supported on concrete blocks and connected to main services, it seemed to the reporter that neither was affixed to the ground in such a way as would preclude it being winched, towed or lifted on to a motor vehicle or trailer for transport off the site. Neither caravan could be regarded as a building. The appeal against the enforcement notice on ground (*c*) of section 85(1) of the 1972 Act therefore failed. (Ref. P/ENA/ST/45, June 7, 1988.)

3.134 Incidental to the enjoyment of a dwelling-house—caravan

This was an appeal against an enforcement notice served in respect of the allegedly unauthorised siting of a caravan on land. Appeal was lodged on ground (*b*) of section 85(1) of the 1972 Act—*i.e.* that the matters alleged in the enforcement notice did not constitute a breach of planning control. The reporter considered that the use of the caravan, situated within the curtilage of a cottage, was not incidental to the enjoyment of the cottage as the house was separately tenanted and the caravan was well removed from the cottage. Other detailed evidence (such as a TV aerial on the caravan) pointed towards separate occupation. It was reasonably practical for the caravan to be occupied by a separate household independent of the dwelling-house for the main functions of sleeping, cooking and eating. It was clearly much more than the limited ancillary accommodation that might be regarded as incidental to the enjoyment of the dwelling-house as such. He therefore found as a matter of fact and degree that the caravan was not incidental to the enjoyment of the cottage. A material change of use had occurred. This represented a breach of planning control. The appeal on ground (b) therefore failed. (Refs. P/ENA/SA/79 and 80, November 8, 1988.)

3.135   Material change of use—caravan—occupancy

The reporter considered that the planning authority had misdirected themselves as to the nature of the planning application which was not to establish a new caravan site but to let to visitors a caravan which had been on the site for several years, perhaps initially to provide personal accommodation while the appellant's new house was being built. Unless there was a direction to the contrary, the planning legislation specifically excluded from development the use of land within the curtilage of a dwelling-house for any purpose incidental to the enjoyment of the dwelling-house as such. It was most important that the occupants of the caravan should be members of the family who continued to use some of the services of the dwelling-house (other than just a toilet or bathroom) because where they did not, the caravan would normally be a separate dwelling and the use could not be regarded as incidental to the enjoyment of the dwelling-house.

Thus the proposed change of use (letting the caravan to the public from April to October) was one requiring planning permission even though no services were connected to the caravan.

However, the reporter granted planning permission for a temporary period of five years, so long as the caravan was provided with water, electrical and waste disposal systems. (Ref. P/PPA/D/160, August 19, 1985.)

3.136   Garden ground—business from home—enjoyment of dwelling-house as such

The garden ground of the appellant's house contained slates, blocks of granite and concrete, timber battens, corrugated sheeting, scaffolding, chimney pots and other building materials. An enforcement notice alleged the land was being used for a demolition contractor's business. The appellant argued that there had been no breach of planning control. In the reporter's view the materials, which took up about one half of the surface area of the garden, were considerably in excess of any requirement which could be regarded as incidental to the enjoyment of the dwelling-house as such. (Ref. P/ENA/GA/57, June 13, 1984.)

3.137 Material change of use—hardstanding—engineering operation—personal bar

An enforcement notice was served in respect of the unauthorised parking of a mobile shop on a hardstanding within the curtilage of a dwelling-house. Appeal was lodged against the enforcement notice on ground (*b*) of section 85(1) of the 1972 Act—that the matters alleged in the notice did not constitute a breach of planning control.

The reporter found that the formation of the hardstanding was an engineering operation. With an area of 48 square metres within a total curtilage, including the house and garage, of 500 square metres, the formation of such a hardstanding was not *de minimis*. The hardstanding therefore amounted to development in terms of section 19(1) of the 1972 Act. The hardstanding was an additional area of paving beside the apron between the double garage and the road. It was therefore not necessary for the use of the garage nor for "visitors'" cars which could use the apron. The hardstanding appeared to have been made to accommodate the mobile shop.

The size and design of the mobile shop clearly showed it was a commercial vehicle, not suitable for normal private, domestic or pleasure purposes. The primary use of the curtilage was residential. The commercial use of the hardstanding was also confirmed by the connection of the mobile shop's refrigerator to the garage electricity supply. The reporter could not accept that regular parking of a commercial vehicle was incidental to the enjoyment of a dwelling-house. He could not accept that it was a *sine qua non* of enjoyment of the house.

The reporter concluded; (1) that a mobile shop was unsuitable for normal private, domestic or pleasure purposes, and its regular parking in the curtilage of the house was not incidental to the enjoyment of the dwelling-house as such; (2) in terms of section 19(1) of the 1972 Act the formation of the hardstanding amounted to development; (3) in terms of section 19(2)(*d*) the use of the hardstanding was primarily for the stationing of the mobile shop and was excluded from the uses of land which did not involve development; and (4) planning permission was required but had not been obtained for the formation and use of the hardstanding for the parking of the mobile shop.

Of the appellant's claim that the authority were personally barred from taking enforcement action, the reporter said that the power to serve an enforcement notice was discretionary. It was not to be expected that the planning authority would serve enforcement notices in respect of every breach of planning control, and evidence of parking of taxis, mobile shops or other vehicles in driveways, without enforcement action, was not evidence of undue discrimination or bias or justification for not taking action here. (Ref. P/ENA/LA/62, October 4, 1983.)

3.138 Caravan—enforcement notice—1972 Act, section 19(2)(*d*)

An enforcement notice required that within 28 days of the notice taking effect a caravan should be removed from the grounds of a house.

On the question of whether planning permission was required the reporter took into account the facts that the caravan was connected to a piped water supply and to mains electricity, that it had its own water closet and that it was approximately 9 metres long by 2.7 metres wide. The reporter concluded that the caravan was an independent residential unit and that its use was not, within the terms of section 19(2)(*d*) of the 1972 Act, incidental to the enjoyment as such of the dwelling-house within the curtilage of which it was situated. For these reasons he was satisfied that planning permission for the siting of the caravan on the appeal site was required.

On the question whether the 28 day period specified for removal of the caravan was sufficient, the reporter took account of the need to disconnect the caravan from the piped water supply and from the mains electricity and also, perhaps, from a sewer. It would also be necessary to arrange for a towing vehicle, to find a site for the caravan and to restore the site to its original state. "Nevertheless," said the reporter, "as the caravan has been on the site since at least early 1979 without the benefit of planning permission—and thus has been an unauthorised development—I consider that the period within which [the appellant] should be required to comply with the notice should be as short as possible. For these reasons I consider the period of 28 days referred to in the notice to be not unreasonable." (Ref. P/ENA/HC/9, September 23, 1980.)

3.139 Development—enforcement—car repairs

An enforcement notice alleged the unauthorised use of a domestic garage as a motor repair workshop. An appeal was lodged on ground (*bb*) of section 85(1) of the 1972 Act—*i.e.* that the breach of planning control alleged in the notice had not taken place.

One of the appellant's hobbies was car mechanics. He had a well-equipped garage in which he worked on his own car and, on a reasonably regular basis, assisted his friends with repairs to their cars.

The reporter said that under section 19(2)(*d*) of the 1972 Act the use of any buildings or other land within the curtilage of a dwelling-house incidental to the enjoyment of a dwelling-house as such was not to be taken to involve development of the land. The use of buildings for a spare time activity would normally come within this exception and the question was whether the same applied to the appellant's vehicle repairing activities. The reporter accepted that the repair and maintenance of one's own car in a domestic garage would come within the scope of the sub-section as would the occasional repair of others' vehicles. However, if the activity changed in either character or extent there came a stage when a material change of use occurred. For example, if the main use of a domestic garage became the repair of motor vehicles, then, independently of any question of financial gain, the reporter would consider the change of use to be a material one. Various letters lodged by the appellant showed that no money changed hands in respect of the repairs but they also confirmed that a significant volume of repair work had been carried on. Further, the garage appeared to be equipped and set up to carry out repairs, albeit modest in scale, rather than as a domestic garage. The reporter was unable to conclude that the use of the garage for repairs was incidental to the enjoyment of the dwelling-house as such. He therefore concluded that the breach of planning control alleged in the enforcement notice had taken place. (Ref. P/ENA/D/65, September 22, 1988.)

3.140 Material change of use—ancillary use—use of house as taxi office
The appellant had been running a private car hire business from his home. The vehicles were private cars and no one called at the house, all hiring being done by telephone. A 24-hour service was provided. Inside the house a desk had been installed in the living room with a telephone and a CB transceiver. An aerial was fixed to the front gable of the house. Two cars were parked in line in the single car port linking the appellant's house to the neighbouring one. A mini-bus was parked at the rear of the property. All three vehicles were used in connection with the car hire business.

The planning authority argued that planning permission was required for the use of the premises, as the operation of a taxi business could not be regarded as incidental to the enjoyment of a dwelling-house as such and was not embraced by the provisions of the Town and Country Planning (General Development) (Scotland) Order 1981.

The reporter said of the question of whether planning permission was required that it was the case that certain developments, specified in Class I of the GDO, could be carried out within the curtilage of a dwelling-house without the need for planning permission and that certain other activities, as envisaged in section 19 of the Town and Country Planning (Scotland) Act 1972 could be accepted where they were incidental to the use of the dwelling-house as such. These tolerances could extend to the use of some small part of a dwelling-house for office purposes, provided that such a use was of a very minor nature which did not affect the residential environment. The dividing line between a use incidental to the enjoyment of a dwelling-house as such and a limited commercial use was frequently a matter of degree but the reporter felt that where the use was, as here, conducted at all hours and on all days, involved the installation and use of radio equipment visible from outside the property and which might result in local radio interference, and resulted in parking and frequent movement of motor vehicles for other than primarily domestic use, it was one which was primarily of a commercial nature involving a change of use for which planning permission was required. The appeal therefore had to fail. (Ref. P/ENA/ GC/39, May 8, 1985.)

Use Classes Order

3.141 Material change of use—vehicle repair shop—sale of motor vehicles

An enforcement notice alleged that the use of a building and an area of land as a coachworks and vehicle repair shop and for the sale of motor vehicles was unauthorised. The original use of the premises had been a workshop for the drying and processing of timber, a general industrial use. From 1975 to 1978 the premises had been used, without planning permission, for the storage of agricultural produce and materials. The latter use being unauthorised, the original use could have been resumed without authorisation. The present use as a coachworks and vehicle repair shop was a general industrial use. In terms of the Town and Country Planning (Use Classes) (Scotland) Order 1973 planning permission was therefore not required. The appeal against the enforcement notice on ground (*b*) of section 85(1) of the 1972 Act—*i.e.* that there had been no breach of planning control—was therefore successful. As regards the sale of vehicles, the reporter doubted if timber had been sold on a retail sales basis from the premises and, bearing in mind that specific reference to the sale of vehicles was made in Class I(v) of the Schedule to the UCO, the reporter considered that the sale of vehicles was development and that part of the appeal failed. (Ref. P/ENA/FB/39, April 18, 1983.)

3.142 Material change of use—Use Classes Order—livestock market—retail market

The previous main use of the land which was the subject of this appeal had been use as a livestock market, with any retail sales being of a minor nature. In the reporter's view the use of the land for livestock auctions was a use *sui generis* (of an individual kind), falling within none of the classes of use specified in the Town and Country Planning (Use Classes) (Scotland) Order 1973. Planning permission would therefore be required for any other use. The appellants now wished to use the premises as an open retail market; in the reporter's view that change of use involved development. (Refs. P/PPA/ST/1; P/ENA/MHW/3, April 7, 1977.)

3.143 Material change of use—Use Classes Order—ancillary use

The reporter concluded, on the authority of *Brazil* (*Concrete*) *Ltd.* v. *Amersham R.D.C.* (1967) 18 P. & C.R. 514, that use as a builder's yard was a use *sui generis* and therefore outside the classes of use specified in the Town and Country Planning (Use Classes) (Scotland) Order 1973. The reporter held that a change from general industrial use to use as a builder's yard was a material change of use and required planning permission. (Refs. P/PPA/FB/121; P/ENA/FB/44, July 28, 1983.)

3.144 Use Classes Order—material change of use—sales from porch

Planning permission had been refused for the use of the front porch of a shop for commercial purposes including the sale of ice cream. The Secretary of State had regard to Class I of the Schedule to the Town and Country Planning (Use Classes) (Scotland) Order 1973 (use as a shop for any purpose) and took the view that the sale of ice cream from part of the shop premises did not involve development. (Ref. P/PPA/TC/32, November 21, 1978.)

3.145 Use Classes Order—scrap-yard—haulage contractor's yard

The reporter took the view that the former use of the appeal premises as a scrap-yard and the present use of the premises for the purposes of a haulage contractor's yard both came within Class IV of the Schedule to the Town and Country Planning (Use Classes) (Scotland) Order 1973 (*i.e.* use for general industrial purposes), with the result that planning permission was not required for the change. (Refs. P/ENA/SL/50–52, March 31, 1977.)

3.146 Material change of use—Use Classes Order—nursing home

Planning permission had been refused for a change of use from a house to a nursing home. The planning authority pointed out that the new use would fall within Class XIII of the Schedule to the Use Classes Order. They argued that the proposal would introduce a form of multiple occupancy into an area of owner-occupied houses. The intensity of use would increase. The reporter saw no reason to believe that there would be such an intensification of activity as to make the new use incompatible with an area made up of private residences. A change to another use within Class XIII could be prevented by way of condition and such a condition was imposed by the reporter. (Ref. P/PPA/SR/120, August 3, 1988.)

3.147 UCO—use "sui generis"

A composite use, whether termed a "car dealership" because it specialises in one make of vehicle or an "all purpose garage" is a use *sui generis* and does not fall within any of the classes of the Schedule to the Town and Country Planning (Use Classes) (Scotland) Order 1973. To change the appeal premises from industrial use to one of these composite uses would require planning permission. Though the composite uses contained possibly a substantial industrial element, nevertheless they did not come within the same use class, *i.e.* Class IV—general industry. (Refs. P/PPA/SS/178 and 183, July 27, 1988.)

3.148 UCO—Class X—boarding house

A consultant psychiatrist had described the proposed use of the premises in question as a "long term special needs boarding house" for ex-psychiatric patients. It did not seem to the reporter that this use fell within Class X (boarding or guest houses) of the Town and Country Planning (Use Classes) (Scotland) Order 1973. In his view the use was *sui generis*. (Refs. P/PPA/SL/478; P/ENA/SL/244, June 27, 1988.)

3.149 Use classes—hostel for homeless young women

Application was made to use premises as a hostel for homeless young women. The planning authority considered that this use would fall into Class XIII of the Town and Country Planning (Use Classes) (Scotland) Order 1973. That class relates to "use as a home or institution providing for the boarding, care and maintenance of children, old people or persons under disability, a convalescent home, a nursing home, a sanatorium or a hospital." Although the distinction might be a subtle one, the reporter considered that a hostel for homeless young women would not come within Class XIII and had to be regarded as a unique use in its own right. (Ref. P/PPA/SL/458, May 17, 1988.)

3.150 Hot food take-away—microwave ovens

Planning permission had been refused for the part use of a shop as a hot food shop with cooking by microwave ovens.

The reporter said that the use of the premises as a delicatessen, including the sale of filled rolls and sandwiches, did not amount to development and neither did the installation of two microwave ovens amount to a material change of use for which planning permission was required. The shop fell within Class I of Schedule 1 to the Town and Country Planning (General Development) (Scotland) Order 1981—a retail shop use. The council had argued that the proposal would constitute over-provision of hot food take-aways. The reporter thought he would have accepted that argument if the proposal had been to convert this Class I retail shop into a specialised hot food carry-out shop equipped with substantial deep frying or similar food heating equipment and with associated fume extraction and ventilation systems which would result in problems of noise, vibration, smell and waste disposal. That, however, was not the case at issue which was to provide a very modest ancillary service to the authorised use of the shop. The service was not seen as having an appreciable impact on the amenity of the area and he considered that it did not affect the Class I use of the premises. The reporter therefore sustained the appeal. (Ref. P/PPA/SL/365, October 27, 1986.)

3.151 Material change of use—Use Classes Order—vehicle repair and storage

An enforcement notice alleged the unauthorised use of land for the repair and storage of accident-damaged and other vehicles and required the removal of vehicles from the site. There were two buildings on the site, one used for storing vehicles, the other a vehicle repair workshop capable of accommodating four vehicles. Though an appeal was not lodged on ground (b) of section 85(1) of the 1972 Act (i.e. that the matters alleged in the enforcement notice did not constitute a breach of planning control), the reporter considered that the evidence suggested that the first question was whether there had been a breach of planning control. In the reporter's opinion the present use had to be classified as general industrial use under the Town and Country Planning (Use Classes) (Scotland) Order 1973 on account of the noise arising from motor repairs in general and panel beating in particular. Information about former uses was limited. The planning authority stated that the site was once used for the purposes of a mushroom farm. At one time the site had been associated with an engineering factory. The reporter took the mushroom farm to be a light industrial use and the use, if any, by the engineering company also to be light industrial. In the circumstances the reporter concluded that planning permission was required. (Ref. P/ENA/SP/22, April 22, 1986.)

3.152 UCO—general industry—special industry

The appellants had obtained planning permission for the use of a site as a garage workshop but the use was not commenced. They now sought planning permission for use of the site as a salvage yard and storage facility. Their intention was that they would bring in various types of salvaged material and also damaged cars for dismantling and the resale of re-usable components. The remainder would be removed. There would be some metal-cutting. The appellants argued that this would be a general industrial use.

The reporter was not prepared to accept that it would be a general industrial use. The operations to be carried out would not fall entirely within the scope of general industry but would involve the recovery of metal from scrap and would therefore fall within Class VI(iii), Special Industrial Group B in the Schedule to the Town and Country Planning (Use Classes) (Scotland) Order 1973. Planning permission was therefore required. (Ref. P/PPA/B/122, November 6, 1985.)

3.153 Material change of use—UCO

The activities in a yard embraced the reception and storage of scrap vehicles and other items, their disposal in part or whole, including stripping down and recovery of materials or components suitable for re-use or re-cycling. In the reporter's view these activities largely involved the recovery of metal from scrap on a scale which brought the use into Class VI(iii) (Special Industrial Group B) of the Town and Country Planning (Use Classes) (Scotland) Order 1973. The previous use was as a mineral goods yard, which would fall into Class IV. Planning permission was therefore required. (Ref. P/ENA/TC/37, October 25, 1983.)

3.154 Vehicle hire site—UCO—maintenance and repair of vehicles

The previous use of part of a site had been the operation of a vehicle hire fleet (mainly taxis). In the reporter's view this use did not come within the Schedule to the Town and Country Planning (Use Classes) (Scotland) Order 1973. As in the case of *Farm Facilities Ltd.* v. *Secretary of State for the Environment* [1981] J.P.L. 42 it was a use *sui generis*. That finding was in line with previous decisions that had upheld a narrow interpretation of the scope of the classes as contained in the UCO. The reporter was therefore unable to treat the former business as coming within Class IV (general industrial use) of the UCO.

However, the maintenance and repair of a large fleet of vehicles was a major operation with specialised equipment and staff and had all the characteristics of a repair garage. That element of the activities at the site was so significant that the reporter considered that it had transformed the simple hire operation to an industrial use falling within Class IV of the UCO. There had therefore been no material change of use of that part of the site used previously as a repair garage. (Refs. P/ENA/ GA/43; P/PPA/GA/127 and 128, June 30, 1983.)

3.155 Material change of use—shop

The appeal premises were formerly a retail shop. There was, however, a question as to whether they were still a shop. The window display lacked an indication of a range of goods for sale and the interior of the shop contained a very small quantity of stock—some shelves held records, patches, badges and T-shirts— described by the appellant as pop merchandise. The merchandise was thinly distributed over the display area. The premises also contained five video game machines. The impression was given that the premises were mainly geared to the provision of entertainment by means of the video machines. The Town and Country Planning (Use Classes) (Scotland) Order 1973 defines a shop as a building where the primary purpose is selling goods by retail. The premises were therefore not now a shop, though retail use remained an ancillary or secondary use. The premises were now predominantly used as an amusement arcade, albeit a small one. A breach of planning control had therefore occurred. (Ref. P/ENA/CB/40, April 5, 1983.)

3.156 Material change of use—enforcement notice—UCO, Classes III and IV

An enforcement notice was served in respect of the alleged unauthorised use of land for the storage and dismantling of scrap cars, trucks and vans and scrap associated therewith.

The planning authority argued that there had been a material change of use when the appellants took entry to the premises in

1980. Prior to that date the property had been in use as a civil engineering and contractor's yard. In 1967 planning permission was granted for a large building. The occupiers at that time had their own plant, machinery and transport and carried out servicing and maintenance of their vehicles and plant.

The reporter could not accept that the previous use of the appeal site as a civil engineering yard and workshop would have been an acceptable use in a residential area. In the reporter's opinion the processes carried on there would inevitably cause noise and vibration from the movement of vehicles, heavy plant and machinery and would more than likely have given rise to some smell, fumes, smoke or dust in the process of, for example, manoeuvring plant, mechanical repairs, coating roadstone for tarmac, depositing stocks of materials, *e.g.* gravel, sand, bricks, etc., and so on. On this basis, and as a question of fact and degree the use would not have come within Class III of the Schedule to the Town and Country Planning (Use Classes) (Scotland) Order 1973. The reporter would place the activity in the category of a general industrial use (Class IV of the Schedule to the UCO). Article 3(1) of the UCO states that: "Where a building or other land is used for a purpose of any class specified in the Schedule to this order, the use of such a building or other land for any other purpose of the same class shall not be deemed for the purpose of the Act to involve development of the land."

In consequence no planning permission was required in this case. (Ref. P/ENA/SL/6, March 11, 1982.)

3.157 Material change of use—UCO—bakery

An enforcement notice required discontinuance of the use of premises as a bakery and retail shop.

The previous use of the premises was a shop within Class I of the Town and Country Planning (Use Classes) (Scotland) Order 1973. The reporter was satisfied that the whole operation of the bakery and shop was a retail operation, notwithstanding the volume of sales which bypassed the shop and which seemed to the reporter to be at an unexceptional level for a business of this type (it was said that about 20 per cent. of the total produce was sold to other shops, hotels, etc.). However, the reporter was unable to accept that in a planning context this provided any justification for regarding such composite use as falling within Class I. It was a use for which the UCO made no specific provision. The use was *sui generis* and constituted a material change of use from the previous use as a shop and therefore required planning permission. (Refs. P/PPA/SL/87; P/ENA/SL/127, September 16, 1981.)

3.158 UCO—GDO—storage of scrap metals—repair of cars

An enforcement notice alleged the unauthorised change of use of land from storage and sorting of scrap metals to parking, repair and servicing of motor vehicles. An appeal against the notice was lodged on ground (*b*) of section 85(1) of the Town and Country Planning (Scotland) Act 1972—*i.e.* that the matters alleged in the notice did not constitute a breach of planning control.

The reporter said that in his opinion the alleged unauthorised use was a general industrial use (Class IV of the Town and Country Planning (Use Classes) (Scotland) Order 1973). The previous use was for the storage and sorting of scrap metal. A vehicle called once a week to uplift scrap materials. On the basis of the council's description of the previous use it seemed to the reporter that the work undertaken could also be construed as a general industrial use, *i.e.* in the same use class as the alleged unauthorised use. Consequently there would be no development (see article 3(1) of the UCO).

Even if it were argued that the previous use of the premises fell within the definition of Class VI(iii) of the UCO (*i.e.* Special Industrial Group B—the recovery of metal from scrap or drosses or ashes), the Town and Country Planning (General Development) (Scotland) Order 1975 (Class III, Schedule 1, Part I) indicated that the change of use from special industry to general industry was development which might be undertaken without permission.

In terms of the legislation the present use was either permitted or did not involve development requiring planning permission. The appeal was therefore sustained. (Ref. P/ENA/LD/8, September 4, 1981.)

3.159 UCO—development plan—vehicle exhaust repair depot

Planning permission was sought for the erection of a vehicle exhaust repair depot. The appellants stated that the principal operation would be the retailing of exhaust systems. It would therefore comply with the development plan which allocated the area for commercial shopping purposes. The planning authority refused permission for the proposed development as being contrary to the development plan. It would result in the undesirable establishment of industrial development in the area. They argued that the proposed premises would not be a shop. Nor would they be light industrial premises. The premises would be a general industrial building since they could give rise to noise, vibration and fumes.

The reporter considered that it seemed from the evidence that while exhaust systems might be sold to customers at retail prices, the sale price including fitting, the activity within the depot would be more akin to that of a vehicle repair garage or petrol filling station than to that of a shop or retail business where the primary business was the selling of goods by retail. He noted that in the Town and Country Planning (Use Classes) (Scotland) Order 1973, "shop" did not include a garage or petrol filling station, whereas "industrial building" was defined as a building used, *inter alia*, for the altering, repairing, etc. of any article, the expression "article" including an article of any description. The reporter considered that the proposed development might come within Class III of the Schedule to the UCO (use as a light industrial building) or Class IV (use as a general industrial building), but not within Class I (use as a shop). (Ref. P/PPA/FB/54, February 25, 1981.)

3.160 Use Classes Order—light industrial use—general industrial use—enforcement action

An enforcement notice had been served in respect of the use for general industrial purposes of premises, the permitted use of which was as a light industrial building. Light industrial building is defined in the Town and Country Planning (Use Classes) (Scotland) Order 1973 as an industrial building, not being a special industrial building, in which the processes carried on or the machinery installed are such as could be carried on or installed in any residential area without detriment to the amenity of that area by reason of noise, vibration, smell, fumes, smoke, soot, ash, dust or grit. Evidence was produced by the planning authority showing that there was material loss of amenity because of noise from the premises (which took them into the category of buildings used for general industrial purposes). The enforcement notice was therefore upheld, without prejudice, however, to the existing (light industrial) use rights. (Ref. P/ENA/EL/2, February 25, 1976.)

3.161 Material change of use—Use Classes Order—guest house—rehabilitation centre

Planning permission had been refused for a change of use from guest house to rehabilitation centre for people in need. The reporter found that the proposed use would not fall within Class XIII of the Schedule to the Town and Country Planning (Use Classes) (Scotland) Order 1973 (use as a home or institution providing for the boarding, care and maintenance of children, old people, or persons under disability, a convalescent home, a nursing home, a sanatorium or a hospital). (Ref. P/PPA/TA/96, June 2, 1986.)

3.162 Use Classes Order—material change of use—billiard hall—prize bingo

An enforcement notice was served alleging the unauthorised use of a billiard hall for prize bingo. The appellants claimed that use of the premises for prize bingo came within Class XV of the Town and Country Planning (Use Classes) (Scotland) Order 1973 ("use as an art gallery (other than for business purposes), a museum, a public library or reading room, a public hall or an exhibition hall"). The appellants argued that use as a public hall included use for prize bingo. The Secretary of State did not agree. The decision letter on the appeal stated that "the Secretary of State does not consider that it is necessary for the purposes of the planning legislation that any use to which land is proposed to be put must be encompassed within one of the classes defined in the Town and Country Planning (Use Classes) (Scotland) Order 1973." The letter also said that "where a use does not clearly come within any of the classes mentioned in the Order the inference must be that a change to or from that use is development which requires planning permission." He therefore considered that a change of use from billiard hall to prize bingo was a material change of use. (Ref. P/ENA/GLW/91, November 24, 1976.)

3.163 Material change of use—UCO, Class III—light industry—plant hire depot

Premises had been used for light industrial purposes (within Class III of the Town and Country Plannning (Use Classes) (Scotland) Order 1973); the use comprised the repair, maintenance and storage of vehicles, plant and machinery. The site came to be used as a plant hiring depot with servicing facilities. The reporter concluded that there had been a material change of use. (Ref. P/PPA/SQ/30, December 30, 1977.)

3.164 Material change of use—Use Classes Order—coal-yard—car repairs

A planning application had been made for a change in the use of a site from coal-yard to garage for the repair of motor vehicles. The Town and Country Planning (Use Classes) (Scotland) Order 1973 provides that a change from one use to another within the same class does not involve development. Article 2(2) of the Use

Classes Order includes within the definition of "industrial building" a building used mainly for repairing any article and a building used for the adapting for sale of any article. Car repairs were covered by the former, a coal-yard with bagging and distribution fell into the latter category. Both uses were general industrial uses falling within Class IV of the Use Classes Order. Planning permission was therefore not required for the change. (Ref. P/PPA/ST/28, January 12, 1981.)

3.165   Material change of use—Use Classes Order—spray-painting—Classes IV and VIII

An enforcement notice alleged that a material change of use had occurred in that there had been a change from a vehicle repair workshop to body-repair shop and spray-painting workshop. The authority claimed that there had been a change from Class IV of the Town and Country Planning (Use Classes) (Scotland) Order 1973 (general industrial use) to Class VIII (which includes the employment of cellulose and other finishes [other than in vehicle repair workshops in connection with minor repairs]). The reporter found the premises to be a vehicle repair workshop and accepted the appellant's claim that only minor repairs were carried on. He therefore found that the appellant was entitled to the benefit of the exception in Class VIII of the UCO. The use of the premises therefore remained within Class IV (though the reporter gave some consideration to the question whether the use was so unusual as to be treated as *sui generis*) and no change of use had occurred. (Ref. P/ENA/D/42, September 7, 1981.)

3.166   Material change of use—Use Classes Order—interpretation of planning permission

Planning permission had been granted for the use of premises as a retail furniture warehouse on condition that the range of goods be restricted. An enforcement notice was served in respect of the use of the premises as an indoor market. One of the grounds on which appeal was made was ground (*b*) of section 85(1) of the Town and Country Planning (Scotland) Act 1972, *i.e.* that no breach of planning control had occurred. It was alleged that the form of retail trading contravened the conditions of the permission in that the form of trading had been changed. The appellant claimed that both the furniture retail warehouse, which he continued to run, and the indoor market use fell within the same class in the Town and Country Planning (Use Classes) (Scotland) Order 1973. Class I of the Schedule to the Use Classes

Order describes a shop use as "A building used for the carrying on of any retail trade or retail business wherein the primary purpose is the selling of goods by retail." The reporter recognised that the change in the form of retail trading could make a significant difference to the number of customers and the extent and nature of turnover but in the absence of a definition of "market" under the planning legislation, he was bound to conclude that such a use of the appeal premises would not, of itself, constitute a breach of planning control. The market operation and the furniture warehouse were both uses within Class I of the Use Classes Order. The planning authority erred in considering that the change of use to an indoor market was in itself a material change of use. (Ref. P/ENA/SG/9, November 11, 1982.)

.167 Material change of use—Use Classes Order—recovery of metal—builder's yard

Activities in a yard embraced the reception and storage of scrap vehicles and other items, their disposal in part or whole, including stripping down and the recovery of materials or components suitable for re-use or recycling. In the reporter's opinion the activities mainly involved the recovery of metal from scrap on a scale which brought the use into Class VI(iii) (Special Industrial Group B) of the Town and Country Planning (Use Classes) (Scotland) Order 1973. The previous use of the site was a mineral goods yard, with some use as a builder's yard. Both of these uses fell into Class IV of the Use Classes Order (*i.e.* general industrial use.)

The present use therefore fell into a different use class and involved a material change in the use of the site. (Ref. P/ENA/TC/37, October 25, 1983.)

.168 Material change of use—Use Classes Order—non-retail uses in retail areas

The planning authority's policy of restricting non-retail uses in retail areas was questioned. It was, thought the reporter, worthy of support in principle, given the pressures to establish themselves in retail areas from non-retail uses such as building society offices, banks, betting offices and amusement centres. The reporter thought some limit to be only prudent, especially when it was appreciated that as a result of the Town and Country Planning (Use Classes) (Scotland) Order 1973 no planning permission was required to change the use of a shop to such non-retail uses (in dictionary terms) as a hairdressers, dry-cleaners, undertakers, etc. (Ref. P/PPA/LA/302, June 20, 1984.)

3.169 Material change of use—Use Classes Order—joiner's workshop—procedure—parking

The reporter considered that use of premises as a joiner's workshop fell within Class IV of the Schedule to the Town and Country Planning (Use Classes) (Scotland) Order 1973. Class IV covers general industrial buildings. It was held that the new use—the packing of produce, mainly vegetables—was also within Class IV of the Use Classes Order. The processes carried on in the packaging building were clearly industrial but did not fall within any of the Special Industrial groups of uses. Nor did the packaging fall within Class III of the Order (light industrial use). Although the sorting, cleaning and packing of produce was likely to generate less noise than a joiner's workshop, vegetables and fruit brought to the site would adversely affect the amenities of some residential areas (and a light industrial use is one which can be carried on without injury to the amenity of a residential area). Planning permission was therefore not required for vegetable packing. If, however, vehicles visiting the site were to be used to bring goods for onward transmission to another destination, without being processed in any way on the site, that would, the reporter thought, constitute use of the site as a contractor's yard. Such a use would involve development. (Ref. P/ENA/TB/31, September 1, 1986.)

3.170 Material change of use—Use Classes Order—guest house—"service flats"

It was agreed that premises had been used since 1981 as an extension to a guest house. The premises therefore fell within the same class, Class X in the Schedule to the Town and Country Planning (Use Classes) (Scotland) Order 1973. Class X relates to "use as a boarding or guest house or a hotel providing sleeping accommodation (except such a boarding or guest house or a hotel licensed for the sale of excisable liquor to persons other than residents or to persons other than persons consuming meals on the premises)." Here the question for the purpose of considering the grant of an established use certificate under section 90(1)(c) of the 1972 Act was whether there had been since the end of 1964 a change of use requiring planning permission. The appellant argued that if the reporter found that the use of the premises prior to 1981 had been use as "service flats," he should treat this as falling within the same use class as a guest house, Class X of the Use Classes Order. There would then have been no material change of use. The reporter's view was that the distinguishing characteristics of Class X were not confined to the explicit single criterion of "providing sleeping accommodation" but would normally also be that meals were supplied on a commercial basis. This was by the interlinked definitions of "boarder," "guest," "inn" and "hotel" in the *Shorter Oxford English Dictionary*.

In particular, the word "boarder" was defined as "one who has his food, or food and lodging, at the house of another" and guest as "a temporary inmate of an hotel, inn or boarding house." In the reporter's view a change of use between guest house (or any use in Class X of the Use Classes Order) and "service flats," which was a form of residential use, required planning permission. Evidence suggested that the premises were "service flats," the term used to describe houses in multiple occupation. The fact that there were two cookers and two kitchens at the time the premises were sold in 1981 suggested that the premises were "service flats" providing self-catering accommodation. As the planning authority had suggested, the premises had been in use for multiple occupation until 1981 but the chain had then been broken by a change of use to a guest house. (Ref. P/EUC/SL/5, April 9, 1987.)

3.171 Material change of use—Use Classes Order—light industrial use—cooked chicken factory

This was an appeal against conditions attached to a planning permission for the extension of a cooked chicken factory. The planning authority considered that the present use fell within the same use class, light industrial use, as the preceding use as an ice cream factory. There had, however, been complaints from people living nearby about the smell and noise from the cooked chicken factory.

The reporter quoted part of the definition of "light industrial building" as one in which the processes carried on "are such as could be carried on . . . in any residential area without detriment to the amenity of that area by reason or noise, vibration, smell, fumes, smoke, soot, ash, dust or grit." The reporter upheld the conditions, saying that it was for the appellant to comply with the statutory provisions of Class III. If he could not do so, he should seek premises outside a residential area. (Ref. P/PPA/TA/114, April 27, 1987.)

3.172 Use Classes Order—store—shop—enforcement action

An enforcement notice had been served in respect of a change of use from a shop to a store for the sale of ice cream freezers. The appellant argued that since freezer stores were not specifically mentioned in any of the classes of use specified in the Town and Country Planning (Use Classes) (Scotland) Order 1973, and since this use had to be classified somewhere in the use classes, no material change of use had taken place. The Secretary of State had no doubt that the appellant's argument was misconceived. Not all uses of land were specified in the Schedule to the UCO; a change from a use specified in the Order to a use not included in any of the use classes was most likely to involve a material change of use requiring planning permission. (Ref. P/ENA/EDB/28, January 19, 1976.)

Section 19(2)(e)

3.173 Agriculture or forestry—estate yard
Section 19(2)(*e*) of the 1972 Act provides that the use of any land for the purposes of agriculture or forestry (including afforestation) and the use for any of those purposes of any building occupied together with land so used is not to be taken to involve development. After lodging an appeal against a refusal of planning permission, the appellants came to the conclusion that their proposed use of land as an estate yard did not involve development on account of section 19(2)(*e*) of the 1972 Act. The Secretary of State agreed that planning permission was not required provided the use of the estate yard fell within the statutory provision. (Ref. P/PPA/LR/1008, July 7, 1976.)

Section 19(3)(b)

3.174 Material change of use—deposit of waste
Section 19(3)(*b*) of the 1972 Act makes it clear that any extension of the superficial area of an existing waste deposit or any extension in height of a deposit above the level of the land adjoining the site involves a material change of use. In this case the reporter was satisfied that excavation and filling with waste since 1948 had gradually extended since then. Consequently, each small horizontal extension of the tipping area had involved a material change of use. (Ref. P/ENA/FC/19, March 24, 1987.)

Determinations under section 51

3.175 Determination under section 51—change of use—new use already started
This was an appeal against a determination given by the planning authority to the effect that a change in the use of premises from office to sun tan treatment establishment constituted or involved development.

The decision letter issued by the Secretary of State stated:

"Section 51(1) of the Town and Country Planning (Scotland) Act 1972 enables a person who is proposing to carry out any operation on land or to make any change in the use of land, but has not yet done so, to apply to the planning authority to determine whether what he proposes to do constitutes or involves development. It is noted that the use of the premises for sun tan treatment had already commenced before the date of application for determination. The view is taken therefore that the application was invalid and that it follows that the appellants were not entitled to a determination under section 51(1). The Secretary of State is therefore turning the appeal away on the grounds that the applicants were not aggrieved within the meaning of section 33 of the Act and for the purposes of formal disposal the appeal is hereby dismissed."

(Ref. P/DEV/1/SP/1, August 13, 1980.)

3.176 Determination under section 51—restaurant—refreshment licence
An application had been made under section 51 of the Town and Country Planning (Scotland) Act 1972 for a determination as to whether planning permission would be required for the addition of a refreshment licence to a restaurant. The reporter found that consumption of drinks by a substantial number of customers not also having a meal would not be ancillary to the consumption of food. That use would not be within the restaurant use. The intended new use would go significantly beyond the activities normally associated with a restaurant and would therefore involve a material change of use. (Ref. P/DEV/1/SL/2, December 13, 1984.)

SECTION 4

GENERAL DEVELOPMENT ORDER—PERMITTED DEVELOPMENT

See generally Young and Rowan-Robinson, *Scottish Planning Law and Procedure*, pp. 171–184.

The current Town and Country Planning (General Development) (Scotland) Order (GDO) has been described as "one of the principal pieces of planning legislation, second in significance only to the Town and Country Planning (Scotland) Act 1972" (SDD letter of July 25, 1990 on the review of the Town and Country Planning (General Development) (Scotland) Order 1981). One of the principal functions of the GDO is to grant automatic planning permission for a wide range of relatively minor developments. This section is made up of summaries of appeal decisions raising issues under the GDO of 1975, now superseded by the similar provisions of the current, but soon to be superseded, GDO of 1981.

In terms of article 3(1) of the GDO planning permission is granted by the order for development falling within any of the 22 classes specified in the First Schedule to the GDO and such development may be undertaken without the permission of any planning authority or of the Secretary of State. It is provided, however, that nothing in article 3 of, or the First Schedule to, the GDO is to operate so as to permit any development contrary to a condition imposed in any planning permission granted or deemed to be granted otherwise than by the Order. Permission granted by the GDO in respect of development of any class specified in the First Schedule is subject to any condition or limitation imposed in the First Schedule in relation to that class. Many of the classes of "permitted development" are governed by one or both of the two "standard conditions" set out in Part II of the First Schedule to the GDO. Either the Secretary of State or the local planning authority may, by direction under article 4 of the GDO, direct that permission granted by article 3 of the Order is not to apply (a) to all or any development of all or any of the classes specified in the First Schedule to the GDO, or (b) to any particular development within any of those classes. The making

112

and effects of such a direction are outlined in Young and Rowan-Robinson, *Scottish Planning Law and Procedure*, chapter 16.

The decisions summarised in this section involve disputes as to whether or not particular works or proposals are "permitted development" under the GDO.

APPEAL DECISIONS

Class I(1)

4.1 GDO—alteration of building—cottage

The appellant proposed to rehabilitate a ruined cottage. It was held that residential use had been abandoned and that the proposed works would involve a material change of use. The appellants advanced the argument that even if the proposed rehabilitation work amounted to development, planning permission was automatically granted for that work—as "enlargement, improvement or other alteration of a dwelling-house"—under Class I(1) of the First Schedule to the Town and Country Planning (General Development) (Scotland) Order 1975 (corresponding to Class I(1) of the 1981 GDO). In the reporter's view, however, the property no longer had the amenities of a dwelling-house; it provided "neither warmth or shelter nor facilities for eating, relaxing or sleeping." The building could no longer be regarded as a dwelling-house. Class I(1) of the GDO was therefore not relevant and the proposed works were not permitted development. (Refs. P/PPA/CC/43; P/DEV/1/CC/1, February 15, 1980.)

4.2 GDO—building operation—imitation stone-cladding

These were appeals against (1) the decision of the planning authority refusing planning permission for an alteration to a dwelling-house and (2) an enforcement notice served in respect of the alleged unauthorised alterations to the said premises by the application of imitation stone-cladding to the front elevation. The appeal against the enforcement notice was on the ground allowed by section 85(1)(*b*) of the 1972 Act—*i.e.* that the matters alleged in the notice did not constitute a breach of planning control but were permitted development.

For the council it was stated that no exemption was given by Class I, paragraph (1)(*c*) or Part I of Schedule 1 to the Town and Country Planning (General Development) Order 1981 which provided that development involving the enlargement, improvement or other alteration to a dwelling-house was permitted development. This was permitted development only where "no part of the building as so enlarged, improved or altered projects beyond the forwardmost part of any wall of the original dwelling-house which fronts on a road." Existing projections such as eaves or gutters were of no relevance.

The reporter said that as regards the enforcement appeal it was noted that there was no dispute over the need for planning

permission, only whether such permission was granted by the
GDO. On that point, notwithstanding the relatively shallow
depth of the new cladding material, the reporter was in no doubt
that the council's interpretation was valid and was supported by
previous appeal decisions—see, for example, [1973] J.P.L. 107.
The enforcement notice therefore failed on ground (*b*) of section
85(1). (Refs. P/PPA/FB/117; P/ENA/FB/42, May 17, 1983.)

4.3   GDO—erection of garage—Class I(1)—road

   Planning permission had been refused for the erection of a
domestic garage. The appellant argued that the garage constituted permitted development under Class I(1) of Schedule 1 to
the Town and Country Planning (General Development) (Scotland) Order 1975. The planning authority considered that it was
not permitted development because Class I(1) of the GDO
requires that no part of any enlargement, improvement or
alteration shall project beyond the forwardmost wall of a dwelling-house fronting on a road. They argued that a driveway to a
garage court constituted a road within the meaning of the GDO;
it was a highway to which the public had access as required by the
Roads (Scotland) Act 1970 (now replaced by the Roads (Scotland) Act 1984). The appellant argued that the proposed garage
would not be in front of the established building line. The
driveway had not been adopted as a road by the highway
authority.

   The reporter said that the wording of the GDO and the Roads
(Scotland) Act led him to the conclusion that the proposal did
not constitute permitted development as the driveway to the
garage court was a road to which the public had access both by
car and on foot and the proposed garage stood nearer to the
driveway than the nearest wall of the original dwelling-house.
(Ref. P/PPA/FB/42, February 11, 1980.)

4.4   GDO—Class I—abandonment

   The appeal premises consisted of a small two-roomed cottage.
It was proposed to extend the cottage under Class I of Part I of
Schedule 1 to the Town and Country Planning (General Development) (Scotland) Order 1981. The planning authority argued that
the premises were no longer a dwelling-house and advantage
could not be taken of the GDO. The appellant argued that the
premises had been used as a dwelling-house since the early 1800s
and had been occupied continuously until 1971 or 1972. Thereafter they had been used and occupied until about 1978 on a
seasonal basis by agricultural workers. The planning authority

argued that the premises were not weatherproof in 1985 and could not then have been occupied by agricultural workers. The reporter found that the premises were still a dwelling-house, concluding that the residential use had not been abandoned. (Ref. P/DEV/1/SM/1, September 24, 1986.)

4.5 GDO—stone-cladding

Stone-cladding had been applied to the front elevation of a dwelling-house; Class I(1) of the Town and Country Planning (General Development) (Scotland) Order 1981, permitting enlargement, improvement or alteration of a dwelling-house, provides that no part of the building as so enlarged or altered is to project beyond the forwardmost part of any wall of the original dwelling-house which fronts on a road. Here, since the stone-cladding projected beyond the original front wall of the house, it was held not to involve permitted development. (Ref. P/PPA/SS/31, March 3, 1986.)

4.6 GDO—stone-cladding

Because stone-cladding affixed to the wall of a dwelling-house projected beyond the forwardmost point of the original wall of the house, it was held that it constituted development which was not permitted by article 3 and Class I of Schedule 1 to the Town and Country Planning (General Development) (Scotland) Order 1981. (Ref. P/PPA/SJ/31, March 6, 1986.)

4.7 GDO—house extension—forwardmost wall of dwelling-house

It was proposed to construct a ground floor extension at the rear of a house. The principal entrance to the house was from a footpath through an area of open grass. There was a vehicular service road at the back of the house. Between this road and its adjoining footway and the appellant's house was a strip of open grassland about 9 metres in width and a further paved footway.

Did the proposed extension amount to permitted development under the Town and Country Planning (General Development) (Scotland) Order 1981? In this case, the reporter said, "it is the back of the house which faces towards a road in an unconventional and unusually spacious layout, but I have no doubt that it is proper to regard the service road and its two footways, separated though they are by a common grass space more than 9 metres wide, as a 'road' within the meaning of the Order; likewise I believe it is right to say that the 'back' of the house 'fronts on' that road; and that in extending further 'backwards' the proposed development would project beyond the 'forwardmost wall of the original dwelling-house in terms of the Order. On a correct interpretation of the General Development Order, the proposal is therefore not development which is permitted by Article 3 of the Order." (Ref. P/PPA/FB/101, April 6, 1982.)

Class I(2)

4.8 GDO—caravan in garden

It was argued for the appellants that one caravan situated within the garden ground of their farmhouse constituted permitted development under Class I(2) of Schedule 1 to the Town and Country Planning (General Development) (Scotland) Order 1975, being development within the curtilage of a dwelling-house and required for purposes incidental to the enjoyment of the house. The caravan was said to be "required" within the meaning of "enjoyment" of a dwelling-house in that it supplemented the restricted income from a tenanted farm by providing accommodation for paying guests during the summer, and by providing extra accommodation for family and relatives. It had also been used by a part-time farm worker.

The planning authority argued that Class I(2) granted permission only for purposes incidental to the enjoyment of the dwelling-house as such—*i.e.*, as a dwelling-house—and that this ruled out a commercial use such as occupation by paying guests. In this respect the GDO allowed no special privileges to farmhouses; temporary accommodation for farm workers was covered by Class XXII of Schedule 1 to the GDO as read with paragraph 7 of Schedule 1 to the Caravan Sites and Control of Development Act 1960 where the use of a caravan is restricted to a particular season and is to cease, with the removal of the caravan, when the particular circumstances cease to exist. The reporter agreed with the planning authority and held that there had been a breach of planning control. (Refs. P/PPA/D/59; P/ENA/D/35, April 18, 1980.)

4.9 GDO—swimming pool—cover

At the rear of a house was a paved patio within which was a swimming pool. A structure was erected over the pool. The cover consisted of a prefabricated timber framed building with a pitched roof 3.6 metres high at the ridge. The structure was free standing. As the eaves of the house overhung the cover by about 1 metre, the pool structure was very close to the roof of the rear wing of the house. An enforcement notice was served in respect of the structure built over the pool.

It was argued for the appellants that planning permission was not required as the structure fell within the terms of Class I(2) of Schedule 1 to the Town and Country Planning (General Development) (Scotland) Order 1981. It was a free-standing structure used for purposes incidental to the enjoyment of the house. The planning authority argued that it was an extension to the house as defined in Class I(1) of Schedule 1 to the GDO since it was linked to the house by a wall. Alternatively, it did not meet the criteria of Class I(2) because the height of the structure, measured from the bottom of the pool, was more than 4 metres.

Class I(1) concerns the enlargement, improvement or other alteration of a dwelling-house. The proposed erection of a screen wall and pergola would have the effect of linking the structure more closely to the house but the two buildings would remain structurally independent. The development would not result in the swimming pool and enclosure becoming part of the house. The development could not therefore be described as coming within Class I(1). Class I(2) concerns the erection, construction or placing within the curtilage of a dwelling-house of a building or enclosure required for a purpose incidental to the enjoyment of the dwelling-house as such. Development permitted under Class I(2) is not to exceed, in the case of a building with a ridged roof, a height of 4 metres. The swimming pool enclosure was 3.6 metres high and was therefore permitted development. The reporter was satisfied that the height of the structure should not be measured from the bottom of the pool. The depth of the pool had no bearing on the external appearance of the structure and the reporter could see no logical reason for taking it into account. (Refs. P/PPA/SP/104; P/ENA/SP/28, December 14, 1987.)

4.10 Permitted development—caravan—siting—curtilage

A large caravan, with hardstanding alongside, had been sited in the large garden of a house. The caravan stood on a concrete slab and was secured by ground anchors. Water and electrical services were connected and there was a direct connection to a sewer. The interior of the caravan consisted of a lounge-dining area with full kitchen facilities, a shower room and two bedrooms. An electrical heating system had been installed.

The planning authority served an enforcement notice, taking the view that the construction of a wall separating the caravan from the house and the provision of a separate parking place and access for vehicles meant that a curtilage separate from that of the house had been created.

On behalf of the appellants it was argued that the caravan was still within the curtilage of the house and was used in connection with the enjoyment of the house by members of the owner's family, etc. Consequently there was, they argued, no breach of planning control; it was permitted development.

The reporter considered, first, whether or not the subject caravan was sited within the curtilage of the house and was incidental to the enjoyment of the house as such. He considered that the appellants had taken positive steps to create a new curtilage for the caravan by (a) breaching a former boundary wall to take in land formerly outwith the original curtilage of the land on which to construct part of the caravan standing and private amenity space around the caravan, and (b) enclosing an area around the caravan and providing a parking area and vehicular access separate from those serving the house. It appeared to the reporter that even if all the land concerned was at one time part of the curtilage of the house, that curtilage had now been effectively subdivided to form two separate and independent curtilages. Class I(2) of Schedule 1 to the GDO specifically excluded from the definition of "development" the use of a building or land within the curtilage of a dwelling-house for any purpose incidental to the enjoyment of the dwelling-house as such. The parking and use of a caravan within the curtilage of a dwelling-house would not therefore involve development if it could be shown that the use was incidental to the enjoyment of the dwelling-house as such. (This is to assume that the siting of a caravan amounts to the use of a building or land rather than the more usual view that the siting of a caravan is a material change in the use of land). The reporter concluded that the parking and use of a caravan within the curtilage of the present house could have been regarded as incidental to the use of that house under section 19(2)(*d*) of the 1972 Act. Consequently, the parking and use of a caravan within the curtilage of the present house could have been accepted as incidental to the use of that house had the caravan been used solely for additional sleeping and living accommodation by members of the household who continued to use the house for other purposes such as for living space or for cooking. "Members of the household" could include children and other relatives of the household but it was important that the occupants of the caravan continued to use some of the services of the dwelling-house other than just a toilet or bathroom. Where they did not, the caravan would constitute a separate dwelling, and the use could not be regarded as incidental to the enjoyment of a dwelling-house.

The reporter's examination of the evidence and inspection of the site, and the works carried out, led him to the conclusion that what had been installed on the appeal site, and was intended to be used as such, was a residential caravan which was a self-contained residential unit. As such, it involved development and required planning permission, and that had not been obtained. (Ref. P/ENA/D/37, July 1, 1980.)

4.11   GDO—dog kennels—curtilage of house
Planning permission had been refused for two dog kennels within the curtilage of the appellant's house. The reason for refusal of permission was that noise might be created in a quiet residential area. Objectors had expressed the fear that commercial dog-breeding might ensue. However, the reporter concluded that the development was permitted by Class I(2) of the First Schedule to the Town and Country Planning (General Development) (Scotland) Order 1975 and did not require a specific grant of planning permission from the planning authority. He stressed that permitted development status did not cover the erection or use of kennels for the commercial breeding or boarding of dogs. (Ref. P/PPA/LD/34, May 11, 1981.)

4.12   GDO—permitted development—caravans in garden ground
These were appeals against (1) the refusal of planning permission for the siting of one static and two touring caravans in garden ground at the appellants' dwelling-house; and (2) enforcement notices served in respect of the siting of the said caravans and requiring their removal.

The reporter noted that there had been partial compliance with the enforcement notices in that one of the caravans, belonging to a tenant, had been removed. In the circumstances the reporter proposed to ignore the fact that the tenant was not served with a copy of the enforcement notice. Similarly, he proposed in terms of section 85(4)(*b*) of the Town and Country Planning (Scotland) Act 1972, to disregard the fact that the notice had only been served on the two husbands who were joint owners of the house with their wives, and had not been served on the wives. He believed neither of the wives had been prejudiced by the failure.

The appeal against the enforcement notice was, *inter alia*, on ground (*b*) of section 85(1)—that the matters alleged in the enforcement notices did not constitute a breach of planning control. The planning authority argued that planning permission was required since the caravans did not satisfy the statutory requirements which would enable them to be classed as "permitted development" in terms of Class I(2) of Schedule 1 to the Town and Country Planning (General Development) (Scotland)

Order 1975. The caravans would be sited forward of one of the two elevations of the house which fronted on a highway and the use had anyway not been shown to be "required for a purpose incidental to the enjoyment of the dwelling-house as such." The appellants argued that the caravans would be used purely for the personal use of the appellants and would be incidental to the enjoyment of the dwelling-house.

The reporter was satisfied that the appellants had no intention of using either of the two caravans remaining on the site other than for purposes incidental to the enjoyment of the dwelling-house as such; and with a total of three households occupying the property it seemed reasonable to assume that the caravans would be "required" during visits by friends and relatives. In these circumstances it was the reporter's view that the appellants could avail themselves of their "permitted development" rights as set out in Class I(2) of the GDO, or of their rights as contained in section 19(2)(*d*) of the 1972 Act. The council's objections to this view seemed to the reporter to be untenable; first, as a matter of ordinary English usage he saw no grounds for interpreting the word "required" as meaning, in effect, "essential"; and secondly, with regard to the argument in relation to Class I(2) of the GDO, although the south elevation of the house was angled slightly towards the public road *ex adverso* the "front" garden of the appeal property, the reporter could not regard that elevation as being one which "fronts on a highway." On the other hand there was no doubt that the east elevation of the house did front on a highway.

The reporter said that a question of interpretation arose as to how permitted development rights were to be quantified. The GDO appeared to place no limit on the number of caravans which might be sited in accordance with the rules but the reporter thought it would be accepted that not more than one caravan per household could reasonably be "required" for the purposes set out. In the present case it was his opinion, as a matter of fact and degree, that this view would permit the siting of one caravan to each of the appellants as joint owners of the house, but not to the tenant. (Refs. P/PPA/D/69; P/ENA/D/39 and 40, July 3, 1981.)

4.13 Timber hut—living accommodation—curtilage

An enforcement notice was served in respect of the placing of a timber structure on land adjacent to a house and its use as residential accommodation.

The structure was rectangular. On one side was a door and at the other a cantilevered extension provided a sleeping shelf. The appellant contended that the site was formerly that of a gardener's hut. He argued that the site was within the curtilage of the house. The building was being temporarily used as living accommodation while a domestic dispute was being resolved. It was now intended to be used as a work hut in connection with the rebuilding of an adjoining wall. The appellant claimed that the use of the hut was incidental to the enjoyment of the dwelling-house and in the appellant's view the siting of the hut did not constitute development within the terms of section 19(2) of the 1972 Act.

The reporter said that section 19(2) had no relevance in the circumstances—it was concerned with the use of land rather than the erection of buildings. Was the hut permitted development in terms of the Town and Country Planning (General Development) (Scotland) Order 1981? It would have been if in terms of Class I(2) of the GDO it had been within the curtilage of the dwelling. However, the land had become detached from the dwelling and was therefore not within its curtilage. The hut was therefore not permitted development. A breach of planning control had therefore occurred. (Ref. P/ENA/SL/41, July 21, 1988.)

4.14   GDO—operations—whether "de minimis"

An enforcement notice required the removal of a radio aerial mast erected in the back garden of the appellant's house. The aluminium mast was of triangular construction, with lattice work, and was bolted into a concrete base. The lattice work section extended to 30 feet, which brought it just above the ridge of the house, and a 6 foot pole extended beyond that and carried two horizontal antennae. By unshackling two bolts the mast could be lowered on a hinge to lie flat in the garden.

The reporter said that the appellant claimed that the aerial constituted permitted development under the Town and Country Planning (General Development) (Scotland) Order 1981. The definition of "building" in article 2 of the GDO included any structure or erection which was not of the nature of plant or machinery. Paragraph (2) of Class I of the GDO permitted the erection of buildings within the curtilage of a dwelling-house, provided (*inter alia*) the height did not exceed, in the case of a building with a ridged roof, 4 metres, or in any other case, 3 metres. The reporter considered the aerial to be a structure not in the nature of plant or machinery which was required for a purpose incidental to the appellant's dwelling-house and which was situated within its curtilage. But for the proviso limiting the height to 3 metres the reporter thought it would be permitted development under Class I of the GDO. The aerial was not, however, permitted development.

The reporter asked himself whether the aerial was *de minimis* or whether it was sufficiently high or prominent to require planning permission. This was a question of fact and degree in each individual case but it seemed to the reporter that a structure which protruded above the level of the roof ridge could not easily be regarded as *de minimis*. He therefore concluded that the erection of the aerial did constitute development in respect of which planning permission was required. (Ref. P/ENA/SR/24, January 20, 1982.)

Class II

4.15 GDO—wall—permitted development—"road"
The appellant had built a wall which had the effect of narrowing an access. It was argued by the appellant that the wall was permitted development in that it came within Class II(1) of the First Schedule to the Town and Country Planning (General Development) (Scotland) Order 1975. That provision grants permission for the erection of a wall not exceeding 2 metres in height.

The planning authority argued, first, that standard condition 1 of Schedule 1 to the GDO was not satisfied in that the building of the wall amounted to the laying out of an access. The Secretary of State concluded that the appellant may have restricted the width of the access by building a wall but since there already was an access, the building of the wall could not be said to constitute the laying out of a means of access.

Article 2 of the GDO defined "road" by reference to the Roads (Scotland) Act 1970 (replaced by the Roads (Scotland) Act 1984) which provided that "road" includes any road to which the public have access. Taking account of the decision in *Young v. Neilson* (1893) 20 R. (J.C.) 62, the Secretary of State was of the view that the entrance road running between a hotel and a house was one to which the public had access and as it was used by vehicular traffic, that it was a "road" for the purposes of Class II of the First Schedule to the GDO. The wall in question abutted on the road. As the wall exceeded 1 metre in height its construction was development for which planning permission was required. The appeal on ground (*b*) of section 85(1) of the 1972 Act (*i.e.* that there had been no breach of planning control) fell to be dismissed.

The reporter found that the end of the wall was about 0.3 metre from the edge of the classified road. The Roads (Scotland)

Act 1970 (now the Roads (Scotland) Act 1984) defines "road" as including any verge. In *Lewisham Borough Council* v. *South-Eastern Railway Co.* (1910) L.G.R. 403 it was decided that "abut" did not necessarily mean "contiguous with." It was, the reporter said, a matter of fact and degree whether a wall "abuts" on a road for the purposes of the GDO. The Secretary of State considered that in this case, where, as the reporter found, the end of the wall was only 0.3 metre from the verge of the classified road, was only 0.7 metre from the edge of the carriageway and obscured the view of drivers from the entrance road to the classified road and *vice versa*, the wall did "abut" upon the classified road for the purposes of the GDO. For this reason also it was considered that the construction of the wall was not development permitted by the GDO and that the appeal against the enforcement notice on ground (*b*) of section 85(1) of the 1972 Act (*i.e.* on the ground that a breach of planning control had not occurred) failed. (Ref. P/ENA/SA/11, June 28, 1979.)

4.16 GDO—"road"

Planning permission was refused to raise the height of a fence from 3 feet to 6 feet high. The fence in question fronted on the private drive serving the appellant's house and two other houses. In the reporter's view there was no need for planning permission since it was permitted development under the Town and Country Planning (General Development) (Scotland) Order 1981, Class II(1) of which states that a fence may be up to 2 metres high but which provides that a fence may not exceed 1 metre where abutting on a road used by vehicular traffic. Article 2 of the GDO provides that the word "road" should have the meaning assigned to it by the Roads (Scotland) Act 1970. That Act was repealed by the Roads (Scotland) Act 1984 which states that "road" means "any way (other than waterway) over which there is a public right of access (by whatever means)." The reporter took the view that a privately maintained drive, even if it served more than one dwelling, did not come within the description of a way over which the public had right of passage. There was therefore no need for an application for planning permission. (Ref. P/PPA/B/120, September 5, 1985.)

4.17 GDO—height of wall

An enforcement notice was served in respect of the boundary wall of a garden, requiring reduction in its height. The appellant argued that there had been no breach of planning control as the wall came within article 3 of and Class II of Schedule 1 to the

Town and Country Planning (General Development) (Scotland) Order 1975 as not exceeding 2 metres in height as measured at any point within his garden. The wall did, however, exceed 2.5 metres on its "outer" side. Of the appellant's case that the wall did not exceed 2 metres when measured from any point within his garden, the Secretary of State said that he could see "no justification for interpreting the relevant provisions in this narrow way as there are no restrictive words in Class II of Schedule 1 to the 1975 Order." (Ref. P/ENA/HF/6, June 13, 1977.)

4.18 GDO—fence—"abutting" on road
Class II of Part I of Schedule 1 to the Town and Country Planning (General Development) (Scotland) Order 1981 provides that a fence is not to exceed 1 metre in height "where abutting on a road used by vehicular traffic." "Road" is defined by the Roads (Scotland) Act 1984 as meaning "any way (other than a waterway) over which there is a public right of passage (by whatever means)."

In this case the fence in question was neither contiguous with nor touched the street at any point. It could not therefore be said to "abut" upon the street. (Ref. P/PPA/SL/352, May 7, 1986.)

Class IV

4.19 GDO—Car boot sales—planning permission required
Planning permission had been refused for the holding of weekend car boot sales in a yard forming part of a large garage complex. A building was used in bad weather. It was argued that the use had permitted development status under the Town and Country Planning (General Development) (Scotland) Order 1981. However, the reporter thought it reasonable to classify the car boot sale as an open air market. Planning permission was therefore required irrespective of whether the sales operated on less than 28 days in any year (see Class IV(2) of the GDO). (Ref. P/PPA/TA/117, July 9, 1987.)

Class V

4.20 GDO—Class V(1)—agricultural development
The appeal site was part of a large field used for the dumping of subsoil from road construction works. Soil was dumped up to a depth of about 5 metres. An enforcement notice was served in respect of the allegedly unauthorised dumping of soil.

The reporter asked himself whether these operations were permitted development under the Town and Country Planning

(General Development) (Scotland) Order 1981 as coming within Class V(1)—namely "the carrying out on agricultural land, having an area of more than 0.4 hectare, and comprised in an agricultural unit, of building or engineering operations requisite for the use of that land for the purposes of agriculture"; and at the same time fall outwith the additional condition imposed on Class V by the Town and Country Planning (General Development) (Scotland) Amendment (No. 2) Order 1985 that "in the case of operations which involve the deposit on or under the land of refuse or waste materials no such material shall be brought on to the land from elsewhere."

The appellants argued that the land had been used for agriculture, had an area of more than 0.4 hectare and was part of an agricultural unit. The land had had drainage difficulties, with choked land drains. The improvement of the land and its productivity was an agricultural purpose and required the drainage difficulties to be overcome. The kind of operations undertaken by the appellants would improve the drainage by natural run off and a deeper water table. The planning authority argued that no evidence had been produced of a previous land drainage problem and that most of the material deposited went far beyond what might be "requisite for the use of that land for the purposes of agriculture." In their view this was substantiated by the fact that the appellants were paying the owner to use the field to dump waste rather than being paid by the land owner to improve his land.

The reporter considered that the relevant test here was whether the operations undertaken had been requisite—*i.e.* reasonably necessary—for the purposes of agriculture. He had no evidence of the drainage problem referred to but as a matter of fact and degree he did not consider that the operations had been carried out for this purpose. The scale and nature of the works, producing a mound of fill 5 metres high, was quite inappropriate if the primary purpose was to drain the land. In the reporter's judgment the purpose of the operations was to dispose of surplus material from the road construction and if there was any agricultural benefit it was entirely incidental to that purpose.

On the second leg of this issue, the appellants argued that the terms "waste" and "from elsewhere" in the Amendment Order did not apply to their operations. The reporter found no basis for reading restrictions into the Order. The subsoil was clearly a surplus arising from the construction of the bypass. In that context it was a waste product of the road works. That the road lay in the vicinity of the appeal site did not alter the fact that the material had been brought onto the appeal site. The reporter's conclusion therefore supported the contention of the planning authority that the operations undertaken satisfied neither of the tests which would be necessary for it to fall within the terms of permitted development.

The appeal against the enforcement notice therefore failed. (Ref. P/ENA/D/67, October 10, 1988.)

4.21 GDO—Class V—nursery—potential development

Planning permission had been refused for the formation of an access, erection of a house and rehabilitation of a nursery. It was agreed that the nursery use could be re-established without express permission. By virtue of Class V(1) of Schedule 1 to the Town and Country Planning (General Development) (Scotland) Order 1975 (which permits the erection of agricultural buildings on agricultural land) the appellant would be able to erect buildings of considerable size on the site, so long as these were for nursery purposes, without the need for express permission. It was therefore possible that the "built up" quality of the area could be increased without reference to development plan policies. (Ref. P/PPA/FA/30, June 9, 1980.)

4.22 Material change of use—agricultural land —tipping—engineering operations—GDO

This was an application for a determination under section 51 of the Town and Country Planning (Scotland) Act 1972 as to whether planning permission was required for the tipping of approximately 1 million cubic feet of infill material in a valley. The work would take from five to ten years and material would be deposited on a site of approximately 43 acres. The infill material was to consist of non-toxic waste. The appellants cited the decision in *Northavon District Council* v. *Secretary of State for the Environment* (1980) 40 P. & C.R. 332 in support of the contention that the proposed activities were engineering operations, that they were, in terms of Class V(1) of the First Schedule to the Town and Country Planning (General Development) (Scotland) Order 1981, "requisite" for the use of the land for agriculture and that they were therefore permitted development not requiring a specific grant of planning permission.

For the planning authority it was argued that the proposal was development requiring planning permission because the importation of such a large quantity of material in order to improve the productivity of some 40 acres of land was not an economically viable proposition and therefore the proposals had to be regarded as a material change in the use of the land to a site for the deposit of waste materials. Planning permission was not, it was argued, granted by the GDO because its criteria were not met in that; (a) in the authority's view, the proposals exceeded what was "requisite" (*i.e.* required) for the successful agricultural use of the land; (b) tipping operations of this kind were not engineering operations; and (c) since part of the site was described as being "unusable" on account of wetness and erosion, that part of the land did not meet the definition of agricultural land as land *used* for agriculture (see Agriculture (Scotland) Act 1948).

The reporter considered that the important issues were; (a) whether the proposals amounted to development by way of operations (see section 19(1) of the 1972 Act) to improve the agricultural quality of the land rather than development by change of use to provide a site for the disposal of refuse and waste materials (see section 19(3)(*b*) of the 1972 Act); and (b) whether the proposal conformed with Class V of the GDO.

As to the first issue, the reporter noted the knowledgeable way that the scheme had been drawn up, that appropriate expert agricultural advice had been sought and that the agricultural quality of a not inconsiderable area of land was likely to be improved. The Department of Agriculture and Fisheries for Scotland had said that it would be difficult to improve the land in any other way and thought that after the scheme the land would be eminently more suited to agriculture than in its present state. These matters led the reporter to conclude that no change of use was involved. It was now well-established by cases such as *Northavon* that the proposals amounted to operations on land and, having regard to the need to achieve certain contours and gradients and providing for drainage and disposal of spring water, they were engineering operations.

Secondly, the reporter accepted that the entire appeal site consisted of agricultural land. It was more than 0.4 hectare in area, was comprised in an agricultural unit and the works were engineering operations.

The only question to arise under Class V of Schedule 1 to the GDO was, therefore, whether the operations were "requisite" for the use of the land for agriculture. *Chambers Dictionary* defined "requisite" as meaning "that which is required, necessary or indispensable" and in the reporter's opinion it was a matter of fact and degree whether the proposed operations accorded with that definition. Both the planning authority and DAFS pointed out that the scheme was not economically viable in purely agricultural terms; it was only feasible as a result of the financial return from tipping and the reporter was therefore led to the conclusion that notwithstanding that there would be a permanent improvement in the agricultural quality of the land, tipping was the primary purpose underlying the scheme. In reaching this conclusion the reporter had regard to the very large amount of infill required, and the loss of agricultural production arising from the considerable duration of the scheme. Most of the land already fulfilled a limited agricultural function, some of the land being of reasonable quality. The reporter was not therefore convinced that a scheme of this magnitude and duration was necessary or indispensable in order to bring about agricultural improvement over the whole site and therefore the proposals failed to satisfy this crucial test for the classification of the proposed works as permitted development (see *MacPherson* v. *Secretary of State for Scotland*, 1985 S.L.T. 134). (Ref. P/DEV/1/ LC/1, May 9, 1983.)

4.23 GDO—Class V—fox farm

An enforcement notice alleged that the appellants had carried out, without the grant of planning permission, certain preparatory works for the further development of a fox farm. The appellants had, it was alleged, constructed an access road, carried out preparatory works for hardstanding and stripped topsoil from the site. The enforcement notice required the developers to restore the site to its original state by respreading and grading the topsoil to the original field level.

The Secretary of State was advised on the legal issues:

(a)   That the breeding and keeping of foxes was included in the definition of "agriculture" as contained in section 275 of the 1972 Act;

(b)   that use of the land for such purposes and the use for any of those purposes of any building occupied therewith, did not constitute development of land by virtue of section 19(2)(e) of the 1972 Act and therefore did not require planning permission;

(c)   that as the agricultural unit in this case exceeded 0.4 hectare, the carrying out thereon of building or engineering operations requisite for the use of the land for the purposes of keeping and breeding foxes was permitted development under Class V of the Town and Country Planning (General Development) (Scotland) Order 1975 (subject to the exclusion specified therein); and

(d)   that accordingly the matters alleged in the enforcement notice did not consitute a breach of planning control.

The appeal was therefore sustained and the enforcement notice quashed. (Ref. P/ENA/HD/7, August 26, 1980.)

4.24 GDO—agricultural use—buildings

An enforcement notice was served in respect of five sectional timber buildings and one corrugated metal and timber building erected on land and the storage of a caravan, sundry quantities of metal, timber and miscellaneous items.

An appeal was made on ground (*b*) of section 85(1) of the 1972 Act, *i.e.* on the ground that no breach of planning control had occurred. The appellant argued that the buildings came within Class V of the Town and Country Planning (General Development) (Scotland) Order 1981 (relating to agricultural buildings, works or uses) and therefore amounted to permitted development. The reporter was satisfied that the appeal site was part of an agricultural unit. However, of the two buildings remaining on the site, one appeared to be used for general storage and the other for housing ponies. The reporter was of the opinion that neither of these purposes was "requisite" for the use of the land for agriculture. The storage use of the appeal site appeared to predominate over any agricultural use and the buildings did not, therefore, benefit from the provisions of Class V of the GDO. The appeal against the enforcement notice therefore failed. (Ref. P/ENA/FA/29, November 7, 1983.)

4.25 GDO—tipping of material—"requisite" for agriculture

The proposals at issue involved the deposit on an 18 acre site of 100,000 cubic metres of waste material and 50,000 cubic metres of soil to achieve a field with a slightly domed surface, capable of arable use in due course. As to whether or not the proposals amounted to permitted development under Class V of the GDO, it was not disputed that the land was part of an agricultural holding. Nor was it disputed that the area of the holding exceeded 0.4 hectare. Part of the site was agricultural land, usable as rough grazing but as regards the remainder of the site an officer of the Department of Agriculture and Fisheries for Scotland said that the land was not capable of supporting livestock and could not be described as agricultural land, *i.e.* land capable of or assisting in agricultural production. On the basis that rather more than half of the appeal site was not agricultural land, it was the reporter's view that the whole could not be described as agricultural land. The poor quality area could be brought into agricultural use merely be spreading topsoil (as little as 100 millimetres). These were operations which could be regarded as reasonably necessary for the use of the land for the purposes of agriculture. The present proposals, involving the tipping of a very large quantity of waste materials and the raising of the level of the area by 2 or 3 metres, exceeded in scale what was "requisite" (or "necessary") for the purposes of agriculture. The appeal therefore failed. (Ref. P/DEV/1/LC/2, June 12, 1985.)

4.26 Caravans—storage—dwelling

Two areas of ground within an agricultural unit of more than 2 acres had been cleared and levelled. A caravan had been stationed on each site for over two years, one used for human habitation, the other for the storage of tools and equipment. As regards the "storage" caravan, the reporter accepted that the erection of a building for the storage of tools and equipment would be requisite for the purposes of agriculture and would fall within the terms of Class V of the Town and Country Planning (General Development) (Scotland) Order 1981. However in this case the caravan was clearly not a structure designed for agricultural purposes. Nor was the land on which the "storage" caravan stood a "caravan site" as defined in section 1(4) of the Caravan Sites and Control of Development Act 1960; there the criterion is that the caravan is stationed on land for the purposes of human habitation. The reporter was therefore of the opinion that the works of clearing and levelling the land on which the "storage" caravan was situated were permitted development, but that the placing of the caravan on that land was not permitted development and constituted a breach of planning control.

As regards the site of the residential caravan, the reporter was of the opinion that the use of the land on which the caravan stood had changed from use for agriculture to use for human habitation, being a material change in the use of that land. The land was clearly a "caravan site" as defined in the 1960 Act but did not fall within Class XXI of the GDO since the caravan had been stationed on the land for more than a year. This took it outwith the April to September period referred to in paragraph 3 of Schedule 1 to the 1960 Act and outwith the "particular season" referred to in paragraph 7 of that Schedule. The use of the land did not fall within any other of the circumstances referred to in Class XXI of the GDO and could not be regarded as permitted development. The reporter was therefore of the opinion that the change in the use of the land, together with the works of clearing and levelling the land for use as a caravan site, constituted "development" as defined in section 19(1) of the 1972 Act, for which planning permission was required but had not been obtained. (Refs. P/PPA/SA/99; P/ENA/SA/44, July 4, 1985.)

4.27   GDO—agricultural development—whether garage or storage use

An enforcement notice was served in respect of the alleged non-compliance with the approved height and roof pitch of a garage previously granted planning permission.

The appellant argued that the "garage" would in fact be used for the storage of farm tools, machinery, equipment, farm transport and seed. He stated that the property—a house and fields—was run as an agricultural unit and that the new building formed an intergral part of the farm. Further, in terms of Class V(1) of Schedule 1 to the Town and Country Planning (General Development) (Scotland) Order 1981, it did not require planning permission. The application had been made in error.

The reporter accepted that the building was intended for and designed for agricultural purposes and that it was, in terms of Class V(1) of the GDO, requisite for the use of land for these purposes. The appeal therefore succeeded. (Refs. P/PPA/SQ/166; HGJ/2/SQ/10, November 1, 1985.)

4.28   GDO—Class V—industrial building

An enforcement notice alleged the unauthorised erection of a building on a farm steading and its use for the sale and repair of motor vehicles. The appellants claimed that the building was permitted development in terms of Schedule 1, Part I, Class V of the Town and Country Planning (General Development) (Scotland) Order 1981. The planning authority said that the building could not be permitted development under the GDO because it did not meet the criteria laid down in the GDO; the building was clearly intended for general industrial purposes and not agricultural use.

The reporter said that in order to benefit from the exemption from the need to seek specific planning permission for agricultural buildings, the terms of Class V(1) of Schedule 1 to the GDO needed to be satisfied. These were specific and required, *inter alia*, that the building must have been designed for the purposes of agriculture. It was not disputed that the previous owner built the building and then used it for industrial purposes. The reporter did not regard the planning authority's submissions that the building was constructed to a significantly higher standard than required for agricultural use as having any relevance, as an agricultural building could be furnished to whatever standards of excellence a farmer required; but he concluded that the intention when the building was designed was that it be used for general industrial purposes. This was the use to which the previous owner put it and at that time the appellants—as farmers—had no interest in the development apart from the sale of the necessary land to that previous owner. The appeal against the enforcement notice failed because the erection of the building clearly amounted to a breach of planning control. (Ref. P/ENA/ D/58, September 1, 1986.)

4.29 GDO—structures not designed for agriculture

On a 7 acre field there were situated five railway wagons to form stables and storage. There had also been erected 7 foot high timber fences around the railway wagons. It was the appellant's intention to breed horses and he desired to obtain some sheep. When the lease was given up the vans and fences would have the benefit of easy removal.

The planning authority accepted the need for some form of accommodation for the animals and had no objection to animals being kept. Their concern was limited to the external appearance of the buildings and their siting on the land. The keeping of horses did not constitute an agricultural use but if a true agricultural use were introduced, Class V of the Town and Country Planning (General Development) (Scotland) Order 1981 specifically excluded from its provisions for building and engineering works on agricultural land the placing on land of structures not designed for agriculture. Railway wagon bodies were obviously not so designed. (Ref. P/PPA/LC/125, November 5, 1986.)

4.30 GDO—Class V—"requisite"—enforcement

The appellant had dammed a river. An enforcement notice was served. The appellant argued that he had various agricultural possibilities in mind such as fish farming, organic farming, irrigation, breeding animals, keeping waterfowl, etc. All these uses were he argued, "permitted development" under Class V(1) of the Town and Country Planning (General Development) (Scotland) Order 1981 as works "requisite" for the use of land for agriculture.

The planning authority relied on the decision of the Court of Session in *MacPherson* v. *Secretary of State for Scotland*, 1985 S.L.T. 134. In that case it was held that "requisite for the use of the land for the purposes of agriculture" was equivalent to "reasonably necessary for the use of the land on which the operations are carried on for the purposes of agriculture."

Permitted development rights could only be claimed in respect of an existing use, not a prospective use. The subsisting use was for grazing sheep and cows. The planning authority considered that the works exceeded those reasonably necessary for the present agricultural use and that they did not therefore constitute permitted development.

The reporter said that although the appellant had suggested a number of ways in which the land might be used, at present it was only registered for small numbers of sheep and cattle. The reporter saw no need for such a volume of water to maintain agricultural activity, nor, in the absence of detailed and specific proposals, was the reporter persuaded that the water would be needed to support the agricultural options which had been put forward. Fish farming would require planning permission. Stocking for private fishing would be development as a recreational use. It was therefore held that the appeal against the enforcement notice on ground (*b*) of section 85(1) of the 1972 Act—*i.e.* on the ground that the matters alleged in the notice did not constitute a breach of planning control—failed. (Ref. P/ENA/FA/54, December 23, 1987.)

4.31   Engineering operations—removal of turf—GDO, Class V—permitted development

An enforcement notice alleged the unauthorised removal of turf and soil from land. An appeal was lodged on ground (*b*) of section 85(1) of the 1972 Act—*i.e.* that the matters alleged in the notice did not consitute a breach of planning control. The appellants stated that the land was used for the purposes of agriculture and that the removal of turf and soil did not therefore involve development and did not require planning permission. Turf was removed by the appellants as part of the farming rotation. The depth of extraction extended to the roots of the grass and no material amount of soil was removed.

The reporter was satisfied that any mechanical operation which involved the removal or movement of soil could be classified as an engineering operation. The determining issue was whether the growing and cropping of turf on a four or five year basis was an agricultural use of land. The definition of "agriculture" in section 275 of the 1972 Act states that agriculture includes *inter alia*, horticulture, the use of land as osier land, market gardens and nursery grounds. These activities involved the growth and sale of plants for purposes other than food production. The growing of grass for sale in the form of turf by, say a horticulturist or nurseryman would therefore be classified as agriculture for the purposes of the Act. There appeared to be no distinction which could seriously be drawn between this activity and the growing of turf on a farm and its subsequent sale for use elsewhere.

The reporter accepted that repeated turf-stripping would have a long term deleterious effect on the quality and structure of the soil. However, it was a matter of fact and degree when turf-stripping could no longer be regarded as a type of rotational crop and became a form of asset-stripping, no longer requisite for the purposes of agriculture. He was satisfied that this stage had not been reached here.

He therefore concluded that the turf-stripping that had taken place was an engineering operation requisite for the use of that land for agriculture and was permitted development under Class V of Schedule 1 to the Town and Country Planning (General Development) (Scotland) Order 1981. (Ref. P/ENA/SL/191, August 12, 1987.)

4.32 GDO—Material change of use—mink farming—buildings
Mink farming is included within the meaning of the phrase "agricultural purposes," so that the use of existing buildings for that purpose does not constitute development requiring planning permission. (Ref. P/PPA/R/1/PtA, August 16, 1978.)

4.33 GDO—infilling—waste material
In terms of section 19(3)(*b*) of the 1972 Act, the deposit of refuse and waste material is, with one exception, a material change in the use of the land in question. Here the appellant intended to infill a gorge. The planning authority argued that it would require 117,000 cubic metres of material to fill the 2.4 hectare site. It was argued that the proposals might amount to permitted development under Class V of Schedule 1 to the Town and Country Planning (General Development) (Scotland) Order 1981. Class V relates to agricultural works.

The reporter concluded that the scale of the proposed works, together with the length of time the works would take, meant that the infilling would not constitute work requisite for agricultural purposes. The prime objective of the infilling would be waste disposal. In arriving at these conclusions the reporter took account of the decision in *MacPherson* v. *Secretary of State for Scotland*, 1985 S.L.T. 134. (Ref. P/DEV/1/SR/1, April 24, 1986.)

Class VII

4.34 GDO—fence—barbed wire
The appeal concerned the erection of three horizontal strands and a roll of barbed wire on top of a metal palisade fence. The

reporter was unable to conclude that the operations constituted permitted development. Class II(1) of the Town and Country Planning (General Development) (Scotland) Order 1981 refers to the erection of low fences but not to something which increases the height of a fence which was already higher than two metres. Under Class VII of the GDO there were difficulties in that the barbed wire could not be considered as "plant or machinery or structures or erections of the nature of plant and machinery," and in any event the provisions excluded any operations "materially affecting the external appearance of the premises of the undertaking." The reporter had already found that the barbed wire did materially affect the appearance of the premises and therefore concluded that planning permission was required for the barbed wire that had been erected at the appeal site. (Refs. P/ENA/SL/234; P/PPA/SL/426, April 28, 1988.)

4.35 Helicopter service base—development—competency of condition

A public inquiry was instructed by the Secretary of State in connection with a proposal to establish a base for helicopter operations and servicing. The application was "called in" by the Secretary of State because of the serious implications which the proposal might have had for a nearby National Nature Reserve. Two interesting questions were raised at the inquiry. First, did the proposal in fact require planning permission and, second, if it did, would it be competent to impose a condition regulating the flight paths of helicopters using the base?

The applicants conceded that planning permission would be required if the site was to be used as a commercial heliport for the collection of passengers or freight in the same way as an airport. What was proposed here, however, was merely a base for the operation and servicing of helicopters and the applicants argued that planning permission was not required for these proposals. The land to which the proposals related was presently used for various industrial purposes (including vehicle repair). Some of the buildings on the site were general industrial buildings as defined in the Town and Country Planning (Use Classes) (Scotland) Order 1973, article 2. The servicing of the helicopters was, it was argued, also a general industrial use and planning permission would therefore not be required for the use of these buildings for the purposes envisaged.

So far as concerned the main physical works involved in the proposals (the construction of a concrete landing pad and a short length of private road), it was argued that these works were permitted development in terms of Class VII of Schedule 1 to the

Town and Country Planning (General Development) (Scotland) Order 1975, the effect of which was to grant planning permission for the carrying out by an industrial undertaker of certain types of development for industrial purposes. The only other physical works which it was proposed to carry-out—the formation of new sliding doors in a vehicle workshop—were, it was submitted, also permitted by the GDO as alterations to industrial buildings.

So far as the operation of the helipad was concerned the appellants argued that planning permission was not required for landing an airborne vehicle on the ground. No permission was required to fly a helicopter over land or for it to hover over any land. Once a helicopter had landed, it became a parked vehicle and the site already had permission for the parking and storage of vehicles.

For the planning authority it was argued that planning permission was required. The reporter took the view that one could not look at the proposal to carry out works separately from the purpose for which the works were intended to be used. In this case the proposal was to create a helicopter operating base with servicing as an ancillary to the main use. Although the servicing operations might closely resemble the operations already carried out on the site in connection with trucks and buses, it was clear that the present use did not, even broadly, resemble an operating base for helicopters. The Secretary of State agreed that planning permission was required for the development.

There also arose the question whether there could competently be imposed on any grant of planning permission for the helicopter base a condition regulating the flight paths of helicopters using the base. The applicants were prepared to accept restrictions of this nature which would, it was said, reduce the danger of disturbance to the nearby National Nature Reserve. The applicants argued that such a condition could competently be imposed by the Secretary of State. In so arguing, they sought to distinguish the decision of the First Division of the Court of Session in *British Airports Authority* v. *Secretary of State for Scotland*, 1979 S.C. 200. In that case a condition regulating the direction of take off and landing of aircraft at Aberdeen Airport was held to be bad because it was concerned with a matter which was outwith the control of the applicants, the BAA. Control of such matters was the legal responsibility of the Civil Aviation Authority and the BAA could not take steps which would secure the desired result. However, the applicants argued that the position in the present case was quite different. The operators of the base were the persons on whom the condition would fall and so there would be no problem of securing compliance with the condition.

The reporter said of the proposed condition that the applicants might be thought to have the same lack of direct control over employees flying their helicopters as the BAA was considered to have over the CAA in the Aberdeen Airport case. He doubted if the planning authority would be able to rely on a condition requiring the operator to have aircraft approach and depart from the site in a specified direction. In the letter giving his decision the Secretary of State said that he was advised that he could not validly impose, as a condition of permission under the planning legislation, a requirement of this nature; regulation of flight paths was a matter for legislation other than the planning code. (Ref. P/PP/70/TC/13, October 2, 1981.)

4.36   GDO—"plant"—stacking of pallets

The planning authority argued that the stacking of pallets and crates in the forecourt of the appeal premises, a dairy, constituted a breach of planning control. It was argued that this activity fell within the terms of Class VII(1)(iv)(*a*) of Schedule 1 to the Town and Country Planning (General Development) (Scotland) Order 1975. That provision excludes from permitted development the installation or erection of plant or machinery materially affecting the external apperance of an industrial undertaking. The Secretary of State held that the stacking of pallets did not constitute the installation of "plant." It was simply storage and as it was ancillary to the use of the premises as a dairy it did not involve development. (Ref. P/ENA/SC/8, December 15, 1978.)

4.37   Engineering operation—GDO—parking and storage area

The planning authority alleged that the levelling and resurfacing of a hardstanding for parking and storage breached conditions on a planning permission. The appellants argued that planning permission was not required.

The reporter agreed with the planning authority that the levelling and surfacing was an engineering operation. Was permission granted by Class VII(1)(i) (development for industrial purposes) or Class VIII (repairs to private streets and private ways) of Part I of Schedule 1 to the Town and Country Planning (General Development) (Scotland) Order 1981? There was a private way through the site but the reporter was not satisfied that works for the improvement of the parking and storage areas were "works carried out on land within the boundaries of a road or street" (Class VIII) or that such works could be regarded as being development carried out by an industrial undertaker for "the provision, re-arrangement or replacement of private ways or private railways, sidings or conveyors" (Class VII(1)(i)). In the reporter's opinion the parking and storage area was a discrete use which was not covered by the definition of a private way as that expression was ordinarily construed.

Planning permission was therefore required and there had been a breach of planning control. (Refs. P/PPA/SS/71; P/ENA/SS/39, June 6, 1983.)

Class XIII

4.38 GDO—permitted development—works affecting stream

The most interesting question to arise in this appeal was whether certain operations, allegedly part of a garden landscaping scheme, required planning permission.

The appellant had placed a length of pipe in the bed of a stream which ran through his garden and had covered the pipe with earth. He had also built a wall in the original bed of the stream. These works had resulted in an increase in the speed and depth of the water downstream from the operations. The planning authority, concerned that the stream was now scouring a wall which supported a public footpath and road, took enforcement action. The appellant argued that the works either did not constitute development or, alternatively, were permitted development and therefore did not require the permission of the planning authority.

The reporter accepted that garden alterations such as the building of a rockery or the laying of concrete slabs to form a path would not normally amount to development, in that operations of that type involved only a small amount of building or engineering work, had no material effect upon the appearance of the garden and did not affect other property. Here, however, the operations were of such a magnitude and had such an effect on other property as to amount to development. The reporter pointed out that section 19(2)(*d*) of the 1972 Act, which excludes from "development" the use of land within the curtilage of a dwelling-house for any purpose incidental to the enjoyment of the dwelling-house as such, refers only to "use" and not to building or engineering operations. Section 19(2)(*d*) therefore had no application in the circumstances of this case.

Nor could the reporter accept that the operations had permitted development status under Class XIII of the Town and Country Planning (General Development) (Scotland) Order 1975, which permits the carrying out of any works required in connection with the improvement or maintenance of water-courses. Since in this case the bed of the stream had been narrowed, the works could not be said to have improved the watercourse. Nor could they be described as maintenance of the watercourse—the works carried out here involved new engineering operations. (Ref. P/ENA/CC/7, February 25, 1980.)

GDO—Caravans

4.39 GDO—caravans—erection of house

Planning permission had been granted for the erection of a dwelling-house on the site of a ruined building. Two caravans and a wooden structure had been sited on the land to provide living accommodation for the appellants. Under Class XXI of the Town and Country Planning (General Development) (Scotland) Order 1981 (which refers, *inter alia*, to paragraph 9 of Schedule 1 to the Caravan Sites and Control of Development Act 1960) a caravan site licence "shall not be required for the use as a caravan site of land which forms part of, or adjoins, land on which building or engineering operations are being carried out (being operations for the carrying out of which permission . . . has, if required, been granted) if the use is for the accommodation of a person or persons employed in connection with the said operations."

In this case, apart from a limited amount of demolition work on the existing derelict house, the rudimentary commencement of a new access and the laying of a water main, there was no evidence that building or engineering operations of an organised or systematic nature were being carried out on the site or had been undertaken with any degree of continuity since the caravans were first sited on the land. In the reporter's assessment, building or engineering operations were not, as a matter of fact and degree, being carried out on the site in accordance with the legislation on caravans. The caravans simply provided a home for the appellants and should therefore have been the subject of an application for planning permission.

The timber shed was linked to and used in conjuction with the two caravans to form part of the living accommodation. It was a readily transportable structure adapted for human habitation and, in the reporter's view, was an integral part of the caravan site and was covered by the same legislation as the caravans. That structure too should have been the subject of an application for planning permission. (Ref. P/ENA/TC/46, July 3, 1985.)

4.40 Caravan—siting on farmland

An enforcement notice alleged the unauthorised siting of a caravan on the appellant's farmland. He alleged that he used the caravan as temporary daytime accommodation during his periodic visits to supervise work on land improvement. The appellant claimed that planning permission was granted for the siting of the caravan by Class XXI of Schedule 1 to the Town and Country Planning (General Development) (Scotland) Order 1981, which in turn referred to paragraphs 2 to 9 of Schedule 1 to the Caravan Sites and Control of Development Act 1960. The land exceeded 5 acres and the appellant did not use the caravan for more than 28 days in any year. The reporter's interpretation of paragraph 3 was that the number of days the caravan was stationed on the land must not exceed 28 days in any year, otherwise it must be removed. The pertinent factor was not whether it was in specific use for human habitation, irrespective of whether it was in operative use.

If the 28 day rule was interpreted as suggested by the appellant, it would allow a caravan to be on any site provided it was not occupied for more than 28 days in any year. Otherwise the Act would have referred to "use" and not "stationing." In practical terms the provision would be unenforceable as no planning authority would find it possible to monitor the use of such caravans. As regards the interpretation of the caravan legislation, the reporter's interpretation was borne out by paragraph 3(1)(*b*) of Schedule 1 to the 1960 Act, for if any owner of 5 acres of land or more was permitted to station up to three caravans on that land on a permanent basis, whether in use or not, then the environmental consequences and the visual intrusion in the countryside would be considerable and hardly supportive of sound land use, of planning practice or of effective caravan site control. (Ref. P/ENA/GD/20, April 11, 1986.)

4.41 GDO—caravan on agricultural land—curtilage

A caravan situated on an agricultural unit was, it was claimed by the appellant, being used in connection with agriculture. Use of a caravan for such a purpose would constitute permitted development under Class XXII of the Town and Country Planning (General Development) (Scotland) Order 1975 only "during a particular season." In this case the caravan had been on the site for some seven years; Class XXII of the GDO was therefore not applicable.

The appellant also claimed that the caravan was within the curtilage of his house and that it was used by family and friends as well as by seasonal agricultural workers. The Secretary of State held that the caravan was not within the curtilage of the house. The Minister noted that the appellant was not seeking planning permission merely for a farm worker's caravan but also for a static holiday caravan. The Secretary of State said that it was desirable for a number of holiday caravans to be accommodated on a relatively small number of sites rather than have them dispersed over the countryside. (Ref. P/ENA/D/13, July 28, 1977.)

4.42 Caravan site—GDO—"rule of three"—enforcement notice—correction

It was a ground of appeal against an enforcement notice relating to a caravan site that as the siting of the caravans in question was the subject of an appeal against refusal of planning permission, an enforcement notice should not have been issued. That was not accepted as a valid ground of appeal.

The view was taken by the reporter that a breach of planning control had occurred because prior to the serving of the enforcement notice in May 1976 there had been five or more caravans stationed at the farm in question without planning permission and because, under Class XXII of Part I of Schedule 1 to the Town and Country Planning (General Development) (Scotland) Order 1975, only three caravans could be so sited without permission.

The Secretary of State said that the terms of the inquiry report suggested that the reporter, the appellants and the planning authority were prepared to accept that the term "use" as used in the GDO in relation to the use of land as a caravan site applied to the occupancy of a caravan and not to its siting. While it was not for the Secretary of State to interpret the statute, the view was taken that the "rule of three" permitted a person in one of the former crofting counties to have on his land, provided it had not been built on and was not less than 2 acres, not more than three caravans in the months between April 1 and September 30, but that it did not allow him to have up to three caravans on his land all the year round even if they were not occupied between October 1 and March 31.

The Secretary of State accepted that there had been a breach of planning control. Because, however, the siting of a caravan without planning permission was not necessarily a breach of planning control, the view was taken that, as presently worded, the enforcement notice did not specify a breach of planning control, as required by the Act. It was clear from the inquiry report, however, that the appellants knew what breach gave rise to the service of the notice and it was considered that there would be no injustice if the Secretary of State were to use his powers under section 85(4)(*a*) of the 1972 Act to amend the notice as described below to remedy this defect by making it clear what breach was being alleged at the time the notice was served. The notice was amended so as to allege, instead of siting a caravan, "you have committed a breach of planning control in that you have used as a site for a caravan [certain land] contrary to the limitation in numbers specified in Class XXII of Article 1 of Schedule 1 to the Caravan Sites and Control of Development Act 1960 as read with paragraph 3(1)(*b*) of Schedule 1 to the 1960 Act and Article 2(iii) of the Caravan Sites (Exemption from Licensing) (Scotland) Order 1961." (Refs. P/PPA/AL/165; P/ENA/SA/5, May 31, 1979.)

General

4.43 GDO—height of wall—traffic hazard

An enforcement notice had been served in respect of the building of a wall which resulted in the alteration of a road junction. The reporter found that drivers of vehicles approaching the entrance road from the east on a classified road could not see vehicles on the entrance road until they had passed the line of the wall, and that drivers of vehicles on the entrance road could not see in either direction along the classified road. The Secretary of State therefore considered that in respect of both categories of driver the wall did not comply with standard condition 2, set out in Part II of the First Schedule to the Town and Country Planning (General Development) (Scotland) Order 1975. That condition provides that no development is to be carried out under the GDO if it creates an obstruction to the view of persons using any road used by vehicular traffic at or near any bend, corner, junction, or intersection so as to be likely to cause danger to such persons. This was one of several reasons for dismissing the appeal against the enforcement notice. (Ref. P/ENA/SA/11, June 28, 1979.)

4.44 GDO—material considerations—extension of flat

The appellant proposed to extend his flat. The planning authority pointed out that the provision of the Town and Country Planning (General Development) (Scotland) Order 1975 relating to deemed planning permission for certain categories of extension to dwelling-houses was not applicable to flats. The authority submitted that this demonstrated that the considerations relevant to the extension of flats were different from those relating to dwelling-houses. With an increased number of occupiers of a flat there could be loss of amenity and conflict between neighbours;

the appearance of the property might be adversely affected; and there could be loss of privacy. (Ref. P/PPA/GC/52, February 18, 1980.)

4.45 GDO—permitted development—dog kennel

An enforcement notice had been served in respect of a large dog kennel situated within the front garden of a flat. Appeal was lodged, *inter alia*, on ground (*b*) of section 85(1) of the 1972 Act, *i.e.* that the matters alleged in the notice did not constitute a breach of planning control. The reporter pointed out that article 2 of the Town and Country Planning (General Development) (Scotland) Order 1981 made it clear that the category "dwelling-house" did not include a building containing one or more flats, or a flat contained within such a building. The types of development within the curtilage of a dwelling-house which would not require planning permission by virtue of article 3 of the Order therefore did not constitute permitted development where, as in this case, the building contained flats. The development which had been carried out did, therefore, require planning permission, and carrying it out without such permission constituted a breach of planning control. (Refs. P/ENA/LA/96; P/PPA/LA/462, March 23, 1987.)

4.46 GDO—road—car park

The question arose whether particular works in a car park fell within the ambit of the Town and Country Planning (General Development) (Scotland) Order 1981 or not. It was held that since the car park in question was public it fell within the definition of a road—"any way . . . over which there is a public right of passage (by whatever means)." (Ref. P/DEV/1/SP/2, January 6, 1988.)

4.47 House in garden—permitted development rights—section 50 agreement

The reporter would have been prepared to grant planning permission for a house in the grounds of another, provided means could be found of ensuring that any future extensions or additions to either house would be subject to planning control. The reporter considered that with the two houses one would have reached the limit of acceptable development. He could have granted planning permission for the proposed house subject to a condition that permitted development rights under the Town and Country Planning (General Development) (Scotland) Order 1981 were removed. He was, however, unable to take such action regarding the existing house. He thought that it might be that, on the basis of his decision letter, the appellants and the planning authority might be able to conclude a section 50 agreement, surrendering permitted development rights attaching to the existing house. (Ref. P/PPA/SQ/225, March 9, 1988.)

SECTION 5

APPLICATION FOR AND GRANT OF PLANNING PERMISSION

See generally Young and Rowan-Robinson, *Scottish Planning Law and Procedure*, pp. 185–206 and 251–275.

Certain exceptional categories of development, set out in section 20 of the Town and Country Planning (Scotland) Act 1972, are declared not to require planning permission. Nor does development by the Crown require such permission. Otherwise planning permission is required for the carrying out of development on land (1972 Act, section 20(1)). However, an express grant of planning permission by the planning authority may not be necessary in order to allow development to proceed; in certain circumstances planning permission for development is deemed to be granted and in other circumstances permission is granted by development order (see Section 4, *supra*). Unless granted in one of the ways mentioned above, planning permission must be obtained from the planning authority. It is with aspects of the application for, and grant of, planning permission that the summaries of appeal decisions contained in this section are concerned.

Among the specific matters with which the appeal decisions in this section are concerned are the consequences following upon an earlier grant of planning permission, proposals found for various reasons to be unacceptable, issues involving outline applications and applications for reserved matters, "specified operations," renewal of lapsed planning permission, reasons for refusal of planning permission, amendment of a planning application at an inquiry, omitting to advertise proposed development in a conservation area or a proposal affecting the setting of a listed building, questions of the applicant's control over the land required for a proposed development, and personal planning permission.

APPEAL DECISIONS

5.1 Planning permission—"future extension"—submitted plans

When planning permission was granted for an extension to a nursing home in 1973, the submitted plans included a dotted outline labelled "future extension," clearly indicating an intention to erect a further extension in due course.

The reporter said in an appeal some 10 years later that it was perhaps unfortunate that the 1973 planning permission had not expressly stated that there was no implied approval for a further extension but the wording of the permission was clear enough; it granted approval for the detailed plans only. In the reporter's opinion the dotted line was not binding on the planning authority, especially after a lapse of 10 years. Any assumed commitment towards a further extension would in any case be affected by the statutory provisions limiting the life of planning permissions. (Ref. P/PPA/SQ/164, July 4, 1985.)

5.2 House in countryside—permission granted for reconstruction—new house built

In 1977 the planning authority had granted planning permission for the reconstruction of an old house. The planning authority stated that that permission was tantamount to permission for the alteration and repair of an existing house. However, problems arose with reconstruction and the appellant proceeded to erect a completely new house on a different part of the site in the belief that he had planning permission. The development would be outwith any settlement and would, as an isolated house in the countryside for which there was no agricultural need, contravene the policy set out in DHS circular 40/1960. The appeal against refusal of planning permission and an enforcement notice were therefore dismissed. (Refs. P/PPA/CB/53; P/ENA/CB/34, December 15, 1981.)

5.3. Planning permission—24 residential caravans—previous permission

Planning permission had been refused for 24 residential caravans on a site. Though the planning authority argued to the contrary, the reporter found that a planning permission granted in 1965 had given approval for 120 caravans on the site in question, subject to a condition that the total number of caravans on the site was not to exceed 43 without the approval of the river purification authority. No planning permission was therefore necessary. (Ref. P/PPA/SU/205, March 9, 1987.)

5.4 Section 50 agreement—"granny flat"—house in countryside

A house in the green belt was linked by a garage to a former barn. It was proposed to make the barn into a "granny flat," a self contained dwelling to be used by dependent relatives of the owner of the house. The planning authority refused planning permission because it would be contrary to their green belt policy to allow a new house in the country.

The Secretary of State did not consider the proposed house to be contrary to green belt policy. An existing building of attractive appearance was to be retained with much the same external appearance; as a new use of an existing building it was acceptable. It would, however, be necessary to ensure that the new house was not used as a separate unit. A condition attached to a planning permission or a section 50 agreement would not be appropriate. The proposal in its existing form was unacceptable. (Ref. P/PPA/SU/159, February 14, 1985.)

5.5 Applications for planning permission—insufficient details
Planning permission had been refused for alternative housing developments on a site. The applications had been refused on the ground that the appellant had failed to provide sufficient details to allow the planning authority to give proper consideration to the applications. The reporter found that the planning authority had complied with the requirements of article 5 of the Town and County Planning (General Development) Order 1975, by (a) notifying the appellant within one month that they were unable to entertain the applications unless further details were submitted and (b) specifying the matters as to which they required further information. (Refs. P/PPA/SU/109–111, July 16, 1982.)

5.6 Application lacking detail—substantial development proposed— appeal dismissed
Outline planning permission had been sought for leisure, recreation and tourist facilities including residential accommodation, self-catering flats, villas, log cabins, a restaurant, a swimming pool and solarium, and a function suite. The reporter considered that the application form and letters in support of the application referred to a great number of facilities but did not include a plan showing where these facilities were to be located. No details of the residential accommodation were given, nor of the amount of land required for the development. The reporter dismissed the appeal for lack of detail. (Ref. P/PPA/SG/52, October 15, 1981.)

5.7 Planning permission—outline or detailed application
This was an application for planning permission for a public house/restaurant. The reporter considered that the development

proposed at the public inquiry was not the same as that applied for. Nowhere in the plans was it indicated that these were illustrative only. Therefore, as indicated in SDD Circular 18/1986, the original plans required to be treated as part of the development in respect of which the application had been made. (Ref. P/PPA/SL/406, September 17, 1987.)

5.8 Outline planning permission—reserved matters

Outline planning permission for development having previously been granted, notice of the planning authority's decision to approve reserved matters was given on March 1, 1984. For the consent to remain valid, it was necessary that the approved development should be taken to have been begun not later than two years following that date. Section 40(1) of the 1972 Act states that development shall be taken to be begun on the earliest date on which any "specified operation" comprised in the development begins to be carried out. The only type of specified operation that had any relevance in this case, and the one on which the appellant founded, was that specified in section 40(2)(*d*)—any operation in the course of laying out or constructing a road or part of a road. The physical work of constructing the road did not begin until May 1986, which was more than two years following the approval of reserved matters. However, evidence had been led on behalf of the appellant to the effect that 8 or 10 garden canes had been placed on the line of the road within the two-year period, in May 1985. The issue to be determined was whether the placing of the garden canes could be considered a specified operation.

The canes were placed 8 metres from a boundary wall. The reporter said that the appellants might have considered that an 8 metre strip was wide enough to allow a road to be constructed but this was about 2 metres less than the road shown on the approved reserved matters plan. The canes could not therefore have been placed in connection with the laying out of the approved road. Canes were wholly unsuitable for laying out a road being much less robust than the type of pegs normally used for this purpose and they could be easily damaged or removed. No steps were taken to protect the canes and there was no evidence that they were still on the site when the construction of the road started one year later. In *Malvern Hills District Council v. Secretary of State for the Environment* [1982] 46 P. & C.R. 58 it was held that the marking of a road did amount to a specified operation. While English decisions could be of assistance in the interpretation of the Scottish legislation, they were not binding in

Scotland. More importantly, the circumstances of that case bore very little resemblance to the present case. In the *Malvern Hills* case three men were involved over three days. The centre line of the road and the line of the pavements were marked with pegs that were 1.5 inches or 2 inches square and 2.5 feet long driven into the ground to leave 6 to 10 inches showing. The pegs were sufficient for the driver of an excavating machine to follow when the construction of the road was begun.

The reporter concluded that the canes were placed on the site as a temporary indicator of the boundary of the proposed site and not as an operation in the course of laying out the roadway. No specified operation had occurred and the appeal against the enforcement notice failed. (Refs. P/ENA/GA/70; P/PPA/GA/406, October 27, 1988.)

5.9 Planning permission—specified operation

Insofar as a claim had been made that a planning permission for a proposed change of use was still extant because of certain work done in implementing that permission, the reporter was of the opinion that the placing for a week or thereabouts of five illumination standards on 3 foot square plates merely staked to the ground, and when the land was not under the control of the developer, did not constitute a "specified operation" in terms of section 40(2) of the Town and Country Planning (Scotland) Act 1972. (Ref. P/PPA/FB/64, July 20, 1981.)

5.10 Planning permission—time limits—specified operations

The appellant claimed that a planning permission for dog and cat kennels granted in 1971 was still extant by virtue of the carrying out of works which the appellant claimed to be "specified operations" within the meaning of section 40(2) of the Town and Country Planning (Scotland) Act 1972. He contended that he had breached a wall, created an access road and a car park off the road, had built a "ranch-style" fence along the back of the houses and had made a trial bore some 10 feet deep. He argued that the decision in *Spackman* v. *Secretary of State for the Environment* [1971] 1 All E.R. 257 supported his view that he had carried out specified operations.

The planning authority denied that he had carried out specified operations, arguing that only works specified in section 40(2) of the 1972 Act might be construed as specified operations and that any operations not so specified could not be deemed part of the development.

The reporter considered that the road widening and the erection of a fence had nothing to do with the proposed kennels development. The works were specifically related to an earlier permission for a workshop. In the reporter's words: "There is no evidence that these works were carried out in furtherance of the kennels development and ample evidence that the road and access have been actively used in connection with the motor repair workshop."

For the car park to be deemed a specified operation it would have had to be regarded as being part of an "operation in the course of laying out a road or part of a road." The small car park lay to the side of the road and it was therefore difficult to see how it could be regarded as "part of a road." In the reporter's view it would be flying in the face of common sense to suggest that this car park was created specifically for the kennels.

The reporter therefore thought that the permission for the kennels had lapsed. (Ref. P/PPA/GC/38, December 13, 1979.)

5.11   Enforcement notice—specified operations—date when development began

An enforcement notice was served alleging unauthorised use of a dwelling-house for office purposes. An appeal was lodged on, *inter alia*, ground (*b*) of section 85(1) of the 1972 Act—*i.e.* that the matter alleged in the enforcement notice did not constitute a breach of planning control.

Planning permission for use of a dwelling-house as offices was granted on appeal by the Secretary of State. The Secretary of State's letter was received by the appellants on July 30, 1975. For the appellants it was argued that on the authority of *R.* v. *Yeovil Borough Council* (1971) 23 P. & C.R. 39 no planning permission existed until written notice was given to the appellant and that therefore the permission ran from July 30, 1975. If that argument was not accepted and it was held that the permission ran from July 29, 1975 (the date of the Secretary of State's letter) it was submitted on the authority of *Cavers Parish Council* v. *Smailholm Parish Council*, 1909 S.C. 197 that the permission expired on the same day in the calendar five years later, *i.e.* on July 29, 1980. The date of expiry of the permission was either 30 or July 29, 1980 and if it was established that the development was begun on July 29, 1980 then there was no breach of planning control.

It was pointed out that in section 40(1) of the Act it is stated that "development shall be taken to be begun on the earliest date on which any specified operation comprised in the development begins to be carried out," and in section 40(2) it is stated that "specified operation" means *inter alia* "any change in the use of any land, where that change constitutes material development." The point to be decided was not whether or not the development had been completed but whether or not it had been begun. It was submitted that one must begin office use by installing furniture— just as one began to build a house by digging a trench—and that there could be no argument about the fact that office furniture was delivered to the appeal premises on July 29, 1980.

The reporter took the view that planning permission for office use of the appeal premises ran from the date of the Secretary of State's decision letter, *i.e.* July 29, 1975, and expired at midnight on July 29, 1980, if the change of use had not been implemented. Some office furnishing had been placed in at least two rooms before midnight on July 29, 1980 but in the reporter's opinion that action was not sufficient of itself to constitute the permitted change of use in terms of section 40(1), (2) and (3) of the 1972 Act. (Ref. P/ENA/GA/29, April 16, 1982.)

5.12   Time limit upon development—demolition—specified operation— licensed premises

Planning permission had been granted in 1975 for the demoli- tion of existing premises and the erection of new licensed premises. A condition required that work should start within five years of the grant of permission. In 1980, after the five years had elapsed, the appellant sought renewal of the permission but this was refused. The appellant then contended that the development had properly commenced in 1976 with the demolition of the existing premises. On this matter the reporter stated that demoli- tion was not included as a specified operation as referred to in section 40(2) of the 1972 Act. He was not convinced that the demolition had been intended as an integral part of the con- struction of the new building. (Ref. P/PPA/SM/54, October 18, 1982.)

5.13   Lapsed planning permission—renewal refused

Outline planning permission for a house had lapsed in 1975. It was agreed that there had been no change in circumstances but a fresh application was refused in 1976. The reporter concluded that the previous decision was misjudged and that the planning authority had properly taken the opportunity that presented itself to repair the mistake that had occurred. (Ref. P/PPA/SQ/9, December 17, 1976.)

5.14   Time-expired planning permission—policy

The appellant had purchased a site for a house with outline planning permission granted prior to local government reorganisation. There was a failure through an oversight to submit an application for approval of details within the statutory time limit. An application for a fresh planning permission had been refused. The reporter stated: "I am satisfied that there is no moral or legal obligation on the present local authority to have regard to a previous lapsed permission if new policies have since been adopted." (Ref. P/PPA/HF/31, March 14, 1980.)

5.15 Reasons for refusal—introduction of new reasons at inquiry— housing in the countryside

Planning permission had been refused for a housing development on the ground of a direction from the Secretary of State on development affecting a trunk road, and on the grounds that the development would constitute ribbon development along a rural section of road and would, by increasing the numbers of vehicles entering and leaving a trunk road, be detrimental to road safety. During the inquiry the planning authority had produced evidence of other grounds of objection, including the fact that the site was not zoned for residential use in the development plan, and that it lay within a National Parks Direction Area. The reporter ruled that these additional grounds were admissible even though they had not been included in the original grounds for refusal of permission. (Ref. P/PPA/AL/180, September 9, 1976.)

5.16 Agricultural use—horses—dwelling-house

The appellant argued that he should be allowed to build a dwelling-house to enable him to care for his horses without inconvenience. The planning authority's view was that the breeding or training of horses was not an activity which would qualify as "agriculture" in terms of the authority's policy on new houses in the countryside. The reporter accepted the view of the planning authority and of the Department of Agriculture and Fisheries for Scotland who expressed the view that the use of the appeal site for the grazing and stabling of horses was not an activity of an agricultural nature. This, it was said, was accepted as "established law." (Refs. P/PPA/GD/67 and 68, April 3, 1981.)

5.17 Power to amend application—reserved matters—public inquiry— alteration of plan by Secretary of State

A reporter dealing with an application for approval of reserved matters suggested revisal of the plans. The Secretary of State accepted that a revision of the plans could be regarded as an acceptable amendment provided that it did not have the effect of altering the whole character of the application; the Minister referred to *Inverclyde District Council* v. *Secretary of State for Scotland*, 1982 S.L.T. 200. The Minister concluded that the amendments would have the effect of altering the whole character of the application and therefore could not be regarded as an acceptable alteration. (Ref. P/PPA/GA/52, July 5, 1983.)

5.18   Application for planning permission—section 23 notice—publication arranged by clerk to planning authority

At an inquiry into a refusal of planning permission it was alleged by an objector to the proposals that the terms of section 23 of the 1972 Act (relating to publicity for certain types of application) had not been complied with. The objector claimed that the press notice concerning the application to which the appeal related had been published by the clerk to the planning authority; it was averred that the clerk had thus become an agent for the applicant and that the planning authority could not give an unbiased judgment on the application. Article 17(2) of the Town and Country Planning (General Development) (Scotland) Order 1975 states that "the form of notice . . . shall be certified by or on behalf of the applicant as having been published on a date specified in the certificate." The Secretary of State considered that the terms of the GDO in conjunction with section 23 had been complied with in that there was no specification as to who might or might not act on behalf of the applicant in so far as the requirement to publish an advertisement was concerned. (Ref. P/PPA/GA/15, June 23, 1978.)

5.19   Application for planning permission—certificate under section 23

An application for planning permission had not been accompanied by a certificate in terms of section 23 of the 1972 Act and article 17 of, and Schedule 5 to, the Town and Country Planning (General Development) (Scotland) Order 1975 (relating to publicity for "bad neighbour" development). The decision letter stated that: "In the absence of the prescribed certificate the view is taken that the application does not conform to the requirement of the Act and the GDO, is therefore invalid, and consequently that there is no valid appeal before the Secretary of State." (Ref. P/PPA/SS/23, February 5, 1979.)

5.20   Application for planning permission—publication of notice—1972 Act, section 23

The planning authority had accepted an application for planning permission and had registered it on the basis of a statement by the applicants that they had posted a site notice and had arranged to have the development advertised, as required under section 23 of the 1972 Act and the GDO. However, no certificate of advertisement under Article 17(2) of the Town and County Planning (General Development) (Scotland) Order 1975 was submitted. The view was therefore taken by the Secretary of State that the application did not conform to the requirements of the Act and the GDO and there was, therefore, no valid appeal before the Secretary of State. (Ref. P/PPA/SA/46, January 25, 1979.)

5.21 "Bad neighbour" development—certificate
No certificate under section 23(2)(*b*) of the 1972 Act, to the effect that an application for "bad neighbour" development had been advertised, had been produced by the appellant, although the development had been advertised in the *Perthshire Advertiser*. The planning authority, after receiving representations that this publicity was inadequate, themselves advertised the proposed development in the *Dundee Courier* and confirmed that they were satisfied that the application had been given adequate publicity both on the site and in the press. The Secretary of State was not entirely satisfied as to the validity of the application. However, he decided to deal with the proposal as a valid application, though without prejudice to the legal position. The Secretary of State dismissed the appeal. (Ref. P/PPA/TC/40, March 30, 1979.)

5.22 Failure to sign section 24 certificate—appeal—application to be dealt with as if made to the Secretary of State
During the examination of the appeal documents, concerned with an appeal against a refusal of planning permission for a caravan, it came to light that the certificate under section 24 of the 1972 Act appended to the application had not been signed. (Section 24 requires that the owner and any agricultural tenant of land should be notified of an application.) However, it was decided to accept the appeal after completion of a fresh section 24 certificate with the proviso that the Secretary of State should deal with the application as if it had been made to him in the first instance. Consequently, the reporter exercised his powers under section 33(3), as read with paragraph 2(1)(*a*) of Schedule 7 to the 1972 Act to consider the issues involved as though the application had been made in the first instance to the Secretary of State. (Ref. P/PPA/LA/138, December 31, 1980.)

5.23   Planning application—error—omission to advertise

Responding to points made by an objector, counsel for the appellant stated firstly that the incorrect naming of the applicant in the planning application form as "Kings Entertainments Ltd." as opposed to "Kings Entertainment" was a mere technicality. It was an error of a type commonly made, and there had been no prejudice to any party with an interest in the proceedings. Secondly, no problems arose because of the decision of the district council not to advertise the proposal under section 25 of the 1972 Act (relating to publicity for planning applications affecting conservation areas). Advertisement was only necessary when the planning authority was of the opinion that a proposed development would affect the character or appearance of a conservation area. Planning authorities had a discretion in this matter, and the district council had not acted in a way that could be described as arbitrary, perverse or capricious. The reporter accepted these submissions. (Ref. P/PPA/TC/253, June 29, 1989.)

5.24   Application for planning permission—certificate under section 24(3)—validity of permission

The planning authority submitted that a certificate under section 24(3) of the 1972 Act (relating to notification of any agricultural tenant) had not been submitted with a planning application which had been granted by the authority some five years previously. They argued that this failure made the permission invalid. The reporter dealing with an enforcement appeal pointed out that the application had been accepted as valid by the authority and had been acted upon. He took the view that it would not be procedurally correct that, in hearing an appeal against an enforcement notice, he should take it upon himself to consider challenge of an *ex facie* valid planning permission. (Ref. P/ENA/GC/24 and 25, June 17, 1982.)

5.25   Application for planning permission—certificate

In making an application for planning permission the applicant certified that he was the owner of two plots of land. Evidence at the public inquiry into his appeal against refusal of permission suggested that the certificate of ownership attached to the application might be incorrect. Contrary to the reporter's view, the Secretary of State stated that this would not render the application invalid. The minister said that it should be left to planning authorities to decide whether they need take action in relation to section 24(5) of the 1972 Act (which provides for a penalty in respect of the making of a false or misleading certificate). (Refs. P/PPA/ST/15; P/ENA/ST/11, December 5, 1978.)

5.26 Application for planning permission—notification of owner

The application was intended to embrace three fields totalling 23.31 acres but the plan enclosed with the application included a further field, not owned by the applicant, which brought the total up to 32.63 acres. The Secretary of State decided to deal with the appeal as in the application, *i.e.* with respect to all four fields. It was appreciated that this meant dealing with land in which the applicant had no interest, and in respect of which the owner had not made any comment. Indeed the owner might not even have been aware of the application or of the appeal. It was considered, however, that in this particular case the owner's interests were not prejudiced as he retained control of the land. (Ref. P/PPA/GC/66, April 6, 1981.)

5.27 Material change of use—Use Classes Order—enforcement notice procedure

The appellants claimed that the use of premises for prize bingo came within Class XV of the Use Classes Order of 1973 (use as a public hall, etc.). The Secretary of State did not agree. "The Secretary of State does not consider that it is necessary for the purposes of the planning legislation that any use to which land is proposed to be put must be encompassed within one of the classes defined in the Town and Country Planning (Use Classes) (Scotland) Order 1973. Where a use does not clearly come within any of the classes mentioned in the Order the inference must be that a change of use to or from that use is a development which requires planning permission." The Secretary of State considered that a change from a billiard hall to use for prize bingo constituted development.

The Secretary of State took the view that although this was an enforcement notice appeal, in terms of section 85(7) of the 1972 Act there was deemed to have been an application for planning permission for the development covered by the enforcement notice. In considering such an application the Secretary of State felt bound to take account of section 23 of the 1972 Act (relating to advertisement of the development). Use of premises for prize bingo would have to be advertised. The Secretary of State therefore considered that it would be wrong to consider granting planning permission before the provisions of section 23 and the GDO had been complied with. (Ref. P/ENA/GLW/91, January 23, 1976.)

5.28 Application for planning permission—advertisement under section 25 of the 1972 Act

It was suggested that an outline planning permission for housing was invalid by reason of the planning authority's failure to advertise the proposals under section 25 of the 1972 Act. In the reporter's view such advertisement was only mandatory if the development would in the authority's opinion affect the setting of a listed building. He considered this was not the case here. (Ref. P/PPA/GD/51, August 14, 1980.)

5.29 Control over land—access

The reporter considered that a proposal for housing development was premature until (*inter alia*) the appellants could clearly demonstrate adequate control over sufficient land to provide and maintain acceptable sight lines at the access to the proposed development. The reporter was not satisfied, on the evidence available, that the appellants yet had control over sufficient land on each side of the limited point of access. (Ref. P/ENA/FB/23, January 30, 1981.)

5.30 Control over land—dispute a matter for courts

Planning permission had been refused for a house and garage. An adjoining proprietor claimed the right to bar vehicular access by a lane to the appeal premises. It was suggested to the reporter that permission should be refused because it was not certain that vehicular access could be obtained. Appeals relating to the provision of external flues were cited to the reporter but he considered these were not really comparable in that in these cases it was not disputed that the objectors had a legal right to prevent a flue being fixed to tenement property. In these cases it was certain that by maintaining this objection an essential condition could not be implemented. In the present case there was a dispute over rights and it was not for the reporter but for the courts to determine the dispute. (Ref. P/PPA/SK/23, January 22, 1981.)

5.31 Control over land—car parking—material considerations

In connection with land for a car park for proposed licensed premises the planning authority argued that the onus was on the applicant to show he had control over the land. The reporter was not satisfied that the applicant had control over the land required for 3 of the car parking spaces shown on the plans, nor was he prepared to consider the appellant's suggestion that some other piece of land might be available. If other arrangements for providing adequate and satisfactory car parking could be made, this should be the subject of a fresh application. (Ref. P/PPA/CB/92 and 101, May 1, 1985.)

5.32 Planning permission—control of necessary land—agreement
The appellant did not control the land necessary to meet the highway authority's access requirements. The Secretary of State said he would be prepared to sustain the appeal but a further condition would have to be attached to that approval—a condition that the access to the site be improved to the satisfaction of the local authority. It was incumbent on the appellant to show, however, that he was in a position to make the required improvements although he was not the owner of the land involved. Accordingly the appellant was requested to submit by January 31, 1980, a formal agreement between himself and the owner of the land authorising the appellant to improve the access as required.

All of the land to which the application related was owned by the appellant's father. The reporter said: "The appellant accordingly does not, himself, possess the necessary ownership or control over this land which would enable application or enforcement of a condition to a grant of planning consent requiring improvement of the access and car park." The reporter concluded that before this condition could be applied it would be necessary for prior proof to be submitted to the Secretary of State that the landowner had given formal consent to the execution of this work on his land. (Refs. P/PPA/SR/16; P/ENA/SR/10, December 20, 1979.)

5.33 Control over land—access
Permission was sought to breach a garden wall to form a vehicular access. Approval from the local authority was required for access over an amenity strip belonging to them. Although the strip of land was not under the applicant's control, the reporter felt able to grant permission as there was no objection from the local authority and there was no prospect of the development being carried out without access across the strip of ground. (Refs. P/PPA/LA/103; HGJ/2/LA/11, July 27, 1981.)

5.34 Access—right—housing site
The reporter accepted that a house could be accommodated on the site in question but it was not clear that the access to the proposed site was within the appellant's ownership. To ascertain this would require close examination of the title deeds to

establish boundaries and rights of access. It was not a matter on which the reporter was enabled to reach a legal conclusion. He could not therefore impose a valid condition over a private lane necessary to ensure safe access. (Refs. P/PPA/HC/102 and 103, January 3, 1986.)

5.35 Planning application—application for approval of details
Planning permission had been refused for 10 houses. Outline permission had been granted in May 1975 and the present application had been made in May 1978. Since the latter application had been accompanied by a section 24 certificate the reporter considered that the planning authority were justified in holding that the present application was a completely fresh one and not an application for approval of reserved matters under the 1975 permission. (Ref. P/PPA/GC/71, January 18, 1983.)

5.36 Planning application—fresh application despite earlier outline permission
The planning authority had failed to determine a planning application for a housing estate within the statutory two months. Outline permission had been granted in 1980 but the current application made no reference to that outline permission. The Town and Country Planning (General Development) (Scotland) Order 1981 requires that reference be made to the previous outline permission when application for approval of reserved matters is made. The current application thus had to be treated as a fresh one for full approval. (Ref. P/PPA/SH/38, July 22, 1982.)

5.37 Outline permission—terms of grant
Two enforcement notices alleged breaches of planning control. In 1972 outline permission had been granted for a residential development on the site. In 1975 the appellant sought planning permission for similar development. This was granted in 1976. The planning authority alleged that the 1976 permission was merely an approval of reserved matters and that permission had therefore lapsed. The reporter concluded that full planning permission had been granted in 1976: there was no reference by the applicant to reserved matters or to the 1972 outline permission; the application was accompanied by a section 24 certificate (relating to ownership) which would not have been required in the case of an application for approval of reserved matters; and the planning authority's decision notice referred to "detailed permission" which was not equivalent to "approval of reserved matters." (Refs. P/ENA/GC/24 and 25, June 17, 1982.)

5.38 Outline permission—approval of reserved matters

Outline planning permission for a house had been granted in 1972. A detailed application presented in 1975 which covered approximately twice the area of the outline permission was refused by the planning authority. An appeal was lodged against the refusal of the application for approval of reserved matters. In the circumstances the Secretary of State could not accept that the application submitted to the planning authority in 1975 was valid insofar as it purported to be an application in respect of matters reserved for subsequent decision by the 1972 planning permission. The planning authority had therefore been right to treat the application as a completely fresh one. (Ref. P/PPA/CB/6, April 5, 1977.)

5.39 Outline planning permission—chalets—houses

Outline planning permission had been granted for the erection of "chalets." Application for approval of details was then made for houses. The Secretary of State refused the appeal on the grounds that the latter application did not conform in a number of significant respects with the outline planning permission originally granted. In particular, the design of the houses was not in accordance with that indicated by the drawing attached to the planning permission and the addition of two houses on a prominent part of the site which the drawing indicated should be left undeveloped would have an effect on the visual amenity of the area. Also, the access to the site had unsatisfactory visibility at the point where it met the main road. (Ref. P/PPA/AL/167, February 2, 1979.)

5.40 Outline planning permission—approval of details—details inconsistent with outline permission

This appeal was based upon an application for the erection of a house and two garages further to a grant of outline planning permission previously granted. The plans accompanying the application were related to a house of two storeys with two garages attached thereto. One of the garages was for the benefit of the house in whose ground the proposed development was to be sited. Part of the boundary wall between the proposed development and the existing property was to be the centre wall dividing the two garages. It was submitted and acknowledged that the rear dimension of the site for the proposed development was some 2 metres or thereby less than the site proposed for the development which was granted outline planning permission. That outline planning permission was granted on the basis of a plan which showed the proposed dwelling-house to be one and a half storeys in height. It was therefore considered by the Secretary of State that the application, although founded upon the earlier outline permission was not in fact an application in detail related to the permission held. It differed in three material factors; (1) the extension of the dwelling-house from one and a half to two storeys; (2) the boundary adjustment effected in the interim period between receipt of the outline permission and the current application; and (3) the addition of a second garage. This being so, it was considered that the planning authority were correct in regarding this application as being one for consideration as a new application. Their consideration was therefore not restricted to a simple determination of the matters normally reserved for approval subsequent to the granting of an outline planning permission. Accordingly the Secretary of State dismissed the appeal. (Ref. P/PPA/SU/21, July 19, 1978.)

5.41 Personal permission—reasons for limiting permission

Since there was no guarantee that a future owner of a pony-trekking centre would manage it with the same care as the present owner, the reporter recommended that permission should inure for the sole benefit of the appellant. The Secretary of State did not agree that permission should be on a personal basis since such a permission is normally only appropriate where there are specific reasons for allowing a development that would not otherwise receive permission or where it was necessary to control closely the management of premises where the development might cause nuisance to neighbours; it was not usual to take into account the competency of the operator. (Ref. P/PPA/GB/37, May 20, 1981.)

5.42 Planning permission—personal—enforcement

In considering whether a planning permission personal to the appellant should be granted, the reporter said that he considered that the principle that planning permission runs with the land should be followed in the great majority of cases. Personal permissions should be granted only to avoid exceptional hardship and he did not accept that such a question arose here, in connection with the use of an outbuilding as a motor vehicle repair workshop. If permission were granted subject to a condition the appellant would be likely to seek to expand business, and the enforcement of such conditions as would have to be imposed was not a practical proposition for any planning authority. (Ref. P/ENA/D/61, January 1, 1987.)

5.43 Extension of garage—local authority proposals for site—suitability of use

The appellants sought to extend a commercial garage. The planning authority proposed to redevelop an area embracing the appeal site for housing. The authority also argued that the use of the garage's existing workshop and the proposed extension fell within Class IV of the Town and Country Planning (Use Classes) (Scotland) Order 1973 (general industry) and that there was a presumption against such a use being located in close proximity to a residential area. The planning authority conceded that their proposals might be delayed.

The reporter considered that delay would be unfair to the appellants in that it would deny them what was otherwise an acceptable use of the land. Whether or not it was viable to proceed with such a development in such circumstances was a decision which had to rest with the developer but the reporter was unable to accept that permission should be refused. The reporter imposed a condition to the effect that the work carried out at the appeal premises was to be without detriment to existing amenity by reason of noise, dust or fumes, and that the permitted development was not to be used for storage other than private motor cars or for any industrial purpose, other than a light industrial use as defined in the UCO. (Ref. P/PPA/FB/49, September 8, 1980.)

5.44 Dog compound—nuisance—operational land

British Rail proposed to form a dog compound, kennels and ancillary buildings on operational land. Planning permission was refused. As the kennels were to be sited only 100 feet from housing, they might constitute a nuisance. Since the land in question was operational land of British Railways the appeal had to be decided jointly by the Secretary of State for Scotland and the Secretary of State for Transport (1972 Act, section 214(1)(b)). The reporter concluded that the development was permitted in terms of Class XVA of the First Schedule to the GDO. The Secretaries of State considered, however, that the proposed development did not come within the terms of the GDO since the development was not required in connection with the movement of traffic by rail. On the planning merits the appeal was upheld. (Ref. P/PPA/SL/59, May 15, 1980.)

5.45 Material considerations—house in countryside—DHS Circular 40/1960—dog-breeding

Permission had been refused for the building of a bungalow and dog-breeding kennels on the site of a derelict cottage in the country. The reason for refusal was the local authority's policy for discouraging isolated development in the countryside, in accordance with DHS Circular 40/1960. Dog-breeding did not, it was considered, constitute a special need for housing in the country. (Ref. P/PPA/AR/274, May 26, 1976.)

5.46 Permission in principle—building operation—garage and workshop
Planning permission had been refused for change of use from vehicle store to garage. Six years earlier, however, planning permission "in principle" had been granted for "the erection of a garage and workshop" (incorporating the existing building). That permission did not reserve any matters for subsequent approval and no time limit had been specified for the start of the development. The Secretary of State took the view that the planning permission covered the development in issue. (Ref. P/PPA/AN/120, October 2, 1976.)

SECTION 6

DEVELOPMENT PLAN POLICY AND OTHER MATERIAL CONSIDERATIONS

See generally Young and Rowan-Robinson, *Scottish Planning Law and Procedure*, pp. 207–230.

In determining an application for planning permission, planning authorities are directed to have regard to the provisions of the development plan, so far as material to the application, and to any other material considerations (Town and Country Planning (Scotland) Act 1972, s. 26(1)).

It is an important part of the development plan's role to provide policy guidance for the making of development control decisions. The planning authority must not, however, adhere so rigidly to their policy that they omit to consider the merits of each individual case. The authority are not bound by the development plan; as Lord Guest said in *Simpson* v. *Edinburgh Corporation*, 1960 S.C. 313; 1961 S.L.T. 17: " 'To have regard to' does not . . . mean 'slavishly to adhere to'. It requires the planning authority to consider the development plan, but it does not oblige them to follow it."

Appeal decisions 6.1 to 6.4 in this section illustrate the weight attached to development plan policies by reporters of the Scottish Office Inquiry Reporters Unit. By far the greater part of this section is concerned with the "other material considerations" to which planning authorities, reporters and the Secretary of State must have regard. A decision will be invalidated if there is a failure to take account of a material consideration or if, on the other hand, an irrelevant consideration is taken into account. It is therefore important to define the scope of "any other material considerations." These considerations are not specifically defined in the 1972 Act and a great deal turns on the particular circumstances of any particular case. Material considerations must be of a "town and country planning" nature but there are no specific statements in the 1972 Act as to the objectives of planning. It seems, however, that "other material considerations" must be concerned with the use and development of land and must be shown to be relevant in the particular circumstances (see *Stringer* v. *Minister of Housing and Local Government* [1970] 1 W.L.R. 1281). The weight to be attached to a particular consideration is generally a matter for the planning authority, the reporter or the Secretary of State to determine.

Appeal summaries numbers 6.5 to 6.163 seek to illustrate the range of relevant and irrelevant considerations. They cover such matters as noise, visual and residential amenity, the amenity of the surrounding area, litter, smell, car parking, anti-social behaviour, nuisance, vandalism, privacy, road safety, over-shadowing, cooking odours, traffic problems or hazards, effect on shopping provision, effect on the green belt or countryside, un-neighbourly uses, need (or lack of it), community views, prox-imity of the development to other forms of development such as schools, houses and churches, loitering, theft, late night distur-bance, congestion, breaking the continuity of shopping frontage, hours of opening, risk of creating an undesirable precedent, effect on the character of the street scene, appearance of a building, adverse effect on a conservation area, cost of reloca-tion, personal circumstances, hardship to the appellant, effect on the setting of a listed building, viability of a project, competition, economic considerations, effect on property values, possible road widening, radio interference, policy on commercial uses in street frontage, encouragement of small business, structural stability, public safety, fairness and consistency, and overlapping controls.

APPEAL DECISIONS

6.1 Houses in countryside—policy—development plan and other material considerations

Planning permission had been refused for houses in the countryside. The appellant submitted that a policy for blanket refusal of all houses in the countryside would be *ultra vires* the planning authority in that it would oblige the authority to disregard considerations which by statute they were bound to take into account, *i.e.* "the provisions of the development plan so far as material to the application and . . . any other material considerations." A policy could not prevent an application from being considered on its own merits. The reporter did not consider that the government circular on houses in the countryside or policies derived from it imposed a blanket policy for refusing all developments in the countryside. They merely provided a pre-argued framework and categories within which individual applications could be considered, so that the policy itself became a "material consideration." On the merits the reporter found the proposal unacceptable. (Ref. P/PPA/GD/66, September 3, 1980.)

6.2 Structure plan—draft—effect of policies

In an appeal against a refusal of planning permission for housing development the reporter placed considerable weight on the draft structure plan which had recently been the subject of an examination in public but on which the Secretary of State had not made a decision. The reporter said: "I think it would be unwise to depart from its stated policies at this relatively late stage in its evolution." (Ref. P/PPA/SU/71, May 20, 1980.)

6.3 Precedent—development plan policy—houses in the countryside

The reporter considered that in this case the consistent application of the development plan's policies required applications for single houses in the country to be refused unless some special case of need could be advanced. He said: "While precedent cannot be an all-powerful argument, consistent decision-taking is essential to ensure public acceptability of development control policies." (Ref. P/PPA/HF/60, June 5, 1984.)

6.4 Material considerations—local plan

The planning authority had refused outline planning permission for the erection of housing on a 4.24 hectare site. The principal reason for refusal was that the land had been identified as being suitable for industrial purposes in the local plan. The reporter acknowledged the priority given by the planning authority to the generation and retention of employment. However, the local plan policy had so far been unsuccessful and was clearly in need of review. The site was surrounded by housing. The reporter considered there was no reason why the proposed development should be held up pending completion of a review of the local plan. If the proposed development was suitable, it ought to be approved. Permission was therefore granted. (Ref. P/PPA/SS/153, January 27, 1987.)

6.5 Material considerations—discothèque

Planning permission was refused for the change of use of a social club to a discothèque and licensed premises. The premises were at first floor level in the main shopping area of the town. The application was refused for the reasons that the application, if approved, could be considered a precedent for applications of a similar nature; and that the proposal would detrimentally affect the character and residential amenity of nearby flats through noise, vibration, general disturbance, etc.

The planning authority argued that the general atmosphere would change dramatically if the premises were used as a dance hall and licensed premises and were open to the general public. A private social club presented a picture of controlled, limited use, restricted generally to local persons. The poor access to the appeal premises was not important in these circumstances. A public dance hall was quite different; it was recognised as a "bad neighbour" use, with late night activity, noise and parking and servicing problems. Some patrons would be likely to behave in a boisterous and noisy fashion to the detriment of the amenity of residents in the vicinity and, although these residents had to expect a measure of inconvenience through disturbance from the present licensed premises, the level of disturbance in the early morning was likely to increase. Such a dramatically different use should be discouraged where there were residential properties nearby, where there were no parking facilities and where the access point was somewhat restricted. Modern dance halls required a greater degree of seclusion than social clubs.

The reporter said that the determining issues in this appeal were the effect of the proposal on the amenity of nearby uses and the relevance of the previous use of the premises. He accepted that an establishment for eating, drinking and dancing would have some effect on the residential amenity of people living in close proximity to the premises. He considered that it was, however, established that matters relating to the suitability of the premises, the likelihood of undue public nuisance, threats to public order, and the safety and the over-provision of facilities in the locality were more properly the concern of the licensing authority who were also able to control opening hours. Many of the problems anticipated by neighbours were capable of control by the effective management of the premises and by other bodies such as the police and environmental health department. In land use terms the environmentally harmful effects of establishments such as that proposed could be minimised by detailed attention to matters such as noise insulation. The reporter did not attach great weight to the objection from the Chinese restaurant as the two uses did not seem to him to be mutually incompatible and the proposed dance floor was to be above the restaurant's kitchen.

The reporter considered that it was significant that the premises were in the town centre which was where one might expect to find licensed premises and a discothèque. In his judgment, neighbours in town centres could not expect the same standards of residential amenity as prevail in, for example, suburban housing areas. The advantages of convenience, etc. associated with living in a central location had to be balanced against the disadvantages that might appear to arise from proximity to commercial and leisure uses. Of even greater significance, in the reporter's opinion, than the central location of the premises was their history of previous similar uses over the past 30 years or so, first as a dance hall and latterly as a social club. The premises were licensed and he understood that functions and social events took place. Residents may have become used to the relative peace and quiet following the closure of the social club, but it was unrealistic to assume that this situation would continue indefinitely. It was obvious that the dance area was purpose-built for entertainment use and the present proposal did not seem to be essentially much different in a planning sense from the previous use of the premises, notwithstanding the change from private to public. Any perceived difference was likely to be a function of management. Accordingly, provided specified steps were taken to minimise noise levels, planning permission was granted. (Ref. P/PPA/TA/147, February 16, 1989.)

6.6 Material considerations—hot food take-away shop—social considerations

The appellants argued that behaviour in the streets outside a hot food take-away and the dropping of litter were not planning considerations, though the former might constitute a breach of the law and the latter was a statutory offence. The reporter agreed that these were not proper planning considerations.

However the social situation in the area was volatile and the vehemence of opposition to the proposed hot food shop was significant and impressive. The reporter concluded that the planning authority were right to say that this use of the site would detract from the social amenity of the area and would upset the flimsy social balance of the surrounding residential area. Most of the population had come in from elsewhere, there was an unusually high turnover of tenants on this estate, it had taken many years for the population to settle down, and it was still socially uneasy, though improving. In the authority's view the social balance could easily be disturbed and the opening of a hot food shop, staying open late in the evening, would be more than enough to upset the delicate social balance. Though the appellants argued that it was wrong to use planning powers to deal with a social problem (see appeal decisions Refs. P/PPA/ LC/93, June 7, 1984 and P/PPA/B/99, December 13, 1983; Nos. 6.12 and 6.17 below), such matters had been held important or decisive in other appeals (see Refs. P/PPA/GLW/875, March 12, 1974 and P/PPA/SH/22, August 28, 1979). The appeal was dismissed. (Ref. P/PPA/SH/51, May 9, 1985.)

6.7 Material considerations—hot food shop—"bad neighbour" development—need

Planning permission was sought for the change of use of a shop to a Chinese hot food carry-out. The reporter found the location of the premises (in close proximity to dwelling-houses and school classrooms) was such that the proposed use would be a "bad neighbour" development on account of the activity, noise and smell that the use would be likely to generate, especially in the late evening. There were other hot food carry-out shops in the neighbourhood and the reporter concluded that there was no local need for the facility which might have offset the disadvantages. The appeal was therefore dismissed. (Ref. P/PPA/SM/118, May 5, 1987.)

6.8 Material considerations—fish and chip shop—disturbance

One of the factors which weighed with the reporter in this appeal was the effect that a proposed fish and chip shop and restaurant would have on the amenity of neighbouring property. He said that motorists would inevitably park outside the front door of a neighbouring house, and continued: "The concentration of activity will affect the quiet enjoyment of this well-maintained house and may well diminish the value. In my view [the occupier of the house] is entitled to look to the planning authority for protection against such a significant change in his immediate environment." (Ref. P/PPA/HF/33, May 28, 1980.)

6.9 Material considerations—litter, noise and disturbance—architectural quality of area

Planning permission had been refused for change of use of an office to a fish and chip shop. The reporter accepted that this would be a well run establishment but considered it inevitable that there would be a certain amount of litter, noise and disturbance outside. Such behaviour would not, of course, be under the applicant's control. The reporter also thought that the proposed shop would be out of character with the architecture of the conservation area in which the appeal premises were situated. (Ref. P/PPA/B/2, May 24, 1982.)

6.10 Material considerations—hot food shop

Planning permission was sought for the change of use from a shop to a hot food shop. The reporter considered it unrealistic to refuse planning permission for the proposed change of use when the pattern of business in the parade of shops in which the premises were situated had already changed in the direction of establishments providing services rather than goods. Restrictions were placed upon the hours of opening. (Ref. P/PPA/SK/68, January 27, 1987.)

6.11 Chinese carry-out establishment—noise, smells, parking—restaurant/tearoom

Planning permission had been sought for a change of use from a restaurant/tearoom to a Chinese carry-out food establishment. Permission was refused on the grounds that the new use would have a detrimental effect on its surroundings through litter, noise, smells and parking. The reporter pointed out that had the intended change been to a Chinese restaurant there would have been no change of use and therefore no need for planning permission. The reporter accepted that smells could be dealt with by a suitable flue liner. Parking was available in the vicinity. He therefore sustained the appeal subject to conditions. (Ref. P/PPA/B/37, March 14, 1981.)

6.12 Material considerations—carry-out restaurant—unsocial behaviour

Planning permission was sought for a carry-out restaurant. The planning authority objected on the grounds of the litter that would result. The reporter said that rowdy or unsocial behaviour in the street was probably unlawful and the deposit of litter was a statutory offence. Powers of law enforcement already existed and it was up to the authorities to use them and for aggrieved persons to make representations to the authorities. It would be an abuse of planning powers to seek, by withholding planning permission, to restrain a legitimate activity for which there was a reasonable demand, solely to avoid situations arising from breaches of the law, which breaches were not inevitable. The planning authority ought, he considered, to be able to secure the standards it required. (Ref. P/PPA/LC/93, June 7, 1984.)

6.13 Material considerations—take-away food sales—restaurant

The reporter stated that it had been normal planning practice in development control to make a distinction between "eating in" restaurant facilities and "take-away" facilities because of the very significant planning differences between them, the main differences being the duration and frequency of customer visits (which had implications for traffic generation, parking and amenity); and a greater tendency for some people consuming take-away food to linger in the vicinity of the shop, sometimes creating disturbance and litter. The reporter considered that take-away food sales would be incidental to a restaurant use only if they were so small as to be insignificant and thus would not cause the potential problems noted above. (Ref. P/PPA/GA/376, February 2, 1987.)

6.14 Material considerations—hot food shop—specific food type

Planning permission had been refused for a change of use from a butcher's shop to a hot food shop for the sale of Turkish kebabs. There were traffic objections, amenity objections and the applicants had failed to demonstrate that flue gases could be satisfactorily dispersed. Nor would the planning authority be able to control possible future change within the same use class to a more noxious type of food preparation, which could then lead to nuisance.

The reporter was not convinced by the objections on traffic or amenity but considered that the ventilation arrangements were unsatisfactory. He pointed out that the planning authority's concern over possible changes were unfounded as it was "quite usual for permission to restrict hot food preparation to a specific food type." (Ref. P/PPA/CC/120, April 26, 1985.)

6.15 Material considerations—litter—chip shop

In granting permission for a chip shop the reporter said on the question of litter: "The deposit of litter in the streets is an offence which can be dealt with under other legislation. It seems to me that it would not be right to seek to deal with a litter problem by refusing to provide a service which people desire to have, namely a chip shop, but to adopt appropriate measures for the control of litter in other ways." (Ref. P/PPA/SD/11, April 28, 1981.)

6.16 Material considerations—hot food carry-out—litter

In granting permission for a carry-out food establishment, the reporter doubted whether the sale of Chinese food for home consumption was likely to cause a street litter problem any more onerous than other town centre retail activities. (Ref. P/PPA/LC/49, July 24, 1981.)

6.17 Hot food shop—complaints—litter—extended hours

Complaints had been made by the planning authority and by local residents that people visiting a shop late at night had caused disturbance by rowdy and unsocial behaviour and had caused annoyance by discarding litter and unwanted food in the streets or in private premises. At the time of the reporter's inspection there was little litter. A litter bin was situated near the shop.

There had been a failure to adhere to the condition of the planning permission for use of the shop as a hot food shop requiring the premises not to open after 11.00 p.m. There was therefore actual experience and not just conjecture about activities in the vicinity of the shop after midnight. Application had been made to open the premises until 12.30 a.m. on Saturdays and Sundays.

The reporter said that: "The deposit of litter is already a statutory offence and the other matters complained of probably also involve breaches of the law as well as departures from ordinary good manners. Powers of law enforcement already exist and it is up to the appropriate authorities to use them, and for local people to make representations to those authorities. Accordingly, it would be an abuse of planning powers to seek, by withholding planning permission, to restrain legitimate activity for which there is a reasonable demand [*i.e.* a hot food shop] solely to avoid situations arising from breaches of the law, which breaches are not inevitable."

In the public interest it was appropriate to grant planning permission but only for a trial period on the assumption that the authorities would use their powers to discourage the deposit of litter and to discourage disorderly behaviour and on the assumption that the developer would adhere to the conditions of planning permission. Temporary planning permission for 12 months was therefore granted. (Ref. P/PPA/B/99, December 13, 1983.)

6.18 Material considerations—hot food shop—disturbance, litter, etc.

Planning permission had been refused for the change of use of premises to a hot food shop and amusement arcade in a residential area. The premises would, it was claimed, appeal to youngsters and would lead to disturbance and anti-social behaviour. It was held that these effects would be unacceptable close to residential premises. (Ref. P/PPA/FA/112, January 12, 1988.)

6.19 Material considerations—hot food shop—competition, disturbance and litter

It was proposed to change the use of a shop to a hot food shop. There was a Chinese restaurant nearby but the reporter could not accept that it was a function of town planning to interfere with commercial competition. Nor did he think it proper for planning to attempt to control matters for which provision was made in other legislation, *e.g.* disturbance, litter, etc. (Ref. P/PPA/SL/374, April 13, 1987.)

6.20 Material considerations—prospects of success—litter

Planning permission had been refused for a carry-out restaurant. The reporter said that the purposes of planning control did not normally include the scrutiny of an applicant's assessment of his or her prospects of success except in so far as they related to such matters as affected amenity, increased noise, disturbance, etc. The reporter also said that it was not easy to determine to what extent litter was a material consideration. He had no doubt that there were places of natural beauty and historic interest where litter-producing uses would be undesirable and might be judged unacceptable, but in a central commercial area it was scarcely practicable to exclude retail outlets for all products which might be consumed on the spot where their wrappers or containers were thrown carelessly away. In the interests of consistency, sweets, sandwiches, biscuits, fruit and canned drinks would have to come under the ban as well as take-away food. The reporter concluded that planning control was not the appropriate method of dealing with the problem in the circumstances under consideration. (Ref. P/PPA/SQ/186, December 2, 1986.)

6.21 Material considerations—Chinese take-away—litter—nuisance

The reporter concluded that the site was suitable for a Chinese take-away restaurant. He said: "I accept that some problems of litter and nuisance already exist in Murray Street, but consider that these are primarily matters to be dealt with under other legislation." (Ref. P/PPA/TA/100, May 21, 1986.)

6.22 Hot food take-away—disturbance—vandalism—litter

The appeal site was situated on the ground floor of a three-storey block of tenements. Planning permission was refused because the use at this location would be injurious to the environmental quality of the adjacent residential premises. The planning authority's experience in the past had been that hot food take-aways in similar locations had led to complaints of odour nuisance, litter, vandalism and late night disturbance.

The reporter said that having regard to the nearby licensed grocer's, the petrol filling station opposite, and the fact that the houses fronted on to a main road, the occupiers of the tenement properties could not be expected to enjoy the same degree of quietness as in a residential suburb. Nevertheless they were entitled to reasonable freedom from unnecessary noise and disturbance, especially in the late evenings.

While problems of litter and vandalism were primarily matters for the police, they could also affect residential amenity and so they were also matters for consideration by the planning authority. The take-away's location on a main road would attract customers from outside the area and the close adjacent to the take-away site would provide opportunities for anti-social behaviour. Planning permission was therefore refused. (Ref. P/PPA/CB/107, January 9, 1986.)

6.23 Material considerations—hot food shop—disturbance and litter—other legislation

It was proposed to change the use of a retail shop to a Chinese take-away. Permission was refused because it would be detrimental to the amenity of nearby housing by reason of smell and disturbance late at night. There was also a fear of increased litter in a well-maintained and pleasant housing estate.

The reporter concluded that the ventilation system would be inadequate to disperse smells. He shared the concern of residents about litter in and around the shop and the disturbance due to the anti-social behaviour of people drawn to the premises. These were, however, considerations which fell to be dealt with under other legislation and not under the planning legislation. (Ref. P/PPA/SL/313, January 3, 1986.)

6.24 Material considerations—hot food take-away—activity, litter, noise, smells and vermin

This was an appeal against a refusal of planning permission for a hot food shop. One of the planning authority's reasons for refusal was that the shop would create unacceptable levels of pedestrian and vehicular activity. There would also be problems of litter and noise. The planning authority were also concerned about traffic hazards through on-street parking. Objectors raised points about litter, smells and vermin problems as well as disturbance.

The appellant said that he considered it inappropriate for the planning authority to concern themselves with questions of litter, vermin, disturbance and parking which could all be controlled under other legislation. The reporter thought the determining issues were whether there would be serious adverse effects on the amenity of local residents because of increased smells, litter, noise and late night disturbance or whether the proposal would result in late night traffic disturbance or in traffic hazard. He said that although these matters might be subject to control under other legislation, they represented potential problems that could result if the proposed development proceeded; they ought to be taken into account in considering whether planning permission should be granted. (Ref. P/PPA/ST/74, July 31, 1985.)

6.25 Material consideration—hot food shop—litter

It was proposed to change the use of a shop to a hot food shop. At the site inspection there were indications that litter from goods purchased at the shop and adjacent licensed premises was being deposited in nearby gardens and along a wire fence to the north of the appeal site though there were indications that the litter was not confined to the area near the shop but was evident all the way along the boundary fence up to 100 metres away from the licensed premises next to the appeal premises. There was a small litter bin at the front of the shop. Among the matters to which attention had been drawn in a petition against the hot food shop was the question of litter nuisance. This was one of the factors taken into account by the reporter. (Ref. P/PPA/SU/168, July 10, 1985.)

6.26 Material consideration—hot food shop—amenity of area—litter

An applicant for planning permission for a hot food shop said arrangements would be made for collecting litter on the premises and on the pavement outside. The reporter referred to local residents' objections to litter and said that he considered that the applicant would be unable to control litter completely. This was one of the reporter's reasons for saying that the use would adversely affect the amenity of the area. The appeal was dismissed. (Ref. P/PPA/SC/112, July 9, 1985.)

6.27 Material considerations—litter—hot food shop
This was an appeal against a refusal of planning permission for a hot food shop. The reporter said there was a general problem of litter associated with hot food take-away shops, particularly when meals were not taken home but were eaten outside the shop. While the proprietors could be expected to make an effort to avoid this nuisance by providing litter bins themselves, provision for litter collection and disposal was a matter for the council. (Ref. P/PPA/FB/178, July 4, 1985.)

6.28 Material considerations—noise
The determining issue in this appeal was whether the grant of planning permission for the use of land for the extraction of coal, fireclay and blaes would have an unacceptable effect on a nearby village in terms of noise. Unacceptable noise might result in proceedings being taken to determine whether the best practicable means of noise abatement had been taken under the Control of Pollution Act 1974. The reporter thought the noise would be intolerable and that some houses would suffer very severe diminution of outlook and visual amenity on account of the proposed workings.

Though local economic benefits, including employment, would stem from the development, the reporter dismissed the appeal. (Ref. P/PPA/SS/102, November 30, 1984.)

6.29 Material considerations—privacy—control over land
It was proposed to build a house in the garden of another with access over an area of grassed public amenity space. A request to purchase the grassed area from the local authority had been refused.

Objections to loss of privacy were lodged by occupiers in the vicinity. The reporter said that there was no law in Scotland that specifically stated that there was a right to privacy but it was a land use matter which a planning authority might reasonably take into account when considering an application. Here, the reporter considered, there was no real loss of visual amenity.

There was no evidence, however, that the owners of the access were prepared to sell or that the appellant had any control over the land. An outline planning permission would have to contain a condition relating to access arrangements but it would be *ultra vires* to impose conditions which related to land not under the appellant's control. The reporter was therefore unable to consider granting outline planning permission. (Ref. P/PPA/SU/185, November 18, 1985.)

6.30 Material considerations—noise—proposed housing

This was an appeal against the refusal of outline planning permission for development of a large site for housing. Nearby was a major chemical manufacturing plant. This had a tall chimney about 450 metres from the nearest part of the appeal site. The reason for refusal was that the site would be detrimental to the amenity of the residents of the proposed housing development by reason of excessive levels of noise generated by the surrounding industrial uses. The chemical factory had been relocated from a site in the inner city to reduce environmental problems.

Complaints about noise affecting existing houses were made in 1982; the noise was produced by fans at the base of the tall chimney but the effect of the noise on the surrounding district varied considerably according to wind and temperature conditions. A nuisance under the Control of Pollution Act 1974 was confirmed in 1982 when the sound level was measured in a bedroom about 1000 metres from the chimney. Complaints had been lodged by individuals, district councillors, community councillors and by various organisations. The noise was not loud but was intrusive. The factory operated for 24 hours a day and the noise became more noticeable when other noise in the area had decreased. Prospective purchasers of houses on the appeal site might well not realise what conditions would be like at night. The planning authority would not like to sanction a situation which might hinder the operation of a newly built factory providing local employment. The planning authority had taken account of the guidance in paragraph 26 of SDD Memorandum 24/1973 "Planning and Noise" which was intended to avoid new residential development being subjected to excessive noise from industrial sources.

The reporter considered that the determining issues were whether, with reasonable precautions in layout and design of buildings, the site could provide an acceptable living environment for the occupants of the proposed houses and whether the development would be likely to inhibit the future operation of the factory. SDD Memorandum 24/1973 would not be satisfied for a significant part of the time. Noise from another factory resulted in a high noise level on the appeal site. If that factory were to operate at night, houses designed to face away from the chemical factory would face towards the other factory. The reporter thought it would be undesirable to permit development to go ahead in view of the noise sources. There were three additional factors: (1) the chemical factory was relocated to this industrial area at considerable expense because of the environmental problems that had occurred at its original site. The reporter thought it would now be a retrograde step to permit a major new housing development so close to the new factory; (2) there was also the possibility of legal action taken on behalf of the residents inhibiting the operation of the factory which could have serious effects on the economy of the local area and further afield; and (3) it was not suggested that there was any particular shortage of land for housing in the area. (Ref. P/PPA/SL/271, December 31, 1984.)

6.31 Material considerations—proposed housing development—noise from factories

Planning permission had been refused for residential development on a site about 800 metres from a chemical factory. The tall chimney of the factory emitted a whine. A steelworks also lay close to the site of the proposed development. The appellants referred to SDD Memorandum "Planning and Noise" and suggested that the standards set out in the memorandum could be achieved. So long as adequate measures were taken in the housing layout, and double glazing was provided in some dwellings, there would be little likelihood of justifiable complaint about the chemical factory.

For the planning authority reference was made to complaints about the chemical factory made by residents living about a half mile or more from the plant and from community organisations. Also if the steelworks, as a result of an upturn in the economy, became more active, there would be a greater noise. Noise would result from a proposed motorway extension. The witness also said that the effect of noise from the new chemical works had been found to vary greatly with climatic conditions and it was therefore a matter of subjective judgment whether there was a noise nuisance under the Control of Pollution Act 1974. The use of the best practicable means to reduce noise could provide a defence against a complaint and efforts were being made by the operators to improve matters.

The chemical company submitted a letter drawing attention to the risk that activity at the factory might be curtailed by legal action.

The reporter said that although it was not a critical issue in planning for noise reduction, he had considered the possibility that complaints from future residents of the site might lead to action for noise nuisance being taken against the factory. As the assessment of noise nuisance under the Control of Pollution Act 1974 was apparently based on subjective judgment it could not be discounted. However, the use of the best practicable means of noise reduction at the source had evidently provided an adequate defence in another case of this type in the district. The position of the factory would therefore be secure if the best practicable means were taken.

The reporter therefore granted outline planning permission subject, *inter alia*, to conditions relating to the need to minimise noise penetration to bedrooms. (Ref. P/PPA/SL/272, March 21, 1985.)

6.32 Parking of lorry—storage of materials—effect on neighbourhood—road safety—amenity

An enforcement notice was served seeking the discontinuance of a site for the parking of lorries and the storage of fish boxes and other materials. The planning authority considered the parked lorries to constitute a traffic hazard. Other people were being subjected to congestion, noise and smell. The reporter accepted that the noise and manoeuvring of heavy vehicles could be disturbing to those living nearby. He concluded that the development was sited in the wrong place, interfered with the free flow of traffic on a trunk road, was a road safety hazard, and detracted from the visual amenity of the area. (Ref. P/ENA/GB/14, March 24, 1981.)

6.33 Material considerations—taxi business—effect on neighbourhood—enforcement

Enforcement action was taken in respect of the use of part of a house for the purposes of a taxi business. The reporter said that, in general, the conduct of a 24-hour taxi business from a house was undesirable on grounds of harm to the amenity of surrounding properties. Here, however, he felt that the taxi business was being operated without offence to the surrounding community. Questions of conflict with the provisions of the local plan and of parking did not alter the reporter's conclusion that planning permission should be granted. (Refs. P/PPA/SR/16; P/ENA/SR/10, December 20, 1979.)

6.34 Material considerations—amenity of houses

Planning permission had been refused for the use of land as a parking area for one commercial vehicle, an articulated lorry, on the ground that it would be detrimental to the amenity of two nearby houses. The reporter noted that although the appellant only intended to park one lorry on the site, if the ownership of the site changed, the new owner might wish to park more lorries there. The reporter therefore considered the potential site as a lorry park. He found that the crucial objection to this use was the close proximity of the two houses. The environment of these houses was not good but whilst they remained, it was important to preserve their environment as far as possible. (Ref. P/PPA/CB/16, September 29, 1977.)

6.35 Material consideration—amenity of neighbouring houses

Planning permission had been refused for the erection of seven houses adjacent to existing dwellings. The latter houses would be overlooked at close range by passing cars and pedestrians, while the noise of passing cars and pedestrians would adversely affect the reasonable amenities of these houses. Because of the adverse effect on amenity the appeal was refused. Another reason why planning permission could not be granted was that the formation of an adequate access would involve the development of land outwith the applicant's control. (Ref. P/PPA/CC/10, August 18, 1987.)

6.36 Relevant considerations—proposed house—site

It was held that a proposed house would lack amenity space and privacy and would be detrimental to the amenity of neighbouring houses, in that it would result in overlooking and loss of privacy, the reporter speaking of "a quite intolerable invasion of privacy" of one of the houses. (Ref. P/PPA/LC/41, October 17, 1980.)

6.37 Car sales showroom—lock-up garages—residential amenity

The appellants proposed to change the use of lock-up garages to a car sales showroom. The reporter accepted that this was not in itself an undesirable form of development and might well be of benefit to the town. However, the reporter considered that any such benefit to the community should not be at the expense of the amenity of a nearby house, the occupants of which were entitled to expect the residential standards of the area to be maintained. (Ref. P/PPA/GE/19, July 11, 1980.)

6.38 Material considerations—amenity—no objection from neighbours

A proposed house extension would have had a detrimental effect on an adjoining house. The fact that the proposed extension was not objected to by the proprietors of the neighbouring house was, it was said, not a very strong factor in favour of the development since it was sometimes difficult for residents who wished to be on good terms with neighbours to object to adjoining proprietors' intentions. Further, over the years owner-ship of the affected property might change. It was therefore the responsibility of the planning authority, in the first place at least, to decide whether a development was acceptable. (Ref. P/PPA/ SB/3, September 9, 1977.)

6.39 Relevant considerations—dwelling-house—overshadowing
The reporter accepted that the scale and appearance of a proposed extension to a house would be similar to that of the existing house. A blank wall of the extension would, however, extend for about 4 metres along the mutual boundary. The reporter considered that it would dominate the outlook from the adjoining house, an effect which would be aggravated by the proposed extension being two storeys in height and thus shading the adjoining property. The appeal was dismissed. (Ref. P/PPA/ HC/115, May 28, 1987.)

6.40 Material considerations—extension of private house—amenity of appellant's house—amenity of neighbour's house
The planning authority had refused planning permission for the erection of a rear extension to the appellant's house. The reporter considered, first, whether the proposed extension would harm the amenity of the appellant's house by excessively reduc-ing the available amount of private amenity open space. He considered that although the back garden was small, others nearby were smaller and he concluded that the proposed exten-sion, occupying 25 per cent. of the back garden, would not be excessive or harm amenity.
Secondly, the reporter considered whether the proposed exten-sion would detract from the amenities of the neighbouring house to a significant extent. The extension would result in a very considerable reduction in direct sunlight reaching the neighbour-ing house and garden. In the reporter's judgment this loss of sunlight was greater than the neighbour should reasonably be asked to bear. (Ref. P/PPA/SU/204, January 19, 1987.)

6.41 Material considerations—effect of building on neighbouring land
The reporter said that overlooking of neighbouring property and restriction of view or light were not of themselves adequate reasons for refusing planning permission but that any developer

was well-advised to take these matters into account in the spirit of good neighbourliness.

The reporter took account of the fact that he was not convinced that construction of the proposed house, to be built on the boundary, could be undertaken without encroachment and disturbance. The proprietor of the neighbouring land had said he would not allow access over his land for construction. Subsequent maintenance of the facades placed on the common boundary would be equally difficult. Quite apart from any legal dispute he considered that this situation could well have a limiting effect by lowering the standard of finish and maintenance of the facades in contention. This, he thought, would be visually unacceptable in a conservation area. (Ref. P/PPA/FC/12, May 3, 1979.)

6.42 Material considerations—advertisements

Planning permission had been refused for the display of three murals in the windows of a bookmaker's shop. The murals depicted sporting scenes. The planning authority considered that the proposed murals would be detrimental to the visual amenity of an outstanding conservation area. The bookmaker's shop was in a street forming part of the main shopping and commercial centre of the town. The shops and commercial premises in the area displayed signage in a wide variety of styles, sizes, materials and colours. Although the merit of the council's ground for refusal was accepted, it was considered that commercial premises which happened to be located in areas of special character and amenity should not be denied advertising media normal to their type of business provided a reasonable degree of restraint was exercised in the display. Each case had to be decided on its merits and it was considered here that the proposed murals, when viewed with the signage displayed in the area, would not detract from visual amenity so as to warrant refusal. The appeal was therefore sustained. (Ref. P/ADA/HB/4, April 20, 1988.)

6.43 Material considerations—multiple occupation

The planning authority refused planning permission for the change of use of part of a four storey tenement to multiple occupation, involving eight occupants. The reporter considered that eight occupants would affect their neighbours by way of noise of movement, the greater noise of radios, etc., more cooking odours, and more demand on car parking in an already crowded street, to the annoyance of other residents in the tenement. (Ref. P/PPA/SL/441, January 18, 1988.)

6.44   Material considerations—traffic—amenity
The reporter was not convinced that a proposed petrol filling station would lead to any appreciable worsening of traffic problems. He considered that a petrol filling station was an acceptable development in the particular location and that it would be likely to enhance the setting of an adjacent conservation area rather than detract from it. (Ref. P/PPA/SC/136, April 4, 1987.)

6.45   Material considerations—effect on shopping provision—effect on amenity of residential property
It was proposed to change the use of two shop units to a coffee shop, an amusement arcade and a pool room. The reporter accepted the planning authority's argument that the loss of retail floor space to non-retail use was unacceptable in this area. Although the block of shops was currently located on the edge of the town centre, it was the planning authority's intention to formally extend the defined shopping area to include the appeal site. In the reporter's view this was a reasonable policy. The reporter was also of the opinion that although residents in the area could not expect to enjoy the same degree of quietness as would prevail in a residential area, the increased noise and disturbance would mean an unacceptable loss of amenity to nearby residents. (Ref. P/PPA/SU/212, March 30, 1987.)

6.46   Material consideration—access to flat
Planning permission for the subdivision of a two storey maisonette into two flats had been granted subject to a condition that a door giving access from the ground floor flat to the common close should be formed. The reporter accepted that in a high amenity area such as this one the carrying of containers of refuse and of laundry from the front door of the flat to the pavement and thence to the common close would be detrimental to the appearance and character of the neighbourhood. (Ref. P/PPA/SL/369, March 16, 1987.)

6.47   Material considerations—licensed leisure club—green belt—effect on house
The appellant proposed to use an existing games room, a single storey outbuilding close to his house, as a proprietor-licensed snooker and angling club.
The reporter said that the proposed snooker and fishing club would be based on one snooker table. There was no suggestion that this would be an organised angling club, with managed

fishing waters nearby. It seemed likely that the main activity would be social gatherings with alcoholic refreshments for sale. The use would be similar to a private licensed social club. The reporter considered that so long as the adjoining house was occupied by the appellant, any disturbance caused by activities at the club need not be a problem.

Satisfactory sight lines for vehicles could be achieved at the access to the property and the existing hardstanding and lay-by could accommodate enough cars for small gatherings at the club. It might, however, be necessary to extend these if the club was successful.

The club appeared to have no special need for a rural location and the reporter considered that the introduction of a private social club use in this rural location would be contrary to the objectives of green belt policy. If the club was successful there would probably be pressures to enlarge the limited snooker, bar and parking facilities that existed. It would be difficult to resist this once the club had become established and enlargement would lead to the existing small cottage and outbuilding becoming a much more conspicuous semi-commercial property with associated parking. The reporter considered that this would detract from the character of this part of the green belt, and that it would be undesirable to authorise the commencement of the private club. (Ref. P/PPA/SJ/35, January 12, 1987.)

6.48 Material considerations—section 50 agreement—sheltered housing

This was an application for outline planning permission for retirement homes. The planning authority said that it was difficult to see the scheme as sheltered housing without a warden. If an alarm system were provided, the scheme might be described as community care. Unless an agreement under section 50 of the 1972 Act were entered into to provide for the availability of a warden off the site, there would be no way to require this and to ensure it continued. The reporter agreed that certain matters could best be dealt with by means of a section 50 agreement. He considered that a grant of planning permission subject to a condition limiting occupation to people over a particular age would be insufficient and inadequate. The appellants were prepared to enter into a section 50 agreement to cover the warden's services, other management services and the age of the occupants. (Ref. P/PPA/FA/68, May 15, 1985.)

6.49 Material considerations—guest house

Planning permission had been refused for the change of use of a property to a guest house. Planning permission for not more than three bedrooms for letting use had been granted in 1985. Because of complaints, the planning authority advised the owner that use of the property at an increased level would require planning permission. The applicant proposed the use of the property as a guest house involving five guest bedrooms. Commercial guests were, said the reporter, more likely than family or friends to disturb amenity, make more noise, create more disturbance and drop more litter. Planning permission was refused. (Ref. P/PPA/SH/112, July 14, 1988.)

6.50 Material considerations—bed and breakfast accommodation—amenity

Planning permission had been refused for the use of three bedrooms in the appellants' house as bed and breakfast accommodation, catering for up to six visitors. The planning authority refused permission on the grounds that the character and amenity of residential areas should be maintained and that here neighbours would see and hear activity at the appeal site. The reporter agreed that residential amenity should generally be protected from the intrusive effect of commercial activities but in the present case the house was on the edge of the residential area, faced onto a busy main tourist route and would not give rise to extra traffic in the residential area. The access to the site was well separated from other houses and the occupiers of most of the nearby houses would be unlikely to see or be affected by the additional traffic. There was adequate space for parking at the front of the house and good sight lines at the access. The appeal was sustained. (Ref. P/PPA/SQ/205, March 31, 1987.)

6.51 Material considerations—guest house—local authority policy

Planning permission had been refused for the change of use of premises from single dwelling-house to boarding house. Four rooms, accommodating eight guests, were used for guest house purposes. The majority of the properties in the immediate vicinity were in residential use but the area was one of mixed residential, commercial and industrial uses. Planning permission was refused for the reasons that the proposal was contrary to the adopted policy of the planning authority relating to guest houses and would detract from the amenity of nearby houses by reason of noise and disturbance. It was agreed that the proposal did not meet the criteria for favourable consideration under the planning authority's policy. The aim of that policy was to prevent guest houses emerging sporadically in residential areas with adverse effects on amenity due to increased traffic, parking, noise, disturbance and visual intrusion from signs and advertisements. The reporter considered that the deciding issue was whether or not a departure from the planning authority's policy on location of guest houses was justified here. He found several reasons why it was. First, the policy was clearly directed towards establishments which provided accommodation for tourists and the relatively short-term visitor to the city but it was evident that the appellant's establishment was much more akin to a traditional lodging house with, in general, long-staying occupants. Secondly, the use for which planning permission was sought had been carried on for a number of years without any record of complaint and without attracting objection when the application was advertised. Thirdly, the location was not such as would attract the average car-owner visiting the city on holiday and in that case he thought the impossibility of providing off-street car parking a matter of comparatively small importance. In order to ensure, as far as possible, that the character of the use was not changed materially, the reporter made the permission personal to the appellant only. (Ref. P/PPA/LA/443, January 21, 1987.)

6.52 Material consideration—business from home—nuisance in neighbourhood

The appellant's retrospective planning application for business use of his home was refused by the planning authority. On appeal the appellant explained that his business involved the delivery of about 4 stones of fish at about 10.30 p.m., the storage of the fish in a garage/shed until about 8.00 a.m., and the overnight parking of a small van on a run-in. The reporter took the view that the deliveries to the appeal site and the uplifting of fish in the early morning could cause disturbance to nearby residents and were for this reason undesirable. He was also of the opinion that the use of the run-in for storage of a commercial vehicle was inappropriate in a residential area, even if cleaning, maintenance and repairs were carried out elsewhere. The reporter concluded that the use of the appeal premises was incompatible with the maintenance of the residential amenity of the area. The appeal was therefore dismissed. (Ref. P/PPA/FA/103, February 10, 1987.)

6.53 Material considerations—retail shop—hot food shop—impact

Planning permission had been refused for the change of use of a shop to a hot food shop. The reporter rejected the planning authority's argument that the proposal would mean the loss of a prime retail shop; a hot food take-away was a type of shop and the authority's policy for non-retail uses in retail areas did not apply. He concluded, however, that the proposed development was unacceptable because of the impact it would have on residential amenity outwith normal shop hours. (Ref. P/PPA/ TA/112, March 5, 1987.)

6.54 Material considerations—change of use from betting shop to amusement centre—residential amenity

The appeal premises—a proposed amusement centre—were situated under residential premises. Planning permission had been refused on the ground that the objectives of the local plan were clearly based on a resolve to control un-neighbourly uses. The reporter considered that the amusement centre, with 12 machines, would be very modest, that noise generation would not be high, and could be further controlled by way of conditions. He did not think the proposed amusement centre would attract many children. The appeal was therefore upheld subject, *inter alia*, to a condition requiring sound insulation of the premises. (Ref. P/PPA/LA/464, March 10, 1987.)

6.55 Material considerations—licensed betting office

The reporter said that while the need for betting offices was a matter for the local licensing board, and public behaviour was primarily a matter for the police, the effect on the amenity of residential areas by the location of a licensed betting office nearby was in his opinion a proper matter for consideration by a planning authority. (Ref. P/PPA/SS/63, January 19, 1982.)

6.56 Material considerations—amusement arcade—prominent site— narrow pavement

Planning permission had been refused for the change of use from a shop to an amusement centre. The reporter considered that objections on the ground that the proposed activity would be out of place in a prominent site with historic associations were not relevant. Permission was, however, refused on account of the narrowness of the pavement. (Ref. P/PPA/D/89, June 3, 1982.)

6.57 Material considerations—local objections—prize bingo

Planning permission had been refused for the use of a shop for prize bingo. Representatives of two local associations objected on behalf of approximately 150 local residents and 20 trading outlets in the area. The reporter said that it was right to take account of those views and not to permit a development in a community which opposed it. (Ref. P/PPA/EDB/379, September 19, 1976.)

6.58 Licensed betting office—local objections

Planning permission had been refused for the change of use from retail shop to betting office. There were a significant number of objections from local people. The reporter considered these were a matter for the licensing board. (Ref. P/PPA/SL/154, August 16, 1982.)

6.59 Relevant considerations—betting office—location

The reporter said:

"While the need for betting offices is a matter for the local licensing board and public behaviour is primarily a matter for the police, the effect on the amenity of residential areas, by the location of a licensed betting office nearby, is in my opinion a proper matter for consideration by the planning authority."

The reporter also accepted that elderly people sometimes suffered genuine alarm from rowdy behaviour. (Ref. P/PPA/SS/63, January 19, 1982.)

6.60 Material considerations—gaming activities—moral objections

The reporter appreciated the concern of a number of local people about the social implications of gaming activities (in this case an amusement arcade was proposed) but considered these matters more appropriate for consideration under the Betting, Gaming and Lotteries legislation. (Ref. P/PPA/LD/31, April 16, 1981.)

6.61 Material considerations—amusement arcade—proximity to schools —exclusion of children

Planning permission had been refused for an amusement arcade with 25 amusement machines. This would normally attract middle-aged lady shoppers. Young people under 18 would not be admitted. The proposal was opposed by the local schools council who considered that children might be inclined to spend their dinner money in the centre and to remain in the centre beyond their lunch break and that the proposed arcade would be on a busy street which could constitute a danger to children. The police suggested that the proximity of the site to local schools could encourage truancy. The planning authority thought the policy objections were not concerned with land use issues and the reporter agreed.

The reporter could find no reason why it would be more difficult for the management of the arcade to control the admission of those under 18 than it was for public house managers. He considered the fears of the objectors on these matters largely unfounded as amusements with prize machines would tend to attract middle-aged women. It was made a condition of permission that no person under 18 should be admitted to the premises. (Ref. P/PPA/ST/51, March 21, 1983.)

6.62   Material considerations—moral issues
Planning permission was sought for the change of use from a betting office to an amusement arcade. Objections, mainly related to a secondary school about half-a-mile distant, were lodged by educational interests. Concern was expressed that the proposed development would act as a temptation to pupils, attract anti-social elements and undermine the work of responsible community institutions.

The reporter said that the concern of the objectors was very real and was not disputed. "However," he said, "Parliament has accepted the existence of amusement centres such as this and has created a licensing system under the Betting and Gaming Act 1963 to control such uses. I find that such matters fall properly to be determined by the responsible local licensing authority and, although sympathetic to the objectors, have to disregard the moral aspect in my planning decision." (Ref. P/PPA/SU/118, June 7, 1982.)

6.63   Material considerations—leisure and amusement centre—proximity to schools—proximity to houses
It was proposed to use a site in a housing area for a leisure and amusement centre. There was a primary school about 400 metres away from the site and a secondary school about 800 metres away. The planning authority referred *inter alia* to DoE Development Control Policy Note No. 11 which advised that amusement centres were not acceptable near residential property and were not good neighbours for schools. The head teachers of both schools had claimed that there was a relationship between the proximity of amusement arcades and increases in truancy and breaking of school rules.

The reporter said that although the Development Control Policy Note was formally an English document, in the absence of any advice specifically designed for application in Scotland, it was fair to look at it for guidance. It was forthright in its advice that amusement centres were not acceptable near residential property. The reporter had no reason for doubting the soundness of this advice.

The DoE's advice was that amusement centres were not good neighbours for schools. There were two schools in the neighbourhood of the appeal site and although neither was close enough for its immediate physical setting to be affected, the milieu in which they were expected to function would be affected, with results likely to be similar to those feared by the head teachers. Pupils were likely to be attracted either during or after school hours and it would be difficult to enforce any condition attached to a planning permission designed to avoid this. The reporter regarded the proximity of the schools to the appeal site as a second major reason for dismissing the appeal. The appeal was therefore refused. (Ref. P/PPA/SQ/154, March 4, 1985.)

6.64   Material considerations—snooker hall and amusement arcade— nearness of secondary school

It was proposed to change the use of premises to a snooker hall and amusement arcade. In reaching their decision to refuse planning permission the planning authority took account of objections to the proposal from the head teacher and the parent-teacher association of a secondary school located about a mile away from the site. Great concern was expressed by the objectors that the centre would tempt school pupils and unemployed young people to spend their time and money unwisely. Pupils might visit the premises in school hours and it was not expected that any restriction on the admission of the young would be effective.

The reporter said that one of the determining issues was whether the proposal would be incompatible with the activities of the educational organisations who lodged objections. Regarding the concern about use of the premises by school pupils and unemployed persons, the reporter considered that moral aspects should have no bearing on the matter. From a land use point of view the site was well away from the secondary school and he did not accept that the site was unsatisfactory on educational grounds. Planning permission was therefore granted. (Ref. P/PPA/ST/71, February 26, 1985.)

6.65   Material   considerations—amusement   arcade—behaviour   of patrons

Planning permission had been refused for an amusement arcade in a city centre location. The appeal premises formed part of a block containing no residential accommodation. The surroundings were devoted to commercial and business uses and there was constant noise and movement of people and vehicles all around. People might loiter outside the arcade and occasionally small groups might form. The next door shop had objected on the ground that the sight of such groups might discourage customers. It was also claimed that the centre would exacerbate existing problems of litter, loitering, drunkenness and rowdiness and thereby detract from amenity. In the reporter's view this kind of occurrence was normal and accepted in a city centre. In this particular location he could not see that the amusement centre would be incompatible with uses in the vicinity. Various behavioural problems might go on but it had not been shown that this centre would add so significantly to the problems as to justify refusal. (Ref. P/PPA/SL/194, March 11, 1983.)

6.66 Material considerations—amusement centre—moral objections

An appeal was lodged against the refusal of planning permission for an amusement centre. The planning authority argued that amusement centres were not good neighbours for schools, churches or hotels. The reporter found that the proposed centre was close to a number of educational and welfare establishments. He therefore dismissed the appeal—the development was out of character with the area and would be socially disruptive—but stated that moral objections did not constitute valid planning considerations. (Ref. P/PPA/GA/51, December 12, 1982.)

6.67 Material considerations—change of use—amusement arcade

The reporter took the view that considerable weight should be placed on the views expressed by local people, the community council and the police on the extent of existing anti-social behaviour and the likelihood that the situation would be exacerbated if a change of use from shop to amusement arcade were allowed. (Ref. P/PPA/SU/113, September 28, 1982.)

6.68 Material considerations—amusement arcade—proximity to residential area, school and church

It was proposed to change the use of a shop to an amusement arcade. The surrounding area was mainly in residential use, there was a church on the opposite side of the road and a secondary school was situated about 70 metres away on the same street. Objections to the proposal were lodged by an MP, several district councillors, two regional councillors, the head teachers of nearby secondary and primary schools, the secondary school's parent-teacher association, the kirk session, three residents' associations and five local residents. Petitions against the proposal had been signed by 1400 local residents. Some of the objections related to fears that the proposed development would attract a greater number of people to this generally quiet residential area with consequent problems of loitering, noise, theft, vandalism and late night disturbance. It was also said that by its proximity to local schools it would be educationally harmful to school children, leading to problems of truancy and addiction to gambling. It was stated that there would be a loss of amenity in the area because of the reduction in the number of shops. The planning authority said that it would be difficult to uphold the disturbance objection as the nearby roads were busy, and that the objection relating to the effect on school children and education was not a valid planning matter.

The reporter agreed with the planning authority about disturbance. As regards the effect on school children and education, he agreed with the planning authority that the moral aspect of how children use their leisure time was not a valid planning objection to the development. However, development so close to a secondary school as the proposed development was, would be disruptive to school activities, with a significant risk that pupils would be late for classes following breaks and that the arcade could become a focal point for activities that would be contrary to educational interests. Though the appellant said he would display a notice saying school children would not be admitted during school hours, the reporter was not confident that the proposed notice would be effective since the criteria specified would be difficult to identify and enforce.

The arcade was also an unsuitable neighbour for the church. The appeal was therefore dismissed. (Ref. P/PPA/SL/283, March 11, 1985.)

6.69 Material considerations—snooker hall—disturbance

The reporter said that snooker and billiards required a good deal of concentration and quietness and involved the use of expensive equipment. He therefore considered that a proposed snooker hall would be unlikely to give rise to the type of noise and unsocial behaviour the objectors feared. He also said that the quietness of a residential suburb could not be expected in the heart of a town centre. (Ref. P/PPA/SC/103, July 30, 1984.)

6.70 Material considerations—change of use from shop to licensed betting office—misbehaviour

This was an appeal against a refusal of planning permission for a change of use from a shop to a licensed betting office. There was evidence of some misbehaviour associated with drink outside the existing betting office nearby. The reporter saw no reason to think that such conduct would change with a change of premises. The Secretary of State agreed with that view and considered that such behaviour would adversely affect the amenity of the shopping mall in which the premises would be situated. (Ref. P/PPA/ SL/49, June 6, 1979.)

6.71 Material considerations—amusement centre—traffic hazards— loitering—effect on residents

Planning permission had been refused for an amusement centre. The police and the highway authority objected, referring to the attraction a centre would have for younger people and children, which might lead to loitering and horseplay on the narrow pavement outside the premises. The premises were located close to a major traffic junction, thus creating congestion and traffic hazards. The education authority also opposed the development in view of its proximity to Ayr Academy. Letters of objection received from residents referred to potential traffic hazards, noise and disturbance, unruly behaviour by some children, the development lowering the tone of the neighbourhood and the lack of any need for further amusement centres.

The planning authority were against the proposal's effect on the character of the surrounding shopping area—it would break the shopping frontage. They also considered it would have an adverse effect on the amenity and character of the surrounding area; on road safety and traffic flow; and on the noise likely to be created. In general, amusement centres were considered incompatible near schools, residential property, churches, hospitals and hotels. They were out of character in conservation areas and within or adjacent to listed buildings. (The appeal premises were listed.)

The reporter considered:

(1) as regards the effect on the appearance and character of the listed building and conservation area, the block in question had been damaged already by a number of unsympathetic business frontages. It was an area of mixed use and it would not be an inappropriate location for a centre. The proposals on design would improve the frontage;

(2) whether the development was likely to aggravate traffic hazards. There would be no sessional games, with the characteristic flow of people at the start and end of sessions, so that it would be unlikely to lead to patrons congregating outside the premises any more than at a café or indeed at any retail outlet. There was always a risk of someone stepping into the carriageway but the proposal would not add to that risk;

(3) as regards the effect on residents, people living above commercial premises alongside busy traffic routes could not expect the same degree of quiet as in a residential area. However they were entitled to have noise emission controlled. (Ref. P/PPA/SQ/119, March 22, 1983.)

6.72 Betting office—moral and social issues

This was an appeal against a refusal of planning permission for a change of use from shop to betting office.

The reporter said that moral and social considerations, of the sort that might be raised by a betting office, were not appropriate to consideration of a planning application and were for the licensing authority to take into account when licensing the premises. It also had to be assumed that the management of the premises would be responsible, while public order was a matter for the police. (Ref. P/PPA/SS/119, May 31, 1985.)

6.73 Material considerations—amusement arcade—moral considerations

This was an appeal against a refusal of planning permission for a change of use from a shop to an amusement arcade. Objectors made representations on moral grounds and the feared social disadvantages of an amusement centre.

The reporter said:

"While I understand the anxiety expressed by the objectors, I require to distinguish between planning and licensing considerations and avoid the temptation to use planning control as a universal long-stop. While gambling can be addictive and there was evidence of unemployment and social problems in this district, these are not sound planning reasons for refusing planning permission for an amusement centre in an appropriate location." (Ref. P/PPA/ST/41, January 21, 1982.)

6.74 Material considerations—amusement centre—moral considerations

This was an appeal against a refusal of planning permission for an amusement centre. The headmaster of a local school said that the centre would be a magnet for the "hard core" of truants. The entertainment offered was addictive. It was likely to distract children from their school work. Some children would direct their lunch money to play the machines. Some might even be tempted to steal. The planning authority thought amusement machines morally bad for young persons. The reporter said: "Whilst I appreciate the objections to the proposed amusement centre that are founded on moral issues and a desire to protect young persons from temptation, I find that such matters fall to be considered by the licensing authority." (Ref. P/PPA/SS/64, January 22, 1982.)

6.75 Material considerations—betting office, pool hall and licensed bar—need and distribution

This was an appeal against a refusal of planning permission for the use of a property as a betting office, pool hall and licensed bar. The reporter considered that neither the question of commercial need nor that of the distribution of licensed premises were primarily matters of planning control. The latter was primarily a matter for the relevant licensing board. (Ref. P/PPA/SL/296, June 7, 1985.)

6.76 Relevant considerations—betting office—moral issues

This was an appeal against a refusal of planning permission for a betting office. A number of objections and a petition had been lodged. There was a local feeling that a licensed betting office would be undesirable in the area on religious grounds. Betting was associated with drinking, which was already a problem, and unemployed young people would, it was argued, be tempted to gamble their limited resources in an attempt to improve their finances. The reporter recognised the strong moral and religious views expressed in the objections. However he had to decide the appeal primarily on the basis of planning considerations—land use and amenity—and to exclude matters which were properly for consideration by the licensing board. (Ref. P/PPA/W/4, March 12, 1982.)

6.77 Material considerations—amusement centre—grounds of objection—moral issues not relevant

An application for permission to use premises as an amusement centre had been refused. The appellant said that the use was intended mainly as one for the tourist season when, in wet weather, there was little for families to do. The machines would be of a type which, it was claimed, were to be found in schools, community centres, swimming pools, colleges, etc.: *i.e.* video electronic games, football, pool tables and mechanical grabs. Gaming matters would be regulated by the terms of a licence issued by the local authority.

Over 200 people objected on the ground of the harmful effect the centre would have on local children. It was at school age children that the centre would be aimed. The effects on children might include truancy, a temptation to acquire money by illicit means to spend on the machines, and exposure to moral danger from association with undesirable elements amongst older age groups. There were also objections on grounds of increased traffic, parking problems, adverse effects on the amenity of nearby residents and the impact on the character of the area.

The reporter took the view that although it was possible to sympathise with the moral judgments expressed, they were of no relevance to the planning merits. The determining issues were the effect on the character of the area, the amenity of nearby residents and traffic considerations. (Ref. P/PPA/GE/39, September 7, 1982.)

6.78 Material considerations—nearness of school to proposed licensed premises

One of the reasons for the refusal of planning permission for the change of use of premises to a public house was that the proposed development would be inappropriately located in respect of a primary school and its playing fields.

Objections were submitted by the school's parent-teacher association, by the head teacher and by the Regional Council's estates department on the advice of the education department, and the divisional education officer. The objectors drew attention to the nearness of the school, the playing fields and a bus stop. They submitted that the proposed public house would be inappropriately sited in relation to the school, attended by some 350 children. Additional traffic attracted to the premises might create a hazard for schoolchildren. Children waiting for the school bus would have to stand close to the entrance to the public house, a highly undesirable situation.

The reporter said he could see no reason to think that the proposed change of use would affect the functions of the school or playing field in any way. Nor did he think that there was any risk of primary-age children being able to enter the licensed premises during school breaks or after school. The adverse effects feared must be those to which a child was exposed as he or she passed by or waited for a bus outside the public house. In the absence of any evidence that the children were at unacceptable risk in the street in the vicinity of a public house he did not think this a supportable reason for the refusal of a public house. (Ref. P/PPA/SG/96, August 23, 1985.)

6.79 Material considerations—shops—competition

Planning permission had been refused for a superstore outside the town centre. The planning authority appeared to be more concerned about the possible effect of the superstore on individual stores within the town centre rather than about the effect on the shopping centre itself. That was clearly a matter of competition and not a relevant planning consideration. (Ref. P/PPA/SM/125, August 1, 1988.)

6.80   Material considerations—view

The view from the back of two houses would be affected by a proposed new house. It was said that it was well-established that rights of view over other property should not and could not be protected by the planning legislation. (Ref. P/PPA/TB/132, September 30, 1987.)

6.81   Material considerations—public house/restaurant

Planning permission had been refused for a public house/ restaurant. The reporter concluded that many of the matters raised by objectors were the concern of the licensing authority and were not relevant in determining a planning application, *e.g.* the possibility of undue public nuisance, over-provision of licensed premises and control over hours of opening. (Ref. P/PPA/SL/406, September 17, 1987.)

6.82   Material considerations—change to use as restaurant and lounge bar—inebriated customers

Planning permission was sought for the change of use of a railway station to a licensed restaurant, lounge bar and flat. Among the issues raised were the possibilities that an inebriated person might fall onto the railway or might annoy or assault passengers; these were held not to be planning matters. (Ref. P/PPA/SB/32, March 9, 1987.)

6.83   Material consideration—shop front—funeral parlour—undertaker's premises

The appellants sought planning permission for alterations to a shop front in order to make it suitable for a funeral parlour. The planning authority refused permission on a number of grounds. They considered that refusal was justified on traffic grounds and on the ground that a funeral parlour was an inappropriate use in an established shopping area. The authority accepted that as the premises had previously been used as a shop, development would not, under the Town and Country Planning (Use Classes) (Scotland) Order 1973, be involved in using the premises as an undertaker's shop. They considered, however, that the formation of a funeral parlour, including a service room used for religious purposes, took the proposal outside the scope of an undertaker's business. The reporter did not accept any of the authority's arguments. In particular he did not accept that any distinction could be drawn between an undertaker's shop and a funeral parlour. That view was accepted. (Ref. P/PPA/SF/24, April 17, 1986.)

6.84 Material considerations—need—public house

Planning permission for a public house had been refused by the planning authority. The reporter stated that the need or otherwise for a public house and possible competition with the existing Miners' Welfare Club were not planning matters. They fell to be determined by the authority as licensing authority and it would be open to residents to raise objections if application were made for a licence. (Ref. P/PPA/CA/47, August 29, 1988.)

6.85 Material considerations—need—public house—licensing

The reporter said, on an appeal against refusal of planning permission for a public house, that on the question of need he had noted that there were already seven or eight public houses within a fairly short distance of the appeal site. However, in the absence of a specific study of this aspect, he could not regard interference with normal commercial competition as being a proper function of planning control. He noted also that the adequacy or otherwise of public house provision was one of the considerations taken into account by the licensing committee. He therefore reached the conclusion that the question of need must be disregarded as a determining factor in this case. The Secretary of State accepted the reporter's reasons. (Ref. P/PPA/LA/67, August 23, 1978.)

6.86 Material considerations—shop—visual amenity—consistency of action by authority—metal roller blinds

Planning permission had been sought retrospectively for the installation of metal roller shutters on the windows of a shop. The shop had been burgled on several occasions, and the shop's insurers required that the owner take some action to improve security. The planning authority conceded the need for increased security and had suggested security glass combined with an open-meshed shutter. The reporter took the view that some increase in security was desirable. However, unless the shop were illuminated at night, there would be little effective difference between the two types of shutter. He considered that the visual effect of the change in question was so small as not to commend one over the other. The reporter also thought it unreasonable to take action in this case and not against other shops in the centre of the town. Planning permission was therefore granted. (Ref. P/PPA/LB/78, May 9, 1985.)

6.87 Material considerations—metal roller shutters—amenity of street-scene

The appeal related to boxed roller shutters over the windows of a shop. The reporter said that the shutters had a significantly detrimental effect, detracting greatly from the appearance of the surrounding buildings and shopping parade. When closed they obscured all view of the window and any display. The character of the shopping area was thus degraded in both visual and social terms. There were other, more acceptable, forms of security available. (Ref. P/PPA/SS/101, February 17, 1984.)

6.88 Material considerations—metal roller shutters—effect on amenity

Planning permission had been (retrospectively) refused for the installation of roller shutters over the shop window and door of a shop. The appellant argued that the premises had been a target for vandalism. The planning authority accepted that there was a problem but did not think solid roller blinds were the right answer here. The reporter could well understand the appellant's problems. It was unfortunate that there had been no discussion with the planning authority before the shutters were erected. The shutters here were ponderous and heavy in appearance, the shutter boxes were particularly obtrusive and the result detracted from the appearance of the property itself and the architectural character of the street-scene. The shutters would be an unfortunate precedent. He therefore refused planning permission. (Refs. P/PPA/LC/101; P/ENA/LC/30, December 6, 1984.)

6.89 Material considerations—canopy—uncharacteristic of townscape

Planning permission and listed building consent had been refused for a canopy above the front entrance of a restaurant. The planning authority considered it would be contrary to the amenity of an outstanding conservation area.

The appellant submitted that the proposed canopy would harmonise with its surroundings and with the permitted use of the premises as a restaurant. The planning authority had a policy of resisting dutch canopies in conservation areas in favour of traditional horizontal, non-curved, retractable sun-blinds. In the authority's view the proposed canopy was uncharacteristic of Scottish townscapes and bore no functional relationship to the building.

In the Secretary of State's view the canopy was of a shape, construction and style foreign to and noticeably out of character with the solid appearance of the traditional flat-fronted building. The addition of the canopy would also diminish the orderly architectural effect of the north and south doorways. Accordingly, the Secretary of State dismissed the appeals. (Refs. P/PPA/ SR/68; HGJ/3/SR/2, October 22, 1985.)

6.90 Material considerations—nuclear power station—railhead

This was an appeal by the South of Scotland Electricity Board against the planning authority's refusal of planning permission for the erection of a railhead facility to serve the Torness Electricity Generating station. The reason for refusal was "[i]n the interests of public safety."

The reporter was of the opinion that the planning authority and various objectors had misdirected themselves as to the proper purpose and remit of the inquiry. He concluded that issues including the validity of international and national regulations relating to the packaging and transport of irradiated nuclear fuels; the design and testing parameters and certification procedures for the packages for nuclear fuels; and national policies relating to the storage, transportation and disposal of nuclear fuels were not matters coming within the ambit of the planning legislation. These matters should be pursued through other channels and not through a planning inquiry.

Relevant issues were:

(a) whether or not there was a need for the proposed railhead; and if so

(b) whether or not the location chosen for the railhead was an acceptable one; and

(c) whether or not the layout, means of access and environmental arrangements were acceptable; and

(d) whether or not the nature of the development was such that special conditions ought to be imposed in any grant of planning permission.

The reporter therefore recommended the grant of planning permission subject to conditions.

The Secretary of State agreed that the decision should be based on local planning issues. He took the view, however, that safety of personnel, one of the matters included in the reporter's suggested conditions, was not a planning issue. (Ref. P/PPA/ LB/72, July 25, 1985.)

6.91 Material considerations—automatic cash dispensing machine—attractive door

A bank proposed to install an automatic cash dispenser in the main entrance. The proposal was refused by the planning authority because this would close the door for access, would detract from the character and appearance of the bank frontage and would be detrimental to public amenity in the pedestrian precinct in which the bank was situated and in the conservation area which included it. The reporter agreed but made a suggestion as to a more acceptable alternative. (Ref. P/PPA/SB/12, November 5, 1982.)

6.92   Material considerations—countryside—caravan storage park
Planning permission had been refused for the use of land in the countryside as a caravan storage site. The reporter pointed out that the National Planning Guidelines on "Agricultural Land," issued in 1987, emphasised the need to ensure that diversification of the rural economy did not undermine or detract from the overall appearance of the countryside. The requirement to protect the countryside from inappropriate development remained unaltered. In consequence the reporter did not find that the latest statement of government policy provided support for the appellant's proposals. Instead it emphasised the need to protect the countryside from developments which were likely to have an adverse visual impact. (Ref. P/PPA/TA/141, August 8, 1988.)

6.93   Material considerations—external steel roller shutters—amenity
Planning permission had been refused for two external steel shutters, one over the window and one over the door, at a general store. External storage boxes were placed across the frontage. The other shops within the building were well maintained and some had been attractively refurbished. There were no other roller shutters in the vicinity. The proprietor of a neighbouring shop, supporting the planning authority, considered the shutters an eyesore, detracting from amenity.

For the appellant it was claimed that the shop window had been broken by vandals and that his insurers then advised him that they were not necessarily prepared to maintain cover unless roller shutters were installed. After the appellant's planning application was refused, his solicitors invited the council to reconsider their decision. They maintained that the appeal premises were not listed as being of special architectural importance, they were not in a conservation area, and they were not a part of the main shopping centre.

The local authority had an established presumption against roller shutters. Depending on the position of the building, the character of the area and the security requirements of the occupier they suggested, in order of acceptability, internally-mounted wrought iron panels; internal open grill shutters; external wrought iron; and external open grille shutters with a concealed storage box. The council did not accept that the preferences of an insurance company should be allowed to determine the design of shop fronts. They regarded the effect of the shutters as unacceptable and stated that there were no other such installations in the vicinity.

The reporter said that the main question was whether a case had been established to justify exceptional treatment against the terms of the council's policy. The council accepted that the appellant needed enhanced security at his premises and had recommended the options they considered could be used to ensure greater security without a significant adverse effect on amenity. The reporter found that the shop was located in an area the character of which was valued; this had led the council to propose its designation as a conservation area. The roller shutters were visually prominent and presented a dead frontage when closed. The options favoured by the council would not have that effect and would not necessarily allow the window glass to be broken. Consequently they could be expected to contribute to the maintenance of the character of the area rather than detract from it. No evidence had been led to show that the appellant's insurers found the council's options unacceptable.

The reporter found that the roller shutters had a significantly adverse effect on amenity and that no case had been advanced to justify exceptional treatment against the terms of the council's policy. (Ref. P/PPA/CC/153, October 29, 1986.)

6.94 Material consideration—house in countryside—agricultural justification

Planning permission for a dwelling-house was refused on the ground that the proposal would be contrary to the structure plan which sought to establish a presumption against new houses in the open countryside unless they could be shown to be essential for countryside needs. The reporter considered that the proposed new dwelling would clearly be contrary to long-established national and local policies seeking to prevent proliferation of houses in the open countryside.

Turning to the agricultural justification for the development the reporter accepted that it would be desirable for the appellant to be able to live in the area which he served as a blacksmith and to live on a farm where he had family links and on which he provided assistance from time to time. However, the reporter considered that this did not satisfy the test of essential need such as that for feeding or supervising livestock. (Ref. P/PPA/D/176, January 28, 1987.)

6.95 Material considerations—development in green belt—cost of relocation

This was an appeal against a refusal of planning permission for the formation of a roofing contractor's yard in the green belt. The reporter considered that the council were right in their contention that the cost to the appellant of relocation was not a material planning consideration. (Ref. P/PPA/LB/46, December 6, 1982.)

6.96 House in countryside—DHS Circular 40/1960—"special need"

The appellant had been refused planning permission for the construction of a new house in the grounds of his existing house. The planning authority considered that this would constitute new housing in the countryside, contrary to the terms of DHS Circular 40/1960 and to the council's policy. The appeal was on grounds of "special need" in that the appellant's wife was suffering from a progressive illness which confined her to a wheel-chair, the present house was unsuitable for her, and suitable alternative accommodation could only be provided by building the proposed new house. The Secretary of State accepted this as a case of "special need." (Ref. P/PPA/AR/254, May 19, 1976.)

6.97 Material considerations—new house—contrary to countryside policy—exceptional need

Planning permission had, in accordance with both local and national policies, been refused for the building of a house in the countryside. The appellants were retiring from a local post office and shop and lived on the premises. They considered it would be almost impossible to sell the shop and post office without the house. The reporter accepted that the appellants had established exceptional circumstances, such that they should be allowed to build a new house near the place they had lived in for a long period. (Ref. P/PPA/SG/57, October 30, 1981.)

6.98 Material considerations — house in countryside — personal circumstances

Planning permission was sought for the erection of a dwelling-house outwith any established settlement. The reporter held that personal circumstances did not provide adequate justification for erecting a house in the countryside contrary to both the structure and local plans. (Ref. P/PPA/SU/204, January 19, 1987.)

6.99 Material considerations—ribbon development—whether house a house in countryside

Planning permission had been sought for the erection of a house and garage on ground forming part of the garden of another house. The site was outside what the draft local plan defined as the urban envelope. The planning authority therefore felt it appropriate to apply countryside policies to the site and refused planning permission.

The reporter found, first, that since the proposed house would not take access from or be visible from the main road, it could not be described as ribbon development. Secondly, the proposed development would not, he thought, be in conflict with the reasoned justification for the council's countryside policy. In the reporter's view positive aspects of the proposal included the fact that the site adjoined the currently designated urban area; that it was already in residential use as garden ground; that the development would not impinge on, or adversely affect the activities at the existing house; that all services were available; and that separate access could be formed to an unclassified road. Furthermore, the reporter did not think that a single infill development of this type would have any significant effect on housing policies. (Ref. P/PPA/CA/38, January 15, 1987.)

6.100 Agricultural use—house in countryside—breeding and training of horses

Planning permission had been granted for the erection of a brood mare barn for the breeding of horses, the erection of a stable block and the formation of a blaes exercise area. Permission was, however, refused for the conversion of a building to a dwelling-house because it would amount to sporadic development in the countryside contrary to DHS Circular 40/1960 (replaced by SDD Circular 24/1985).

The reporter said that the council did not dispute that a countryside location was suitable for the breeding and training of horses. In the reporter's opinion it could be argued that such activities were a branch of agriculture since the definition of "agriculture" in section 275 of the 1972 Act "includes the breeding and keeping of livestock." A dwelling would not always be an essential adjunct for the keeping of horses. Obviously, the mere grazing of horses would not require a house for their supervision. However, he considered that the breeding and training of a substantial number of horses would require substantial supervision. He concluded that there were adequate grounds for a new house in the country. Its occupation would, however, be restricted to the person (and his immediate family) engaged in the breeding, training and care of horses on the site. The reporter considered such a condition important, its imposition being a good guide to the appellant's *bona fides*. (Ref. P/PPA/CB/116, March 14, 1986.)

6.101 Material considerations—travelling person—green belt—scrap cars

An enforcement notice alleged the unauthorised use of a site for the storage of cars. The appeal site consisted of a cottage and attached ground. At the rear of the cottage were two caravans and about 50 scrap cars. The appellant said he was a member of a family of travelling people. He spent the summer months pursuing agricultural activities. He also dealt in scrap which had now become established as a traditional activity of travelling people. Wishing to improve his standard of living, he bought the cottage as a base. He had not been aware that planning permission was required for his activities.

The reporter did not think an exception to the green belt policy was justified. He thought it would be preferable for the business to be located at an industrial site where it could operate and expand without planning restrictions. He accepted that the appellant wished to combine scrap-dealing with summer travelling. He therefore considered that the period for compliance with the enforcement notice should be extended so as not to interfere with the appellant's travelling activities in the summer and to allow the appellant to make arrangements to transfer his business to a suitable location during the coming winter period. (Ref. P/ENA/SC/36, June 24, 1985.)

6.102 Material considerations—personal circumstances—new dwelling-house—outside established settlement

Personal circumstances did not provide adequate justification for the erection of a house outwith a settlement in contravention of established countryside policies in both the structure and local plans. (Ref. P/PPA/LC/130, January 15, 1987.)

6.103 Material consideration—agricultural use—house in countryside

The aim of the planning authority's policy and of national policy was to seek to direct new development to towns and villages unless there was a clear and overriding need to site a house in a position in the countryside suitable for the development of agriculture or forestry. The appellant claimed that the exercising, training and grazing of his driving horses necessitated constant supervision and justified a house in the countryside. The reporter considered the appellant's need was not an agricultural one because the horses had no agricultural relevance as they were kept purely for the purpose of the appellant's hobby. The proposal was therefore inconsistent with the planning authority's policy for houses in the countryside. (Ref. P/PPA/HC/96, June 24, 1985.)

6.104   Amenity—detriment—failure to take action—green belt

Planning permission was refused for change of use from a derelict gun-site (latterly used for stabling horses) to greyhound kennels. Some 30 greyhounds were accommodated within the buildings associated with the former gun-site. Planning permission was refused on the ground that the proposals, involving the siting of a residential caravan on the land, would be detrimental to the visual amenity of this attractive part of the green belt. It was submitted that if the use of the land could not be carried out without the siting of a caravan, that was indicative that the use was unacceptable in the green belt. In the planning authority's view the caravan was an eyesore, visually intrusive and detrimental to the amenity of the area, particularly as it was visible to the occupiers of nearby houses and users of surrounding roads.

The appellant submitted that he had been assured by council officials that he would not require planning permission as the previous use had been for the stabling of horses. He had incurred expense in renovating buildings and in removing rubbish, car body shells and vehicle components from the site, the son of the previous owner having carried out car repairs at the site.

In the reporter's view the determining issue was whether the development was detrimental to the visual amenity of the attractive surrounding landscape and the green belt. The site was fairly isolated and the present use as greyhound kennels was similar to the previous use for stabling and grazing horses. No action had been taken to discontinue that use or to prevent the use of part of the site for car repairs, both activities having been carried on at the site for a number of years. The remoteness of the site from residential property had advantages in that any noise from the barking of the dogs was unlikely to be disturbing. The reporter did not consider, provided that certain conditions as to landscaping and the design of the perimeter fence were carried out, that the use of the land and buildings for greyhound kennels would detract from the visual amenity of the surrounding area. As regards the caravan, however, the reporter found this to be an obtrusive feature, detrimental to the visual amenity of the area, especially as seen from a well-used highway and attractive approach to the city. A better solution would be to convert part of the existing buildings to provide a shelter-cum-office or to construct a small single-storey building adjacent to an existing structure. Planning permission was therefore granted subject to appropriate conditions. (Ref. P/PPA/LA/305, October 22, 1984.)

6.105 Material considerations—natural justice—site for dwelling—village extremity

Planning permission had been sought for the erection of a dwelling-house on former garden ground at the edge of a village. The site was now being cultivated as part of adjoining land, though apparently without the appellant's consent. The planning authority argued that the proposed house would amount to development in the open countryside.

In the reporter's view the planning authority's arguments were somewhat specious. It was true that the appeal site could not now be distinguished visually from the remainder of the field, but the incorporation of the site into the field was done without the consent of the owner and was therefore unlawful. The reporter considered that it would be contrary to natural justice for the authority to be allowed to invoke an unlawful use in support of their case. He considered that the current use of the site had to be ignored. It followed that for present purposes the site must be regarded as being former garden ground lying within the urban area as defined in the local plan. On that basis the development would constitute a natural rounding off of the settlement. (Ref. P/PPA/CB/95, October 16, 1984.)

6.106 Material considerations—local acceptability of proposal—prize bingo

The appellant had been refused permission for the change of use of two shop units to prize bingo premises. The reporter noted that it was the responsibility of the licensing authority to judge the demand for such facilities, and that there were no valid physical objections in relation to noise or the effects on visual or residential amenity. However, he thought it was right to take account of local opposition to the proposal. A petition against the proposed development had over 230 signatures and representations opposing it had been made on behalf of several bodies, including the local Residents' and Community Association. In dismissing the appeal, the Secretary of State said that due weight must always be given to the local acceptability of any proposed development. (Ref. P/PPA/GLW/983, December 30, 1976.)

6.107 Automatic bank teller—pedestrian congestion—danger—vehicles stopping—relevant considerations

Planning permission and listed building consent had been refused for the installation of an automatic cash dispensing machine in a listed building. It was argued by the authority that the pavement width at this point was such that the proposed development would be detrimental to pedestrian movement and road safety. The Secretary of State expressed the view that queues at autotellers were seldom very long and congestion should not be a reason for refusal. Car drivers would be unlikely to stop so near to a busy junction merely to obtain cash. The effect on the amenity of the area of the autoteller would be negligible. Listed building consent was, however, refused. (Refs. P/PPA/SL/165; HGJ/2/SL/23, November 29, 1982.)

6.108 Material considerations—hardship to appellant—dormer window

Listed building consent had been sought for the construction of a dormer window in a listed building. One of the grounds of appeal was that there were already many dormers in the same street. The planning authority and the reporter agreed that the applicant had suffered hardship in that he had correctly applied whereas others, in a similar situation, had not done so. However, the reporter did not see this as a sufficient reason for treating the application as a special case. (Refs. HB/AR/LA/2; P/PPA/EDB/37, September 22, 1976.)

6.109 Material considerations—personal hardship

Planning permission had been refused for the siting of a mobile home in an area of great scenic beauty. However, the appellant stated that the caravan provided accommodation for his brother, who was waiting for a council house. In view of the circumstances of the appellant's brother, the reporter considered that an exception should be made to policy. The Secretary of State agreed and sustained the appeal subject to a condition that permission enured solely for the benefit of the appellant's brother. (Ref. P/PPA/HD/7, October 28, 1977.)

6.110 Material considerations—proposed house—listed building nearby

Outline planning permission for a house was refused for a number of reasons. Necessary road improvements would require the removal of gates and piers forming part of a nearby listed building. Mature trees within the surrounding conservation area would have to be removed and this would adversely affect the setting of the listed building and the visual amenity of the conservation area. The design of the proposed house was not compatible with that of the listed building and the erection of a house here would adversely affect the setting of the listed building.

The appellant argued (*inter alia*) that the designs for the proposed house were illustrative only and that it was intended to design a house compatible with its surroundings.

The reporter concluded that the proposed house would adversely affect the setting of the listed building. It would diminish the public enjoyment of the listed building. The appeal was therefore dismissed. (Ref. P/PPA/CB/111, April 17, 1986.)

6.111 Material considerations—viability of project

Outline planning permission was sought for the erection of a dwelling-house and buildings appropriate to a market garden. The planning authority did not believe that a market garden at this site would be viable and the Department of Agriculture and Fisheries for Scotland supported the authority's view. On appeal it was argued for the appellant that the planning authority had no right to take the possible viability of the enterprise into account in reaching their decision and that the profitability of the enterprise was not a town planning consideration. The reporter considered that in this case, where the sole justification for the erection of a dwelling in the green belt was that it was necessary for the establishment of a market garden, the planning authority were perfectly justified in regarding the viability of the proposed enterprise as a material consideration and that the authority would be failing in their duty if they behaved otherwise. (Ref. P/PPA/TB/28, December 17, 1980.)

6.112 Material considerations—sheltered housing—viability

This was an appeal against a refusal of planning permission for a sheltered housing development comprising 46 flats, a residents' lounge, guest accommodation, five shops, a car park, a service area and a riverside park. Permission had been refused because of the scale and general bulk of the building. It represented an over-development of the site. Two elements in particular were criticised—the relationship of the main block to the smaller scale of the buildings in the surrounding area and the over-dominant feature formed by the south-facing wing.

The reporter considered that the overall effect of the design would be one of a solid massive building alien to the character of this part of the town. In his view a smaller scale scheme would be more appropriate and would allow the adoption of a design more in keeping with the domestic scale and discontinuous pattern of uses in the area. The reporter appreciated that in the private sector a minimum of 35 units, and in this case 45, might be required to achieve financial viability. However, he did not regard this factor as being of sufficient importance to override the need for a smaller scale of development on this site. The appeal was therefore dismissed. (Ref. P/PPA/GC/117, December 7, 1984.)

6.113 Material considerations—change of use—flats to offices—economic considerations

Planning permission had been refused for change of use of four flats to use as office accommodation. The premises were in an area zoned for commercial purposes. The reporter stated that as an aid to economic prosperity, it had to be an objective of the planning authority to foster and encourage the expansion of successful businesses within the city, and that of the appellants fell within that category. (Ref. P/PPA/GA/130, April 7, 1982.)

6.114 Material considerations—market forces

Application had been made for the change of use of a former dry cleaners/laundry service outlet to an amusement centre.

The reporter had "no doubt that the excellent new development and redevelopment proposals now far advanced for the west end of High Street will raise this end of the street to the status of a prime shopping location where the emphasis should be on high quality retail outlets for goods and services. This may well come about naturally through the operation of market forces but in my opinion the process should be aided by the intervention of planning control when opportunities arise. Your client's proposal, if allowed, would absorb a potential retail outlet only a few metres from a future shopping magnet (Littlewoods) and in my opinion would interfere to a material extent with the anticipated prime retail function of this part of High Street." The reporter therefore accepted the planning authority's first reason for refusal—that the site was in an area being considered for redevelopment and the proposal would not accord with approved and projected proposals for nearby premises. (Ref. P/PPA/GE/40, August 12, 1982.)

6.115 Material considerations—material change of use—house to office—locality

Planning permission was refused for the change of use of a six apartment first-floor flat to an office. The proposal was contrary to local plan policy which sought to prevent the loss of housing of a tolerable standard.

The reporter considered that there were special circumstances which allowed an exception to the plan to be made. The appeal premises were located above a restaurant and fish and chip shop. Two of the bedrooms fronted on to the pavement outside the shop and the locality was primarily commercial in appearance and character. As a result, a house would suffer from a very poor environment. Planning permission was granted. (Ref. P/PPA/ ST/82, January 22, 1986.)

6.116 Material considerations—shopping policy—solicitors' office

The reporter recognised that most shoppers found continuous parades of shops more attractive and convenient than those interrupted by non-shopping uses. He found that a change in the appeal premises from shop to solicitors', estate agents' and building society agents' office "would represent a non-retail and alien intrusion in a parade of premises in which shops predominated." (Ref. P/PPA/CB/91, July 13, 1984.)

6.117 Material considerations—material change of use—shop—estate agent's office

Planning permission was sought for a change of use from a shop to an estate agent's office. Local plan policy attempted to prevent loss of prime retail floorspace to other uses. The reporter took the view that an estate agent's office, although classified as an office, was by nature a quasi-retail function involved in the buying and selling of property. The frequently changing window display was compulsive viewing for many people, necessary for others and had a drawing power that could benefit other enterprises. The appeal premises were slightly detached from the town centre. The proposal was not likely to run counter to the attractions of the town centre as a lively shopping and commercial area. (Ref. P/PPA/SC/131, March 20, 1986.)

6.118 Material considerations—retail warehouses—traffic—effect on shopping in town centre

Outline planning permission was refused by the planning authority for the erection of three non-food retail warehouses with a total area of 5950 square metres on a site about 1 kilometre from the town centre. Permission was refused for the reason that the proposals would, by virtue of their scale and location, be contrary to the provisions of the structure plan, contrary to the provisions of the local plan and contrary to the interests of road safety.

On traffic safety the reporter was satisfied that the appellants' proposal to build a new roundabout could overcome any problems.

From his inspection of the existing retail centre the reporter was impressed by the quality and range of shopping and was especially impressed by the provision for car parking, coupled with the ready availability of public transport. This lent credence to the planning authority's submission that the centre catered for all sections of the public including persons with or without access to a motor car.

The reporter found it disturbing that there was a considerable amount of unlet floor space within the new shopping malls in the town centre and that numerous established businesses were being advertised for sale or for letting. In these circumstances the reporter found himself in agreement with the planning authority that the appellants had failed to make a convincing case that retail development on the scale proposed would not seriously affect the viability of the existing centre. (Ref. P/PPA/FB/213, January 8, 1987.)

6.119 Material considerations—guest house—commercial use in street block

This was an appeal against the planning authority's decision to refuse planning permission for the change of use of a dwelling-house to a guest house. In the planning authority's view if permission were granted the commercial use of the street frontage would exceed 50 per cent., contrary to the authority's policy on guest houses.

The reporter took the view, however, that the street block was to be taken as the residential terrace in which the appeal subjects were situated and not a longer stretch of road. There was therefore no clear cut reason for refusal on grounds of policy alone. (Ref. P/PPA/LA/435, January 15, 1987.)

6.120 Material considerations—policy on non-retail uses—office

The appellants had been refused planning permission for the change of use from an empty shop to an office. Permission was refused on the grounds that the proposal was contrary to the planning authority's non-statutory policy on non-retail uses in shopping centres and if approved could lead to an erosion of the shopping centre. The appellants argued for the application of the policy in (English) Development Control Policy Note 11 which stated that banks and building societies, the type of use to which the appellants proposed to put the site, might often be acceptable uses in retail centres. The reporter accepted that Note 11 provided sound general guidance. Here, however, the planning authority had reached the conclusion that the limit of non-retail uses had been reached. The reporter concluded that the local planning policies should, in the circumstances prevailing in the prime shopping area, be upheld. The appeal was therefore dismissed. (Ref. P/PPA/TA/111, March 2, 1987.)

6.121 Development plan and material considerations—change from licensed restaurant to lounge bar and restaurant

It was proposed that the use of premises be changed from licensed restaurant to lounge bar and restaurant. The reporter noted that the finalised local plan showed the site in a primarily residential area in which there would be a presumption against commercial uses. The reporter considered that the planning authority had given insufficient weight to the fact that the premises were already in commercial use and that the proposed change of use affected an area of less than 30 square metres, considerably less than half of the area already in restaurant use. The reporter accepted that there would be more comings and goings, but considered that a small lounge bar, closely associated with, and entered through, the restaurant, was unlikely to share the less attractive characteristics of a traditional public house. Additional comings and goings might be a nuisance to residents but since the nearest house was some 50 metres away, the reporter was not persuaded that the risk to residents' amenity was sufficient to justify refusal of planning permission for this modest proposal. (Ref. P/PPA/SQ/207, May 21, 1987.)

6.122 Material consideration—replacement house—equity

The appellant's house lay on the line of a proposed bypass road. He sought planning permission for a new house nearby. Permission was refused on the grounds (1) that the site was within the green belt, within which it was the council's policy not to permit the erection of individual houses unless there was some proven local need for agriculture, forestry or some other appropriate use; and (2) that it was undesirable to permit new housing immediately adjacent to the line of a trunk road.

Here demolition would be caused by a public project and it would thus be in the public interest to allow the appellant to build a house; the public interest here overrode the planning presumption. In equity the new house should be permitted on a site not markedly inferior to the existing site. (Ref. P/PPA/GC/147, September 30, 1987.)

6.123 Material considerations—car parking restrictions
The reporter considered that it was competent for a planning authority, in considering whether or not to grant planning permission for a hot food shop, to take into account the likelihood that nearby traffic waiting restrictions would be ignored. (Ref. P/PPA/SL/176, March 21, 1988.)

6.124 Material consideration—property values—travelling people's site
The reporter commented that allegations that a proposed development such as a travelling people's site would serve to depress property values in the vicinity was seldom a material consideration in determining planning applications. In this case he found no evidence that lent support to this contention. It seemed to him from experience of another travellers' site that the close proximity of such a site had not deterred either developers or purchasers of new property in the medium-price range. (Ref. P/NID/LD/17, July 11, 1988.)

6.125 Material considerations—extension of house—road widening
Planning permission for the extension of a house had been refused by the planning authority on grounds of road safety. The extension itself would not further have impaired visibility on the adjoining road but the planning authority argued that if the appeal were allowed, the life of the building would be prolonged and this would prejudice the likelihood of an arrangement for demolition of the property being made by the roads authority. The planning authority submitted that the future use of the land as a highway was a relevant planning consideration as in *Westminster Bank Ltd.* v. *Minister of Housing and Local Government* [1971] A.C. 508. The Secretary of State distinguished the *Westminster Bank* decision on the ground that in that case there was evidence that road widening was a firm proposal, which was not the case here. (Ref. P/PPA/SA/17, January 10, 1977.)

6.126 Material consideration—radio interference—taxi business
Planning permission had been refused and an enforcement notice served in respect of the use of a transport depot as a taxi radio base. Permission had been refused on the ground of unacceptable interference with electrical equipment within other property in the vicinity. The reporter noted that SDD Circular 25/1985 made it clear that the question of radio and television interference was not normally a relevant town planning consideration since there were other controls designed to minimise such problems. However, it was accepted that significant interference

could sometimes arise lawfully and unavoidably. Where there was clear evidence that interference would arise and that no practical remedy was available, interference was a material planning consideration. (Refs. P/PPA/ST/90; P/ENA/ST/40, July 7, 1987.)

6.127 Material consideration—SEPD Circular 2/1978

Planning permission had been refused for the change of use of a dwelling-house to a coach hire business. The reporter was in no doubt that the area was residential and he could not therefore grant a permanent permission. However, bearing in mind, *inter alia*, Scottish Economic Planning Department Circular 2/1978, in which local authorities were encouraged to support small local industries, a temporary condition for two years could be granted. (Ref. P/PPA/MB/30, June 24, 1980.)

6.128 Material considerations—neighbour

The appellant sought to extend his house. The reporter said that the fact that the appellant's neighbour had consented to the extension was, in his view, irrelevant since houses change hands and the planning authority had a duty to maintain an acceptable standard. (Ref. P/PPA/HC/41, August 28, 1980.)

6.129 Material considerations—policy—tenement in Edinburgh's New Town

Permission had been refused for the formation of a car park for four cars at the rear of a three-storey building in Edinburgh's New Town. The land in question was overgrown and untidy and the only difference the car park would make would be to create a gap in the wall. The proposal was, however, contrary to the authority's policy and would, by making the building more attractive to commercial users, have the effect of discouraging the building's reversion to residential use. It was the council's policy to maintain and encourage residential use in the area. Planning permission and listed building consent were therefore refused. (Refs. P/PPA/LA/89; HGJ/A/LA/1167, November 2, 1979.)

6.130 Material considerations—reservation of site

Planning permission had been refused on the ground that the area in the vicinity had traditionally been used for activities related to the fishing industry and it was the authority's intention that it should continue to be so used. It was felt that the present oil-related development should be sited elsewhere. The reporter accepted that the site was suitable for the proposed development but also accepted that the authority had followed a consistent policy, looking to the time when the oil industry would taper off. The reporter upheld the authority's decision for the reasons they gave and also to avoid creating an unfortunate precedent. (Ref. P/PPA/Z/6, March 14, 1979.)

6.131 Material considerations—house in country—kennels and dog track

The planning authority had refused outline planning permission for the erection of a house and garage and greyhound kennels, and the formation of a training trials track. The authority argued that the site of the house was in the green belt and that it should therefore be refused. They also said that in their view the accommodation and training of greyhounds could not be considered as outdoor sport of the type that would be allowed in the green belt. The reporter considered that the countryside was an appropriate place for kennels and that since the house and kennels lay within the curtilage of a former farmhouse, this would form an appropriate re-use of the land. (Refs. P/PPA/SU/80; P/PPA/SU/88, September 15, 1981.)

6.132 Material considerations—subsidence—proposed houses

One of the reasons for the refusal of planning permission for the erection of two houses was public safety in that it could not be guaranteed that mineral support for the site would be satisfactory. The National Coal Board had advised that the site was close to a coal outcrop and it was considered that there might well be problems of support. The planning authority had an obligation to consult the board over proposals in areas of past, present and future coal-working. The authority therefore considered it essential that the NCB's views were seriously considered on public safety grounds.

The reporter accepted that outline planning permission might be framed in such a way as to require the results of test bores to be submitted as part of any later, detailed application for approval of reserved matters. He considered that the planning authority would be failing in their development control role if they did not draw the potential danger to the notice of an applicant for planning permission or if they allowed a development to proceed on land on which test bores might indicate a risk of future subsidence. (Ref. P/ENA/SS/49, February 3, 1986.)

6.133 Material considerations—subsidence

One of the reasons for the refusal of planning permission for two houses was public safety in that it could not be guaranteed that mineral support for the site would be satisfactory. The appellant argued that this was not a matter for the planning authority but for the developer alone. The National Coal Board had advised that the site was close to a coal outcrop and it was considered there might well be problems of support. The planning authority had an obligation to consult the board regarding proposals in areas of past, present and future coal-working. They therefore considered it essential that the NCB's views were seriously considered on public safety grounds.

The reporter accepted that outline planning permission might be framed in such a way as to require the results of test bores to be submitted as part of the later, detailed application for approval of reserved matters, but he considered the planning authority would be failing in their development control role if they did not draw the potential danger to the notice of the applicant for planning permission or if they allowed a development to proceed on land on which test bores indicated might give rise to future subsidence. (Ref. P/PPA/SS/131, February 3, 1986.)

6.134 Material considerations—structural stability

The appellant had applied for planning permission for the erection of a house. The planning authority were, however, advised by the National Coal Board that the site could not be guaranteed free from mineral subsidence. Planning permission was therefore refused.

The reporter concluded that the letter from the NCB could not form the basis of a valid reason for refusal. In his view the planning authority could do no more than draw the attention of the applicant to the mineral surveyor's views. It seemed to the reporter that structural stability was a matter to be considered under the building regulations; it could not properly amount to a valid planning reason for refusal in these circumstances. (Ref. P/PPA/CB/22, July 24, 1978.)

6.135 Material considerations — mineral working — strengthened foundations

In granting planning permission for two bungalows the Secretary of State imposed a condition regarding strengthened foundations because of the possibility of future mine workings in the area. (Ref. P/PPA/ML/141, June 30, 1980.)

6.136 Need for development—chalets

This was a proposal for seven new chalet sites. The planning authority argued that there was already adequate provision of chalet sites. The community council supported the planning authority. The developer argued that the question of the adequacy of the provision was one for him and that the possibility of the site becoming disused or falling into disrepair was irrelevant.

The reporter took the view that the need for more chalets had not been demonstrated. He accepted that commercial justification for the proposal was a matter for the developer but he also believed that the planning authority had a *locus* to consider the overall provision of accommodation in any particular area. He further concluded that the proposal did not accord with the local plan policy for the area and that there was no justification for overriding that policy. (Ref. P/PPA/CC/131, January 3, 1986.)

6.137 Relevant considerations—need—asphalt

The reporter regarded the question of need in the area for sand asphalt and the related arguments on supply and demand to be relevant considerations. (Ref. P/PPA/FC/86, May 31, 1988.)

6.138 Relevant considerations—safety

Application had been made for outline planning permission for a house. Permission was refused because of the appeal site's proximity to the route of a wayleave for an ammonia pipeline. The Health and Safety Executive pointed out that in the event of the failure of the pipe resulting in even a comparatively small leak, no part of the appeal site would give an adequate separation distance from concentrations of ammonia which could prove fatal. The reporter said that it would be "wrong . . . for any planning authority to take a conscious decision which would add to the number of persons already exposed to such a serious risk." He therefore dismissed the appeal. (Ref. P/PPA/GB/35, January 12, 1981.)

6.139 Material considerations—conversion of Tollcross House—road safety

The reporter found that it was clear that the listed Tollcross House, Glasgow would have to be demolished if remedial action was delayed. This would be regrettable since the building added great interest to the park and every user of the park would suffer some loss of amenity by the demolition of the house. He accepted the appellants' scheme for the conversion of the house into 13 dwellings. Implementation of the scheme would mean that a greater number of vehicles would use the driveway. "Sleeping policemen" in the drive would ensure that a speed limit was observed. Widening the gateway would minimise risk to pedestrians, and barriers could be placed on the footpath if it were thought there was a risk of children running across the drive. Regarding the question of danger to traffic on Tollcross Road from vehicles emerging from or entering the drive, the reporter relied on the fact that the roads authority had not seen fit to object to the proposals. The Secretary of State accepted the reporter's recommendation and granted planning permission and listed building consent. (Refs. P/PPA/SL/339; HGJ/2/SL/43, March 12, 1987.)

6.140   Material considerations—pedestrian access—safety
The appellant had formed an unauthorised pedestrian access at his house, the access giving on to an adjoining road. The planning authority considered the development to be unsatisfactory in that it would lead to vehicles stopping at the access. The reporter concluded that the pedestrian access was not unacceptable on road safety grounds, nor would it create a precedent for other accesses. Planning permission was therefore granted. (Refs. P/PPA/GC/138; P/ENA/GC/42, March 16, 1987.)

6.141   Material considerations—safety
Planning permission had been refused for a compound for the storage and sale of liquefied petroleum gas. The site was near the centre of town. On one side was a bungalow, on a second side a church with houses beyond and on the third side the playground of a primary school.
The reporter considered that the most important issue was whether there was an unacceptable hazard to the public. He found the planning authority's policy on liquefied petroleum gas to have strayed into areas which were not strictly planning considerations. It was clearly quite proper for the planning authority to formulate policies which took account of amenity but on matters of public safety it seemed to him that that was the function of the Health and Safety Executive. He considered that the planning authority should only seek to impose a higher safety standard than the HSE where there was a sound reason for doing so. The proposed site met the HSE standards. (Ref. P/PPA/ST/97, September 22, 1987.)

6.142   Material considerations—safety and security
Planning permission had been refused for the erection of two explosives depots on land about two-thirds of a mile from a village. The reporter was satisfied that the access road was of a suitable standard. Questions of safety and security were matters

for the Health and Safety Executive. (Ref. P/PPA/LD/43, May 11, 1982.)

6.143 Material considerations—income from bed and breakfast— precedent

The appellant had been refused planning permission for a bed and breakfast establishment on grounds of amenity and the creation of a precedent. The appellant stated that the only way he could continue to maintain his large house was by earning the extra money which a bed and breakfast business would provide. The Secretary of State dismissed the appeal, commenting that he did not consider that the desirability of obtaining an income from the use of the property was enough to outweigh the planning considerations. (Refs. P/PPA/LR/1032; P/PPA/SM/2, September 9, 1976.)

6.144 Precedent—application for planning permission

Dealing in 1979 with an application for planning permission for a house, the reporter, in refusing permission, said that the planning authority had been mistaken in granting permission in 1978 for a house close to the appeal site. However, he could not accept that an unwise previous decision should set a precedent for future applications. The present appeal was dismissed. (Ref. P/PPA/GC/44, November 2, 1979.)

6.145 Material considerations—competition—precedent

Planning permission had been sought for change of use from retail shop to hot food shop. The reporter said that the question of commercial competition was not normally a planning matter, but in the circumstances of this case there was a balance to be struck between the protection of residential amenity and the operation of this shopping street as a district centre and its service to a wider area. A hot food take-away shop would increase the attraction of the area to customers arriving by car as well as local residents. With three off-licences, two hot food take-aways, a take-away sandwich bar and a licensed restaurant all within 200 metres of the appeal site, the reporter was of the opinion that further concentration of service retail uses in this area was undesirable if residential amenity was to be adequately protected and the district centre promoted as a convenience shopping area. On the question of precedent the reporter stated that while every case had to be assessed on its own merits, the approval of this use at the appeal site, on a major radial route where car-borne customers were likely to be attracted, would make it more difficult to resist other similar applications in nearby premises. (Ref. P/PPA/GA/373, May 18, 1987.)

6.146   Material considerations—precedent—lapsed planning permission

The appellant had been refused planning permission for the erection of a house on a smallholding. One of the reasons for refusal was that if the development were approved it would create an unacceptable precedent, making other similar applications difficult to resist. The reporter considered that the planning implications of the current proposal were not sufficiently different from that granted permission some years previously to justify the refusal of planning permission. (Ref. P/PPA/SR/90, March 31, 1987.)

6.147   Material considerations—dwelling-house—need—precedent

The proposed erection of a dwelling-house would run counter to the planning authority's policies and to the provisions of the structure plan in that it would constitute isolated housing development in the countryside. The house was not required to assist the rural economy and if it were allowed the planning authority would have great difficulty in maintaining control over further similar developments. (Ref. P/PPA/SR/80, January 22, 1987.)

6.148   Material considerations—condition—precedent—house extension

In granting planning permission for an extension to a house the planning authority imposed a condition restricting the size of the extension. The appellant argued that extensions similar to his proposed extension had been granted planning permission in the vicinity. The reporter stated that the planning authority were not bound by precedent, especially where the previous decisions had been granted by an authority now abolished. (Ref. P/PPA/FA/29, April 22, 1980.)

6.149   Precedent—fairness and consistency

Application was made for the erection of a single house in the green belt. The reporter said that as the appellant's case was based mainly on the alleged precedent resulting from the approval of a house in 1978 on the site to the north of the appeal site, he had considered whether the appeal should succeed for reasons of fairness and consistency. Several other applications for individual houses in the green belt had been refused planning permission since the one approved. The reporter said that in his view it would be a greater inconsistency to grant permission for the appellant's proposal to conform with the single house granted approval by the planning authority than to refuse permission in conformity with the other six applications for houses determined by the planning authority. (Ref. P/PPA/FA/25, March 10, 1980.)

6.150 Material considerations—dwelling-house—proposed extension— precedent

It was proposed to build a flat-roofed extension extending back from the ridge of a cottage roof. The village in which the cottage was situated had been declared a conservation area. The reporter considered that the transformation of a small single-storey pitch-roofed cottage into a two-storey flat-roofed house of approximately four times the original floor area would constitute a gross over-development of the site, would completely change the character of the cottage and would create a dangerous precedent which could result in a change in the present attractive character of the village. (Ref. P/PPA/LC/138, May 20, 1987.)

6.151 Material considerations — solicitor's office — shopping area — precedent

Planning permission had been refused for a change of use from a small shop to a solicitor's office. The question of precedent in permitting a non-retail use of retail premises in the town centre was raised. The reporter thought this a relevant question and that the change of use of even a small unit could be seriously damaging if it was likely to lead to a substantial number of similar applications which could not reasonably be resisted. However, he found the proposal to be acceptable because of its location and the size of the premises. Similar proposals for similarly-sized premises in similar locations would probably be equally acceptable, but he did not consider they would be so numerous as to have a serious impact on the retail attractiveness of the town centre. (Ref. P/PPA/SS/173, March 22, 1988.)

6.152 Material considerations—precedent—fairness—erection of house

This appeal arose out of a refusal of planning permission for a single house in the green belt. The appellant's case was based mainly on the fact that permission had been granted for a house on a nearby site quite recently. The reporter considered whether the appeal should succeed for reasons of fairness and equity. He found that 6 other applications for houses in the vicinity had been refused in the period since the single house had been approved. It would therefore be consistent to refuse the present appeal. (Ref. P/PPA/GC/56, June 9, 1980.)

6.153 Material considerations—consistency—each case to be dealt with on own merits

In considering whether the access to a proposed house would create an unfortunate precedent the reporter declared that it was important for district councils and the Secretary of State to be seen to apply policies consistently. However, applications for planning permission were rarely identical and for that reason each must be considered on its own merits. (Ref. P/PPA/CC/66, October 31, 1980.)

6.154 Cumulative effect of development—relevant considerations—section 50 agreement

Planning permission had been refused for a chalet development on the grounds that there already were a number of outstanding permissions and it would, as the reporter said, be very easy to lose control if all the permissions were implemented. On the other hand one witness said that it seemed "unethical" to withhold planning permission for a development that was likely to go ahead immediately if allowed, on the ground that development which had been granted permission had not been carried out. On matters of detail the developers intended that the owners of the chalets should not be permitted to keep caravans on the site or to build garages, car ports, sheds or greenhouses and owners would not be permitted to launch boats from the site. Those matters would be dealt with in an agreement under section 50 of the 1972 Act. Counsel for the appellants pointed out that these prohibitions would then run with the land. The planning authority said that they intended that conditions be imposed on matters such as replanting, road works and water supply. These could be incorporated in an agreement.

The reporter considered that the development would, in his view, be acceptable if various matters were regulated by conditions or by section 50 agreement. He believed however that it would not be right to attempt to give planning permission subject to a condition that a section 50 agreement be entered into. An attempt to do so might be of doubtful validity, he thought.

The Secretary of State accepted the reporter's general recommendation. (Ref. T/NP/7/1/HF/IC9, February 2, 1980.)

6.155 Material considerations—"non-planning" controls—bingo hall

One of the Secretary of State's reasons for upholding an appeal against a refusal of permission for a change of use from cinema to bingo hall was that the question of the need for, or desirability of, additional bingo facilities was properly one for the licensing authorities. (Ref. P/PPA/ML/179, June 29, 1976.)

6.156 Material considerations—competency of operator
The Secretary of State disagreed with one of his reporters that planning permission should be granted on a personal basis so as to allow continuing control over the competence of the operator. The Secretary of State said that this would be most unusual. Applications for planning permission for shopping development were not, for example, considered in relation to the capability of the person who was to run the business. "Generally speaking, where other controls are deemed necessary by Parliament, separate arrangements will be made, such as, for example, the licensing arrangements under the Riding Establishments Acts 1964 and 1970." (Ref. P/PPA/GB/37, May 20, 1981.)

6.157 Material considerations—overlapping legislation
The appellant argued that the need for a planning condition on the opening hours of a hot food shop had been superseded by the licensing requirements of the Civic Government (Scotland) Act 1982. The reporter agreed that the planning legislation should not duplicate control exercised under separate legislation but pointed out that planning control related to the juxtaposition of land uses. Unrestricted opening hours would mean that a hot food shop would be an unacceptable use of land, irrespective of licensing considerations. A condition on opening hours was therefore necessary. (Ref. P/PPA/LA/421, October 3, 1986.)

6.158 Material considerations—non-planning legislation
In the course of this appeal the question arose whether the quantity and pressure of water would be adequate to ensure the effective operation of fire equipment at proposed chalets. The decision letter stated that this question was one to be dealt with under the building regulations. (Refs. P/PPA/SP/2; P/ENA/SP/4, March 15, 1977.)

6.159 Material considerations—overlapping powers—toilets
It was a ground of refusal for a proposed extension to a tea bar that adequate provision was not made for toilet accommodation commensurate with the projected requirements. This issue seemed more appropriate to public health legislation relating to shops and public eating places and any necessary provision for additional toilets could be dealt with under legislation other than the planning Acts. (Ref. P/PPA/CB/22, July 24, 1978.)

6.160 Material considerations—view
The owner of a house considered that a proposed house on an adjoining site would adversely affect the occupiers of the existing

house. The reporter said that it might be noted that the occupiers of the house had no statutory rights to the protection of the view from that house and in other respects he did not consider they would suffer material loss of amenity from the development of the adjoining house. (Ref. P/PPA/CB/95, October 16, 1984.)

6.161   Material considerations—view

The reporter said: "While a householder in buying a house does not buy the view from its windows, he can reasonably, in a high quality residential area such as this, expect a degree of protection from inappropriate and disharmonious developments in the near vicinity." (Ref. P/PPA/SL/106, November 27, 1984.)

SECTION 7

CONDITIONS

See generally Young and Rowan-Robinson, *Scottish Planning Law and Procedure*, pp. 231–250.

In *Grampian Regional Council* v. *City of Aberdeen District Council*, 1984 S.L.T. 197, Lord Keith stated that the power conferred by section 26(1) of the Town and Country Planning (Scotland) Act 1972 to impose conditions on a grant of planning permission "is expressed in the widest possible terms. 'A local planning authority may grant planning permission, either unconditionally or subject to such conditions as they think fit.' The power is not, however, unlimited. The nature of the limitation is well settled by authority and is compendiously stated by Viscount Dilhorne in *Newbury District Council* v. *Secretary of State for the Environment* [1981] A.C. 578 at p. 599: 'it follows that the conditions imposed must be for a planning purpose and not for any ulterior one and that they must fairly and reasonably relate to the development permitted. Also they must not be so unreasonable that no reasonable planning authority could have imposed them.' " In addition to the three tests laid down by Viscount Dilhorne, conditions may be void from uncertainty and it seems that they may now be open to challenge on the ground that they are unnecessary—see *British Airports Authority* v. *Secretary of State for Scotland*, 1979 S.C. 200; 1979 S.L.T. 197.

The summaries of appeal decisions contained in this section are mainly concerned with legal restrictions on conditions.

APPEAL DECISIONS

7.1 Private hospital—reason for refusal—invalidity of condition

A planning authority had refused planning permission for a private hospital on the ground that the development would have a detrimental effect upon Health Service resources, particularly qualified and experienced nursing staff, in the area. The Secretary of State concluded that this reason was not a planning matter and was therefore invalid. (Refs. P/PPA/LB/48; HGJ/2/LB/5, April 20, 1983.)

7.2 Condition — clearance of material — related to permitted development?

Planning permission had been granted for alterations to form a dwelling out of part of a mansion. A condition was imposed on the permission to the effect that before development took place, the site had to be tidied, the curtilage of the mansion containing a considerable amount of material including timber, steel girders, disused cookers, a caravan and a semi-derelict car. The reporter said that he did not consider that the complete removal of the material could reasonably be related to the limited development proposed. The requirement to remove most of the material was not, in the reporter's view, expedient for the purpose of or connected with the authorised development. (Ref. P/PPA/GD/59, June 26, 1981.)

7.3 Condition—invalid

In granting planning permission to Central Regional Council for the construction of a new road, Clackmannan District Council imposed a condition which stated that no work was to commence on "land within the present site of St. Mungo's School until such time as adequate alternative educational provision has been made elsewhere with the agreement of the District Council." The planning permission stated that this condition was imposed in order to avoid "undue nuisance and disturbance, during site work, to the operation of the school." An enforcement notice was served in respect of an alleged failure on the part of the regional council to comply with the condition.

This was an appeal against the enforcement notice. The Secretary of State took the view that the condition attached to the planning permission was invalid. His reasons for taking this view were, it was stated, "that a planning condition must fairly and reasonably relate to the planning permission sought and must not be imposed for an extraneous objective, or have the effect of deferring the grant of planning permission, or deal generally with educational provision for an area, which is a matter for the Regional Council as education authority."

In any event, the Secretary of State considered that the wording of the condition went beyond what was necessary to achieve the planning authority's desired purpose. He also took the view that the invalid planning condition was not severable from the grant of planning permission and that accordingly the planning permission was itself invalid.

The Secretary of State therefore quashed the enforcement notice and granted a fresh planning permission for the development. The regional council's victory in this respect was, however, in the nature of a Pyrrhic one; the new permission was granted subject to a condition that no work was to start on the school site until such time as either (a) the school ceased to be used for educational purposes, or (b) the school was operated within buildings on one side only of the route of the proposed road and a scheme for protecting the school buildings from the road traffic noise was approved by the district council. (Ref. P/ENA/CA/3, June 25, 1982.)

7.4 Conditions—not reasonably related to permitted development—inappropriate

This was an appeal against conditions imposed on a grant of planning permission for the change of use from cinema and storage to bathroom and kitchen centre and electrical and plumbing spares distribution centre. Five conditions were the subject of appeal. These were as follows:

"1. This permission shall not enure for the benefit of the land, but for the benefit of the present applicant, John R. Mowbray personally (and 'for a Company in which he has a controlling interest').

"2. Notwithstanding the terms of the Town and Country Planning (Use Classes) (Scotland) Order 1973, the use of the site (and buildings) shall be restricted to premises for the retailing and wholesaling of kitchen and bathroom fitments and the retailing and distribution of electrical and plumbing components and spares and no other use shall be undertaken unless previously agreed in writing by the planning authority.

"3. Within two months of the date of this consent, a scheme for the external decoration and refurbishment of the main facade shall be submitted to and approved in writing by the planning authority and thereafter all such approved works shall be carried out within two months of the date of that approval.

"4. The unkempt yard area to the rear of the building shall be tidied and improved in accordance with a scheme which shall be submitted to and approved in writing by the planning authority within two months of the date of consent and thereafter all such approved works shall be carried out within two months of the date of that approval and shall thereafter be regularly maintained in a tidy condition to the satisfaction of the planning authority.

"5. Notwithstanding the provisions of the Town and Country Planning (Control of Advertisements) (Scotland) Regulations 1961, no advertisements shall be displayed without the prior consent of the planning authority."

The reasons for the imposition of these conditions were as follows:

"1. To ensure that the planning authority can control a use which has been granted owing to the special circumstances of the applicant.

"2. In order that the planning authority can control the further use of the site (and buildings).

"3. and 4. To ensure that the appearance of the building and site is improved in the interests of amenity of the area as a whole.

"5. In order to safeguard the amenity of the area."

For the appellant it was argued that, regarding condition 1, there were no "special circumstances" or grounds for granting the permission on a personal basis. Using Ministry of Housing and Local Government Circular No. 5/1968 as the basis of advice on the framing of conditions, condition 1 failed all the tests. The condition would effectively restrict the type of business which the appellant could conduct to one in which he had a controlling interest and would render the premises unsaleable as they would not be capable of any legal use by another person without first obtaining planning permission. The planning permission included the use of the premises as a shop and condition 2 was inappropriate in that it was not legitimate to restrict the actual range of products to be sold. The condition was badly worded, imprecise, incapable of enforcement and it did not achieve any reasonable planning objective. The fears of the planning authority that the site might be developed as a major multiple store were unfounded. Conditions 3 and 4 did not relate to the development to be permitted and were beyond the scope of the planning authority. It was not now possible to comply with the time limits imposed. Condition 5 was inappropriate in that powers to control advertisements already existed in the Town and Country Planning (Control of Advertisements) (Scotland) Regulations 1961.

The planning authority were concerned about the unnecessary dispersal of shopping facilities when there were adequate prem–

ises available for retail purposes in the town centre. Traffic generation was an important issue, the local residents having enjoyed relatively undisturbed conditions in the years since the closure of the cinema in 1958. However, taking account of the character of the area at the level of use of the premises which had taken place over the last two years without complaint, it was considered unreasonable to withhold consent. The special circumstances applying to the appellant, given in the reason for condition 1, were the type of business he was running. Another operator could introduce an entirely different scale of retail activity. If there was a substantial intensification of use, the car parking facilities available were inadequate. Condition 2 was related to but independent of condition 1 and restricted the type of retailing to that sought in the application. Under article 4 of the Town and Country Planning (General Development) (Scotland) Order 1975, the planning authority had adopted powers to control developments under Class II of Schedule 1 (sundry minor operations) for all conservation areas and it was the duty of planning authorities to preserve and enhance the character of conservation areas. Conditions 3 and 4 were therefore appropriate, reasonable and capable of enforcement. Other powers under section 49 or section 50 of the 1972 Act were not considered suitable. Condition 5 was a standard condition applied frequently in change of use cases. It was emphasised that if these conditions had not been imposed it was unlikely that planning permission would have been granted.

Taking each condition in order, the reporter was of the opinion that condition 1 was unnecessarily restrictive to the operation of the business in that by it the appellant was required to have a controlling interest in any company using the premises and that if the appellant were to die or to transfer the premises to another person, no legal use of the building would subsist until a planning application had been made and granted either for a new use or for the transfer of the "personal" permission to another person. He also considered that the objective of the condition, that the level of use should be restricted to that carried on now, would not necessarily be achieved since the appellant himself would remain free to intensify the use to the limit permitted by the capacity of the premises and would therefore not be in a different position from any other owner or occupier. He therefore considered condition 1 to be inappropriate.

Condition 2 restricted the uses of the premises precisely to those for which permission was sought and to no other. Although the appellant's intention was to use the premises partly for the retail of bathroom and kitchen fitments etc., that intention did not extend to the use of the premises as a shop in the normal sense of being primarily for the sale of goods by retail. It was therefore reasonable for the planning authority to limit the scope of permission so as to avoid it being extended to allow for the retailing of other types of goods without a fresh application being made in that behalf; the proper planning consideration here was the protection of the retail uses in the town centre.

The reporter considered the question of whether the planning permission granted on June 9, 1978 on an application for change of use of the appeal premises to shop and auction hall included permission for their use as a shop. Additional condition 1 attached to that permission stated: "this permission shall relate solely to the change of use in principle to an Auction Hall with related storage facilities." In the reporter's opinion the use as a shop was excluded by that condition.

Conditions 3 and 4 both required works to be carried out to the premises for the purpose of improving their appearance. Powers existed under section 49 and section 63 of the 1972 Act by which alterations to buildings and abatement of injury to amenity of land could be obtained by a planning authority. It had also been held by a court that a condition must be reasonably related to the permitted development. Here the permitted development was a change of use not involving any alteration to the building. Because the need for the improvements did not arise from the proposed use of the premises, the two conditions were in the reporter's opinion outside the scope of the development permitted and did not reasonably relate to it, despite the desirability of their objective. The reporter was also in doubt about the enforceability of the time conditions and considered the wording was incorrect in that it was not within the power of the appellant to ensure approval within two months of any scheme submitted.

Similarly, for condition 5, the reporter's attention was drawn to a decision by the Secretary of State under reference P/PPA/TB/2 in which he took the view that control of advertisements was a matter to be dealt with under the provisions of the Town and Country Planning (Control of Advertisements) (Scotland) Regulations 1961 and that it was inappropriate to seek to regulate advertisements by attaching conditions to a planning permission.

For the above reasons the reporter concluded that conditions 1, 3, 4 and 5 were inappropriate but that condition 2 ought to be retained in order that the planning authority could control the further use of the site and buildings.

The reporter therefore sustained the appeal in respect of conditions 1, 3, 4 and 5 attached to the planning permission. (Ref. P/PPA/CC/83, August 6, 1982.)

7.5 Material considerations—condition not relevant to development

In granting planning permission for the renovation of part of a house, two of the conditions imposed were as follows:

3. Drainage to be to a septic tank with adequate capacity and suitable vehicular access, to the satisfaction of the planning authority in consultation with the Forth River Purification Board;

4. All roof and surface water from both the renovated and the existing part of property to be separated out of the foul water system.

The appellants pointed out that there was already a septic tank with adequate capacity and suitable vehicular access thereto. It was already drained by the district council. The surface water flow was essential if the system was to function properly and pipework joints were not to dry out. The planning authority said it was now common practice to separate foul and surface water systems.

The reporter said that so far as drainage was concerned the planning authority had gone beyond questions of legitimate planning concern. He considered it appropriate for a planning authority to examine matters specifically covered by other legislation to establish general feasibility, in that it would be unsatisfactory to grant permission for development which was incapable of implementation. Such conditions stopped short of duplicating, in a planning permission, the requirements of another authority operating under separate powers, and under which they retained control regardless of their requirements being repeated in, or omitted from, a planning permission. The adequacy or otherwise of the existing septic tank, and the specification of any new one was a matter for the district council as building control authority in consultation with the River Purification Board regarding the standard of any discharge. The reporter therefore considered that condition 3 was inappropriate. On the question of surface water disposal and the merits of a combined or separate drainage system, the reporter likewise considered this matter would be more appropriately resolved in response to any application for a building warrant in much the same way. Planning conditions should in any case be relevant to the development approved. To the extent that condition 4 attempted to dictate the question of drainage for the existing building (which would remain whether or not this proposal proceeded), it sought to achieve a fringe benefit. This might be very desirable but it was accordingly not sufficiently relevant from a planning point of view to the approved development. The reporter therefore found condition 4 was inappropriate. (Ref. P/PPA/CC/203, February 20, 1989.)

7.6   Conditions—footpaths—unnecessary, irrelevant and unreasonable
Planning permission had been granted for a housing estate subject to conditions which required footpaths to be constructed along two roads. In the case of the first road the occupiers of the houses would not be able to reach the proposed footpath directly. Accordingly, the reporter found that the condition was not relevant to the development and was therefore *ultra vires*. As regards the second road, the reporter accepted that a footpath along this frontage would be unnecessary in regard to the housing development. In any case the reporter considered that it would be unreasonable to require the developer to provide a facility that was principally intended to serve another development—see *Hall & Co. Ltd.* v. *Shoreham-by-Sea Urban District Council* [1964] 1 W.L.R. 240. The reporter also concluded that most of this footpath would not be relevant to the permitted development. (Ref. P/PPA/GD/156, November 20, 1986.)

7.7   Condition—time limit—not related to permitted development
A condition attached to a planning permission for the siting of a residential caravan provided that "[c]onsent is for three years only and is not renewable." The reporter found that the phrase "and is not renewable" could not prevent the appellant from making a future application and was therefore of no practical effect.

Another condition required a screen fence and planting around two adjacent sides of the site. The reporter found that the condition was *ultra vires* since it was not related to the development sanctioned by the planning permission but was imposed against the possibility that the appellant might resume business as a haulage contractor at the site. The appeal against this condition was therefore sustained. (Ref. P/PPA/H/2, August 13, 1977.)

7.8   Condition—validity—change of use—reinstatement of site
A condition had been attached to a grant of planning permission for a change in the use of premises from shop to licensed betting office. The condition provided that "the use shall be discontinued and the land restored to its former condition at or before the expiry of a period terminating on September 29, 1980" (about a year ahead). The authority's stated reason for imposing

the condition was that "the continued use of the premises beyond the period specified would be prejudicial to the realisation of the proposals of the council for the future development of the area."

The reporter said that the determining issues in this case were (a) whether the condition appealed against met the normally accepted criteria for the attachment of conditions to a planning permission, and (b) whether, in particular, it was a proper use of planning conditions to impose a time limit condition on a planning permission for the purpose of warning the applicant about the impending redevelopment. He suggested that the generally accepted criteria for planning conditions were that they should be (1) related to the development authorised by the planning permission; (2) necessary in order to achieve the objectives of the planning authority; and (3) enforceable. In the reporter's view conditions which failed to satisfy all or any of these criteria had to be regarded as unreasonable and should not be imposed on a grant of planning permission. It seemed to the reporter that the condition failed to meet the first of the three criteria. Since no works had been authorised by the permission, it was unreasonable for there to be a requirement for the land (including buildings) to be reinstated to its former condition. It was doubtful whether the condition could be enforced. The reporter therefore considered that the condition should be deleted. He did not consider that the condition could be satisfactorily amended.

The Secretary of State did not consider that the imposition of a time limit on the planning permission for change of use was necessary in order to avoid prejudicing the future development of the area. He considered that the condition was not needed to warn the appellants about the possibility of future development, because, even if they had not already been aware of it, a covering letter with the planning permission would have sufficed. In its operation the condition would have meant uncertainty or possibly the need to reinstate (at some cost) premises which were in any case to be demolished under redevelopment proposals. The condition would not be beneficial to the planning authority in making their redevelopments easier to bring about. For these reasons the Secretary of State accepted the reporter's recommendation and accordingly decided that the condition ought to be deleted. (Ref. P/PPA/GA/51, July 19, 1979.)

7.9 Extension to haulage yard—screen fencing—condition invalid

This was an appeal against a condition attached to a grant of planning permission for an extension to a haulage yard. The appellant submitted that the condition was *ultra vires* in that the fence required by the condition would be outwith the application site. It was, however, on land under the applicant's control and in terms of section 27(1)(*a*) of the 1972 Act was competent. The principal effect of the fence was, however, to reduce the visual impact of the present yard rather than to conceal the extension. The condition did not therefore relate primarily to the permitted development and had to be quashed. (Ref. P/PPA/SC/86, November 30, 1982.)

7.10 Condition—unreasonableness

The decision letter on this appeal stated that the view was taken that it would be unreasonable to impose conditions that the development match any or all of the design suggestions made in the planning authority's letter since this would result in radical alteration of the proposals which were the subject of the planning application and of the inquiry. (Ref. P/PPA/SQ/7, May 6, 1977.)

7.11 Condition—enforcement notice—provision of lay-bys at new houses

Enforcement notices were served on separate parties on the ground that they had failed to comply with a condition requiring them to construct a lay-by in front of their houses. The appellants challenged both the validity and the merits of the condition. The reporter found the condition to be an unhappy compromise which involved the appellants in an expense out of proportion to the marginal road safety improvement claimed. On the merits the reporter therefore dismissed the appeal. It was thus not necessary for him to deal with the extensive legal arguments advanced by the parties. The reporter did, however, record his reservations on the validity of the conditions in that they required the provision of a lay-by, which could not be for the exclusive use of the appellants, on land not owned by them. This went, he said, beyond what was expedient for the purposes of, or in connection with, the development. He considered that dicta in *Hall & Co. Ltd.* v. *Shoreham-by-Sea UDC* [1964] 1 W.L.R. 240 had to be applied with caution but he considered them relevant in this case. The requirement here was, in effect, for the construction of a public lay-by at private expense. (Ref. P/ENA/ST/15, April 17, 1980.)

7.12 Condition—public open space

A condition attached to a planning permission for a house required that land shown on the plan should be maintained as open space associated with a coastal footpath. The reporter found that the planning authority had made a fundamental error in presuming that the condition established the subject land as open space available for public enjoyment. It had no such status, being private land, part of the feu of the dwelling-house. The condition could not have the effect of requiring land to be dedicated for public use, a requirement which would have to be achieved by negotiation, with compensation being payable to the person being deprived of his use of the land. (Ref. P/ENA/FA/41, April 10, 1986.)

7.13 Condition—pedestrian access—"ultra vires"

It was a condition of planning permission for two houses that a 3 metre strip of land be reserved along two sides of the site boundary to allow for pedestrian access from a private road. The appellants asserted that the condition was invalid in that it failed to pass any of the six basic tests for a condition. It was unnecessary; it was not relevant to planning; it was not relevant to the permitted development; it was not enforceable; it was not precise; and it was unreasonable in all other respects. In effect the planning authority were requiring the owner of the land to dedicate part of the site to public use. The development could be implemented without such a condition which was therefore *ultra vires*. The condition was also lacking in precision; it referred to a 3 metre strip of ground when a 3 metre *wide* strip was meant, and it did not specify on which side of the boundary the land was to be reserved (the appellants owned the land on both sides of the boundary).

The reporter agreed that it was well-established that conditions must fairly and reasonably relate to the development being permitted and he found that that was not the case here. The condition was not necessary or relevant to the erection of two dwelling-houses. In addition it seemed to the reporter that the condition was unreasonable. It was also doubtful whether the condition had any relevance to planning since there was no evidence that the planning authority had ever resolved to proceed with the footpath project, nor that any such proposal had been included in a draft local plan. Indeed it had been categorically stated that "there were no district council policies . . . relating to this matter." In the reporter's view in imposing the condition the planning authority had an ulterior motive and were acting *ultra vires*. He considered that the condition ought to be discharged. (Ref. P/PPA/LD/101, June 10, 1986.)

7.14 Conditions—"ultra vires"—retail warehouse

This was an appeal against refusal of amendment of two conditions:

"(a) The use hereby permitted shall be carried on only by the Reid Group or its successors;

(b) The retailing of products shall be restricted to furniture and furnishings, and 75 per cent. of the goods for retail at the site in any one year shall be manufactured by the Reid Group or its successors in their premises in Strathclyde Region."

The reporter said that it seemed to him that whilst the conditions imposed highlighted the special circumstances of the decision, they did little or nothing to sustain the structure plan policies. The relevant considerations from the standpoint of strategic planning were the floor space involved and the nature of the goods sold. Conditions (a) and (b) had no direct bearing on these issues and, as a means of preserving the structure plan were, in his view, unnecessary.

As regards relevance to planning, he accepted that the provision of employment was a material consideration. However, the reporter considered that the creation of jobs in one area of high unemployment rather than another or in one region rather than another, was of doubtful relevance in the absence of other planning considerations.

On enforceability the reporter was bound to conclude that it would be impossible for the planning authority to tell from a normal inspection of the premises whether the Reid Group were complying with condition (b) or not. In view of the nature of the operation, whereby goods were ordered from the store on the basis of room displays, it would not be easy for the Reid Group themselves to know whether they were in breach of that condition. The problem of enforceability was compounded by the lack of precision in the wording of the conditions. It would have needed to be made clear exactly what was meant by the term "successors" in condition (a) and how the percentage referred to in condition (b) was to be calculated. Such ambiguities could be met by amendment, but the reporter did not consider that this would overcome the other objections to the conditions.

On the criterion of reasonableness, it could, the reporter said, be argued that a condition which failed to satisfy three or four of the other tests was *ipso facto* unreasonable, but the question was whether it was reasonable "in all other respects" (see SDD Circular 18/1986). In this case it was clear that the two conditions in combination would have a serious financial effect on the Reid Group's operations. Whilst this was not so severe as to negate the planning permission granted, it had made it unusually difficult to implement, and served to highlight the need for considerable caution in imposing personal conditions. Paragraph 79 of SDD Circular 18/1986 made clear that personal conditions would scarcely ever be justified in the case of a permission for the erection of a permanent building. The reporter did not consider it justifiable in this instance and concluded that the imposition of conditions (a) and (b) was unreasonable. (Ref. P/PPA/ST/103, July 13, 1988.)

7.15 Condition—negative—suspensive—footpath

The planning authority served an enforcement notice on a developer requiring the provision of a section of footpath. This section of footpath would have to be built partly on land owned by the roads authority. The reporter said that the law had evolved since the planning permission was granted in 1980, to facilitate this procedure by recognising the validity of negative suspensive conditions requiring off-site works, provided that there was a reasonable prospect that it would be feasible to carry out the works. In this case the owners of the land were anxious to have the footpath constructed and were willing to co-operate and give access to the site. Thus the reporter thought that the circumstances were appropriate for a negative suspensive condition. (Ref. P/ENA/CC/22, April 18, 1988.)

7.16 Condition—suspensive—road improvements

New road improvements required for a proposed superstore would involve work on land which was not under the appellant's control. The reporter did not agree with the planning authority that this necessarily ruled out any consideration of the improvements in the context of the appeal. On the contrary, it seemed to the reporter a good example of the sort of case where a suspensive condition worded in negative form would be appropriate. The important question was, as stated in SDD Circular 18/1986, whether there were at least reasonable prospects of the action in question being performed. It was not certain who owned the land required for the road improvements. Nevertheless, in the absence of known opposition and in view of the committed approach of the appellants to the development, the reporter found there to be a reasonable prospect of the land becoming available. He therefore concluded that a suspensive condition was appropriate. (Ref. P/PPA/SM/125, August 1, 1988.)

7.17 Condition—reasonableness and necessity

Developers had obtained planning permission for housing on a 1.26 hectare site. This was an appeal against a condition which required "all uses to be removed from the site and the ground cleared of all buildings prior to the commencement of building works." The owners of one building refused to sell their building to the developers.

The planning authority maintained that the condition passed the test of reasonableness which the House of Lords imposed in *Grampian Regional Council* v. *City of Aberdeen District Council*, 1984 S.L.T. 197 and it was perfectly proper that such a condition should be imposed in the circumstances of the case.

The appellants said that when considered against the terms of SDD Circular 18/1986, "The Use of Conditions in Planning Permission," the condition nullified the permission which was granted and prevented the erection of the residential development. The condition could only be met if the owners of the building acquiesced. Since the owners were not prepared to sell, the condition was unreasonable in terms of the tests set out in paragraphs 35 and 38 of the circular. They also argued that a condition could only be imposed if it were shown to be necessary. They maintained that a suspensive condition was inappropriate in this case as the appellants had no power to influence the situation in the manner which was required.

The reporter considered that the determining issues in this case were whether the disputed condition was both reasonable and necessary. The 1972 Act and the Town and Country Planning (General Development) (Scotland) Order 1981 allowed for planning permission to be sought and granted in circumstances, such as were involved here, where at the time of the application the developer did not own or control all of the land necessary to complete the development. The condition was imposed to ensure that a planning objective, the separation of industrial and residential land uses, was achieved. The condition related to land within the site of the planning application and was suspensive on the entire development. The reporter found the principle of such a condition acceptable within the terms of both paragraphs 37 and 29 of the circular. He did not find in favour of the argument that the condition could be held to come within the terms of paragraph 35, to have removed the benefit of the permission. The appellants sought planning permission to develop the whole site and the condition simply required that development should proceed on that basis. In relation to paragraph 38 of the circular the reporter did not find support for the appellants' argument that the condition was unreasonable because its terms could only be met if the owners of the building, third parties, acquiesced. In effect, these were the terms on which planning permission was sought, because, although the appellants did not then control the entire site, there was a reasonable prospect of achieving control within the time limit of the planning permission. The implied argument that the condition should now be regarded as unreasonable because the owners of the building were not prepared to accept the appellants' offer for the building was not tenable.

As to whether the condition was necessary, the approved development, proposed works and landscaping intended to integrate the buildings with the appellants' earlier development and with the listed buildings in an adjoining street. If the condition were to be set aside then development would proceed on all but the site of the building which could not be acquired. That building had an established industrial use which was capable of resumption without planning permission. There was therefore the prospect that the residential amenity of the new householders could be adversely affected by noise and intrusion from those industrial premises. The reporter found as a matter of fact and degree that should the condition be discharged, the resultant form of development would be unsatisfactory.

In the circumstances the reporter found the condition to be reasonable and also to be necessary within the context of the planning permission. The appeal was therefore dismissed. (Ref. P/PPA/SL/449, March 7, 1989.)

7.18 Condition—time limit on permission

A condition was imposed on a planning permission for a petrol filling station requiring that the development should begin within nine months. The reason for the condition was to ensure the expeditious development of the site which was in a poor condition and harmful to the amenity of the locality. The reporter was not prepared to accept the appellant's argument that the condition effectively nullified the permission because the appeal had delayed the start of the development—whatever period was set would commence on the date of the appeal decision. It was reasonable to impose such a condition because of the desirability of obtaining an improvement in the appearance of the site. (Ref. P/PPA/SL/142, October 7, 1986.)

7.19 Helicopter service base—development—competency of condition

A public inquiry was instructed by the Secretary of State in connection with a proposal to establish a base for helicopter operations and servicing. The application was "called in" by the Secretary of State because of the serious implications which the proposal might have had for a nearby National Nature Reserve.

Two interesting questions were raised at the inquiry. First, did the proposal in fact require planning permission and, second, if it did, would it be competent to impose a condition regulating the flight paths of helicopters using the base?

The applicants conceded that planning permission would be required if the site was to be used as a commercial heliport for the collection of passengers or freight in the same way as an airport. What was proposed here, however, was merely a base for the operation and servicing of helicopters and the applicants argued that planning permission was not required for these proposals. The land to which the proposals related was presently used for various industrial purposes (including vehicle repair). Some of the buildings on the site were general industrial buildings as defined in the Town and Country Planning (Use Classes) (Scotland) Order 1973, article 2. The servicing of the helicopters was, it was argued, also a general industrial use and planning permission would therefore not be required for the use of these buildings for the purposes envisaged.

So far as concerned the main physical works involved in the proposals (the construction of a concrete landing pad and a short length of private road), it was argued that these works were permitted development in terms of Class VII of Schedule 1 to the Town and Country Planning (General Development) (Scotland) Order 1975, the effect of which was to grant planning permission for the carrying out by an industrial undertaker of certain types of development for industrial purposes. The only other physical works which it was proposed to carry out—the formation of new sliding doors in a vehicle workshop—were, it was submitted, also permitted by the GDO as alterations to industrial buildings.

So far as the operation of the helipad was concerned the appellants argued that planning permission was not required for landing an airborne vehicle on the ground. No permission was required to fly a helicopter over land or for it to hover over any land. Once a helicopter had landed, it became a parked vehicle and the site already had permission for the parking and storage of vehicles.

For the planning authority it was argued that planning permission was required. The reporter took the view that one could not look at the proposal to carry out works separately from the purpose for which the works were intended to be used. In this case the proposal was to create a helicopter operating base with servicing as an ancillary to the main use. Although the servicing operations might closely resemble the operations already carried out on the site in connection with trucks and buses, it was clear that the present use did not, even broadly, resemble an operating base for helicopters. The Secretary of State agreed that planning permission was required for the development.

There also arose the question of whether there could competently be imposed on any grant of planning permission for the helicopter base a condition regulating the flight paths of helicopters using the base. The applicants were prepared to accept restrictions of this nature which would, it was said, reduce the danger of disturbance to the nearby National Nature Reserve. The applicants argued that such a condition could competently be imposed by the Secretary of State. In so arguing, they sought to distinguish the decision of the First Division of the Court of Session in *British Airports Authority* v. *Secretary of State for Scotland*, 1979 S.C. 200. In that case a condition regulating the direction of take off and landing of aircraft at Aberdeen Airport was held to be bad because it was concerned with a matter which was outwith the control of the applicants, the BAA. Control of such matters was the legal responsibility of the Civil Aviation Authority and the BAA could not take steps which would secure the desired result. However, the applicants argued that the position in the present case was quite different. The operators of the base were the persons on whom the condition would fall and so there would be no problem of securing compliance with the condition.

The reporter said of the proposed condition that the applicants might be thought to have the same lack of direct control over employees flying their helicopters as the BAA was considered to have over the CAA in the Aberdeen Airport case. He doubted if the planning authority would be able to rely on a condition requiring the operator to have aircraft approach and depart from the site in a specified direction. In the letter giving his decision the Secretary of State said that he was advised that he could not validly impose, as a condition of permission under the planning legislation, a requirement of this nature; regulation of flight paths was a matter for legislation other than the planning code. (Ref. P/PP/70/TC/13, October 2, 1981.)

7.20 Condition—control over land

In exercising their powers to determine an application for planning permission, the planning authority took into account the objections of the occupier of the neighbouring land. The objector suggested that the applicant might not be able to implement an essential feature of his proposal in that the objector claimed to have a property right in the wall to which the applicant would have to fix a flue if his proposal were to proceed. The Secretary of State agreed that the planning authority were right to refuse the application. (Ref. P/PPA/SL/58, February 15, 1979.)

7.21 Appellant's interest—conditions—under appellant's control
This was an appeal against an enforcement notice served in respect of an open-air retail market. The question was raised whether the appellant came within section 85(4) of the 1972 Act (*i.e.* was he owner, lessee, or occupier of the land or a person having an interest in the land for the purpose of serving an enforcement notice?). The Secretary of State considered that the fact that the appellant had lodged an appeal against the enforcement notice implied that he had an interest in the land.

The decision letter in this case pointed out that the power to impose conditions, as contained in section 27(1)(*a*) of the 1972 Act, was a power for regulating the development or use of any land under the control of the applicant (whether or not it was land in respect of which the application was made). It was brought out during the inquiry that the planning authority had taken court proceedings to obtain an interdict on the appellant's activities. In such circumstances the Secretary of State could not be satisfied that the land in respect of which the proposed condition would be imposed was under the control of the appellant. It therefore seemed to the Minister that the proposed conditions might be *ultra vires*. He therefore upheld the enforcement notice. (Ref. P/ENA/FB/5, June 6, 1977.)

7.22 Conditions—access
Application had been made for planning permission to erect housing on an area of land. Access to the site was by means of an unsurfaced track. The appellant owned only about 20 metres out of the track's total length of 80 metres. He merely had a right of access over the 75 per cent. of the track outwith his ownership. The reporter considered that the planning authority were correct in taking the view that planning conditions relating to the access could not validly be attached to any planning permission affecting the appeal site only. Further, any such conditions would have carried no prospect of implementation, given the necessary participation of other owners, including objectors. The reporter considered that for these reasons conditions would have run counter to the advice in paragraphs 29 and 37 of SDD Circular 18/1986. (Ref. P/PPA/CB/163, April 20, 1989.)

7.23 Condition—access—outwith applicant's control
The access which formed part of the application for a house depended on a connection with an adjacent road which was to be

provided as part of a development by others on land outwith the applicant's control. The test of whether a condition depending on land outwith the applicant's control is strict and the circumstances under which such a condition may be imposed are set out in SDD Circular 18/1986; it depends on the likelihood of the condition being fulfilled within such time as may enable the development to be commenced within the time limit imposed by the planning permission. This would normally be three years. There was no explicit commitment to build the access road. The appeal was therefore dismissed. (Ref. P/PPA/SN/83, October 26, 1987.)

7.24 Condition—control of land—dwelling-house

Application had been made for the erection of a dwelling-house and a garage in the grounds of a large house.

The reporter would have granted planning permission but the appellant neither owned nor had control of all the ground on which the access to the house would be formed. The reporter agreed with the appellant that ownership of land was not a prerequisite of an application for planning permission and had considered whether it would be possible to grant outline planning permission, leaving the means of access as a reserved matter for which a detailed application could be submitted at a later date. However, in view of what was known about the legal position— the access would require in part to be constructed over land owned by the district council who would not sell or lease the necessary land—he considered this was the stage at which the matter should be addressed.

In the reporter's view any approval of the appellant's proposal would have to be accompanied by a condition requiring the construction of the access before the house was occupied, otherwise there was a risk of the house being built without an access, which would lead to problems of enforcement. SDD Circular 18/1986 suggested that it would not be *ultra vires* to impose conditions relating to land which was not under the appellant's control (provided that—as in this case—such land was situated within the application site), but the circular made it clear that such a condition should only be imposed if the circumstances were such that "it would not be unreasonable to expect that the construction of an access would be carried out." In the present case the district council had refused to sell or lease the ground. Such a condition could not therefore be imposed and it followed therefore that planning permission could not be granted. (Ref. P/PPA/SU/217, May 12, 1987.)

7.25 Condition—failure to comply—land not under applicant's control
This was an appeal against the planning authority's failure to give a decision within the prescribed period on an application for planning permission. The application was for the substitution of a pair of semi-detached houses for a different house type shown in the planning application for the final phase of a large housing development. Planning permission had originally been granted in 1978; subsequently, in 1982 an altered planning permission had been granted and changes in some of the house types had been permitted.

Though the plan which accompanied the planning application showed a strip of ground linking the final phase to a nearby street, the applicants had explained to the planning authority, after the 1982 permission, that they did not own the strip of ground, nor could they acquire it at a reasonable price and they would therefore be unable to construct the pedestrian link shown on the plan.

The planning authority claimed that the pedestrian link was an essential part of the housing development and a condition requiring its construction had been included in each of the planning permissions referred to above. Though the planning authority had no objection to the substitution of house types, it considered the substitution to be part of an application for a revision of the whole final phase. The authority therefore considered it competent to withhold planning permission for the appeal proposal until the developers showed they were willing and able to construct the pedestrian link.

The reporter saw no objection to the proposed substitution and believed that the planning authority's action in withholding planning permission in order to secure the implementation of a condition imposed on a different application for planning permission was not within the powers of the Town and Country Planning (Scotland) Act 1972. (Ref. P/PPA/SR/58, December 11, 1984.)

7.26 Condition—"ultra vires"—mobile home
Planning permission for the erection of a house had been granted subject to a condition that allowed a mobile home on the site until the occupation of the dwelling-house. At that time the mobile home was to be removed. The house was now occupied and the planning authority served an enforcement notice requiring removal of the mobile home.

In the reporter's view section 27(1)(*a*) of the 1972 Act (conditional grant of planning permission) could not be construed as enabling a planning authority when granting planning permission for one development (the house) to approve another development (the mobile home) which clearly required planning permission and which did not form part and parcel of the application for the first development by means of a condition imposed on the former. Planning permission for the retention of the mobile home could only have been granted following submission of a planning application under the Act.

Because the planning authority's case was based on non-compliance with an *ultra vires* condition, it was, in the reporter's opinion, so materially defective that it was incapable of correction. (Ref. P/ENA/GD/23, June 27, 1988.)

7.27 Planning permission—condition—advertisement display

Planning permission relating to a fascia sign at office premises was granted subject to a condition that "notwithstanding the Town and Country Planning (Control of Advertisements) (Scotland) Regulations 1961," details of any advertisement, fascia signs or projecting signs should be submitted for the approval of the planning authority. The Secretary of State stated that control of advertisements was generally a matter to be dealt with under the regulations and that it was inappropriate to seek to regulate advertisements by attaching conditions to a planning permission. (Refs. P/PPA/HF/45; and P/ADA/HF/1, May 4, 1982.)

7.28 Condition—uncertainty

An enforcement notice was served in respect of the planning authority's refusal to amend or delete several conditions imposed on the grant of planning permission for the use of a site as a metal container storage area. One of the conditions provided that the site was to be kept in a clean and tidy condition at all times to the satisfaction of the Director of Planning. The reporter said that he could appreciate the authority's concern to protect residential amenity but he had to say that SDD Circular 18/1986 made it quite clear (paragraph 31 and paragraph 10 of Appendix B) that this condition was *ultra vires* as the appellants could not be sure what standard of tidiness was required by the authority. (Ref. P/PPA/SL/524, January 30, 1989.)

7.29 Condition—garage shop—items permitted for sale

A condition attached to permission for the erection of a shop and pump control at the appellant's petrol filling station provided that "the type of goods to be sold in the shop be restricted to garage trade related or motor accessories." The reason given was "in the interest of amenity."

It was submitted that the appellant's intention was to sell both the items mentioned in the condition and also consumer items. The planning authority claimed that the shop would attract customers from surrounding residential areas and from a nearby school. The site was, they argued, unsuitable for use as a "corner shop." They feared that if sales were unrestricted, the shop would attract customers on foot with consequent danger to both pedestrian and vehicular traffic.

The reporter considered that the range of goods covered by the words "motor accessories" and "garage trade related" was unclear. At the inquiry no precise definition was put forward. The reporter found the situation unsatisfactory in that in drafting conditions it was essential to make clear to a developer what he was required to do or was not allowed to do. Here the appellant had permission for a shop but the condition made it impossible for him to be sure what he might sell in it. It would be impracticable to require the shopkeeper to obtain consent from the planning department every time he wished to vary the range of goods sold. The reporter also found the reason for the condition too vague—"amenity" was a word open to wide interpretation. Not only was the condition imprecise, impracticable and therefore unreasonable, it was unnecessary to restrict the goods sold. The reporter therefore excised the condition. (Ref. P/PPA/TA/95, June 6, 1986.)

7.30 Condition—breach—gas meter boxes
An enforcement notice alleged the unauthorised installation of four gas meter boxes at the front of a building. The notice required the removal of the boxes. The building was a two-storey red sandstone mid-terraced property with a basement. The meter boxes were situated beside the main door. The property was in a conservation area. There were also two burglar alarms on the front of the building. Planning permission for sub-division of the property into four flats had been granted subject to a condition that the gas meter boxes be installed in an existing outhouse at the rear of the property.

The reporter said that by painting the boxes brown the visual impact of the meter boxes had been reduced but they were still an alien intrusion on the attractive front of the property. He considered that planning permission should therefore be refused. (Ref. P/ENA/SL/228, September 15, 1987.)

7.31 Condition—occupancy—over-restrictive
The planning authority stated that the occupation of a house on an estate was contrary to a condition limiting occupancy to a

person employed on the estate. The appellant stated that it was difficult to find suitable staff at short notice and in the meantime he had let the house. The appeal was dismissed but the condition was amended to restrict occupancy to estate workers only except "with the prior written consent" of the planning authority "which shall not be unreasonably withheld." (Ref. P/ENA/GD/12, April 23, 1980.)

7.32 Green belt—occupancy condition—cemetery

This was an appeal against a condition attached to a planning permission for the erection of a single-storey house. A condition was imposed providing that occupation of the house should be limited to a person employed in Sandymount Cemetery or a dependant of such a person residing with him. The appellant argued that the purchaser of the house was prepared to regard himself as a security agent for the cemetery company but it might not be possible to ensure that that relationship would continue following any future change of ownership. The planning authority submitted that the site was in the green belt and that without the proposed condition, the development would simply be a speculative residential proposal. The Secretary of State took the view that as the council had granted planning permission they appeared to have accepted that the appellant's case related to the needs of an approved green belt function. He dismissed the appeal. (Ref. P/PPA/SL/20, May 13, 1977.)

7.33 Material considerations—agricultural occupancy condition—qualified occupier

The reporter was satisfied that a proper and sustained effort had been made to dispose of a house which was subject to a condition restricting occupation to persons employed in agriculture or forestry but that no one qualified to occupy it had come forward to purchase it. He was also satisfied that there was no foreseeable agricultural need for the house and that it would be wasteful to leave it empty and deteriorating. He concluded that to remove the condition would not weaken the proper operation of development control. (Ref. P/PPA/FB/227, May 28, 1987.)

7.34 Motel—use by non-residents

In granting planning permission for a motel, a condition was imposed to the effect that facilities forming part of the proposed development should be restricted to use by residents only. The appellants challenged the condition as unduly restrictive. The reporter could see no objection to the opening of the restaurant to non-residents and that a table licence for non-residents would be reasonable. Availability of bar facilities to non-residents was a matter for the licensing authority. No sound reason had been demonstrated for the condition and the reporter therefore discharged it. (Ref. P/PPA/SU/106, November 30, 1981.)

7.35 Conditions—retrospective planning permission

On a point of legal principle, counsel for the appellants argued that since retrospective grants of planning permission were dealt with under section 29 of the 1972 Act and since section 29 made no reference to sections 26 and 27 (the statutory provisions dealing with the imposition of conditions on planning permissions), the planning authority had no power to impose conditions on a grant of retrospective permission.

No legal authority was offered for this proposition and in the absence of such authority the reporter could see no reason why conditions should not be imposed on retrospective planning permissions. He could not agree that the use in section 27(1) of the phrase "Without prejudice to the generality of section 26(1) of this Act, conditions may be imposed on the grant of planning permission thereunder" precluded the imposition of conditions on a grant of retrospective planning permission under section 29. If this were not the case, there would be serious problems in regularising the position of many unauthorised uses. (Ref. P/PPA/SK/74, August 25, 1987.)

7.36 Condition—appeal—refusal of planning permission

An appeal was lodged against a condition imposed on a grant of outline planning permission for a house. Under section 33 of the 1972 Act the Secretary of State or the reporter may, on appeal, reverse any part of the original decision. Here the reporter employed section 33 to hold that planning permission should not be granted. (Ref. P/PPA/HE/15, November 11, 1987.)

7.37 Conditions—inconsistency—challenge

In granting outline planning permission for a development the reporter attached two conditions to the permission. The conditions were; (a) that the layout of the driveway and sight lines at the entrance to the site should meet the requirements of the highway authority; and (b) that steps should be taken in the detailed design and construction of the development to retain and protect all trees and hedges along the boundaries of the site. The district council made application to the Court of Session to quash the conditions on the ground that they were inconsistent. No

answers to the application were lodged on behalf of the Secretary
of State and the conditions were therefore quashed by the court.
(Ref. P/PPA/SC/145, July 15, 1987.)

7.38 Conditional planning permission—personal planning permission

Acting in breach of planning control, the appellant repaired
one vehicle at a time at his premises. Given that the adverse
effect of the use was thus likely to be as small as it could be, the
reporter gave careful consideration to the possibility of making
planning permission personal to the appellant and so circumscrib-
ing the permission by conditions that any change from the
present level of use would be prevented.

He found this course to be unsatisfactory. For administrative
reasons the principle that planning permission runs with the land
should be followed in the great majority of cases. Personal
permissions should, he thought, be granted only to avoid exceptional hardship and he did not accept that such a question arose
here. An attempt to bind the use by conditions was likely to fail
because it was natural that as time went by the appellant would
seek to expand his business as far as the size of the premises
allowed and enforcement of such detailed conditions as would
have to be imposed was not a practical proposition for any
planning authority. (Ref. P/ENA/D/61, January 22, 1987.)

7.39 Failure to comply with planning permission—implied condition

An extension to a building did not conform in a number of
respects with the development for which planning permission had
been granted. The planning authority served an enforcement
notice, maintaining that the building was constructed contrary to
an implied condition requiring compliance with the plans accompanying the application for planning permission. The reporter did
not accept that there could be any implied conditions in a grant
of a planning permission. Here the grant of permission was
unconditional and he found no substance in the planning authority's argument that the breach of planning control amounted to a
failure to comply with an implied condition requiring conformity
with the approved plans. The breach of planning control was
clearly the carrying out of development without the benefit of
planning permission as the building actually constructed was not
the building which received planning permission. Section 85(4)(*a*)
of the 1972 Act allows the Secretary of State to correct a defect
or error in an enforcement notice provided the error is not
material. In this instance the defect was material and was not
open to correction in this way. The reporter therefore found that

the enforcement notice was a nullity. (Ref. P/ENA/HE/25, September 29, 1986.)

7.40　Condition—occupancy—dwelling-house—personal circumstances

Planning permission was granted for a house subject to a condition that the permission should enure only for the benefit of the applicant, her heirs and successors and any other person showing a special need to live in the area. After her marriage, an application for outline permission was made in the name of husband and wife. A similar condition was imposed, amended so that the permission enured for the benefit of the husband as well as the wife.

On their wishing to sell the house, the appellants said that if the meaning of the condition had been obvious to them, they would not have purchased the site. The husband had not expected to be in the area for more than five years. It had appeared to him that the condition stated only that the opportunity to build a house was limited to certain persons. He only discovered the council's meaning in 1984. The husband had been sent to England and it was necessary to sell the house if the family were not to be split up.

Evidence was given by an estate agent that the house had been advertised in the newspapers over a period of three weeks. Likely purchasers were sent a brochure which mentioned the condition. About 10 or 12 recipients of the brochure had gone further. Offers over £105,000 had been invited, but none had been received. The estate agent believed that it was the condition rather than the price that was the obstacle. Since then the agency had continued its efforts to sell the property by circulating clients.

The appellant submitted that the condition, though not devoid of meaning, was ambiguous and was capable of being read by both laymen and solicitors in a different way from that of the council.

The council argued that the removal of the condition would devalue their policies. The condition had been imposed in the interests of the amenity of the area. Personal circumstances were relevant considerations but each case had to be looked at on its own merits. There had to be a planning reason to remove the condition and here there was none. The property had not been on the market for an excessively long time. The condition was clearly intended to restrict occupation, and its continuing nature was demonstrated by the reference to heirs, successors, etc. Under any other interpretation the condition would have little or no value in achieving a planning purpose. In *Fawcett Properties*

Ltd. v. *Buckingham County Council* [1961] A.C. 636 Lord
Denning said that a planning permission was only void for
uncertainty if it could be given no ascertainable or sensible
meaning. It was not enough that it was ambiguous. That dictum
was followed in Scotland in *Caledonian Terminal Investments
Ltd.* v. *Edinburgh Corporation*, 1970 S.C. 271; 1970 S.L.T. 362.

The reporter said he considered the condition to be badly
drafted and capable of misinterpretation by those not familiar
with the planning authority's policies. However, in the light of
Fawcett Properties the reporter held with some reluctance that
the condition had to be held to refer to the occupancy of the
house. (Ref. P/PPA/SH/54, December 19, 1985.)

7.41 House—agricultural occupancy condition

An agricultural holding had been subdivided. The reporter
granted planning permission for a new house subject to a
condition that it be occupied by a person working on the
agricultural holding. The reporter also imposed a condition to the
effect that an existing cottage on the land, presently occupied,
should, when the premises were vacated, cease to be used as a
dwelling-house. (Ref. P/PPA/SU/193, August 8, 1986.)

7.42 Estate yard—agriculture or forestry—occupancy condition

Planning permission had been granted for the use of a site as
an estate yard. It was considered essential for proper management and maintenance that a residence for an employee should
be provided on the site. The Secretary of State agreed that the
yard was a suitable use in the green belt and considered that the
appellants had made out a reasonable case. In granting planning
permission the Secretary of State imposed a condition that "the
occupation of the dwelling-house shall be limited to a person
solely or mainly employed, or last employed, in the locality in
agriculture as defined in section 275(1) of the Town and Country
Planning (Scotland) Act 1972, or in forestry (including any
dependants of such person residing with him), or a widow or
widower of such a person." (Ref. P/PPA/SC/3, July 7, 1976.)

7.43 House in country—occupancy condition

Planning permission had been granted for a house subject to a
condition that the house should only be occupied by an employee
of a nearby manufacturer. The appellant said that this condition
would make the house unsaleable and made it impossible for him
to obtain a mortgage. The reporter agreed with the council's
policy on houses in the countryside but considered the condition

to be unreasonable. The house would not be allowed without the condition and therefore, exercising his powers under section 33 of the 1972 Act to treat the application as if it had been made to the Secretary of State in the first place, he refused permission for the erection of the house. (Ref. P/PPA/D/51, October 24, 1979.)

7.44   Condition—restriction on occupancy

Planning permission was granted for the erection of five houses, each subject to a condition that:

> "The occupation of the dwellings hereby approved shall be limited to those instances where the first occupation will be by persons already resident in the area or by other persons who are otherwise entitled to such accommodation by virtue of their employment or other direct interest in the economic or social structure of the area."

The condition was stated to be imposed "in order to comply with the terms of policy 6 within the Loch Lomond Subject Plan." Policy 6 was not applicable to the site and even if it had been the reasons for it could only be achieved by refusing to permit development which would have an adverse effect on landscape, agriculture, forestry and nature conservation interests. They would not be achieved by placing a restriction on the occupancy of new dwellings.

In paragraph 82 of SDD Circular 18/1986 there is an unequivocal statement that the Secretary of State rejects domestic occupancy conditions of the kind under consideration. The undesirable consequences of the imposition of such conditions are set out and it is made clear that only in exceptional cases involving individual houses might such a condition be appropriate. They were not appropriate here. (Ref. P/PPA/CC/139, July 31, 1986.)

7.45   Conditions—modification of permission

A planning application had been made for a block of six two-storey terraced houses set at right angles to a road. Permission was granted for a maximum of three dwellings. A further condition was that the dwellings were to be single-storey dwellings. The reason for the conditions was in order to secure the proper development of the area with regard to the size of the site. The reporter said that it was inappropriate to use planning conditions to modify a proposal so that it became substantially different from that for which the applicant was seeking approval. In determining a planning appeal it is open to the Secretary of

State to consider the application as if it had been made to him in the first place and that is what occurred here. The reporter considered that the site could only accommodate two houses. It was not competent to use a planning condition to change a project so that it became substantially different from that proposed by the applicant; he was therefore unable to approve the development of two houses in response to an application seeking permission for six houses. Permission was therefore refused. (Ref. P/PPA/TC/193, June 2, 1986.)

7.46 Conditions—power of reporter—discothèque
This was an appeal against two conditions attached to a grant of planning permission for a discothèque. The conditions required that the premises should not operate after 1 a.m. on Friday and Saturday and after 12 midnight on Sunday to Thursday. The use caused considerable disturbance to the occupiers of adjacent premises. The reporter pointed out that under section 33(3) of the Town and Country Planning (Scotland) Act 1972 the Secretary of State was empowered to decide an appeal as if the application had been made to him in the first place. The reporter said he intended to exercise that power and to impose fresh conditions. As required, notice of that intention was given to the parties. He imposed conditions requiring that all persons should have left the premises by midnight on Mondays to Saturdays and that the premises should not open at all on Sundays. (Ref. P/PPA/CC/128, December 17, 1985.)

7.47 Conditions—contradictory—dwelling-houses
Planning permission in outline was granted for the demolition of a house known as Garden House and for the erection of three detached houses on the site. The planning permission was subject to three standard conditions regarding submission of detailed plans and reserved matters. However, condition (4) stated: "Notwithstanding conditions (1), (2) and (3) above, no consent is given or implied for the three detached dwellings, and the detailed application shall consist of a compact development based on the existing courtyard concept, being either a conversion of the existing Garden House . . . or a new development on the solum of Garden House itself and which should be designed by a principal in a registered architectural practice." The reason for the condition was "to ensure that the proposed development does not detract from the existing character of the site and surrounding area."

The reporter said that in granting planning permission the planning authority had accepted residential use of the appeal site and, specifically, the demolition of the Garden House and the erection of three detached houses on the site. The wording of condition (4) clearly contradicted this decision and offered the retention of the Garden House as an alternative. The reporter considered that condition (4) in its present form was invalid. The removal of the condition would not prevent the authority from exercising control over the development when a detailed proposal was submitted. (Ref. P/PP/75/GD/3, November 18, 1985.)

7.48   Conditions—claim that compliance impracticable—conditions accepted

This was an appeal against four of 10 conditions imposed on a grant of planning permission for a change of use to a paint-spraying workshop. Included in the four conditions were conditions concerning access and prohibiting Sunday work.

The appellant said that it was not practicable to comply with the conditions on access and Sunday working; these were essential to the viability of the business.

The reporter concluded that the planning authority's decision was correct in the context of a non-conforming use in a residential area. He considered the conditions imposed by the authority to be the minimum necessary to make this "bad neighbour" use acceptable in the area. However, it was the appellant's contention that compliance with the conditions was not feasible and would impose unacceptable operational and financial burdens on him. In the circumstances the reporter considered that the test of acceptability could not be met and was forced to the conclusion that this meant planning permission should be refused. The decision letter therefore stated the intention of the reporter to refuse permission unless representations were received persuading him otherwise.

The appellant then wrote withdrawing his appeal and stating he was prepared to accept the conditions. This withdrawal was accepted. The permission granted by the planning authority therefore stood. (Ref. P/PPA/TA/80, October 8, 1985.)

7.49   Condition—agricultural track—erection of house

Planning permission had been granted for the erection of a house subject to a condition that an existing agricultural track within the site be retained as a means of access to adjacent agricultural land, the reason for the condition being that it was not always easy for the farmer of the adjoining land to use alternative accesses. The reporter said the access was convenient to the farmer who had the use of it. However, the retention of the means of access by way of a planning condition should not be imposed in this fashion. It was not for a planning authority to intervene in a dispute of this kind between individual adjoining proprietors. If the farmer had a right of access, then the condition was unnecessary; if no such right existed the condition was onerous in requiring such access to be allowed. If the parties wished to pursue the question it had to be for the courts to decide ultimately. (Ref. P/PPA/CB/103, September 13, 1985.)

7.50 Section 50 agreement—condition
    The main issue in this appeal was whether a cottage should be refurbished as one of the three dwellings the planning authority were prepared to permit on the site. Once that issue was decided, and demolition allowed, it was thought it would be possible to conclude a section 50 agreement to resolve a drainage problem which affected land outwith the appeal site.

    A minute of agreement inviting the reporter to issue planning permission and containing a requirement to impose a condition suspending the operation of the permission until one or more section 50 agreements had been concluded raised doubts in the mind of the reporter. Although both parties had agreed in principle to the need for agreements, their terms were not known, even in outline, and he felt that a planning permission subject to such a condition would lack adequate specification. Instead, therefore, of granting a conditional permission, the reporter considered that the proper course was to issue a letter of intent, so allowing the parties to adjust matters of detail and execute appropriate agreements. The appeal therefore remained before the reporter for decision; he was prepared to issue a formal permission, with detailed conditions, when the remaining matters had been resolved. Alternatively, if the agreements were concluded and the planning authority felt able to do so, they could issue a detailed planning permission and the appeal could be withdrawn. (Ref. P/PPA/GA/245, June 18, 1985.)

7.51 Performance bond—opencast mining
    A scheme for opencast mining and rehabilitation of pit bings was granted permission by the reporter subject to the conditions that:
    "Before the development is begun the applicants shall give the planning authority an undertaking in writing to implement a scheme of containing and surfacing of the pit bings in accordance with the regional council's designs and specifications"; and
    "Before the development is begun a performance guarantee bond in the sum of £250,000 shall be lodged by the applicants with the planning authority." (Ref. P/PPA/LC/114, July 3, 1985.)

7.52 Condition—bond required

The reporter, in granting planning permission, imposed a condition to the effect that the development was not to be begun until the developer had delivered to the planning authority a bond or surety covering the estimated cost of completing the roads and footpaths relating to the development, all to the satisfaction of the planning authority. (Ref. P/PPA/B/117, April 4, 1985.)

7.53 Condition—retail warehouse—restriction

Planning permission was granted in respect of a retail furniture showroom for the display and sale of hard and soft household furnishings but for no other purpose (notwithstanding the provisions of the Town and Country Planning (Use Classes) (Scotland) Order 1973). The planning authority considered that a different type of retail use might have very different parking requirements. The reporter saw no reason why a condition restricting the use of premises to a retail furniture warehouse was not valid or enforceable. (Ref. P/PPA/SQ/149, August 27, 1984.)

7.54 Conditions—market garden/garden centre—items permitted for sale

The reporter granted planning permission for a market garden/garden centre subject to a condition that retail sales should be of plants grown or propagated on the site together with such items as seeds, fertilisers, weedkillers, etc., but excluding other manufactured items such as powered tools, greenhouses, huts and garden furniture (or otherwise as might be agreed with the planning authority in terms of an agreement under section 50 of the 1972 Act). (Ref. P/PPA/SC/102, July 20, 1984.)

7.55 Condition—restriction of range of goods—retail warehouse

The planning authority argued that if a large retail store were to be permitted, a condition should be imposed restricting the range of goods that might be sold. Their desire for such a condition rested on a fear that some established shopping centres with a current surplus of space or with under-used space might have their trading position undermined by competition from elsewhere.

The reporter said: "Whilst appreciating this desire of the council to protect existing commercial outlets in order to foster their continuing viability, I am not convinced that it is a proper function of a district planning authority to restrict by means of development control conditions the precise range of goods which a retail firm may legitimately offer for sale. Where special restrictions are in the public interest, Parliament makes provision for them—if necessary by a licensing system or other means of control . . . It is axiomatic that no condition should be imposed on a grant of planning permission unless it is necessary, reasonable, relevant to planning, precise and enforceable. The specific condition advocated by the council at this inquiry does not meet these criteria." (Ref. P/PPA/TB/59, June 18, 1984.)

7.56 Conditions—limitations

The appellants, a building society, sought permission to change the use of shop premises to a building society office. These premises were only a short distance from the society's present office but were slightly larger. The planning authority refused permission on the ground that the proposal would lead to the unnecessary loss of a shop and of "live" frontage on a main shopping street. The appellants stated that if permission were granted they were prepared to accept a condition to the effect that their present office should not be used otherwise than as a shop.

The reporter considered that the proposed change of use would not be prejudicial to what was described as "the delicate balance of the retail pattern" in the area, provided that the society's present office reverted to shop use. He therefore found it necessary to consider how such reversion could be legally secured.

He said: "I take the view that it is inappropriate that a condition of planning permission for the change of use of [the premises proposed for the new office] should be the means, in effect, of granting planning permission for the change of use of [the present office], notwithstanding the fact that both properties are in [the society's] ownership." He said he had considered "the possibility of imposing conditions relative to an order or agreement under sections 49 and 50 of the [1972] Act" but concluded that "such conditions would not be valid" since it was not known that the society would be able to secure the planning authority's cooperation in fulfilling them. (Section 49 of the 1972 Act empowers a planning authority to make an order discontinuing the use of a building, while section 50 enables an authority to enter into an agreement restricting or regulating the development or use of land.)

The reporter also considered the default powers provided by section 260 of the 1972 Act. By means of this provision the Secretary of State could himself make an order under section 49.

In the reporter's view, however, there was "no call for the employment of these powers in a case where the public interest is not involved."

The reporter concluded that it was not apparent that the reversion of the present building society office to shop use could be secured in the granting of planning permission for the change of use of the shop premises which were the subject of the appeal and since the reversion of the present office to shop use was an essential precondition of a favourable decision on the proposal, the appeal had to fail. (Ref. P/ENA/GA/29, April 16, 1982.)

7.57 Condition—no breach

Planning permission had been granted in 1975 for housing development, the permission being subject to a condition that certain landscaping works be carried out on the site. An enforcement notice was served by the planning authority in respect of the alleged failure on the part of the appellants to carry out landscaping works on the appeal site. The Secretary of State concluded that no breach of planning control had occurred. The condition in question merely required the submission to the planning authority of detailed plans and particulars of certain matters, including landscaping, before any work was begun. Detailed approval of these matters (including landscaping) had been obtained before work started on the housing development. The condition in the planning permission had therefore been complied with; there was nothing in the condition which required that any of the permitted development, be it the houses, landscaping or whatever, should actually be carried out. The appeal against the enforcement notice was therefore upheld. (Ref. P/ENA/SR/14, December 19, 1980.)

7.58 Condition—restriction on occupancy

A condition attached to a planning permission for a dwelling-house limited occupation of the dwelling to "a person employed locally in agriculture as defined in section 113(1) of the Town and Country Planning Act 1947, or in forestry or a dependant of such a person living with him." Though the appellant interpreted this condition as requiring the occupant of the house to be engaged full-time in agriculture or forestry, the planning authority considered the condition less restrictive than that. (Ref. P/PPA/SS/66, December 16, 1977.)

7.59 Condition—failure to state reason

Failure to state a reason for the imposition of a condition was held not to invalidate the condition. (Ref. P/PPA/LA/42, November 23, 1977.)

7.60 Condition—limit on number of houses

Planning permission had been granted in outline for two houses subject to a condition that "the number of houses be limited to one only." The reason for the condition was in order that the general amenity of the area should not be affected.

Given their view that two dwelling-houses would be inappropriate, the correct course of action would have been to invite a voluntary reduction of the application from two houses to one. Failing agreement on such a revision, outright refusal of permission for two dwelling-houses would have presumably followed. The appeal was dismissed. (Ref. P/PPA/TA/145, November 23, 1988.)

7.61 Condition—suspensive

The reporter's one concern about the grant of planning permission for a particular development was that he considered road operations were required before the development could go ahead. The land required for these works was not owned by the appellants. Could a condition be imposed requiring that the developers should not carry out the development before the road works were carried out? SDD Circular 18/1986 states that: "the test of whether such a condition is reasonable is strict; it amounts to whether there are at least reasonable prospects of the action in question being performed . . . The reasonableness of such a requirement in all cases depends on the likelihood of the precondition being fulfilled within such time as to enable the development to be commenced within the time limit imposed by the permission." It was not certain who owned the land required for the road improvement. Nevertheless, in the absence of known opposition and in view of the committed approach of the appellants, the reporter found there to be a reasonable prospect of the land becoming available. The reporter therefore concluded that a suspensive condition was appropriate in this case. (Ref. P/PPA/SM/125, August 1, 1988.)

7.62 Planning permission—condition—whether competent—whether necessary—amusement machines

A condition attached to a grant of planning permission for use of part of premises as an amusement arcade restricted the arcade to six machines. The reporter considered whether it was competent and necessary for the planning authority to control the scale of an operation that had been approved. He said that it was often appropriate for a planning authority to control the scale of operation of a change of use that had been approved, as what would be acceptable on a small or medium scale might be unacceptable on a large scale. Such control was particularly important where the site approved for change of use had a large or variable potential capacity. A condition controlling the scale of operation would be competent, provided that it met the usual criteria regarding relevance, reasonableness, precision, etc. Here, however, the reporter thought the area capable of accommodating a larger number of amusement machines than the authority specified in the condition attached to the planning permission. (Refs. P/PPA/LD/44; P/EUC/LD/2, March 9, 1983.)

7.63 Condition—unenforceable

A standard condition attached to a grant of planning permission required the fulfilment of two separate requirements: (a) that details were submitted (which had been done); and (b) that these details be approved by the Director of Planning. The latter requirement was in the reporter's opinion outwith the control of the appellant and therefore could not be enforced. On this and other grounds the reporter found the condition unreasonable and held that it ought to be discharged. (Ref. P/ENA/GA/46, January 19, 1983.)

7.64 Condition—unenforceable

A condition of planning permission for a housing estate required the erection of a screen fence before occupation of the houses. The reporter was in no doubt that a breach of the condition had occurred but since the houses were now occupied there was no way of enforcing the condition. (Ref. P/ENA/SC/17, July 15, 1981.)

7.65 Condition—time limit—not complied with—whether enforceable

Planning permission had been granted subject to conditions for the change of use of premises to a motor vehicle, tyre repair and exhaust-fitting centre. One of the conditions was to the effect that all alterations and building works were to be completed by September 30, 1983. An enforcement notice was served alleging breach of that (and other) conditions.

An appeal was lodged on the ground that the condition alleged not to have been complied with ought to be discharged (section 85(1)(*a*)). The appellant argued that the condition was totally unenforceable since it was impossible to comply with the requirement—the date specified in the condition—by which time the work was to have been completed. In support of this view the appellant quoted from DoE Circular 5/68 which stated, *inter alia*:

"A condition requiring that the development permitted should be completed within a specified period should never be imposed: it is in practice incapable of enforcement. Once a time limit has expired, it is too late to require compliance with the condition and impracticable to enforce against the development already carried out."

On this basis the appellant asked that the enforcement notice be quashed.

The planning authority said that the appellant was stating the obvious. But compliance with the time condition was not a requirement of the enforcement notice which allowed until April 27, 1985 for completion of the outstanding work.

The reporter said that in general he would agree with the appellant's view and with the advice in DoE Circular 5/68. A more usual solution to ensure that conditions were implemented would be to require them to be completed prior to the land or premises being occupied or operated for the approved proposal. However, there were situations where a specified period for compliance was reasonable and in his opinion that was so where development had taken place and was operational (as here) without the grant of planning permission but where the authority were disposed to grant retrospective planning permission subject to certain conditions (as here). In these circumstances the reporter did not find it necessary or appropriate to discharge the condition. Though it was no longer capable of enforcement, its purpose was primarily to underline the importance and urgency of the measures required to be taken to secure a satisfactory form of development.

The appeal therefore failed and the enforcement notice was upheld. (Ref. P/ENA/FA/33, August 13, 1985.)

7.66 Condition—unenforceable

There was a failure to implement a condition relating to sight lines at an access. The requirements of the condition could not be met. If the requirements could not be met, the condition could not be enforced; and a condition which could not be enforced should not have been imposed in the first place. (See SDD Circular 18/1986, paragraphs 12, 29, 37 and 38). (Ref. P/PPA/TA/104, August 15, 1986.)

SECTION 8

SECTION 50 AGREEMENTS

See generally Young and Rowan-Robinson, *Scottish Planning Law and Procedure*, pp. 276–288; and Rowan-Robinson and Young, *Planning by Agreement in Scotland*.

Section 50 of the Town and Country Planning (Scotland) Act 1972 provides that a planning authority may enter into an agreement with any person interested in land in their area for the purpose of "restricting or regulating" the development or use of land. The use of such agreements in Scotland appears to be on the increase. If recorded in the Register of Sasines or the Land Register, as appropriate, such an agreement will be enforceable at the instance of the planning authority against singular successors in title.

Planning appeals are seldom likely to be concerned with agreements made under section 50 of the 1972 Act but this section contains summaries of three appeal decisions in which questions relating to planning agreements arose.

APPEAL DECISIONS

8.1 Section 50 agreement—interpretation and effect

The appellant submitted that an agreement under section 50 of the 1972 Act which he had entered into at the time of receiving planning permission for a garden centre, shop, etc. fell if a new planning permission were granted. The reporter pointed out that there was no provision in the 1972 Act for the overriding of a section 50 agreement by the Secretary of State. In the case of a successful appeal here, the appellant would, if some matter covered in the agreement were affected, have to seek to renegotiate an amendment of the agreement.

The planning authority argued that the section 50 agreement regulated the type of goods that might be sold over the whole 4 acres occupied by the appellant. The reporter did not accept this interpretation. In his view, a section 50 agreement being one which creates conditions which run with the land, had to be construed strictly. The preamble to the agreement did narrate that the appellant owned the whole 4 acres but did not specifically provide that the agreement affected the whole area. That being so, the scope of the restrictions effected by the agreement had to be deduced from the clauses specifying them. The first clause stated that only horticultural goods might be sold from the garden centre. The second clause declared that certain categories of goods (including household goods, other than those directly related to gardens) could not be sold. That passage did not specify the area to which it was applicable and the only safe deduction was that as the sale of garden goods was prohibited, the restriction had to be implied as applying to the garden centre and the garden shop. The second clause also provided that in the retail shop there might be sold such general items as were normally to be found in a country general merchant's shop.

That declaration was not specifically restrictive but even if it were treated as a restriction on what might be sold in the shop, it was, in the reporter's view, limited in its effect to the retail shop. The third clause stated that the appellant was permitted to sell caravans but that the display and storage thereof had to be kept inside certain buildings. To the reporter's mind that did not restrict the appellant as to where the sale of caravans might take place, it only restricted the place they were to be kept. The reporter therefore accepted the argument for the appellant that the section 50 agreement affected only the garden centre and shop, the retail shop and the snack bar for which permission was granted in 1982. The agreement did not prevent a change of use from selling caravans to selling furniture in a building not covered by the agreement. (Ref. P/PPA/CB/83, April 19, 1984.)

8.2 Section 50 agreement—encouraged by reporter

The reporter had stated in a letter to the parties to an appeal that he was disposed to grant outline planning permission for the development of a hotel, marina and self-catering holiday complex but, before doing so, he wished to see a concluded agreement made under section 50 of the 1972 Act relating to the provision and maintenance of the wildlife area and related matters. If an agreement could not be concluded he said that he would have to consider whether, as a second best, these matters could be made the subject of enforceable conditions. He also said that he would welcome suggestions as to appropriate conditions from the planning authority. He hoped his statement of intent would encourage both parties in drafting a section 50 agreement with reasonable restrictions and undertakings. (Ref. P/ENA/B/6, November 28, 1983.)

8.3 Section 50 agreement—supermarket—additional parking spaces

An application had been made for a retail supermarket. The appellants accepted the need to enter into an agreement guaranteeing that they would meet the cost of implementing a traffic management scheme. They were also prepared to accept the confirmation of a traffic management order. In addition, they would accept a condition that the development should not be begun until the necessary improvements had been carried out. To compensate for the 40 or so street parking places that would be lost when the order was made, the appellants offered to provide additional parking spaces within the site to an agreed total of 20 spaces. (Ref. P/PPA/LA/377, February 25, 1986.)

SECTION 9

ENFORCEMENT OF PLANNING CONTROL

See generally Young and Rowan-Robinson, *Scottish Planning Law and Procedure*, pp. 289–352.

The legislation on the enforcement of planning control is intrinsically very complex. The law relating to enforcement is an area in which legalism flourishes. The Town and Country Planning (Scotland) Act 1972 makes specific provision for the enforcement of control over listed buildings, trees, advertisements, mineral development, etc., but the present section deals with appeal decisions concerned with the enforcement of control over development which has been carried out without planning permission or which has been carried out in contravention of a condition attached to a grant of planning permission. The present law is to be found in Part V of the 1972 Act (as amended).

Under the 1972 Act unauthorised development is not of itself a criminal offence. Before prosecution can be undertaken or before the planning authority can enter on the land and carry out the necessary works, an enforcement notice must have come into effect without the required steps having been taken.

Any breach of planning control which took place before the end of 1964 is immune from enforcement action. Further, where the breach consists of—

(1) the carrying out without planning permission of building, engineering, mining or other operations; or

(2) failure to comply with any condition or limitation relating to the carrying out of such operations; or

(3) the making, without planning permission, of a change of use of any building to use as a single dwelling-house;

an enforcement notice can only be served within four years of the breach occurring. It is for any person claiming the benefit of the "four year" immunity to establish the date on which the breach of planning control occurred.

An enforcement notice is to be served on the owner, lessee and occupier of the land to which it relates, and on any other person having an interest in that land if, in the authority's opinion, that interest is materially affected by the notice. An enforcement notice cannot take effect until a period of not less than 28 days has elapsed from the date on which the last person was served with the notice. When an appeal against an enforcement notice is lodged, the enforcement notice is of no effect pending the final determination or withdrawal of the appeal.

Under the 1972 Act (as amended) an enforcement notice must specify—

   (1)   the matters alleged to constitute a breach of planning control;

   (2)   the steps required to be taken to restore the land to its condition before the breach took place; the notice may also specify, as an alternative, the steps to bring the land to a condition acceptable to the planning authority;

   (3)   the date on which the notice is to take effect;

   (4)   the period or periods within which any steps specified are to be carried out;

   (5)   the precise boundaries of the land to which the notice relates;

   (6)   the reasons why the authority consider it expedient to serve an enforcement notice;

   (7)   an explanation of the rights of persons to appeal against the enforcement notice.

Appeal to the Secretary of State may be made on any one or more of the eight grounds specified in section 85(1) of the 1972 Act. On an appeal against an enforcement notice the Secretary of State or appointed person (the reporter) may correct any informality, error or defect if he is satisfied that the informality, error or defect is not material.

In the case of all unauthorised changes of use (except those relating to a change of use to a single dwelling-house) the only restriction on service of an enforcement notice is that the breach of planning control must have occurred after the end of 1964. This might make it difficult for a person with an interest in land to establish (notably for the benefit of an intending purchaser) that the use to which the land is being put is safe from enforcement action. In order to overcome this difficulty, the 1972 Act provides that where a person having an interest in land claims that a particular use of that land has become "established," he may apply to the planning authority for a certificate to that effect. Such a certificate is termed an established use certificate.

APPEAL DECISIONS

9.1 Enforcement notice—validity

An enforcement notice required the multiple occupation of a flat to be terminated. The appellant claimed that the boundaries of the flat were incorrectly shown on the plan which accompanied and formed part of the enforcement notice and that the notice was therefore invalid in terms of the Town and Country Planning (Enforcement of Control) (Scotland) Regulations 1984. In respect of this claim the reporter noted that regulation 3 of the Regulations required an enforcement notice to specify "the precise boundaries of the land to which the notice relates whether by reference to a plan or otherwise." The plan merely identified the tenement property shown on the ordnance survey map based on the street frontage at the close entry. This was inaccurate but as the notice described the premises as "Flat 1/2, 12 Clouston Street, Glasgow G20" the reporter considered that there could have been no doubt as to the location of the property affected by the notice. Accordingly the notice was not invalid. (Ref. P/ENA/SL/246, October 11, 1988.)

9.2 Enforcement notice—failure in service—prejudice

An enforcement notice must be served on the owner, lessee and occupier of the land in question and on any other person having an interest in the land, being an interest which in the opinion of the planning authority is materially affected by the notice (1972 Act, section 84(5)). Here an enforcement notice had not been served on heritable creditors (a bank). The reporter was satisfied that the appellants had not established that the bank's interest was materially affected by the failure to serve notice on them, or that the appellants' interest had been substantially prejudiced by the failure. The Secretary of State agreed. (Refs. P/ENA/GLW/54, 58–62, October 18, 1976.)

9.3 Enforcement notice—service—defect

An enforcement notice was served in respect of the stationing of two mobile homes at a hotel. It was claimed, *inter alia*, that the enforcement notice was not served as required by section 84(5) of the 1972 Act. From his study of the plan attached to the application for planning permission in 1974 and the plan attached to the enforcement notice, the reporter found that the area for which the temporary planning permission had been granted overlapped with and was not wholly within the area delineated on the plan attached to the enforcement notice, the latter being less than the total area now within the curtilage of the hotel. However, the reporter was satisfied that it was clear to the appellants which mobile homes were referred to in the notice. While the plan attached to the notice was defective in that it did not depict the land on which the mobile homes stood, the reporter considered that neither the appellants nor the planning authority had been in any way prejudiced. He was therefore of the opinion that the defect was not material and could be corrected in terms of section 85(4)(*a*) of the Town and Country Planning (Scotland) Act 1972 by reference in the enforcement notice to the plan attached to the temporary permission. The reporter also considered that the date referred to in the planning permission and in the enforcement notice, namely November 31, 1980, was a minor error, that the planning permission should be read as referring to November 30 and, also, in reliance on the power of correction contained in section 85(4)(*a*), that the enforcement notice could accordingly be corrected by substituting the date November 30, 1980. (Ref. P/ENA/W/27, March 20, 1985.)

9.4 Enforcement notice—non-service on owner—prejudice
   A husband and wife were joint owners of a property but an enforcement notice was served on the husband alone. The appellants (the husband and wife) argued that the requirements of section 84(5) (requiring service on the owner, lessee and occupier of land) had not been complied with. The planning authority argued that the wife's presence at the inquiry, and the fact that she gave evidence, showed that she had not been prejudiced by any failure in service. The wife had admitted that she had seen the notice. The Secretary of State accepted the reporter's view that she had not been substantially prejudiced by the failure. He therefore exercised his powers under section 84(5)(*b*) to disregard the failure. (Refs. P/EUC/EDB/2; P/ENA/ LA/1, October 12, 1976.)

9.5 Enforcement notice—service—error in notice
   An enforcement notice was served on the managing director of Kydd Produce Ltd. as occupier and lessee of a site and on another concern as owners of the site. Kydd Haulage Ltd. were not served though they also occupied the site. The appellants argued that the plan which had accompanied the enforcement notice had not identified the right site and premises. They claimed that the error was so fundamental that the notice should be quashed.

The reporter considered the determining issue to be whether the deficiencies in the enforcement notice made it incapable of correction. It was clear that as the notice was not served on Kydd Haulage Ltd., one of the occupants of the site, it did not comply with section 84(5) of the 1972 Act. Also, although Mr. A. H. Kydd might have been served as a member of the boards of both Kydd Produce Ltd. and Kydd Haulage Ltd., the reporter could not conclude that because the enforcement notice was served on the former company, the latter company would automatically have been aware of it, or that it should have interpreted the notice as applying to its operations on the site as well as to those of Kydd Produce Ltd.

Further, as the coming into operation of the enforcement notice could have resulted in the extinguishment of their business, the reporter could not conclude in terms of section 84(5)(*d*) of the 1972 Act that the omission of service of the notice on Kydd Haulage Ltd. did not substantially prejudice the interests of that company.

Finally, by referring to the yard and associated buildings occupied by Kydd Produce Ltd. and to the subjects delineated on the plan attached thereto, Schedule 1 of the enforcement notice was clearly ambiguous in that it referred to two different properties. Such a defect or error, it seemed to the reporter, was so material as to be incapable of correction in terms of section 85(4)(*a*) of the 1972 Act. For these reasons the reporter concluded that the enforcement notice was so defective and fundamentally flawed as to be incapable of rectification in terms of the Act and should therefore be quashed. (Ref. P/ENA/TB/31, September 1, 1986.)

9.6　Enforcement notice—service—parties omitted
An enforcement notice had been served on the owner of the Shalimar Restaurant Ltd. and on Mr. Paul Chima as lessee. Mr. Chima owned 50 per cent. of the shares in the company, Mrs. K. S. Chima senior and Mrs. S. K. Chima junior owning 25 per cent. each. The notice was therefore served on the person who owned 50 per cent. of the shares and who, along with two others living at the same address were the only directors of the company. The Secretary of State considered that it was difficult to sustain the argument that Shalimar Restaurant Ltd. had not in fact been served with the notice. In any case it seemed to the Secretary of State that subsequent events had shown that Shalimar Restaurant Ltd. had suffered no prejudice. (Refs. HGJ/6/TC/4 and 4/1; P/ENA/TC/61, April 8, 1988.)

9.7   Enforcement notice—service

An enforcement notice had been served on a company. The notice had not been served on the regional council, the owners of the land. The regional council was well aware of the situation and was keen that the objectives of the notice should be achieved. The reporter considered that neither the regional council nor the company had been substantially prejudiced by the failure to serve the notice on the regional council. The reporter exercised his powers to disregard the failure. (Ref. P/ENA/CC/22, April 18, 1988.)

9.8   Enforcement notice—service

The appellant claimed that an enforcement notice had not been properly served upon him as it had been pushed through the gate of his premises and had been retrieved by a dog which had chewed and damaged the document. The reporter was not persuaded that the notice had been served incorrectly as it was delivered in duplicate to both the company of which the appellant was a director and to the company secretary. (Ref. P/ENA/SL/214, July 7, 1987.)

9.9   Enforcement notice—advertisement—service

The appellants argued that an enforcement notice had not been properly served on them. It had been served on Guthrie Bros. (Craigo) Ltd., but not on David Guthrie, the owner of the land on which the allegedly unauthorised advertisement was situated. In terms of regulation 25(4)(b) of the Town and Country Planning (Control of Advertisements) (Scotland) Regulations 1984 the Secretary of State may disregard a failure in service provided that neither the appellant nor the person who was not served with the notice has been substantially prejudiced by the failure. It was a fact that Mr. Guthrie was a director of Guthrie Bros. (Craigo) Ltd. and as such signed the application for consent to display the advertisement. In the light of this the view was taken that the failure to serve the enforcement notice on Mr. David Guthrie had not substantially prejudiced him or the appellant. (Refs. P/ADA/TA/27; P/ADE/TA/4, July 8, 1987.)

9.10   Enforcement notice—service—superior

An enforcement notice served on the superiors of an area of land required the cessation of the use of the land for the parking of commercial vehicles. The superiors appealed against the notice on ground (e) of section 85(1) of the 1972 Act on the ground that their only interest in the land was that of superiors. They were, however, considering what steps they might take as feu superiors to have the use cease.

The planning authority claimed they had been scrupulous in complying fully with the requirements of section 84(5) of the 1972 Act and that it was right to serve notice on the superiors as having an interest in the land.

The reporter was of the opinion that the superiors' interest was one which was materially affected by the notice. The 1972 Act required that those with a legal interest in the land had to be served with an enforcement notice and to be given an opportunity to appeal should they wish. As a result, enforcement notices would often be served on persons who were not responsible for the breach. The Act does not provide for the identification of the person responsible for complying with the notice or for apportioning the costs involved. The reporter was satisfied that the superiors' interest was one which required the enforcement notice to be served on them. The appeal on ground (*e*) therefore failed. (Ref. P/ENA/SC/60, June 9, 1988.)

9.11 Enforcement notice—service—defect

This was an appeal against an enforcement notice served in respect of the allegedly unauthorised use of premises as a commercial garage for the maintenance and repair of motor vehicles.

An appeal was lodged, *inter alia*, on ground (*e*) of section 85(1) of the Town and Country Planning (Scotland) Act 1972—that the enforcement notice was not served as required by section 84(5) of the 1972 Act. There had been a failure to serve notice on the owner of the land. The notice was, however, served on the owner's husband and the reporter disregarded the failure on the ground that he was satisfied on the evidence that neither the wife nor the husband had been substantially prejudiced by the failure. (Ref. P/PPA/TB/10, May 20, 1981.)

9.12 Enforcement notices—service—requirements

Enforcement notices were served in respect of the allegedly unauthorised use for multiple occupation, including "bed and breakfast" accommodation, of all 6 floors of terraced premises in the New Town of Edinburgh. On both sides of the appeal property, which was listed as a building of special architectural or historic interest, were individually occupied residential flats.

At the time of the reporter's site inspection most of the appeal subjects appeared to be let. The "bed-sits" contained between one and three beds, and bathrooms and toilets were shared.

Some kitchens were shared and others were located in individual "bed-sits." The general condition of the property was poor, as was its appearance, with broken windows, sections of handrail missing from stairs, graffiti on the walls and evidence of a recent fire on the top floor. The enforcement notices were served because the change in the use of the premises to use for multiple occupation was considered to be detrimental to the amenity of neighbouring residents by reason of noise and other disturbance.

Copies of the enforcement notice were served on the owners of the property, on a Mr. Lennie, as the assumed lessee of the premises, and on a company with which he was associated, on the individual who applied for planning permission to use the premises as a guest house, and on the various occupants.

The appellants claimed that the notices had not been properly served. First, they alleged, mere service of a notice on "the occupant" of part of the premises, without naming him or her individually, meant that the notices were fatally flawed. Secondly, it was claimed that from a date prior to service of the notices, the lessees had been a limited company different from that on which the notices had been served: this, it was argued, was a defect which invalidated the notices.

As regards the first point, service on the occupants, the reporter pointed out that the premises were occupied by a large and essentially transient population; in his opinion it would have been impractical for the authority to have sought to establish the name of every occupant and to have served individual notices on such occupants. He therefore found no fault in the local authority's action.

However, the appellants' second contention succeeded. The authority said that they had served notices under section 270 of the 1972 Act, requiring the provision of information as to interests in the land. They pointed out that neither of the two companies alleged to be the new lessees appeared in any public record available at the time of service of the notices. The appellants denied having received any notice under section 270 and averred that the planning authority should have used a pre-paid registered letter or the recorded delivery service, as provided for in section 269(1)(c) of the 1972 Act.

The reporter found the evidence on this matter to be unclear but considered that if the planning authority had done all in their power to establish the correct lessees of the premises by issuing the section 270 notices by registered post or recorded delivery, he would have felt obliged to dismiss the appeal. He considered, however, that the authority's failure to act as provided for in section 269(1)(*c*) had prejudiced the interests of the lessee or lessees. In his judgment that provided sufficient justification for finding in favour of the appellants.

Following an appeal to the Court of Session, the reporter's decision was quashed. On the question of service of the notices, the reporter stated that though it would have been preferable if the planning authority had followed the procedures contained in section 269 of the 1972 Act (relating to service of notices), these procedures were not mandatory. More importantly, the appellants had failed to produce, in the form of either leases or official extracts, evidence to show that the persons on whom the enforcement notices were served were not the lessees of the properties on the dates when the enforcement notices were served. No explanation for this failure was offered. He therefore had to treat as unproven the claim regarding the transfer of leases. The reporter had no evidence that either the appellants or any lessees had been prejudiced by any failure in service. Accordingly the appeal on ground (*e*) of section 85(1) of the 1972 Act (that the enforcement notice was not served as required by section 84(5) of the 1972 Act) failed. (Refs. P/ENA/LA/87 and 92, December 1, 1986 and May 24, 1988.)

9.13 Enforcement notice—service—contractors

An enforcement notice had been served on the owner of land and on a company who were dumping material on the land. Appeal was made on ground (*e*) of section 85(1) of the 1972 Act (that the enforcement notice was not served as required by the Act).

The reporter pointed out that section 84(5) of the 1972 Act stipulates that an enforcement notice shall be served on the owner, lessee and occupier of the land to which it relates and on any other person having an interest in the land, being an interest which in the opinion of the authority is materially affected by the notice. The word "interest" was normally taken to mean "legal interest" in land and the reporter accepted that as the company were merely contractors, their interest was not a "legal" one in the normal sense of the word. However, the service of an enforcement notice on a number of people did not imply that all of these people were equally, or even partly, responsible for the alleged breach. More importantly, the fact that the Act required service on certain classes of person did not preclude service on someone else who did not belong to one of those classes. (Ref. P/ENA/CB/51, June 30, 1988.)

9.14   Enforcement notice—omission of service—owner of part of site

That part of a site which was the subject of an enforcement notice was owned by a person who had not been served with a copy of the notice. The reporter noted that there had been no appeal on ground (*e*) of section 85(1) of the 1972 Act (that the notice had not been correctly served). The reporter took account of section 85(4)(*b*) of the 1972 Act, to the effect that the Secretary of State may disregard non-service of a notice if neither the appellant nor the person on whom the notice should have been served has been materially prejudiced by the planning authority's omission. In this case the owner who had not been served with the notice fully supported the enforcement notice and had already taken steps to have items removed from her land. The reporter was satisfied that none of the alleged breaches had occurred with that owner's consent. He was satisfied that her interests had not been prejudiced by non-service of the notice. (Ref. P/ENA/SA/68, July 13, 1988.)

9.15   Enforcement notice—advertisement—service

The appellant alleged that an enforcement notice had not been served as required by regulation 24 of the Town and Country Planning (Control of Advertisements) (Scotland) Regulations 1984. The first enforcement notice had been sent by registered letter but was not collected from the Post Office. The planning authority issued further notices by mail and by hand. The view was taken that the planning authority had taken all reasonable steps to ensure that the enforcement notice was served in accordance with the regulations. (Refs. P/ADA/FB/35; P/ADE/FB/4, August 3, 1988.)

9.16   Enforcement notice—service

This was an appeal against an enforcement notice served in respect of the allegedly unauthorised siting of a caravan on land. The reporter considered that one of two people on whom the enforcement notice was served did, contrary to the appellant's view that the notice was incompetent, have an interest in the appeal site in the sense of being an occupier from time to time. He therefore found that on the question of validity the notice was properly served under section 84(5) of the 1972 Act. The reporter was also of the opinion that the caravan could be considered to lie within the curtilage of one of a row of cottages despite the lack of physical boundaries and the appeal site's physical separation from the row of cottages. (Refs. P/ENA/SA/79 and 80, November 8, 1988.)

9.17 Enforcement notice—service—scope

An enforcement notice contained, *inter alia*, an allegation that a breach of planning control had occurred through the use of part of the roadway in front of the appellant's home for parking and storing damaged vehicles. The enforcement notice was not, however, served on the regional council, the authority responsible for the highway. The Secretary of State can, under section 85(4)(*b*) of the 1972 Act, disregard a failure in service of an enforcement notice but in view of the requirement in the enforcement notice to remove all vehicles from the street in question (and not merely those owned by the appellant and his wife) he decided he could not disregard the failure in this case. (Ref. P/ENA/SL/32, October 18, 1976.)

9.18 Enforcement notice—failure in service

An enforcement notice was served in respect of the siting of a caravan. The land on which the caravan stood, a showground, was occupied by Mr. C. D. Smith (the appellant) and his father. They were joint lessees of the land. The enforcement notice was not served on the father. It was alleged on behalf of the appellant that the enforcement notice was bad in that Mr. Smith senior had an interest in the land. Nor was the notice served on Mrs. Smith and her children who were undoubtedly occupiers of the caravan.

The reporter considered that it was clear that all persons having an interest in the land were aware of the enforcement notice having been issued; no one with an interest had been substantially prejudiced by the failure in service. On the question whether the notice had been properly served, the Secretary of State agreed that all persons materially affected by the notice had been aware of it and that no one with an interest had been substantially prejudiced by any failure in service of the notice. The Secretary of State concluded that failure to serve on Mr. Smith senior, or on the appellant's wife and daughter had not substantially prejudiced any of these parties. He therefore took the view that under section 85(4)(*b*) he could disregard the fact that the notice was not served on them. (Refs. P/PPA/LB/13; P/ENA/LB/14, November 16, 1979.)

9.19 Enforcement notice—service—correction

Two identical enforcement notices were served on different parties on different dates. The Secretary of State was, however, satisfied that, although the notices took effect on different dates, the powers conferred upon him by section 85(4)(*a*) of the 1972 Act (relating to correction of informalities, defects, or errors which are not material) allowed him to correct the defect. (Refs. P/PPA/SL/70; P/ENA/SL/92 and 93, January 1, 1980.)

9.20   Enforcement notice—condition

An enforcement notice alleged failure to comply with a condition requiring the landscaping of a site. Appeal was lodged on, *inter alia*, ground (*e*) of section 85(1) of the 1972 Act—*i.e.* on the basis that the appellants had no legal interest in the land to which the notice related. The appellants claimed that they were not responsible for the alleged breach of planning control, nor were they in a position to comply with the requirements of the notice.

The planning authority accepted that the appellants might have no legal interest in the land designated for landscape purposes which was the subject of the notice. Nevertheless, the land in their possession formed part of the overall development on the site for which planning permission was granted and to which the condition applied. In the authority's opinion the appellants had an interest in the land which was materially affected by the notice and were therefore entitled to be served with the notice in accordance with the requirements of section 84(5) of the 1972 Act.

The reporter said that section 84(5) required that an enforcement notice should be served on the owner, lessee and occupier of the land to which it related and on any other person having an interest in that land, being an interest which in the opinion of the authority was materially affected by the notice. In this case the land to which the notice related was the site covered by the permission granted in October 1984 and the conditions imposed thereon. The appellants clearly had an interest in part of that land and therefore had to be served with the notice and given the opportunity to appeal should they wish to do so. The requirements of this section of the Act might well result in enforcement notices being served on persons who were not responsible for the alleged breach of control and who were not in a position to comply with the requirements of the notice. It was important to note that the notice did not seek to apportion responsibility for the breach, nor did it stipulate who should carry out the steps that were specified. The appellants' appeal therefore failed on this point.

Appeal was also lodged on ground (*f*) of section 85(1)—that the steps required by the notice to be taken exceeded what was necessary to remedy any breach of planning control. The planning authority did not accept this, contending that the steps specified were the only ones which could remedy the breach. The reporter said that again, looked at solely in the context of the land in the appellants' control, the appellants' submission had some justification. However, in the context of the whole site the breach lay in the failure of the persons responsible to submit a detailed landscaping plan and to landscape the site accordingly. In this respect he agreed with the planning authority that the steps required by the notice represented the only ones which could remedy the breach of control. The appeal on this ground therefore failed. (Ref. P/ENA/LB/55, December 28, 1988.)

9.21 Enforcement notice—defects

An enforcement notice did not specify the date on which the notice was to take effect or the period at the end of which it was to take effect. It therefore failed to comply with section 84(7A)(*a*) of the Town and Country Planning (Scotland) Act 1972. The Secretary of State declared that the notice was a nullity and that there was therefore no valid appeal before him. (Refs. P/ENA/GD/2; P/WEN/GD/1, June 16, 1978.)

9.22 Enforcement—specification of breach—specification of requirements—notice quashed

An enforcement notice was served in respect of a mobile snack bar. The reporter pointed out that the wording of the enforcement notice referred to the *siting* of a caravan and the *use* of a caravan as constituting development. In the reporter's view neither the act of siting (or "stationing") a caravan on land nor the uses to which a caravan might be put, constituted development. Section 19(1) of the 1972 Act refers to development as meaning "the carrying out of building, engineering or other operations . . . on . . . land, or the making of any material change in the use of any buildings or other land." These meanings did not, the reporter said, embrace the siting or use of any vehicle or trailer such as a caravan.

Even if the reference to siting the caravan (adapted as a snack bar) and its use for retailing snacks to the public were sufficient to allege a material change of use of the land, it did not exactly match what had happened. The evidence at the public inquiry indicated that the grass verge at the lay-by was in regular use for the retailing of snacks from a caravan adapted for the purpose. The caravan was not there every day, being removed every weekend and on the days when it was at the lay-by, it was not there for 24 hours. However, the use of the grass verge for the stated purpose did occur on more than 28 days in the year in 1982 and any material change of use created would not therefore enjoy the "permitted development" status granted by Class IV of Part I of Schedule 1 to the Town and Country Planning (General Development) (Scotland) Order 1981.

The reporter was therefore of the opinion that in order to be valid, the enforcement notice would have had to have referred to the use of the land at the lay-by, should have stated that the caravan had been on land for more than 28 days in a calendar year and that such stationing constituted a material change of use of the land without the grant of planning permission in that behalf, that the change of use constituted development and that therefore there was a breach of planning control.

In paragraph 2 the notice required the recipient to remove the caravan adapted as a snack bar and discontinue the said unauthorised use thereof. Again, to be valid, reference should have been made to the unauthorised use of the land and not to the unauthorised use of the caravan. The reporter considered that the enforcement notice wrongly identified the breach of planning control, that in this respect the defects in the notice were material, and that they were of too substantial a nature to be capable of correction. The notice was therefore quashed. (Ref. P/ENA/TA/2, May 13, 1983.)

9.23 Enforcement notice—steps required

In this appeal the reporter had to consider, *inter alia*, whether the steps required by the enforcement notice exceeded, in terms of ground (*f*) of section 85(1) of the 1972 Act, what was necessary to remedy any breach of planning control. The reporter considered that in a very small shop which sold a very limited range and quantity of goods, the installation of even one amusement machine would have a significant effect on the retail use and character of the premises and that the breach of planning control would not be completely removed unless all the machines were completely removed. (Ref. P/ENA/SL/188, May 28, 1985.)

9.24 Enforcement notice—alterations to shop—failure in specification—notice quashed

An enforcement notice alleged unauthorised alterations to a shop front. The reporter regarded the colour, design, proportions, detailing and the materials used in the development as contributing to its incongruous and unacceptable visual impact. However, the enforcement notice required only that a new specified finish be applied in place of the stall risers and that the red perspex moulded fascia panel and the canopy should be removed.

In specifying that the replacement fascia panel should be a maximum of 0.5 metre deep, the notice did not specifically require the removal of the band of tiles located over the fascia. The reporter regarded that omission as being significant. If works were undertaken to comply with the terms of the enforcement notice as currently drafted, the visual impact of the unauthorised works would not be entirely excised and the incongruous effect of the remaining band of tiles would remain. The reporter regarded this defect in the notice as being material. It was not therefore susceptible of correction within the terms of section 85(4)(a) of the 1972 Act. Consequently, the reporter had no alternative but to quash the notice. He added, however, for the avoidance of doubt, that the development was unauthorised and remained susceptible to further enforcement action. (Refs. P/PPA/GA/405; P/ENA/GA/71, August 8, 1988.)

9.25 Enforcement notice—specification

An enforcement notice had been served alleging the removal of part of a concrete retaining barrier from a loch. The authority were concerned about the environmental effect of lowering the water level of the loch. The owner alleged that he had only dug away a mass of stones and soil, revealing what would appear to be a sluice gap in the wall. He appealed against the notice on ground (*bb*) of section 85(1)—that the breach of planning control alleged in the notice had not taken place.

The reporter said that the first question to be considered was whether the enforcement notice adequately described the work that had been done. The enforcement notice spoke of a "section of concrete." This was an imprecise description of materials; the notice should have described the materials as "cemented stones." However, the Secretary of State may correct any informality, defect or error in an enforcement notice if he is satisfied that the error is not material. In *Miller-Mead* v. *Minister of Housing and Local Government* [1963] 2 Q.B. 196 Lord Denning had stated that "no informality, defect or error is a material one unless it is such as to produce injustice." In this case it was quite clear what work was the subject of the enforcement notice and no injustice had occurred because of the use of the word "concrete." The error was therefore corrected. (Ref. P/ENA/FA/62, April 5, 1989.)

9.26 Canopies—external appearance of building—specification

Three canopies had been fitted to small windows of a large building. An enforcement notice was served requiring removal of the canopies. Appeal was made (*inter alia*) on the ground that planning permission was not required. The reporter found, however, that it was undeniable that the canopies materially affected the appearance of the building and that there had therefore been a breach of planning control.

The reporter found the enforcement notice to be lacking in specification in that it did not explain in what way the canopies failed to comply with the council's policy. It was not necessary to decide whether this defect could be remedied since, on the merits, the reporter considered that these small canopies had no adverse effect on the appearance of the building. (Ref. P/ENA/TC/62, April 28, 1988.)

9.27   Enforcement notice—specification
An enforcement notice alleged that there had been a material change in the use of a former domestic garage to use as housing for an industrial compressor. The reporter considered that there had been a material change of use but that the authority could only require cessation of the use of the premises for housing a compressor since there was no evidence to show that the premises had ever been used as a domestic garage. (Ref. P/ENA/GA/66, March 31, 1987.)

9.28   Enforcement notice—defect—specification of period for compliance
An enforcement notice required the appellant to discontinue the use of an access to his house and to form a different access. The Secretary of State found the enforcement notice to be invalid since it did not, as required by section 84(7)(*c*) of the 1972 Act, specify the period for compliance with the requirements of the notice. (Ref. P/ENA/SQ/1, August 15, 1978.)

9.29   Enforcement notice—description of breach
The reporter found that the stationing of a caravan on agricultural land amounted to development for which planning permission had been required but not obtained.

However, the breach of planning control stated in the enforcement notice was only that of clearing and levelling the site and not the material change of use of the land. The works appeared to involve only the removal of turf and the laying of a bed of stones. The caravan was not supplied with water, electricity or drainage services. In the reporter's opinion the works were so slight as to be *de minimis*. The planning authority explained that the enforcement notice was intended to include the use of the land as a caravan site and that it was unlikely that enforcement action would have been taken in respect of the site works only. In these circumstances it appeared to the reporter that the breach of planning control was either wrongly defined or related to works which were *de minimis*. In the first case the wrong definition was a material and therefore fatal defect which could not be remedied in terms of section 85(4) of the 1972 Act and in the second case the works were not such as to amount to a breach of planning control. Therefore in either case the appeal against the enforcement notice had to succeed on ground (*b*) of section 85(1) of the 1972 Act, *i.e.* that the matters alleged in the enforcement notice did not constitute a breach of planning control.

With regard to the planning authority's request that the enforcement notice be varied to include the site of a "storage" caravan in its terms, the reporter considered that it would be improper for him to do so, since this would extend the scope of the notice and would not be within the powers granted to the Secretary of State in section 85(5) of the 1972 Act, which restricts any such variation to one which favours the appellant. (Refs. P/PPA/SA/99 and 101; P/ENA/SA/44, July 4, 1985.)

9.30 Enforcement notice—validity—description of breach

It was submitted for the appellant that the position of an allegedly unauthorised dam was incorrectly shown on the plan accompanying the enforcement notice. The site was identified on the plan by a circle but none of the unauthorised works had been carried on within the area of that circle. This, it was alleged, constituted a material error in the notice which it was beyond the powers of the Secretary of State to correct. In the words of SDD Circular 6/1984: "It is . . . essential to identify precisely the boundary of the land or premises to which the notice relates." It was submitted, on the basis of *Miller-Mead* v. *Minister of Housing and Local Government* [1963] 2 Q.B. 196 and *TLG Building Materials* v. *Secretary of State for the Environment* (1980) 41 P.&C.R. 243, that the notice was "hopelessly ambiguous" and incapable of correction without injustice.

The planning authority conceded that the plan and the notice were erroneous but submitted that the defect was not material or incapable of correction. Referring to *Miller-Mead*, the council argued that correction of the notice could be achieved without injustice to the appellant.

The reporter considered that although in most cases the locus of an alleged breach must be precisely defined in order to avoid any confusion with other land or buildings in the vicinity, in this case there was only one dam across the river and the operations were therefore of such a singular nature that there could be no doubt in the mind of any reasonable person as to the location of the works described. Having regard to the judgments of Upjohn and Denning L.JJ. in *Miller-Mead*, it was the reporter's opinion that the error in this case did not give rise to so serious a lack of certainty as to render the notice a nullity. The Secretary of State has power under section 85(4)(*a*) of the 1972 Act to correct any defect or error in an enforcement notice if he is satisfied that the error or defect is not material. The reporter considered that the notice could properly be corrected under these powers and that such correction would not give rise to injustice to the appellant. He therefore concluded that the notice as served was not so fatally flawed as to be invalid. (Ref. P/ENA/FA/54, December 23, 1987.)

9.31 Enforcement notice—description of breach—hostel or house in multiple occupation

Section 84(7) of the 1972 Act requires that an enforcement notice shall specify the matters alleged to constitute a breach of planning control and the planning authority in this case described the unauthorised use as a hostel. The reporter took the main characteristics of a hostel to be a degree of supervision, provision of certain communal services and some community of interest or purpose among the occupants. The first two did not apply here and he considered that the most appropriate description of the use was multiple paying occupation. Normally this defect could be corrected, said the reporter, but because of the imminence of the planning authority's policy on multiple occupation he decided to treat the defect as a material one, not capable of correction. The notice was therefore held to be invalid. (Ref. P/ENA/SL/152, July 21, 1982.)

9.32 Enforcement notice—defect—development

An enforcement notice was served in respect of the use of an area of ground for the display of vehicles for sale. There was a defect in the enforcement notice in that the word "Limited" appeared in the address after "Blackadder Motor Co.," the appellants. The appellants' solicitors observed that the notice could therefore be held to be inept. The reporter accepted this as an additional ground of appeal under section 85(1)(*e*) of the Town and Country Planning (Scotland) Act 1972 (that the notice was not served as required by section 84(9)). The reporter did not consider this to be a material defect and corrected it in exercise of his powers under section 85(4)(*a*) of the 1972 Act.

The reporter was satisfied as regards the appeal on section 85(1)(*b*)—that the matters alleged in the notice did not constitute a breach of planning control—that the appeal site had been used for the display of vehicles in the process of retailing them to the public and that this constituted a material change of use. Development in terms of section 19(1) of the 1972 Act had therefore taken place without planning permission.

As regards the appeal on ground (*d*) of section 85(1)—that in specified cases the breach of planning control alleged by the notice occurred before the beginning of 1965—the reporter said that to claim immunity from enforcement procedure it was necessary for the appellants to present a conclusive case that the land was in use for the display of vehicles for sale before the beginning of 1965 and this they had failed to do satisfactorily. (Refs. P/ENA/CB/32 and 33, February 18, 1981.)

9.33 Enforcement notice—defect

The reporter found that an enforcement notice failed to specify sufficiently clearly the matters alleged to constitute a breach of planning control as it did not state, clearly or by implication, whether the alleged breach was constituted by the carrying out of development without the grant of planning permission or by a failure to comply with a condition or limitation attached to a planning permission. This was a fundamental defect which the Secretary of State could not correct. (Refs. P/ENA/GA/43; P/PPA/GA/127 and 128, June 30, 1983.)

9.34 Enforcement notice—defects

An enforcement notice alleged the unauthorised use of farm buildings and land for the breaking, sale and repair of motor vehicles. The notice required cessation of the use and the removal of all vehicles, materials and plant connected with the use. The plan attached to the enforcement notice showed an area considerably larger than that occupied by the appellant. There was also a reference in the notice to "development in terms of section 84 of the Town and Country Planning (Scotland) Act 1972" whereas development is defined in section 19 of the Act. The reporter considered these errors were not material, that the appellant was not prejudiced by them and that they could be corrected.

However, the appellant said (and the planning authority did not dispute the claim) that the current use of the appeal site was primarily for storage of accident-damaged vehicles and not for the breaking, sale or repair of motor vehicles. The reporter accepted that the notice wrongly stated the nature of the alleged breach of planning control. He was of the opinion that the defect or error was material and was therefore incapable of correction in terms of section 85(4)(*a*). The notice was therefore quashed. (Ref. P/ENA/FB/54, February 6, 1985.)

9.35 Enforcement notice—defective plan—not material

The plan attached to an enforcement notice was defective in that it showed an area different from that for which conditional planning permission had been granted. However, the reporter was satisfied that it was clear to the appellant which mobile homes were being referred to in the notice. Neither the appellant nor the planning authority had been prejudiced by the error. The defect was therefore not material and could be corrected. (Ref. P/ENA/W/27, March 20, 1985.)

9.36 Enforcement notice—corrections—planning unit

An enforcement notice served on the appellants was alleged to be defective and to result in injustice to the appellants. The notice referred to "operations" and not to "material change of use" in its preamble. This was clearly an error since only one of the six alleged breaches was an operation. However, the reporter took the view that the description of the breaches left no doubt about which were material changes of use and which was an operation. He did not consider that this error was material. The description of four of the alleged breaches as "use of . . ." and the absence of the phrase "material change of use" was in his view a matter of little consequence. The notice clearly implied that these items described alleged material changes of use. The wording of two of the alleged breaches contained a number of errors or ambiguities. These points were, thought the reporter, more important since it could be argued that they created confusion as to the precise nature of the planning authority's complaint. However, he thought the essence of the council's position to be reasonably clear and he did not accept that injustice had been caused. All in all, the reporter was not persuaded that the defects were of sufficient importance to warrant quashing the notice on that basis.

On the facts of the appeal the reporter said that the disagreement between the appellants and the planning authority related to the relevance or otherwise of the change in the planning unit. An additional site had now to be regarded as part of the planning unit. In planning terms the main change that had occurred was the increase in use of a particular access, especially by articulated lorries. The reporter said that he was aware that a change in the boundaries of a planning unit can result in a new phase in a site's history, and the extinguishment of existing use rights. However, in this case all that had happened was the rearrangement of the boundaries of occupation within a large area in general industrial use and a redistribution of traffic amongst different accesses. As a consequence it was arguable that there might have been an intensification of the use of one of the sites. In the reporter's view this intensification did not amount to a material change in the character of the site. In any case, both the original and the present uses fell within the same class of the Town and Country Planning (Use Classes) (Scotland) Order 1973 and so no development was involved. There had therefore been no breach of planning control so far as the use of this site was concerned. (Ref. P/ENA/SS/57, February 22, 1988.)

9.37 Enforcement notice—defects
   Planning permission had been granted subject to conditions for residential development. An enforcement notice was served in respect of the alleged breach of two of the conditions.
   A telephone box restricted the sight line at a junction. The box was under the control of British Telecom. They had not been served with a copy of the notice, though they had an interest in the land in question. Under section 84(5) of the 1972 Act an enforcement notice must be served on the owner, lessee and occupier of the land to which it relates and on any other person having an interest in the land if that interest is materially affected by the enforcement notice. The reporter considered that there would be substantial prejudice if the enforcement notice were to proceed when affected parties had not been served. He therefore quashed that part of the enforcement notice.
   A car park for the village hall had not been formed as required by the planning permission. Section 84(7) of the 1972 Act requires an enforcement notice to specify the matters alleged to constitute a breach of planning control. Here the terms of the condition sought to be enforced were that all the required car parking was to be formed "before the development hereby approved is completed or brought into use." The reporter considered that the use of the word "or" introduced uncertainty and implied choice. It could not be assumed that the condition took effect whichever criterion was first satisfied, or prior to the whole development being completed or brought into use. Part of the development had been brought into use but because of the wording of the condition, no breach could occur until the whole

development had been completed or brought into use. That had not yet happened and there had therefore been no breach of the condition. (Ref. P/ENA/SR/55, April 4, 1989.)

9.38   Enforcement notice—defects

An enforcement notice had been served in respect of the change of use of premises from a barn to use for five-a-side football. A preliminary question was raised as to possible defects in the enforcement notice.

First, it was claimed that there had been a failure to establish expediency within the notice itself. Section 84(1) of the 1972 Act sets out the powers to serve an enforcement notice if the planning authority consider it expedient to do so. The Town and Country Planning (Enforcement of Control) (Scotland) Regulations 1984 indicate that the enforcement notice should specify the reasons why the planning authority consider it expedient to issue the notice. Whether or not expediency was incontrovertibly established was, in the reporter's opinion, another matter. He was satisfied that the notice left the appellant in no doubt about the reasons why the district council considered it expedient at the time, whether or not the appellant was aware of wider reasoning, which in this case the reporter was sure he was.

Secondly, there was omitted from the plan accompanying the notice details of toilet accommodation associated with the development. On the question of the site boundary on the plan, there was no evidence of other toilet provision at this location, nor was its location disputed at the site inspection. The reporter found that the appellant was left in no doubt about the works to which the notice referred. This matter might, he said, represent a minor imperfection but certainly not a fatal flaw. He found that the enforcement notice did not fail in either respect. (Refs. P/PPA/SC/210; P/ENA/SC/68, March 29, 1989.)

9.39   Enforcement notice—not internally consistent—correction

An enforcement notice was served in respect of the alleged unauthorised use of land as a permanent residential caravan site. The breach of planning control alleged in the enforcement notice consisted of the "unauthorised use of land . . . for permanent parking of four showmens' caravans" without the grant of planning permission required for that development. The steps required to remedy the breach were to "discontinue the unauthorised parking of caravans on the site" within a period of six months. The reasons given for the service of the enforcement notice were that "the use of the land for residential purposes is inappropriate within an industrial area and this is likely to be prejudicial to the viability of firms in the area and in consequence of the jobs of those employed therein."

The reporter noted, however, that the breach of planning control was referred to under the heading of "operations on land or premises." In response to the reporter's questions it was accepted by the planning authority that the enforcement notice should have referred to a change of use throughout. Though the reporter accepted the authority's point that as the caravans became adapted over time, it was a matter of fact and degree whether the breach alleged was considered to be a change of use or an operation, that was not at issue here; the reporter's concern was that as it stood the enforcement notice was not internally consistent.

The reporter said that while a misclassification of an enforcement notice might be fatal, under section 85(4)(*a*) of the 1972 Act the Secretary of State could correct any informality, defect or error in an enforcement notice if he was satisfied that the informality, defect or error was not material. The interpretation of this power had been clarified in *R.* v. *Tower Hamlets London Borough Council, ex parte Ahern (London) Ltd.* (1989) 59 P.&. C.R. 133, drawing on *Eldon Garages Ltd.* v. *Kingston-upon-Hull Corporation* [1974] 1 W.L.R. 276. These cases confirmed that the test of what was material was if the correction could be made without injustice to either party. In the present case it was clear that the appellant knew precisely what was being alleged and therefore the reporter considered no prejudice had arisen. He therefore amended the enforcement notice to refer to a material change of use, consistent with the references to an unauthorised use of land. (Refs. P/ENA/SL/251; P/PPA/SL/501, July 26, 1989.)

9.40 Enforcement notice—material change of use—interpretation of enforcement notice

An enforcement notice was served in respect of the use of a building as an indoor market. One of the grounds of appeal was ground (*b*) of section 85(1) of the 1972 Act—*i.e.* that no breach of planning control had occurred. The enforcement notice required the appellants to discontinue the sale of goods other than furniture, carpets, bedding, etc. (sale of which was permitted) to comply with the conditions of the planning permission relating to the premises. The notice went on to allege that this breach occurred "by the use of the land for the purposes of an indoor market." The point of law was whether this narrative was sufficiently specific to inform the appellant of the alleged breach.

There was no dispute on the facts as to what goods were sold at the market. Taken together, the facts persuaded the reporter that the appellant could have been in no doubt that the breach concerned the wider range of goods sold at the market than was authorised by the planning permission. In the reporter's view the notice was slightly defective in failing to include a phrase such as "at which are sold goods other than furniture, carpets, bedding, etc. such as clothing and footwear." The reporter was not, however, convinced that that omission was material. Having considered the cases of *Miller-Mead* v. *Minister of Housing and Local Government* [1963] 2 Q.B. 196 and *Hammersmith LBC* v. *Secretary of State for the Environment* (1975) 30 P.&C.R. 19, which dealt with analogous English legislation, the reporter believed that the breach had been correctly described and the lack of a recital itemising the specific facts of the breach could be remedied under the powers conferred by section 85(4)(*a*) of the 1972 Act without injustice to the appellant. (Ref. P/ENA/SG/9, November 11, 1982.)

9.41　Enforcement notice—deemed application for planning permission—publicity

When an appeal is made against an enforcement notice, there is deemed to have been an application for planning permission for the development to which the enforcement notice relates (see 1972 Act, section 85(7)). However, where an enforcement notice had been served in respect of a bingo hall, the Secretary of State concluded that it would be wrong to consider such an application without its having been publicised (by way of a newspaper advertisement and a site notice) under section 23 of the 1972 Act. (Ref. P/ENA/GLW/91, January 23, 1976.)

9.42　Enforcement notice—deemed application for planning permission—departure from original application

The decision letter in this appeal stated that in the context of an appeal against an enforcement notice, planning permission could only be granted for the development to which the enforcement notice related. Here, however, the conditional planning permission suggested by the reporter would be for planning permission on a different site, for a building which would probably be of a different size, and for a building constructed, perhaps, of different materials. The decision letter declared that the view was taken by the Secretary of State that such a permission could not be said to be a planning permission for the development to which the notice related. A development of the kind indicated would need to be the subject of a separate planning application to the planning authority. (Ref. P/ENA/LC/3, February 24, 1978.)

9.43 Enforcement notice—reversion to earlier use—house—office

An enforcement notice was served in respect of a change of use from an office to a house. Until 1978 two small rooms in the house were used as offices. From 1978 until 1982 the whole house was used as offices by a construction company. No application for planning permission had been made. The appellants now occupied the premises as a family dwelling-house. Planning permission for use of the premises was refused for the reason that there were risks inherent in its proximity to a garage and workshop.

The appellants claimed there had been no breach of planning control. However, the reporter said he had to have regard to *Young* v. *Secretary of State for the Environment* [1983] 2 A.C. 662, in which the House of Lords affirmed the decision in *LTSS Print and Supply Services* v. *Hackney London Borough Council* [1976] Q.B. 663, in which the principle was laid down that the effect of section 20(9) of the Town and Country Planning (Scotland) Act 1972 was that where an enforcement notice had been served, reversion was allowed only to that use which was current immediately before the development which was the subject of the enforcement action, and if that use was not lawful then planning permission would be required for any use it was proposed to adopt. Here, therefore, the matters alleged in the enforcement notice did constitute a breach of planning control and planning permission was required to revert to the former use as a dwelling. Planning permission was, however, granted. (Refs. P/ENA/TB/21; P/PPA/TB/68, July 13, 1984.)

9.44 Enforcement notice—caravan—owner not available—removal

An enforcement notice had been served in respect, *inter alia*, of the parking of a caravan on a site. Appeal was made on ground (*g*) of section 85(1) of the 1972 Act—*i.e.* that the specified period fell short of what should reasonably have been allowed for removal of the caravan. The appellant, the owner of the land, did not own the caravan and had no legal right to remove it. The caravan had been brought onto the site by another person.

The reporter said that the caravan's removal need not be time-consuming. In so far as there might be a legal impediment to the removal of the caravan because of ownership, it seemed to him that the necessary works could be executed expeditiously by the appellant as landowner, his expenses being recoverable under section 88 of the 1972 Act. The planning authority were also entitled to remove the caravan with consequent claims for expenses being made against the caravan owner. In the circumstances the period of one month allowed for removal was held to be reasonable. (Ref. P/ENA/SA/45, December 9, 1984.)

9.45 Enforcement notice—steps required

An enforcement notice required the use of land as a caravan site to cease and required that the land be reinstated "to its condition prior to its development as a caravan site." On the question of the steps required to be taken, the reporter considered it reasonable and necessary for the use of the caravan site to cease and for all caravans to be removed from the site. In relation to the site residents, but not to the site owner, he considered the requirement of reinstating the site to be too onerous in view of their occupying their pitches only on monthly tenure. He therefore recommended that in the case of the site residents requirement (3) of the notice (regarding reinstatement) should be deleted.

In his decision letter the Secretary of State said that it was reasonable to assume that any owner or occupier of a caravan on the site who was served with the notice need contribute to the steps required by the notice only to the extent to which it was within his or her power to do so, *i.e.* caravan occupiers would be expected to comply with requirement (1) (cessation of use), owners with (1) and (2) (cessation of use and removal of buildings and caravans) and the site owner with requirements (1), (2) and (3) (cessation of use, removal of buildings and caravans, and reinstatement of the site). In this connection the view was taken that no injustice would result if, for the avoidance of doubt, paragraph 2 of the enforcement notice was corrected, in accordance with section 85(4)(*a*) of the 1972 Act, to avoid the use of the second person. It was changed from "require you to take the following steps" to "require the following steps to be taken." (Ref. P/ENA/W/7, January 29, 1980.)

9.46 Enforcement notice—appeal—ground of appeal invalid

One of the grounds of appeal against an enforcement notice relating to the siting of a caravan was that since the siting of the caravan was also the subject of an appeal against a refusal of planning permission, an enforcement notice should not have been served. This was not accepted as a valid ground of appeal against the enforcement notice. (Refs. P/PPA/AL/165; P/ENA/SA/5, May 31, 1979.)

9.47 Enforcement notice—requirements—lapsed conditions

Appeals had been lodged against a refusal of planning permission for a retail market and against an enforcement notice. The Secretary of State considered that the enforcement notice could never have any effect because it required compliance with conditions attached to an expired planning permission. The appellants could not now be penalised for non-compliance with lapsed conditions. (Refs. P/PPA/LB/12; P/ENA/LD/2, November 3, 1980.)

9.48 Enforcement notice—"four year rule"

This was an appeal against an enforcement notice which alleged non-compliance with a condition attached to a grant of planning permission for the erection of a house. The condition required construction of a fence of specified height and design along the rear boundary of the plot.

The appellant argued, *inter alia*, that since the enforcement notice had not been served within four years of the date on which planning permission for the development was granted, the breach of planning control had become immune from enforcement action. The planning authority argued that the date of the grant of permission could not be taken as the date of the breach; the date of substantial completion of the development should, it said, be regarded as the effective date of the breach and, therefore, as the date from which the four years began to run. The enforcement notice had been served within four years of that date.

The authority's argument was upheld by the reporter. (Ref. P/ENA/LB/24, July 31, 1981.)

9.49 Enforcement notice—"four year rule"

These were appeals against (1) the refusal of planning permission for the change of use of part of an opencast mine site to a haulage yard and (2) an enforcement notice alleging unauthorised use of land and buildings in connection with a haulage yard. The appeal was made on the ground that the breach of planning control had occurred more than four years previously. This ground was inappropriate since the change of use of land and buildings is not protected by the "four year rule." (Refs. P/PPA/SS/113; P/ENA/SS/46, December 24, 1985.)

9.50 Enforcement notice—"four year rule"—roller shutters

An enforcement notice alleged a breach of planning control in that externally-boxed roller shutter security windows had been erected over the windows of a shop.

The reporter considered that because of their adverse effects on the property itself and on the street in general they ought not to be permitted. However, the physical condition of the shutters and their security boxes and fixtures was such that he was convinced that they had been installed on the property some considerable time before its acquisition by the appellant in 1977. Section 84(3) of the 1972 Act states that where an enforcement notice relates to a breach consisting of building, engineering, mining or other operations in, on, over or under land, it may be served only within four years from the date of the breach. An appeal under ground (*c*) of section 85(1) (*i.e.* claiming the benefit of the "four year rule") had not been lodged. Nevertheless, the reporter found that the breach of planning control alleged in the enforcement notice occurred outwith the period of four years prior to August 1985 and consequently the enforcement notice was invalid. The reporter therefore quashed the notice. (Refs. P/PPA/SS/135; P/ENA/SS/50, April 23, 1986.)

9.51   Enforcement notice—"four year rule"—condition—amenity areas
It was a condition of planning permission for a housing development that areas be planted as amenity areas. The reporter was clear that the "four year rule" (see section 84(3)(*b*) of the 1972 Act) applied where an enforcement notice related to a breach of planning control consisting in failure to comply with any condition or limitation which related to the carrying out of operations and subject to which planning permission was granted for the development of that land. The reporter considered that the "four year rule" should apply to all conditions attached to this planning permission on the basis that the permission itself involved operational development. The enforcement notice was served more than four years after the date when details of landscaping had to be submitted. The appeal therefore succeeded. (Refs. P/ENA/SJ/10 and 11, March 10, 1988.)

9.52   Enforcement—"four year rule"—caravan—curtilage
Planning permission had been refused and an enforcement notice served in respect of the siting of a single static caravan. The appellant claimed that the appeal site was used as a site incidental to and within the curtilage of her dwelling-house and therefore did not require planning permission. The appellant claimed there had been a caravan on the site since 1962. The planning authority argued that if the caravan was used by the appellant while accommodating paying guests in her house, such use of the caravan was not incidental to the use of the dwelling-house as such. The authority also argued that the "four year rule" in section 84(3) of the 1972 Act did not apply. The reporter thought the appeal site was not part of the curtilage of any

dwelling, so that the siting of the caravan was not "permitted development" on that account. It was development requiring planning permission which had not been obtained. The reporter had no doubt that the caravan had been stationed on the land for more than four years and was almost persuaded that an established use prior to 1965 could be claimed under section 85(1)(*d*). The reporter concluded that "as the notice was served outwith the period of four years from the date of the breach of planning control, that service was incompetent as the breach enforced against, the stationing of the caravan on the site, was an operation referred to in section 84(3)(*a*) of the 1972 Act." (Refs. P/PPA/D/90; P/ENA/D/43, November 23, 1981.)

9.53 Material change of use—"four year rule"

In 1972 planning permission had been granted for the use of the appeal site as a scrap-yard for a period of five years. That period having expired, an enforcement notice was served. The appellant argued that an enforcement notice could only be served within four years of the breach. The "four year rule" applies only to "operations" and the appellant argued that the dictionary definition of "operations" related to activities and functions and that in the planning context operations might include making a material change of use of land by virtue of the provisions of section 40(2) of the Town and Country Planning (Scotland) Act 1972. This argument was not supportable because subsections (1), (2) and (3) of section 40 are stated to relate only to the purposes of sections 38 and 39 of the Act, *i.e.* those subsections only provide means of determining whether or not development under a grant of planning permission has been begun within the prescribed period. The appeal therefore failed. (Ref. P/ENA/FB/64, April 16, 1986.)

9.54 Enforcement notice—"four year rule"—use pre-1965

This was an appeal against an enforcement notice alleging the unauthorised use of a building for car repairs. An appeal was lodged on grounds (*c*) and (*d*) of section 85(1) of the 1972 Act (*i.e.* that the period of four years had elapsed at the time of the notice and that the breach of planning control had occurred before the beginning of 1965). The appellant stated that he had operated the business for five years. A previous occupant had operated the same type of business since about December 1963. The appellant believed that the subjects had been used as a car repair shop for over 20 years. The planning authority pointed out that the "four year rule" did not apply to changes of use and that there was no evidence that the property had been continuously used for car repairs since 1964. The reporter agreed that there was no supporting evidence for ground (*d*) of the appeal and he could not be satisfied on that ground. The appeal was dismissed. (Ref. P/ENA/SL/210, April 3, 1986.)

9.55 Enforcement—"four year rule"—contractor's yard—established use certificate

An enforcement notice had been served requiring cessation of use of a site for a haulage contractor's yard and the removal of a workshop, oil tank, diesel fuel tank and an articulated platform. The appellant argued that an enforcement notice could only be served within four years of a breach of planning control and that that period had elapsed before the date of service of the notice. The Secretary of State accepted this ground of appeal since the evidence indicated that the buildings had been erected more than four years before service of the enforcement notice.

An established use certificate governing the uses of the site was not granted. (Refs. P/ENA/LA/37; P/EUC/LA/7, July 11, 1987.)

9.56 Enforcement notice—out of time

An enforcement notice was served in respect of the making up of the foot-pavement in front of a house. The appellants claimed that the enforcement notice had been served out of time since the house had been occupied for more than four years before service of the notice. The planning authority argued that though it had been occupied for more than four years prior to the notice under a temporary occupation certificate, it could not be regarded as finally occupied until the full completion certificate was issued. The enforcement notice had been issued within four years of the latter date. The reporter considered that there was no stipulation that the certificate had to be a final one and held the enforcement notice to be out of time. (Ref. P/ENA/LD/18, December 29, 1987.)

9.57 Enforcement notice—immunity from enforcement action

The appellant claimed that prior to his purchase of a property it was in a state of semi-dereliction and for at least 25 years had been used openly as guest/boarding house with rented rooms which had their own washing facilities and communal bathrooms. He argued that multiple occupancy of the dwelling had occurred before 1964 and that the premises were therefore immune from enforcement action. The contention that it had been used as a guest house or boarding house had not however been supported by any documentary evidence and was disputed by local residents. As the onus of proof on this matter rested on the appellant, the reporter found his claim had not been substantiated. The appeal therefore failed. (Ref. P/ENA/SL/232, February 29, 1988.)

9.58 Enforcement notice—whether use immune from planning control
The appellant stated that his premises had been used since 1960 for the receiving, sorting and processing, storage and despatch of scrap metal. He appealed against the enforcement notice served on him on ground (*d*) of section 85(1) of the 1972 Act (*i.e.* on the ground that the alleged breach of planning control occurred before the beginning of 1965).

The reporter considered that there was a reasonable basis for the planning authority's allegation that scrap storage covered only part of the site in 1965; that there was a significant extension of the area used for scrap purposes between 1965 and 1968; and that from the late 1960s onwards there was increasing use of equipment on the site for the sorting and processing of scrap. The reporter concluded that the breach did not occur before the beginning of 1965 and did not therefore enjoy immunity from enforcement action. (Ref. P/ENA/SP/24, March 23, 1987.)

9.59 Reversion to previous use — body repair shop — temporary permissions
An enforcement notice was served in respect of the allegedly unauthorised use of premises as a workshop for panel-beating, vehicle body and engine repairs and sale of motor vehicles.

The appellant argued that the appeal premises had been used for mechanical and bodywork repairs by a series of owners since 1949 or earlier. The present use was similar to what had happened in the past.

The planning authority stated, however, that the appeal premises were originally a domestic garage which had been granted temporary planning permission as a panel-beater's workshop in 1949. A succession of temporary permissions for this use, and for use as a motor repair workshop, continued until the end of 1979. The authorised use therefore reverted to domestic garaging. There had been complaints from nearby residents about noise, smell, dust, smoke, outdoor paint-spraying, and congestion and obstruction in the street.

The reporter was satisfied that from 1980 onwards there was no authorisation for industrial use at the premises. Authority for vehicle repairs ceased with the expiry of the last temporary planning permission in 1979. It was therefore clear that the breach of planning control alleged by the notice had not continued since before 1965 and the breach of planning control was therefore not immune from enforcement action. The enforcement notice was therefore upheld. (Ref. P/ENA/GA/60, November 28, 1984.)

9.60 Enforcement notice—use pre-1965—vehicle repairs
An enforcement notice had alleged the unauthorised use of a lock-up garage for vehicle repairs. The appellant claimed that the use had begun before 1965 and produced a letter dated in 1962 which indicated that the premises had then been used for vehicle repairs. This led the reporter to quash the enforcement notice. (Ref. P/ENA/SL/148, July 14, 1982.)

9.61 Enforcement notice—use pre-1965—caravan site
An enforcement notice was served in respect of an allegedly unauthorised caravan site. One of the grounds on which appeal was made was ground (*d*) of section 85(1) of the 1972 Act—*i.e.* that the alleged breach of planning control, the use of land as a caravan site, had occurred before the beginning of 1965. The reporter found that the caravan use prior to 1965 had been of a casual nature and therefore the claim that the use had been established prior to that date could not be substantiated. (Ref. P/ENA/GD/5, February 26, 1979.)

9.62 Enforcement notice—caravan site
It was argued for the appellant that any breach of planning control involved in stationing caravans on a site occurred before the beginning of 1965. The reporter concluded that there was some use of part of the land for the occasional and infrequent holding of caravan rallies supervised by an exempted caravan organisation but that at all material times any other siting of a caravan thereon had been so infrequent that existing use rights pertaining to the land could not be discerned.

Concerning another part of the site the position was more complex; caravans had been seen on it from time to time during holiday seasons between May and September in a number of years before and after World War II. Sometimes there were two or three such caravans on the site. It was in effect "wild camping," no caravan remaining for more than two or three weeks. The caravan use was never regulated by the owner, tenant or factor of the land. There was increasing use of the site prior to 1960, when up to 16 caravans might be seen on the land. In the reporter's view it was, however, clear that in 1960 there was no organised or "existing site" as defined in section 13 of the Caravan Sites and Control of Development Act 1960, and that on the day the Act came into force there were no caravans on the land.

Use thereafter was sporadic, confined to a short summer season. The reporter drew the conclusion "that the subject land is not and never has been, a recognisable caravan site in either the planning or the legal sense, and that the unauthorised stationing of up to a score or so of touring caravans from time to time during the summer holiday season on part of the substantial area has, in land use terms, been *de minimis*." It followed, he considered, that the appeal under section 85(1) should not be upheld.

The Secretary of State accepted the recommendation that the notice should be upheld because "(i) the land in question has never been a recognised caravan or camping site and the occasional unauthorised use of the land for camping and caravanning in the past was not significant in land use terms; and (ii) the site is unsuitable for caravans and camping since its use would lead to damage to a site of special scientific interest and would have an adverse effect on the scenery of an area of great landscape value." (Refs. P/ENA/D/28 and 42, May 9, 1979.)

9.63 Enforcement notice—caravan site—use before 1965
An enforcement notice had been served in respect of the siting of a caravan in a field. The appellant had appealed against the notice on ground (*d*) of section 85(1) of the 1972 Act (that the caravan had been on the site since before the beginning of 1965). The present caravan was sited within a short distance of the site of a static caravan occupied since 1964 but since removed. The reporter found that the present caravan was sited in a position significantly different from that used in 1964. The present caravan had not been brought on to the site until 1979 and a breach of planning control had therefore taken place. The appellant also sought a determination under section 85(5)(*b*) of the 1972 Act as to whether the caravan could remain on the farm land from April to September. The reporter stated that if the farm were of the appropriate size, then up to three caravans could be stationed on it for holiday purposes. (Ref. P/ENA/HF/31, November 25, 1980.)

9.64 Enforcement notice—use pre-1965—furrier's workshop
This was an appeal relating to an enforcement notice served in respect of the use of a tenement flat as a furrier's workshop. The

main ground of appeal was that the breach had occurred before
the beginning of 1965 (see section 85(1)(*d*) of the 1972 Act). The
planning authority produced evidence from the valuation roll
which suggested that the premises had not been in continuous use
since before 1965 as a tailor's workshop. On the other hand the
appellant produced witnesses—a former employee and a customer—who stated that the use had been continuous; if accepted
that evidence would mean that the use was immune from
planning control. The reporter accepted the witnesses' evidence.
However, the appellant had, after 1965, increased the workshop
use from two to four rooms in the flat without planning permission. The reporter agreed with the planning authority that this
was an undesirable intensification of use which removed residential accommodation from the area. The enforcement notice was
therefore upheld as it applied to the two recently-converted
rooms. (Ref. P/ENA/SL/12, October 24, 1979.)

9.65 Established use certificate—change of use

Application had been made for an established use certificate in
respect of the use of a former byre as a joiner's workshop. The
reporter found that the byre had been used for occasional joinery
work associated with the farm between 1963 and 1969. In 1969 a
joinery firm entered into a lease with the owner of the farm to
use the byre for a commercial joinery business. Only in 1969,
therefore, did the byre cease to be a building used for purposes
ancillary to the farm. An established use certificate can only be
granted in respect of a use begun before the end of 1965. A
certificate could not therefore be granted here. (Ref. P/EUC/
LR/8, August 25, 1976.)

9.66 Established use certificate—lack of specification

An application for an established use certificate did not specify
the use which was claimed to be established. The application was
therefore inept and no valid decision had been made by the
planning authority. There was therefore no appeal before the
Secretary of State. The appeal premises had previously been in
use as a hostel for unmarried mothers but that had changed in
1974 when the premises came to be used to accommodate
persons of a "disturbed background." The reporter found that
the latter use had not begun before the beginning of 1965, so that
an established use certificate could not have been issued in terms
of section 90(1)(*a*) of the 1972 Act, but that since the change of
use from that of a hostel for unmarried mothers to the present
use did not require planning permission it might have been

possible to grant a certificate under section 90(1)(*c*). (Ref.
P/EUC/LA/1, September 23, 1977.)

9.67 Established use certificate—previous use unlawful—particular use
This was an appeal against the refusal of an application for an
established use certificate for the use of premises as a hotel and
restaurant. Premises consisting of two houses came to be used as
a hotel under a restricted hotel liquor licence. This involved a
breach of planning control before 1965. There was a change in
1975 when the premises came to be used under a full hotel
certificate. This change was held to be a material change,
involving as it did a change from the last authorised use of the
premises as two dwelling-houses.

Subsection (2) of section 90 of the 1972 Act provides that a
claim that a use has become established should relate to a
particular use of the land. The reporter stated that since the
particular use of the hotel premises did not exist before 1975, that
particular use could not become an established use within the
meaning of the Act. The appeal against refusal of an established
use certificate was therefore dismissed. (Ref. P/EUC/SL/1, July
12, 1978.)

9.68 Established use certificate—caravan site—site licence
An inquiry report stated that there had been reference in the
course of the inquiry to a suggestion that the applicant might
apply for an established use certificate under section 90 of the
1972 Act in respect of the stationing of caravans on the site. The
reporter pointed out, however, that such an application would do
no more than grant immunity from enforcement action under the
1972 Act; it would not entitle the applicant to a caravan site
licence (which can only be issued if planning permission has been
granted for specific use). (Refs. P/ENA/D/28 and 42, May 9,
1979.)

9.69 Established use certificate—ancillary use—waste land notice
A waste land notice had been served in respect of the deposit
of scrap materials in a garden and in respect of the repair of the
roof of a house which stood in the garden. There was also a
deemed refusal of an established use certificate. The property
had been occupied by the appellant and his mother until 1967.
Some vehicles and materials had been stored in the garden but
this had been ancillary to the residential use of the house and
garden. There was, therefore, no ground for issuing an established use certificate. (Ref. P/EUC/TA/1, September 5, 1979.)

9.70 Established use certificate—grounds not made out—enforcement notice—breach of planning control

An enforcement notice alleged unauthorised use of agricultural land for the storage of goods on a commercial basis and for the parking of commercial vehicles. An application for an established use certificate was made. The latter application was refused because (a) the use subsisting at the relevant date (January 1, 1965) was predominantly agricultural and the storage of goods or parking of vehicles was ancillary to the main agricultural use of the farm steading; and (b) that planning permission had never been granted for the use of the site for the above purposes.

An appeal was made, *inter alia*, on ground (b) of section 85(1) of the 1972 Act, *i.e.* that a breach of planning control was not involved. The reporter did not think that it had been shown that the land for which the established use certificate was sought had been devoted to the particular use claimed before the beginning of 1965. A certificate could not in consequence be granted. (Refs. P/ENA/GB/8; P/EUC/GB/1, February 12, 1980.)

9.71 Enforcement notice—established use—intensification of use

This was an appeal against an enforcement notice which required that the use of a dwelling-house for multiple occupancy, guest house or any purpose other than a private dwelling-house should cease. The appeal was made on ground (d) of section 85(1) of the Town and Country Planning (Scotland) Act 1972— *i.e.* that the breach of planning control alleged in the enforcement notice had occurred before the beginning of 1965 (and was on that account immune from enforcement action).

Two main issues had to be considered. First, was use as a guest house the predominant use of the premises before 1965, and secondly, if that was so, had there been in 1969 or 1970 such an intensification of the guest house use as amounted to development? An application for an established use certificate had been refused by the planning authority before the enforcement notice was served.

The reporter found that before 1965 the premises were used both for guest house and private residential purposes. At that time the whole upper floor was used for paying guests while on the lower floor, four rooms were used exclusively for private residential purposes. The kitchen, bathroom and dining-room were used for both purposes. The reporter considered, taking account of the floor area allocated to each use and the number of persons resident in each part of the house, that during the period of dual use the predominant use was as a guest house.

It was then necessary to consider the position after 1969 or 1970, when the owner stopped living on the premises, the private residential use ceased and the whole premises came to be used for guest house purposes. The planning authority claimed that this, together with the resultant increase in the number of paying guests, was such an intensification of the guest house use as to amount to development. The number of paying guests had, it seemed, increased from about eight or 10 to 18.

The reporter did not consider that an increase of that order could be considered conclusive. Complaints about disagreeable incidents were relevant but the reporter did not think there was any firm evidence to show that there had been a change in the character of use after 1970 as compared with the period from 1964 to 1970. In his view there had been no such complete change in the character of the use of the premises as would amount to development. He therefore sustained the appeal and quashed the enforcement notice. (Ref. P/ENA/LA/17, June 29, 1981.)

9.72 Established use certificate—granted in part

An established use certificate was sought in respect of premises currently being used for the repair and storage of motor vehicles. The reporter considered that prior to 1965 the principal use of the premises had been as a lock-up garage with incidental maintenance of the vehicles normally kept there. An established use certificate excluding the workshop element could therefore be issued. (Refs. P/PPA/LD/40; P/EUC/LD/1, September 10, 1982.)

9.73 Established Use Certificate—UCO—unlicensed private hotel

This was an appeal against a determination by the planning authority that planning permission would be required for the proposed change of use of an unlicensed private hotel to a private hotel with a restricted hotel licence.

No planning permission had been granted for the use as a private hotel but a certificate of established use was issued on August 21, 1972 to the effect that the use of the subjects "was established as a private hotel on June 27, 1972." The reporter said that an established use certificate was not equivalent to a planning permission. Section 90(7) of the 1972 Act provides that "[a]n established use certificate shall, as respects any matter stated therein, be conclusive for the purposes of an appeal to the Secretary of State against an enforcement notice served in respect of any land to which the certificate relates." It was agreed that the premises had never been licensed for the sale of liquor.

The appellant claimed that the terms of Class X of the Town and Country Planning (Use Classes) (Scotland) Order 1973 meant that "a hotel providing sleeping accommodation," which described the appeal subjects, could have a restricted hotel licence within the same use class. That was exactly what was proposed and it was therefore permitted development. The planning authority's view was that the specific rights conferred by an established use certificate did not extend to all the statutory rights enjoyed as the result of receiving planning permission for that use. In particular the certificate did not confer the right to change without planning permission to other uses within the same use class as permitted development.

The reporter said that while this might seem a narrow view, he accepted the correctness of the legal interpretation. In Classes III and IV of the UCO, for example, the scope for what started as an unauthorised use could result in a quite incompatible development being allowed.

The appellant's final submission was that the expression "private hotel" did not exclude the sale of liquor under a restricted hotel licence. The appellant did not point to any definition of "private hotel" but claimed that Scottish usage recognised as a private hotel one where the facilities were limited to residents and their guests and to persons taking meals. A private hotel might be licensed or unlicensed but, if it was licensed, it would only have a restricted hotel licence to serve residents and people taking meals.

The reporter considered that the question whether the appellant's proposal amounted to development depended upon the interpretation of the established use certificate. It certified the use of the subjects as "a private hotel." While the terms of such a certificate required to be interpreted strictly, he did not feel entitled to look behind the certificate for evidence of any further qualification which it might have contained. He considered it significant that the use was not certified as "an unlicensed private hotel." As the change from an unlicensed private hotel to one with a restricted hotel licence did not amount to a material change of use, the reporter thought he therefore had to conclude that the appellant's proposal did not amount to development. He accordingly determined that the proposed change of use did not require planning permission. (Ref. P/DEV/1/SL/1, June 14, 1983.)

9.74 Established use certificate—enforcement notice—fish offal from outside

The appellant was a fish merchant engaged in storing, handling and processing fish at the appeal site. In terms of an established use certificate issued in 1982 he was not liable to enforcement action in respect of the use of the site for "fish storage, handling and preparation and the incidental parking and repair of commercial vehicles related thereto." An enforcement notice was served in respect of the handling and storage of fish offal produced elsewhere. For the appellant it was submitted that the storage of fish offal on the site did not constitute "development" in terms of section 19(1) of the Town and Country Planning (Scotland) Act 1972 because it was not a building, engineering, mining or other operation nor a material change of use because fish offal had always been produced in the course of the appellant's activities. He denied that there had been any intensification of use; the nature of the business had not changed since the appellant took over the site in 1965. He alleged that the amount of offal stored on the site was no greater than the previous amount.

The planning authority agreed that fish offal was a necessary by-product of the appellant's operations as authorised by the established use certificate and that the appellant was entitled to continue these operations. They contended, however, that a material change of use had occurred in so far as the appellant handled fish offal collected from various premises elsewhere. It was submitted also that even if the collection, storage and disposal of fish offal produced by other fish merchants were held not to constitute a material change of use, the substantial increase in volume of offal stored on the site represented an intensification of use amounting to development.

The reporter said that since an established use certificate was designed to provide immunity from enforcement action, he considered that it had to be interpreted strictly, and on careful consideration of the certificate in question, he found no reason to hold that it encompassed storage of offal which was not derived from fish stored, prepared and handled on the site. There had therefore been a breach of planning control. (Ref. P/ENA/FC/17, May 6, 1986.)

9.75 Established use certificate—planning permission—Use Classes Order—restricted hotel licence

This was an appeal against an enforcement notice on ground (*b*) of section 85(1) of the 1972 Act (*i.e.* that the matters alleged in the enforcement notice did not constitute a breach of planning control). The appellants claimed that an established use certificate issued by the planning authority in 1981 granted planning permission for the use of the appeal premises as a guest house. The appellant also produced a certificate issued by the local authority under section 23 of the Licensing (Scotland) Act 1976. This was issued to a previous owner and stated that "a determination under section 51 of the Town and Country Planning (Scotland) Act 1972 that planning permission in respect of the said premises for the purposes of a restricted hotel certificate is not required." The appellant claimed that this showed that planning permission for use of the premises as a hotel was not necessary.

The planning authority said that there was no record of planning permission ever having been granted for the use of the appeal premises for any purpose. The authority claimed that an established use certificate was not equivalent to a grant of planning permission—it was only a defence against an enforcement notice issued in respect of that use. When the certificate was granted in 1981 no licence for the sale of alcohol existed and they contended that there was no reference in either the application or the certificate to the serving of drinks to residents. The authority accepted that the appellant had the benefit of a restricted hotel licence which allowed the service of drinks to non-residents but maintained that planning permission for that use had never been granted. The authority contended, in consequence, that planning permission was required for a change of use from the established use to any other use.

The reporter said that the determining issues were whether the use of the premises as a hotel and the service of meals and refreshments to non-residents constituted development requiring planning permission and, if so, whether the use of the premises as a hotel was feasible without adverse amenity consequences. When the established use certificate relating to the premises was issued, a licence to serve alcohol was not in force. In the reporter's view the established use certificate only provided immunity from enforcement action against the use specified. It was not analogous to a grant of planning permission and therefore, in this case, there was no planning permission in force. In consequence the provisions of the Town and Country Planning (Use Classes) (Scotland) Order 1973, which would allow use for another purpose within the same class, did not apply. He therefore found that planning permission was required for use of the premises as a hotel and also for the use as a guest house where meals and refreshments were served to non-residents. (Ref. P/ENA/SR/36, May 13, 1986.)

9.76 Established use certificate—use prior to 1965

This was an appeal against the planning authority's refusal to grant an established use certificate in respect of a 1.7 acre site for the storage of materials and the parking of commercial vehicles.

The planning authority claimed that the requirements of section 90 were not met as regards an established use certificate. They pointed out that on March 16, 1965 planning permission was granted for stacking of coal and other materials (but excluding scrap) and for ancillary purposes. The latter included use of the site for transport. This planning permission ended any breach of planning control and therefore the unauthorised use of the site had not continued since the end of 1964. The appellant claimed that this planning permission had never been implemented. The planning authority also claimed that at various times since 1964 the site had been used for paper-baling, car body repairs, car-breaking and as a caravan site.

The appellant claimed that use of the site for the parking of commercial vehicles and the storage of material was established under the Town and Country Planning (Scotland) Act 1947, prior to 1965. When, in 1965, planning permission was granted for the stacking of coal, the other uses were already immune from control. The 1965 planning permission was never implemented. The uses for which the established use certificate were now claimed had never been interrupted. The operation of a transport depot was suspended temporarily on the death of the owner but there was never any intention to abandon the use.

The reporter declared that section 90 requires, for an established use certificate to be granted, that the uses specified in the application must have been begun before the beginning of 1965 without planning permission, must have continued since the end of 1964 and must subsist at the time of the application. It seemed to the reporter that the appellant's application satisfied the first of these requirements but not the other two. At the time of the inspection it did not seem to be in use. Moreover, the appellant had said that the use of the site for storage of materials and transport was diminished in 1982. Although the appellant said operations were suspended and not abandoned, the reporter could not see how it could be held that the uses specified subsisted when the application for a certificate had been made in 1986. The appellant's argument had to fail. An application for an established use certificate made in 1981 had stated that the uses of the site included car-breaking and car repair. The reporter could not accept that the planning permission had not been taken up—and it was for storage and ancillary works—the latter presumably including storage of vehicles. (Ref. P/EUC/LB/1, June 30, 1987.)

9.77 Established use certificate—multiple occupancy

The appeal premises were a five-storey terraced house. The appellant sought an established use certificate for "multi-occupancy bed sits." Photocopies of the valuation roll made clear that from 1964 to 1971 the use of the premises had been described as six houses, and from 1971 to 1986 as service flats. The appellant argued that in terms of the planning legislation this meant that the appeal premises had been in continuous multiple occupancy since before the end of 1964. As no structural alterations had been made, the six houses mentioned in the earlier valuation rolls had actually been six service flats. For a period of five to six months in 1978 and in order to avoid the terms of the Rent Acts, some of the tenants had been provided with continental style breakfast. The large front ground floor room had been used as a breakfast room. Tenants from other flats also breakfasted there. For the rest of the day the room had been used as a lounge.

The reporter accepted that the house had been used to provide accommodation for a number of families since before the end of 1964. The six months use of the breakfast room was not enough to change things. However, the application for a certificate of established use was not for multiple occupation, but for the necessarily more specific "multi-occupancy bed sits." The reporter considered that on the latter aspect the evidence was insufficient to justify the issue of an established use certificate. The accommodation of the flats at first and second floor levels did not have private front doors and were not traditional flats. However, they could not be considered as traditional bed-sits either. The grounds for issue of an established use certificate were therefore not satisfied. (Ref. P/EUC/SL/6, September 30, 1987.)

9.78 Enforcement—established use certificate—establishing position pre-1965—amusement arcade

This was an appeal against refusal of an established use certificate in respect of the use of part of café premises. The appellants said that a back room had been used for amusement machines and a juke-box in 1955. The number of machines then increased to 10. In 1964 planning permission was obtained for a new building, the permission showing a café or coffee bar. Trading continued while, in 1965, demolition was going on and the transfer from the old to the new building took place in 24 hours, so that there was no break in continuity.

The appellants acknowledged that the particular portion of the appeal premises for which the established use certificate was requested was not the same area as that which accommodated the machines prior to 1965 but it was argued that taking the "broad use" approach to premises accommodating a café and amusement machines, the amusement machine use had continued since before the end of 1964. The number of machines had grown to 18. The reporter thought this argument would have some validity if the "broad use" of the land was a combination of activities that were so interdependent and inextricably linked as to be an integral and indivisible package. However, this did not appear to be the case at present as the three uses of the ground floor of the new building occupied separate areas and were reasonably independent of each other.

On the second part of the appellants' argument, on the slight geographical shift in the location of the amusement arcade, it was quite clear, said the reporter, that the particular "land" for which the certificate was sought had not been used as an amusement arcade prior to the beginning of 1965. The form of the building on the site and the disposition of particular uses was radically altered in the middle of 1965 when the new building was completed and occupied and the old building demolished. In the absence of more specific arguments that the continuation of the particular use under consideration could survive such a drastic upheaval on the site and a geographical shift to the south, the reporter was unable to accept that the appellants' claim had been made out.

The reporter said he had sympathy for the appellants because, had their new premises been ready a few months earlier, or if the planning permission for them had specified an amusement arcade as one of the authorised uses, the status of the use would have been much clearer. However, on the evidence, the reporter found the planning authority's decision well-founded. (Refs. P/PPA/LD/44; P/EUC/LD/2, March 9, 1983.)

9.79 Established use certificate—use not established—enforcement notice successful—vehicle parking—storage use
An application for an established use certificate had been sought in respect of agricultural land. The planning authority had refused a certificate on the grounds that the use subsisting before the beginning of 1965 was predominantly agricultural, any use for the storage of goods or the parking of vehicles being ancillary to the dominant use of the farm steading. Only a small part of the whole area of agricultural land was covered by the application for the established use certificate. The reporter was unable to accept that the land for which the certificate had been applied had been devoted to the storage of goods or the parking of vehicles. He

concluded that only a small, and not readily identifiable, part of the land had been used for these purposes. In his view a certificate should not be granted. The enforcement notice therefore succeeded, the use not having begun before 1965 or under a grant of planning permission. (Refs. P/ENA/GB/8; P/EUC/GB/1, February 12, 1980.)

9.80 Development—established use
The planning authority had served an enforcement notice in respect of the use of a number of lock-ups within the curtilage of a dwelling-house. The authority were unable to confirm or deny the appellant's claim that the site had been used for industrial purposes for 80 years but they noted that, by the appellant's own admission, the lock-up garages had only been in use for their current commercial/industrial uses since 1977. For that reason the council maintained that there could be no question of the use being "established"—*i.e.* that in terms of section 90 of the 1972 Act the use had been begun before 1965 and had subsisted continually thereafter. The reporter agreed. (Refs. P/ENA/ST/27 and 28, June 24, 1985.)

9.81 Enforcement notice—successful—determination of purpose for which premises in question might be used
In determining under section 85(5)(*b*) of the 1972 Act the purpose for which the premises in question might lawfully be used, the reporter considered the drafting of condition 2 of an earlier planning permission to be unfortunate. It restricted sales to "furniture, carpets, bedding, etc." It allowed scope for argument as to what "etc." added to furniture, carpets and bedding. It would be absurd to expect "etc." to include all other goods, and both parties appeared to accept that the *euisdem generis* rule applied in interpreting the condition. In the reporter's view the most generous interpretation which the expression could bear was to extend the range into other goods in the nature of furniture, carpets and bedding. This would therefore include all forms of bedding, floor coverings other than carpets and a range of fancy goods, such as ornaments or accessories in the nature of furniture. While the classes of accessories almost defied clear description, he had little difficulty in deciding that sports goods, clothing, garden tools, plants, handbags, books, wool, and shoes were not goods in the nature of furniture, carpets and bedding. China, cutlery and kitchen utensils were nearer the borderline but they too were not in the same category as furniture. (Ref. P/ENA/SG/9, November 11, 1982.)

9.82 Enforcement notice—unauthorised replacement windows—appellant's ignorance of policy

An enforcement notice was served in respect of the installation of new windows in a dwelling-house. The windows did not comply with the planning authority's policy for replacement windows in conservation areas. The appellant had moved to the house in 1986 and did not know it was in a conservation area. Nor was the appellant aware of the authority's policy on windows.

The reporter said that the planning authority deserved praise for its sound and strenuously defended policy on windows in conservation areas. It was most unfortunate that the appellant had fallen through the "information net" on the subject.

The enforcement notice required the substitution of the new aluminium windows with more appropriate timber windows. The reporter was satisfied that it would be over-zealous to require reinstatement in the case of the rear elevation. So far as the front windows were concerned, his consideration of the appeal on ground (*f*) of section 85(1) of the 1972 Act (that the steps required by the notice to be taken exceeded what was necessary to remedy the breach of planning control) hinged on the extent to which the front windows might be adapted as a possible alternative to total removal. The reporter saw no reason why a suitable white paint should not suffice to cover the aluminium and look like timber. Variations from traditional windows would remain but he considered that these were fairly subtle and, though sufficiently material to amount to development, were likely to be lost on the vast majority of people. Though the council was strictly correct in its view that the appellant's ignorance of the situation on replacement windows was not an "excuse" the reporter gave the case the benefit of the doubt because the district council's commendably strict policy would benefit from a more rigorous publicity programme. The authority might usefully review how best to extend its information service in this respect, given the priority it attached to these matters. (Ref. P/ENA/LB/46, August 17, 1988.)

9.83 Enforcement notice—amendment—material change of use

An enforcement notice alleged that there had been a material change in the use of premises from lock-up garages to a car repair business. The reporter dismissed all the grounds of appeal against the notice but considered that the requirement in the enforcement notice to restore the premises to their former condition was not reasonable; that requirement might well result in restored buildings which would not comply with the building regulations. The enforcement notice was therefore amended by the reporter. (Ref. P/ENA/LA/29, October 5, 1979.)

9.84 "Chalet"—accommodation for agricultural worker—enforcement
An enforcement notice had been served by the planning authority in respect of a chalet, said to be for the accommodation of an agricultural worker. The reporter considered that there were reasonable arguments for allowing the chalet to remain. He said, however, that:

"The chalet has been designed and laid out internally as holiday accommodation . . . and would be capable in its present form of sleeping up to six persons. The design fails to reflect the altered purpose for which the building is now required and I am not prepared to grant even temporary, conditional planning permission for this design owing to the additional burden of enforcement which would be placed on the district council in an area where problems of enforcement are already apparent."

The reporter added that the planning authority might perhaps be prepared to consider a restricted permission for the chalet "suitably modified as to internal layout in order expressly to accommodate a single farm worker." (Ref. P/ENA/GD/11, October 12, 1979.)

9.85 Enforcement notice—denial of breach
It was argued for the appellants that they did not use a site for the purposes of a road haulage business. This depended on the assertion that road haulage operations were almost entirely associated with and subsidiary to the vegetable preparation and packing operations which were legitimately carried on at the site and that any other haulage operations were too insignificant to merit enforcement action. The reporter found that it was the appellants' policy to use their vehicles to carry not only vegetable produce that was or was about to be processed at the site but also goods of any description on trips where the vehicles would otherwise travel unladen. Considering that drivers started and ended their day at the site, and the vehicles were maintained there and fuelled there, the reporter thought it quite improbable that vehicles laden with goods other than vegetables were not brought to the site in an emergency. That opinion was borne out by a witness. It was admitted that when vegetable processing was in abeyance, six or so drivers were continued in work, and an

advertisement in *Yellow Pages* included the company under the heading "Road Haulage." A breach of planning control had therefore occurred. (Ref. P/ENA/TB/38, October 26, 1987.)

9.86 Enforcement notice—remedying breach of control—roof tiles

An enforcement notice alleged a breach of planning control in that the roofing of two houses with interlocking clay pantiles was not in accordance with the approved plans. An appeal was lodged against the notice on ground (*f*) of section 85(1) of the 1972 Act (*i.e.* on the ground that the steps required by the notice to be taken exceeded what was necessary to remedy any breach of planning control). The decision letter stated: "It is considered that, even if the appellant's contention that there would be no material difference in the appearance of the roofs if roofed with non-interlocking tiles were correct, the breach cannot be remedied without complying with the steps required by the enforcement notice. For this reason the appeal on ground (*f*) fails and is therefore dismissed." (Refs. P/ENA/LB/9 and 10, April 27, 1979.)

9.87 Enforcement notices—caravans—permanency of service connections—within curtilage of house

Enforcement notices had been served in respect of the use of land as a caravan site. Appeal was lodged under section 85(1)(*b*) of the 1972 Act (that the matters alleged in the enforcement notices did not amount to development). It would have been legitimate to have one caravan on the property, provided its use was incidental to the use of the house. The house had, however, been burnt down, with the result that any caravan on the land for more than 28 days in any period of 12 months was unauthorised.

Appeal was also made on ground (*c*) of section 85(1) of the 1972 Act (that the notices could only be validly served within the period of four years after the breach). For this ground to succeed, the installation of the caravan would have had to be treated as a physical operation rather than as a change in the use of land. The appellants argued that whether a caravan was a "building" or not was a matter of circumstance. In a judgment delivered by a sheriff in 1979 under the Building (Scotland) Act 1959, it had been stated that the word "building" included a caravan. The appellants also made reference to the permanence of the caravan—it was fixed to the ground, had drainage connections and had water and electricity fed into it.

Although flimsy plywood-clad extensions had been added at both ends of the caravan, the reporter did not accept that the caravan was a building. He considered that the mobile home was capable of being transported in finished sections on a trailer, the service connections being of a rudimentary and impermanent nature. The Secretary of State took the view that the grounds of appeal under section 85(1)(*c*) were incompetent. (Refs. P/ENA/ LC/9, 12–16; P/WEN/LC/2, 5–9, November 16, 1979.)

9.88   Enforcement notice—fresh planning permission granted
An enforcement notice was served in respect of non-compliance with conditions attached to a temporary planning permission issued on November 15, 1977 and expiring on March 31, 1978. An appeal against the enforcement notice was lodged on January 20, 1978 but on March 7, 1978 the planning authority issued a fresh temporary planning permission in almost identical terms to the earlier permission. The Secretary of State would have been inclined to substitute different conditions for those attached to the planning permission of November 15, 1977, but saw no purpose in doing so because, irrespective of what conditions one attached to the 1977 permission, the enforcement notice could never have any practical effect because the schedule thereto required compliance with conditions attached to a planning permission which no longer existed. It appeared that the appellants could not now be penalised for non-compliance with lapsed conditions. The Secretary of State therefore considered that the enforcement notice should be withdrawn. (Refs. P/PPA/ LD/12; P/ENA/LD/2, January 31, 1980.)

9.89   Enforcement notice—period for compliance—residential caravan
An enforcement notice had been served in respect of the use of a caravan as a residence by the appellant and his family. The notice required the removal of the caravan within six months. Appeal against the notice was lodged, *inter alia*, on ground (*g*) of section 85(1) of the 1972 Act, *i.e.* on the ground that the period for compliance fell short of what should reasonably be allowed. The appellant explained that some three years previously he had, in desperation, bought the caravan as accommodation for his family and himself. Subsequently he had been offered a council house but was unable to pay both rent and hire purchase payments on the caravan, and that he could not afford the penalties involved in a forced sale of the caravan. The payments would be completed in a little over a year's time and he sought permission until that date. On compassionate grounds the reporter extended the period for compliance from six to 15 months. (Refs. P/PPA/FC/20; P/ENA/FC/5, May 12, 1980.)

9.90 Enforcement of planning control—breach of condition—responsibility of developer—responsibility of householder

An enforcement notice had been served on a housing developer in respect of an alleged breach of planning control. It was claimed that whereas the approved plans for a housing estate had indicated a timber screen fence at the rear of two gardens, a post and wire fence had been erected. The reporter noted that at no time had the planning authority formally accepted substitution of this kind. He was therefore of the view that a breach of planning control had occurred. The owners of the relevant houses had also had enforcement notices served on them.

One of the householders had appealed against the notices on several grounds. The planning authority expressed their sympathy that the householder had had to be served with the notice and had felt he had to appeal despite his view that a screen fence was essential to enhance the outlook and security of his house and garden. The authority pointed out, however, that to comply with the legislation, an enforcement notice had to be served on all those with an interest in the land. The reporter pointed out that the Act did not make provision for apportioning either the blame or the cost of complying with an enforcement notice. It was, however, the developers who had not complied with the conditions of planning permission and the reporter considered that they might reasonably be expected to assume that responsibility now. (Ref. P/ENA/SC/18, July 15, 1981.)

9.91 Enforcement—caravan in lay-by—role of regional council

Enforcement notices were served by the planning authority in respect of the siting of a mobile snack bar on the grass verge of a lay-by on a trunk road. The regional council appealed under section 85(1)(*f*) of the 1972 Act on the ground that the council had no power to comply with the notice and therefore, as far as they were concerned, all steps required by the notice were excessive. The Sheriff had already ruled that the regional council had no power to prohibit the owners of the caravan from selling refreshments on roads or lay-bys.

The planning authority argued that the enforcement notice had to be served on those persons with an interest "materially affected" by the notice. As roads authority the regional council had an interest. The reporter stated that as the region was the highway authority, with the right to maintain roads, footpaths, lay-bys and verges, he was bound to agree that the regional council had an interest in the appeal site which was materially affected. Therefore, in terms of section 84(5), the regional council was one of the parties upon whom the planning authority had to serve the enforcement notice. If the planning authority were to take action to secure compliance with the enforcement notice, a judgment in the Sheriff Court would appear to offer a complete defence to the regional council. (Ref. P/ENA/TA/2, May 13, 1983.)

9.92   Enforcement notice—purpose incidental to use of dwelling-house

An enforcement notice alleged that a breach of planning control had taken place on the appeal site, a yard behind a dwelling-house. It was alleged that there had been a material change in the use of the yard to storage of scrap motor vehicles and parts. An appeal was lodged on grounds (*b*) and (*bb*) of section 85(1) of the 1972 Act (*i.e.* on the grounds that the matters alleged in the enforcement notice did not constitute a breach of planning control and that the breach of planning control alleged in the notice had not taken place). The appellant claimed there had been no development whatsoever, that he did not own any scrap vehicles or run a scrap-yard, and that vehicles for his family's domestic use were repaired at the yard. Having considered the correspondence and documents submitted, the reporter was satisfied that the appeal site had recently been in use for the storage of motor vehicles and motor bicycles in excess of that which could reasonably be interpreted as being for a purpose incidental to the enjoyment of the dwelling-house. He was therefore of the opinion that the facts stated in the enforcement notice were correct and that the matters alleged constituted a breach of planning control. The appeal on grounds (*b*) and (*bb*) therefore failed. (Ref. P/ENA/TC/49, March 26, 1986.)

9.93   Enforcement notice—breach discontinued—permanence of notice

An enforcement notice required discontinuance of the use of the curtilage of a dwelling-house for the parking of earth-moving machinery, lorries and vans. Appeal was made on grounds (*b*) and (*f*) of section 85(1) of the 1972 Act (that the matters alleged in the notice did not constitute a breach of planning control or that the steps required to be taken exceeded what was necessary to remedy any breach of planning control). The appellant argued that the alleged breaches no longer occurred and that enforcement action was no longer necessary. In the reporter's view, even if these claims were substantiated, they did not amount to a valid ground of objection to an enforcement notice. He stated: "Even if the parking had totally ceased, the planning authority is entitled to pursue enforcement action if it believes there is a risk of recurrence. If there is a risk, they have not wasted time and money in pursuing the action and if [the appellants] are certain there is no risk of recurrence, they do not suffer by allowing the notice to be upheld." (Ref. P/ENA/SN/2, January 16, 1981.)

9.94 Enforcement notice—continuing effect

In the course of dismissing an appeal against an enforcement notice the reporter pointed out that compliance with an enforcement notice did not discharge its effect. (Ref. P/ENA/HE/2, August 28, 1981.)

SECTION 10

SPECIAL CONTROLS

See generally Young and Rowan-Robinson, *Scottish Planning Law and Procedure*, pp. 429–469.

The planning legislation makes provision for a number of special controls, the object of which for the most part is, as with general planning control, the protection and improvement of the physical environment. These special controls are directed at buildings of special architectural or historic interest ("listed buildings"), conservation areas, trees, advertisements, waste land and caravan sites.

Although the object of these special controls is the protection and enhancement of the environment, the ways in which they achieve that object differ. The general nature of these controls and the means by which they are tied into the development control process reflect their different characteristics. Listed building control operates as an addition to ordinary planning control; it is an offence to demolish a listed building or to alter or extend it in any manner which would affect its character unless listed building consent has first been obtained. Interior alterations to listed buildings may be subject to control. Planning authorities may designate particular areas as conservation areas. These are areas of special architectural or historic interest, the character or appearance of which it is desirable to preserve or enhance. One of the objects of designation is to stimulate interest in the preservation or enhancement of the amenity of such areas; in furtherance of this objective it is provided that publicity must be given by the planning authority to any application for planning permission which would in the opinion of the planning authority affect the character or appearance of a conservation area. Further, demolition of unlisted buildings in a conservation area is brought under control by the 1972 Act.

Works on trees do not amount to development but the 1972 Act recognises the importance of trees by providing for the making by planning authorities of tree preservation orders, relating to individual trees, groups of trees or woodlands.

Outdoor advertisements are subject to a complex and largely self-contained code of control. This code is currently contained in

318

the Town and Country Planning (Control of Advertisements) (Scotland) Regulations 1984. The central provision of the 1984 Regulations is regulation 5 which declares that no advertisement may be displayed without consent granted in that behalf by the planning authority or the Secretary of State or deemed to be granted by virtue of the Regulations themselves.

If it appears to the planning authority that the amenity of any part of their district is seriously injured by reason of the ruinous or dilapidated condition of any building in their district or by the derelict, waste or neglected condition of any other land in their district, the authority may serve on the owner, lessee and occupier of the building or land a notice under section 63 of the 1972 Act, referred to as a waste land notice. The notice must specify the steps to be taken for abating the injury and the period of time within which the steps must be taken. In the event of failure to comply with a waste land notice the planning authority may themselves take the necessary steps.

APPEAL DECISIONS

Listed buildings

10.1 Listed building—whether building a listed building

The reporter identified the determining issue in the appeal as being whether the appeal premises were properly described as a listed building. He concluded that although 491 Lawnmarket (the appeal site) was not included in the Secretary of State's list of buildings of special architectural or historic interest, it could be regarded as coming within the listed building item (1482) described as 495–509 Lawnmarket and 11, 15 and 17 James Court. This conclusion was based on the decision of the Court of Appeal in *Attorney-General* v. *Calderdale Borough Council* [1983] J.P.L. 310 in which it had been found that an unlisted terrace of mill cottages fell to be treated as part of the listed mill to which the cottages were attached by means of a linking bridge, despite the separate ownership of the mill and the terrace.

The reporter also concluded that the existing paintwork on the shop front and the east gable with its sheep logo adversely affected the character of the listed building and the conservation area in which the building was situated. His conclusion that the appeal failed on all five of the stated grounds of appeal was based on his view that:

(1) the appeal site was a building of special architectural or historic interest;

(2) the matters alleged in the enforcement notice constituted a contravention of planning control;

(3) the notice was served as required by section 92(3);

(4) the steps required by the notice would serve the purpose of restoring the character of the building to its former style; and

(5) the breach of listed building control alleged in the notice had taken place.

The Secretary of State was unable to accept the reporter's conclusion that the appeal property was a listed building for the reason that it was not included in the statutory list and it was not ancillary to the listed item (1482) as would be, for example, the mill cottages in relation to the mill as in the *Calderdale* case or the steading of a farmhouse. This view was borne out by a judgment of the House of Lords in *Debenhams plc* v. *Westminster City Council* [1986] 3 W.L.R. 1063.

Consequently, the Secretary of State took the view that the matters alleged in the notice did not constitute a contravention of section 53 of the 1972 Act, that a notice should not have been served under section 92(3) of the 1972 Act and that the breach of listed building control alleged in the notice had not taken place. While he agreed with the reporter that the character of the conservation area had been adversely affected by the paintwork which was the subject of the listed building enforcement notice, he was unable, for the foregoing reasons, to accept the reporter's recommendation that the listed building enforcement notice be upheld. Accordingly the Secretary of State upheld the appeal. (Ref. HGJ/6/LA/48, April 29, 1988.)

10.2 Listed buildings—failure to notify owners

Appeals were lodged against listed building enforcement notices served in respect of the installation of replacement windows in three listed dwelling-houses. The Secretary of State decided to determine the appeals. The planning authority had omitted to notify the owners of the houses that the Secretary of State had decided to include the buildings in the statutory list of buildings of special architectural or historic interest. The reporter considered that that omission did not mean that the buildings had not been included in the list. Nor did it mean that the Secretary of State was thereby barred from including them. He therefore concluded that the buildings which were the subject of the appeals were incorporated into the Secretary of State's statutory list in 1971, despite the subsequent lack of notification to the owners. He stated that although the former Ayr County Council should have informed the owners of the situation, nevertheless information on listing was held by district councils and should be available on request. He sympathised with the appellants in their situation but considered that the district council were right in their claim that the burden of establishing the status of any building prior to its alteration lay with the owners. He did not think that the district council was precluded in any way from taking enforcement action to have the original windows replaced.

The Secretary of State also regretted the failure of the former Ayr County Council to inform the owners that their buildings had been listed, but he could not in this case condone unauthorised alterations affecting the character of the listed buildings. (Refs. P/LBE/SP/5; P/LBE/SP/6; HGJ/6/SP/5, May 2, 1989.)

10.3 Listed building—automatic cash-dispensing machine—effect of alteration—relevant considerations

Listed building consent was refused for the installation of an automatic cash-dispensing machine at a listed building occupied by a bank. In the Secretary of State's view the installation of the teller would result in jagged interruptions of the clean lines established by the building's granite plinth and in the bronze grille above the plinth. The proposal would result in the virtual destruction of the grille as an interesting architectural feature. The character of the listed building would be adversely affected and listed building consent was refused. (Refs. P/PPA/SL/165; HGJ/2/SL/23, November 29, 1982.)

10.4 Listed building—replacement windows—"character"

Replacement windows had been inserted in the upper floors of a listed building. They differed from the traditional windows in that the horizontal division did not occur at the mid-point of the vertical division and in that the glazing of the opening sash and the fixed light was in approximately the same plane. It was clear to the Secretary of State that the windows in the front elevation of the appeal property, forming part of a terrace in a prominent position in the town centre, ought to be returned to their original appearance. The appeal was therefore dismissed as regards the front windows, but the Secretary of State considered that those at the back could remain. (Ref. HGJ/2/SF/1, January 31, 1985.)

10.5 Listed building—"character"—material consideration

The planning authority had granted planning permission and listed building consent for a three year period for the continued use of the ground floor of the appeal premises to house a computer. The council argued that the computer use had adversely affected the "character" of the listed building in question. The Secretary of State found it unfortunate that part of the listed building should have been allowed to house a computer, even temporarily. He was, however, prepared to extend the period of the permission to 10 years. (Ref. P/PPA/LA/113, August 26, 1980.)

10.6 Listed building—"character"—colour

Listed building consent had been refused for the painting in yellow and green of the shop part of a listed building. The building was in an outstanding conservation area. In the Secretary of State's view the main issue was whether the paintwork affected the "character" of the building and its setting to a degree which justified the refusal of listed building consent. The shop front was of modest proportions and was situated in the narrower part of the street; it was considered that the effect of the paintwork, which could be said to provide a modest counterpoint to the overall theme in the street, on the "character" of the listed building and on its setting was not so damaging that consent for it could not be granted. Consent was, however, granted on a personal basis only. (Ref. HGJ/2/TA/15, July 6, 1988.)

10.7 Listed building—onus of proof

Appeal against a refusal of listed building consent for new windows was made, *inter alia*, on the ground that the building was not of special architectural or historic interest (see paragraphs 7 and 8 of Schedule 10 to the Town and Country Planning (Scotland) Act 1972 and regulations 6 and 7 of the Town and Country Planning (Listed Buildings and Buildings in Conservation Areas) (Scotland) Regulations 1975, as amended). The reporter said on that point that in the absence of any supporting information he was unable to agree that the building should be removed from the list of buildings of special architectural or historic interest. In his view it was a good example of an early nineteenth century building which grouped well with others in the surrounding conservation area and the frontage of which was an important element in the townscape of the main street frontage. (Ref. P/LBE/SP/4, May 25, 1988.)

10.8 Listed building—material considerations—"character"

Listed building consent had been refused for the erection of a Dutch canopy on a listed building.

In the Secretary of State's view the main issue was whether the canopy affected the "character" of the building. Commercial advertising in the street had in the Secretary of State's opinion reached the stage where it was severely detrimental to the listed buildings and to the overall environmental quality of the conservation area. The impact of the canopy was not great if compared with the overall impact of advertisements in the street. However in this location, where the buildings were essentially of identical design, there was no doubt that the protruding canopy destroyed the overall unity of the terrace, as well as masking the architectural features of the linking arched doorpiece. There was also the question of precedent; it was considered that a number of canopies would serve to emphasise the problems and would be quite unacceptable. (Refs. P/PPA/LA/509; P/ENA/LA/99; HGJ/6/LA/51; HGJ/2/LA/77, March 4, 1988.)

10.9 Listed building—material considerations—slates

The appellant appealed against a condition attached to a grant of planning permission and of listed building consent. The condition required that second-hand Scotch slates be used for the roof covering of a building included as category B in the Secretary of State's list of buildings of special architectural or historic interest. The appellant wished to use modern tiles. The reporter found that these were less in harmony with the building than Scotch slates for the reasons that the colour and texture were different and that even laid broken-bond, the interlocking tiles had a smooth line and provided quite a different appearance from slates. There were no exceptional reasons to overcome the presumption that the listed building, which had a slate roof, should be re-roofed in the same material. No proof had been offered that the cost of using slate was unreasonable.

The appellant argued that second-hand slates had faults and limitations as a roofing material. They were more difficult to lay, requiring greater skill, and were of unpredictable quality. Tiles had a 50 year guarantee from the manufacturer, whereas second-hand Scotch slates were of inconsistent quality and seldom, if ever, had a guarantee beyond one year. If the condition remained, the re-roofing scheme was not viable. There was much more difficulty in patching a slate roof than a tiled one.

The reporter recommended that the appeal against the condition should be dismissed. The Secretary of State accepted this recommendation. (Refs. P/PPA/GA/233; HGJ/3/GA/1, December 6, 1984.)

10.10 Listed building—automatic teller machines—"character" of building
Planning permission and listed building consent for the installation of automatic teller machines had been refused. In the Secretary of State's view the proposed alteration would adversely affect the "character" of the listed building. (Refs. HGJ/2/LA/74; P/PPA/LA/495, November 23, 1987.)

10.11 Listed building—"character"—bank—automatic teller machine
Listed building consent had been refused for the installation of an automatic teller machine in a window opening at a listed bank. The bank argued that listed building consent was not required since the proposed works would not affect the character of the bank building. On the basis that a modern, non-traditional feature was to be introduced into the little-altered front of a nineteenth century classical design, the planning authority's view that the bank's "character" would be affected and that listed building consent was required was accepted. (Ref. HGJ/2/SQ/13, December 9, 1987.)

10.12 Listed building—disposal

A fine example of a nineteenth century mill was thought by the reporter to have no immediate alternative use. The Secretary of State said that where an owner was unable or unwilling to restore a listed building and where demolition was proposed, he would expect to see evidence that the property had been extensively marketed with a view to attracting a restoring purchaser. (Ref. HGJ/2/SU/3(2), December 9, 1987.)

10.13 Listed building—war memorial—removal

Planning permission and listed building consent had been refused for the removal of a war memorial from the precincts of a listed church to those of another church. The planning authority's reasons for refusal were to protect the setting and "character" of the listed church; that the location of the war memorial was an integral part of the churchyard; and that the removal of the memorial was regarded as neither appropriate nor necessary.

The reporter took the view that the churchyard comprised the curtilage of the listed church and the ecclesiastical exemption from listed building control applied to objects within that curtilage as it did to the church itself (see 1972 Act, section 52(7)). He concluded that a case could be made that the removal did not require the approval of either the planning authority or the Secretary of State. The Secretary of State agreed with the reporter's view that planning permission was not required for the removal of the memorial in the absence of the necessity for works which could reasonably be described as development for the purposes of the planning legislation. Conditions could not therefore be applied to the removal of the memorial and the making good of the site of the memorial at the listed church but he recommended that every care should be taken to ensure that the memorial was carefully taken down and transported without damage and that its former site be restored in a manner which did not detract from the appearance of and the approach to the listed church. (Refs. HGJ/2/FA/9; P/PPA/FA/102, November 12, 1987.)

10.14 Listed building—alteration—"character"

A new bathroom was constructed in a listed building, the works involving alteration of a bedroom.

The reporter identified the determining issue in the case as whether the unauthorised alterations which had been carried out were seriously damaging to the character of the listed building. It was the planning authority's policy that principal rooms should not be subdivided; the reporter considered this policy important. In the reporter's view the altered bedroom was a principal room because of its architectural features; its detailing matched that of the drawing room and it was of a carefully designed symmetrical layout. The principal effect of the alterations had been to alter the overall symmetry and proportion of the room. The most significant loss was the fireplace. The elaborate ceiling cornice had been faithfully copied on the length of new wall and the room was still an attractive one.

The reporter considered that it was important to see the alteration of the bedroom in the context of the works undertaken throughout the house. These he considered to be of an impressively high standard, resulting in the upgrading of an original Georgian house of considerable quality to provide accommodation compatible with a twentieth century pattern of living. Although there had been a breach of listed building control and a loss of architectural "character" to a principal room, there had been gains arising from the upgrading of the house. The change in "character" did not justify the withholding of listed building consent. The Secretary of State agreed. (Ref. HGJ/A/LA/3023, June 30, 1987.)

10.15 Listed building—conversion—"character"
A category A listed building had already been partially converted into flats. It was now proposed to convert the ground floor and basement into flats. The Secretary of State considered that the works would not affect the "character" of the building. (Refs. P/PPA/LA/447; HGJ/2/LA/68, May 28, 1987.)

10.16 Listed building—alteration—"character" of building
PVC windows had been installed in a listed building. In the Secretary of State's view the main issue was whether the introduction of outward opening PVC windows would affect the "character" of the B-listed property and the listed terrace of buildings to an unacceptable degree. The terrace still retained its "character" as an early nineteenth century terrace and, in the Secretary of State's view, justified its inclusion in the statutory list. In the Minister's opinion, to replace the existing windows with PVC windows which had a noticeably different profile and method of opening would add to the harm which had already been done and would be seriously damaging to the "character" of the terrace. The "character" of buildings such as those in the terrace depended to a great extent on the traditional treatment of door and window openings and the use of PVC windows was

considered inappropriate by the Secretary of State. Accordingly the appeal was dismissed. (Ref. HGJ/2/D/7, April 15, 1987.)

10.17 Listed building—replacement windows—material considerations
Traditional timber sash-and-case windows in a building had been replaced by aluminium windows. The Secretary of State considered the aluminium replacement windows to be noticeably non-traditional. In his opinion they detracted to an unacceptable degree from the quality of the building. He therefore dismissed the appeal against the enforcement notice requiring replacement of the windows. (Ref. HGJ/6/D/4, March 6, 1987.)

10.18 Listed building—first-floor room—partitioning
The planning authority had refused listed building consent for the partitioning of a first-floor room in a listed building. Their reasons were that this would adversely affect the "character" of a principal room in a listed building and that subdivision would be contrary to the authority's policy for subdivision of older property.

The appellants said the room was too large for economic use for single occupancy or for use as a meeting room and was not wholly suitable for open plan accommodation because of the sound amplification caused by the ceiling. A refusal of listed building consent would result in inefficient usage of existing space which would, in the long run, have a detrimental effect on the occupiers' rate of growth. Any division would be temporary and the appellants would undertake to remove the partition and reinstate the room on vacating the property.

The Secretary of State supported the local authority's policy on subdivision. In his view the proposal would affect the internal "character" to an unacceptable degree. Although the work would not be permanent, the proportions of the room would be changed and the moulding would not be properly seen. Although the division would be of a temporary nature, in practice the property was likely to remain in commercial use and it was very likely that a future user would have the same wishes as the present occupiers. Listed building consent was therefore refused. (Ref. HGJ/2/LA/61, June 23, 1986.)

10.19 Listed building—removal of mantelpieces and surrounds—architectural or historic interest
A listed building enforcement notice was served in respect of the removal of two fireplaces from bedrooms in a Grade A listed castle. The bedrooms had been fitted with new hand carved

waxed pinewood surrounds in "Adam" style. The surrounds which had been removed were probably of nineteenth century manufacture, possibly fitted when the building was altered in 1890.

An appeal was lodged on grounds (*a*), (*b*), (*d*) and (*g*) of section 93 of the 1972 Act—that the building was not of architectural interest; that the matters alleged did not involve a contravention of section 53 of the 1972 Act; that listed building consent ought to be granted for the works; and that the period specified in the notice as the period within which the steps were to be taken was too short. The appellant said that the proceeds of the sale had been spent in conversion work and maintenance at the castle.

In the Secretary of State's view the main issues were whether the chimney-pieces were features of special architectural or historic interest integral to the listed building and whether their removal affected the character of the building to an unacceptable degree. The building had been extensively restored and altered in the 1890s. It was possible that the late-Georgian marble fireplaces had been installed then. There was no dispute that they were *in situ* when the castle was listed in 1971. The Secretary of State agreed with the planning authority that the chimney-pieces were integral to the building as listed.

Section 54(3) of the 1972 Act requires that in considering whether to grant listed building consent for any works to a listed building, the planning authority (or the Secretary of State) shall have special regard to the desirability of preserving any features of special architectural or historic interest which it possesses. In this regard the Secretary of State's view was that the chimney-pieces were features which were of historic interest in relation to the development of the castle and of architectural merit in their own right and he considered that, as features contributing to the character and interest of the castle, their removal affected the character of the listed building to an unacceptable degree. It was not a desirable principle in the Secretary of State's view that important features of a listed building should be removed to finance its maintenance nor that the unauthorised alteration to the character of the building should be condoned.

The Secretary of State therefore dismissed the appeal. It was agreed that as the chimney-pieces had been installed elsewhere, the original 28 day period for compliance with the notice was insufficient for their reinstatement and three months were allowed for compliance. (Ref. HGJ/6/SP/4, March 4, 1986.)

10.20 Material considerations—listed building—internal alteration
Listed building consent had been refused in respect of proposed internal alterations to a category B listed building. It was proposed to form a hallway separating the lounge from the main entrance. The Secretary of State considered that the proposals would adversely affect the "character" of the main front room to an unacceptable extent. Consent was refused. (Ref. HGJ/2/SL/21, October 29, 1982.)

10.21 Listed building—church—extension
This was an appeal against a refusal of planning permission for the erection of an extension to a church. Although it was listed, the building was still in use for ecclesiastical purposes and was therefore exempt from listed building control. The reporter concluded that the design of the proposed extension would not harmonise with the existing building. Though the purpose was worthy, the disadvantages of the design were so great that they could not be disregarded. (Ref. P/PPA/SL/303, June 18, 1985.)

10.22 Listed building—material considerations
An appeal against a refusal of listed building consent was upheld on the ground that although the Secretary of State would usually expect efforts to be made to dispose of the house on the open market or find a fresh use for the property, the setting of the house was such that it was unlikely that a purchaser would be found who would ensure the retention of the building. (Ref. HGJ/2/SP/5, May 3, 1985.)

10.23 Listed building—curtilage—car park—material considerations
It was proposed to form a car park in garden ground at the rear of a listed building. Listed building consent was refused by the planning authority on the ground that a large paved area would adversely affect the "character" of the listed building. The planning authority said that there was as much need for care in the consideration of applications for listed building consent affecting the curtilage of a listed building as in the consideration of applications affecting the listed building itself.
The Secretary of State thought that the introduction of cars and extensive areas of hard paving would radically change the character of the garden. They would have a seriously detrimental effect on the "character" of the curtilage of the listed building. The appeal was dismissed. (Refs. P/PPA/LA/321; HGJ/2/LA/48, February 12, 1985.)

10.24 Listed building—"character"—listed building enforcement notice
A listed building enforcement notice was served requiring the reinstatement of five ornamental fireplaces in a B-listed mansion

house. Appeal was lodged on grounds (*b*) and (*h*) of section 93(1) of the 1972 Act, namely (1) that the matters alleged to constitute a contravention of section 53 of the 1972 Act did not involve a contravention and (2) that the steps required by the enforcement notice would not serve the purpose of restoring the "character" of the building to its former state.

The appellant submitted that listing should cover period detail and features and not items which had been grafted onto the building. The fireplaces had originally belonged to a house in Sussex, the "character" of the interior had already been drastically eroded by unsympathetic alterations prior to the appellant's purchase of the property, and in the light of these changes reinstatement of the fireplaces would not serve to restore the building's "character" internally.

The Secretary of State's letter said that the main issue was whether the five fireplaces contributed to the "character" of the listed building and whether their removal detracted from the building to an unacceptable degree. He said that although the chimney-pieces may have been brought up from England, it was probable that the architect conceived his designs to include the fireplaces as features of the rooms in question, as was the case in the rooms where the fireplaces remained. They were therefore considered features contributing to the "character" of the listed building. In the Secretary of State's view all the chimney-pieces had been important elements in the design of the rooms in which they had been situated and he considered the loss of three of them (from virtually unaltered rooms) to represent unacceptable changes in the "character" of these rooms. Listed building consent had been granted for alteration of the two rooms which contained the other two fireplaces. These changes would have the effect of altering the rooms' "character" to the extent that reinstatement of the fireplaces would not, in the Secretary of State's view, serve to preserve their "character." (Ref. HGJ/6/CC/1, December 13, 1984.)

10.25 Listed building—"character"—wet-dash harl

Roughcasting was held by the planning authority to be one of the features that might affect the "character" of a listed building. The authority offered, instead of modern dry-dash roughcasting to permit the alternative of finishing the front elevation with a traditional wet-dash harl. The Secretary of State agreed and granted planning permission for the latter or for a smooth-cement render with margins to be applied in smooth cement to the door and windows and painted. (Ref. HGJ/3/GE/1, April 2, 1982.)

10.26 Listed building—setting—advertisement of application

An application for outline planning permission for the erection of three dwelling-houses had been granted. The application site adjoined the grounds of a listed building. The reporter said that the planning authority had stated that the appeal site could be developed for housing with no detriment to the listed building. On this point it was the reporter's view that press advertisement under section 25 was only mandatory if the development would affect the setting of a listed building "in the opinion of the authority," which was clearly not the case here. In any event, it was the reporter's view that administrative defects did not invalidate a planning permission once issued; it remained valid, he said, unless revoked or successfully challenged in the courts. (Ref. P/PPA/GD/51, August 14, 1980.)

10.27 Listed building—paving of garden—removal of walls—whether necessary for safety or health or preservation of building

An enforcement notice was served in respect of the paving of the garden ground of a listed building and the removal of walls. The appellants claimed that the paving was necessary to eliminate a flow of surface water and to operate the building (a hotel) with the minimum of soil being brought into the kitchen. The paving had thus been laid in the interests of safety and health and for the preservation of the building.

The removal of walls, some of which were crumbling or in a dangerous condition, was in the interests of extra light. The walls were not of special interest.

The planning authority denied that the work was urgently necessary in the interests of safety or health or for the preservation of the subjects. The elimination of surface water and the operation of the subjects with the minimum of soil brought in did not necessitate the paving of the whole garden. The removal of the walls had little effect on light.

The Secretary of State agreed with the planning authority but allowed extra time for negotiation on a suitable scheme for the restricted paving of the garden. (Ref. HB/AEN/LA/3, July 17, 1978.)

10.28 Listed building—article 4 direction—painting of building

A building was listed and was also the subject of an article 4 direction made under the Town and Country Planning (General Development) (Scotland) Order 1975 taking away the right to paint the building. The lower part of the facade of the building was painted. It was the planning authority's policy that stonework should, if possible, be cleaned by an approved method if this would result in acceptable restoration of the natural surface. Failing this, new painting in an approved stone colour should be carried out.

The Secretary of State upheld the enforcement notice. (Ref. HB/AEN/SL/1, May 26, 1977.)

10.29   Listed building—refusal of consent—listed building purchase notice

This was a listed building purchase notice served in respect of a disused church and an appeal against the refusal of listed building consent for the demolition of the church.

So far as the appeal was concerned the appellants stated that they did not consider the property to be of such special architectural or historic interest as to warrant its retention at any great expense. The planning authority submitted that they considered the church to be a good example of Gothic Revival architecture. Their main reason for the refusal of listed building consent was that they considered the church building to be of considerable architectural merit and to be of high townscape value.

The reporter recognised the architectural qualities of the church which had led to its listing. He considered the church to be a good, although not outstanding, example of its category and this, together with its townscape value, caused him to comment that he was of the opinion that the church deserved further efforts to secure its preservation in its entirety.

As regards the purchase notice, the owners had advertised the church for sale. While the property remained on the market, the owners, in anticipation of the property being eventually sold for demolition and redevelopment and oblivious of its listed status, did not incur greater expense than was necessary for its maintenance. However, as dry rot was discovered in the upper hall of the church an application for planning consent for demolition was made. While the planning authority accepted the fact that the church had been advertised for sale, they pointed out that the services of the Historic Buildings Bureau (which had been brought to the owners' attention) had not been utilised. The Scottish Civic Trust maintained that not all avenues had been explored for an alternative use for the church building.

The reporter was of the opinion that the church deserved further efforts to secure its preservation in its entirety. He did not consider that the owners had exhausted all the possibilities open to them. He concluded that he would not accept that the owners had been deprived of reasonably beneficial use of the land without a further round of advertisement being undertaken and the services of the Historic Buildings Bureau being enlisted.

The reporter therefore recommended that the appeal be dismissed and that the listed building purchase notice should not be confirmed. The Secretary of State saw no reason to disagree. (Ref. HB/PN/CC/1, October 26, 1976.)

Conservation areas

10.30 Conservation area consent—workshop—need for consent

The planning authority had refused conservation area consent for the demolition of an engineering workshop. The reporter discussed the statutory provisions for the demolition of unlisted buildings in conservation areas which had come into force since the appeal was lodged. He concluded that the provision in Annex IV to SDD Circular 17/1987 (relating to the Town and Country Planning (Listed Buildings and Buildings in Conservation Areas) (Scotland) Regulations 1987) for the exclusion of buildings with a total cubic capacity not exceeding 115 cubic metres from the requirement for conservation consent to be obtained for their demolition was a new provision and that demolition of the engineering workshop might no longer require conservation area consent. In any event the reporter recommended that consent be granted for demolition. (Refs. P/PPA/SC/57; P/ENA/SC/52; P/WEN/SC/7; HGJ/C/SC/4, July 18, 1988.)

10.31 Conservation area—advertisement—material considerations—amenity

A non-illuminated signboard had been erected above a shop. The planning authority refused consent for the reason that the sign, by reason of its design, size and location was detrimental to the visual amenity of the shop front and the surrounding outstanding conservation area.

The Secretary of State considered the planning authority's efforts to improve the standard of signage in the area to be worthy of support. While accepting that commercial premises which happened to be located in areas of special character and amenity should not be denied advertising media normal to their type of business, there had to be a reasonable degree of restraint exercised in any display. Here the view was taken that the sign, because of its size and location, was detrimental to the amenity of the building and of the area in general. (Ref. P/ADA/SL/553, January 7, 1988.)

Tree preservation orders

10.32 Tree preservation order—"trees" or "woodland"

Section 60 of the 1972 Act was amended by the Town and Country Planning (Amendment) Act 1985 in order to remove an anomaly in the 1972 Act whereby if a tree in a woodland which was protected by a tree preservation order were destroyed, the planning authority had no power to order replacement though an authority did have that power in respect of a protected tree which was not in a woodland.

The planning authority served a notice in respect of the alleged unauthorised felling of trees. It was agreed that the felling took place before the coming into force of the 1985 Act. The reporter accepted that the notice served related to trees and not to woodland. Paragraph 1 of the tree preservation order referred to any of the trees, groups of trees or woodland but the schedule specified only woodland. No trees or groups of trees were separately identified and had it been intended to protect trees or groups of trees, then paragraph 1 of the order should have stated "and" and not "or" and the particular trees or groups of trees should have been separately identified. The map also showed a woodland. The reporter was therefore satisfied that the only protection which the tree preservation order conferred was on trees as part of a woodland. As a consequence the replanting obligations of section 60, and the power of the planning authority to enforce such replanting did not apply in this case.

Accordingly, the notice was quashed. (Ref. P/TEA/LA/3, March 17, 1987.)

10.33 Material considerations—tree subject to preservation order

The planning authority had refused permission for the felling of a tree covered by a tree preservation order. The appellant argued that it encouraged insects and thus caused a nuisance especially for the drying of clothes. Removal of the tree would have little effect on amenity as it was seen against a woodland background. Permission was therefore granted for the felling of the tree. (Ref. HGM/3/4/SK/2, June 14, 1982.)

10.34 Tree preservation order—felling of trees—nuisance

Trees in a front garden were subject to a tree preservation order. The appellant contended that in terms of section 58(6) of the 1972 Act nothing in a tree preservation order prohibited the felling of a tree if it was urgently necessary for the abatement of a nuisance. In his view the partial denial of light, the dirtying of cars parked for no more than a few hours, and the failure of plants within the umbrella of the trees to flourish constituted real nuisance. The appellant argued that where an occupier was disadvantaged by a real nuisance, the argument for removal of the nuisance had to outweigh any argument based on preserving unchanged the view of passers-by. He maintained that the sycamore trees were not appropriate to the house and he knew of no other situation in the district where similar trees stood in a similar relationship to similar houses.

The Secretary of State considered that the felling of the sycamores would impair the townscape of the street. They were sound, healthy trees which did not endanger the safety of the public. Most of the nuisances to which the appellant referred were fairly commonplace and were applicable generally to trees in private gardens. Though the trees were not unusually close to the house, they created a significant loss of light to parts of the building. The detrimental effect on the dwelling justified a substantial reduction in their height and spread. He therefore approved the pollarding of the sycamores. (Ref. P/TPO/2/SB/1, March 6, 1986.)

Advertisements

10.35 Advertisement—unauthorised display

An advertisement enforcement notice alleged the unauthorised display of an advertisement measuring 10 by 20 feet on the gable of premises. An appeal against the enforcement notice was based on regulation 25(1)(*a*) of the Town and Country Planning (Control of Advertisements) (Scotland) Regulations 1984, *i.e.* that the matters alleged in the notice did not constitute a display of an advertisement without a consent required by the regulations. The appellants contended that the display had been erected in terms of Class IV of regulation 10 of the 1984 regulations and enjoyed deemed consent.

The planning authority disagreed. In their view the advertisement under appeal did not comply with the description of the advertisements allowed by Schedule 4, Class IV of the regulations in that the advertisement was designed to promote sales of a brand name product which was widely available as opposed to an advertisement which was specifically designed to promote sales of a product or products produced on the premises on which the advertisement was displayed. It was not therefore an advertisement "wholly with reference to . . . the goods sold or services provided . . . on the premises." They also considered that the advertisement did not comply with the regulations in that the height of the highest part of the panel was greater than the bottom of the first-floor level of the building on which the advertisement was displayed. In addition, in their view the advertisement did not comply with one of the other conditions contained in Schedule 4, Class IV, relating to shop premises, which stated that advertisements were not to be displayed on the wall of a shop unless the wall contained a shop window. The wall on which the advertisement was displayed had no window and deemed consent could not therefore be alleged or implied. The appeal was dismissed. (Ref. P/ADE/ST/6, March 15, 1989.)

10.36   Advertisements—whether consent required
   Consent had been refused and an advertisement enforcement notice served in respect of the allegedly unauthorised display of six non-illuminated window panel signs. The signs were displayed in the windows of premises partly used as a dwelling-house and partly as offices. Appeal against the enforcement notice was lodged on ground (*a*) of regulation 25(1) of the Town and Country Planning (Control of Advertisements) (Scotland) Regulations 1984—*i.e.* that the matters alleged in the enforcement notice did not constitute a display of an advertisement without a consent required by the regulations. The reporter agreed with the planning authority that each of the six panel signs—comprising green sheets of glass with black borders and black lettering—constituted advertisements rather than the lettering alone. The reporter stated that it was the totality of the elements that constituted the sign. Each advertisement exceeded 0.3 square metre in area and deemed consent was therefore not granted by Class II of Schedule 4 to the regulations. The signs were displayed behind windows and could not therefore be considered in terms of Class IV which related to advertisements on business premises. There was also an element of doubt about whether two rooms—the kitchen and a bed-sitting room—could be strictly defined as "business premises" as that expression was defined in regulation 2(1). Class V covered advertisements *within* buildings, but the extent of the six signs was such that they failed to meet the criteria relating to covering less than one-tenth of the area of window within which they were displayed. The reporter concluded that the signs required a consent and that the appeal on ground (*a*) should therefore fail. (Ref. P/ADA/SL/544, March 14, 1989.)

10.37   Advertisement—business premises—shop window
   An appeal was lodged against an advertisement enforcement notice on the ground that by virtue of regulation 25(1)(*a*) and

Schedule 4, Class IV of the Town and Country Planning (Control of Advertisements) (Scotland) Regulations 1984 (deemed consent for advertisements on business premises wholly with reference to the business carried on, the goods sold, etc.) the advertisement in question enjoyed deemed consent.

The planning authority pointed out that in terms of Class IV of Schedule 4 to the Regulations an advertisement on business premises was subject to a condition that it was not to be displayed on the wall of a shop unless that wall contained a shop window. In this case the wall in question contained no window. The advertisement did not therefore enjoy deemed consent.

The official view was taken that the advertisement panel did not enjoy deemed consent in terms of Class IV of Schedule 4 because it was designed to promote sales of a brand name product which was widely available as opposed to an advertisement which was specifically designed to promote sales of a product or products produced on the premises on which the advertisement was displayed. It was not therefore an advertisement "*wholly* with reference to . . . the goods sold or services provided . . . on the premises." (Ref. P/ADE/LA/3, June 20, 1988.)

10.38 Advertisement hoarding—enforcement notice—deemed consent

An advertisement enforcement notice required the removal from the gable wall of a shop of an allegedly unauthorised hoarding. The appeal was based on regulation 25(1)(*a*) of the Town and Country Planning (Control of Advertisements) (Scotland) Regulations 1984, *i.e.* that the matters alleged in the enforcement notice did not constitute a breach of the regulations. The appellants claimed that the advertisement had the benefit of consent by virtue of Schedule 4, Class IV of the regulations (deemed consent). The planning authority disagreed with this interpretation of the regulations, pointing out that one of the standard conditions of the deemed consent provision (Schedule 4, Class IV) is that advertisements on business premises shall not be displayed on the wall of a shop unless the wall contains a shop window. Here there was no window in the gable wall.

There was therefore no doubt that the advertisement required consent under the 1984 Regulations. (Ref. P/ADE/LA/2, August 25, 1987.)

10.39 Advertisements—road safety

Consent had been sought for the erection at a football ground of eight hoardings, each measuring 10 feet by 20 feet. The proposed display would be seen above the boundary wall of the ground and the overall height would be about 17 feet. The appeal site was within 30 metres of a major six-way roundabout at which there were a number of statutory directional and warning signs.

Agreeing with the planning authority, the Secretary of State found that although the proposed display would be set back from the road, there could be no doubt that the hoardings would be a very prominent feature of the street-scene. It could not be assumed, he said, that the advertisement display would not tend to impair the degree of concentration required by motorists at this location. (Ref. P/ADA/TB/9, January 20, 1986.)

10.40 Shop fascia—listed building

Consent had been sought in respect of an acrylic advertising fascia on a shop which formed part of a listed building. The premises were in a conservation area. The planning authority's reasons for refusal of consent were that the material proposed to be used was inappropriate in a conservation area and that the material would adversely affect the "character" of the listed building. The authority had been concerned about the variety of shop signs in the area. Their policy now was to restrict new fascias to hand-painted timber signs designed in accordance with advice issued by the authority.

The appellant argued that the acrylic material was appropriate for a shop front, would be less costly to maintain than painted timber and would retain the shop's high standard and appearance. The shop was part of the Mace group and it was important that the public should be able to recognise it as such so that the shop might benefit from national advertising. There were other shops in the vicinity with plastic fascias.

The Secretary of State accepted that the use of traditional materials was an important element in the preservation of "character." He therefore supported the planning authority's policy which sought to halt the erosion of traditional signs. (Ref. HGJ/2/CA/3, January 27, 1986.)

10.41 Advertisements on listed building

The planning authority had refused advertisement consent for the erection of company logos on the front of a listed building. In the authority's view the proposed signs would be detrimental not only to the visual appearance and character of the building but also, by reason of the bulk, position and colours of the proposed signs, to the surrounding area. The architectural merit of the building was not in dispute. The building also formed an attractive group with other buildings nearby. The building was on the south side of the Clyde and from the pedestrian promenade on the opposite side of the river the building was a prominent feature. The carving on the front of the building gave it richness and splendour. A building of this type could, it was argued, only take a limited number of brightly coloured additions in light modern materials. The Secretary of State considered that the erection of the proposed logos on the front of the building would detract from the grandeur and dignity of the building. Listed building consent and advertisement consent were therefore refused. (Ref. HGJ/2/SC/33, July 12, 1985.)

10.42 Advertisements—figurines—appearance of building
This appeal against a refusal of advertisement consent and an advertisement enforcement notice in respect of figurines at an establishment called *Oscars* was, unusually, dealt with by way of a public inquiry. The planning authority considered that illuminated figurines, facsimiles of film "Oscars" and each about six feet tall, were out of scale and character with the attractive building, a building of considerable architectural merit, on which they were displayed. The figurines detracted from the appearance of the building and of the street-scene generally.

The reporter was of the view that the appeal premises were the only significant ones in the area, that the refurbishment of the building had undoubtedly emphasised its classical design, and that the figurines themselves were obtrusive and had an unfortunate effect on the building's symmetry by almost obscuring the pilasters. However, he also thought that the figurines had to be considered in the context of the fascia and other advertisements on the building, the neon-strip illumination and the rigid canopies. Thus viewed, the figurines did not, the reporter concluded, have adverse consequences for visual amenity.

There had arisen the question whether the figurines were advertisements or whether their erection involved development requiring planning permission. The reporter concluded that the figurines were advertisements as they were devices used for purposes of announcement and that their erection would have served no purpose had the premises not been called *Oscars*.

The Secretary of State accepted both of the reporter's conclusions. Consent was therefore granted and the enforcement notice quashed. (Refs. P/ADA/FB/29; P/ADE/FB/2, April 14, 1987.)

10.43 Advertisement hoardings—screening
This was an appeal against the refusal of advertisement consent for four advertisement hoardings, each measuring 10 feet by 20

feet, to be erected alongside a busy road. The planning authority considered that by reason of their size, bulk and location the proposed hoardings would be detrimental to the amenity of the area.

The Secretary of State noted that the appeal site was situated in a predominantly commercial area where a certain amount of advertising was to be expected and that the land in the area, including the appeal site, was unattractive. There appeared to be no imminent prospect of the site being developed. The appellants proposed to remove an untidy stone and brick wall on the boundary of the site, to landscape the area in front of the advertisement panels and to remove an existing advertisement panel.

In the circumstances the Secretary of State considered that in this setting an advertisement display would not so detract from amenity as to justify the refusal of consent. (Ref. P/ADA/SL/449, May 10, 1985.)

10.44   Advance directional signs

Consent had been refused for the erection of three advance directional signs, two on one side of a food bar and one on the other. It had been proposed to site the signs, each measuring 8 feet by 4 feet, on land adjacent to a trunk road in an area of outstanding natural beauty. The planning authority stated that the signs would, if permitted, create an undesirable precedent, that the size of the signs was excessive and that the signs were contrary to the authority's policy of not allowing advance signs for roadside establishments except where such signs were necessary in order to reduce the incidence of vehicular stopping and manoeuvring on the highway.

In his decision letter the Secretary of State declared that it was his general policy that, outside built-up areas, advance directional signs alongside main roads should be kept to a minimum. This was because of the adverse effects which such signs might have on amenity and road safety. Exceptions to this general policy might be made where premises were in a remote or isolated position or where, in the absence of a sign, premises might pass unnoticed. Here the food bar could not be said to be in a remote or isolated position. There should not be any difficulty in identifying the premises for persons approaching them from the west. It was, however, accepted that because of the road alignment and level, the absence of a sign for the eastern approach might result in a loss of trade as the premises did not come into the view of a driver from any great distance away. There was, therefore, a case for an advance sign to the east of the food bar. However, a sign of the size proposed would be out of place; a smaller sign containing only the name of the food bar and the distance to it was permitted. Since there appeared to be no similar premises in the area, the decision could not be seen as setting a precedent that would result in a proliferation of such signs. (Ref. P/ADA/SA/34, June 11, 1986.)

10.45 Material considerations—advance directional signs—when permissible

It was pointed out that advance directional signs on main routes should be kept to a minimum because of their effect on amenity and road safety. It was established policy that such signs should be permitted only where there were special circumstances sufficient to outweigh these considerations. Usually they were only permitted in open countryside outside towns. Where, however, the premises were located within a town or village and were clearly visible or readily identifiable, there could not be the same justification for advance signs. Here the premises were located in a main street, were visible from the main road and from a road junction, and had signage which clearly identified their presence. There was no special need for an advance directional sign. (Refs. P/ADA/TA/26; P/ADE/TA/3, July 2, 1987.)

10.46 Advertisement—condition

In granting permission for a change in the use of premises to office use the planning authority imposed a condition to the effect that, notwithstanding the provisions of the Town and Country Planning (Control of Advertisements) (Scotland) Regulations 1961, details of any advertisement or sign on the premises were to be submitted for the authority's approval. The reason given for this condition was to enable the authority "to retain control of proposed signs in the interests of amenity." In the authority's view the consent automatically granted by the 1961 Regulations for certain sorts of advertisements might well result in the erection of signs which would be incompatible with the building and would detract from the amenity of the street in question. The authority also pointed out that section 26(1) of the 1972 Act empowers a planning authority to grant planning permission subject to such conditions as they think fit.

The condition was discharged by the Secretary of State, the decision letter stating that "generally the control of advertisements is a matter to be dealt with under the provisions of the

Control of Advertisements (Scotland) Regulations 1961 and that it is inappropriate to seek to regulate advertisements by attaching conditions to a planning permission."

It does not seem that the Secretary of State intended to imply that such a condition is legally invalid; it appears that on policy grounds he disapproved of powers under the planning Acts being used to control matters which are the subject of other, more specific, legislation. (Refs. P/PPA/HF/45; P/ADA/HF/4, May 4, 1982.)

10.47   Advertisements—material considerations

Consent had been refused for the display of two advertisement hoardings, each measuring 10 feet by 20 feet. The Secretary of State noted that the hoardings would be erected in an area of mixed amenity, and that the panels would be mounted on a 6 foot wall and therefore be partially visible against the skyline. The hoardings would not, however, be directly overlooked by any residential property. The decision letter stated that it was normally the practice to allow hoardings only in situations where they were likely to be beneficial to the visual amenity of the area, as for example by screening untidy buildings or land. Such a claim could not be made here. The display would introduce an over-conspicuous and obtrusive feature in the street-scene, to the detriment of the visual amenity of the area as a whole. (Ref. P/ADA/SL/535, May 11, 1987.)

10.48   Advertisement—material considerations

It was proposed to erect an internally-illuminated projecting box sign. The sign was to be of perspex with a white background and purple squares and yellow letters advertising "Silk Cut" cigarettes. Consent was refused for the reason that "[t]he installation of product-only signs is contrary to the Regional Council's policy on signposting and would be detrimental to the visual amenities of the surrounding area."

The decision letter stated that the content or subject matter of an advertisement should have no bearing on the question whether or not a sign would be detrimental to the visual amenity of an area. (Ref. P/ADA/B/21, January 1, 1988.)

10.49   Advertisements—material considerations

Consent had been refused for the display of two advertisement panels, each measuring 20 by 10 feet, with associated screen fencing on an area of vacant land.

It was noted that land use in the area was mixed but that commercial/industrial use predominated in the vicinity of the appeal site; that the display would not be directly overlooked by the occupants of the nearby flats; and that the Divisional Road Engineer had no objection to the proposal. Notwithstanding the proposed landscaping works in the vicinity, the view was taken that the proposed display would not be so detrimental to the visual amenity of the occupants of the nearby flats in particular or the area in general as to warrant a refusal of consent. (Ref. P/ADA/SL/574, July 14, 1988.)

10.50 Advertisement hoarding—material considerations—discontinuance notice

A notice requiring discontinuance of the use of a site for the display of an advertisement was served by the local planning authority. The authority's reasons for service of the notice were that the advertisement contravened their advertisement policy; the hoarding, by reason of its bulk and location, detracted to an unacceptable degree from the amenity of the surrounding area and of local residents; and the advertisement's proximity to a trunk road and its prominence made it likely that motorists' attention would be distracted by it.

Regulation 14 of the Town and Country Planning (Control of Advertisements) (Scotland) Regulations 1984 provides that where a planning authority, if they consider it expedient to do so in order to remedy a substantial injury to amenity or a danger to members of the public, may serve a discontinuance notice. They can, however, only serve such a notice in respect of an advertisement displayed with consent deemed to be granted by the 1984 Regulations themselves. Here the advertisement was not being displayed with deemed consent. The discontinuance notice was therefore invalid and the appeal upheld.

The advertisement's reprieve was, however, short-lived in that within a few months an enforcement notice was served in respect of the display. Advertisement consent was sought and refused. On appeal, the Secretary of State found that the display was in an area which was mixed residential/commercial in character and that the advertisement occupied a prominent position in the street-scene. The Minister noted that the display was contrary to the planning authority's policy which provided that advertising panels should normally only be permitted where the scale and design were in keeping with the locality and where they made a positive contribution to the environment. The roads authority had recommended removal of the display on grounds of road safety. The Secretary of State found that the wall to which the panel was affixed was in good condition and considered that the panel detracted from the appearance of the building and of the general area. It could not be said with certainty that the degree of concentration required by motorists would not be impaired by the display. The enforcement notice was therefore upheld and the appeal against the refusal of consent was dismissed. (Refs. P/AAD/FB/1, October 5, 1987; P/ADA/FB/36 and P/ADE/FB/3, May 10, 1988.)

10.51 Advertisement hoardings—material considerations—unsuitable location

It was proposed to erect hoardings on a tidy area of landscaped land. The appeal site was in a mixed residential/commercial area. The proposed site was directly overlooked by a number of houses. The planning authority recognised the usefulness of advertisements in improving local amenity—as, for example, in screening unsightly gables, closing up gap sites and screening unsightly vistas. Here there would be no such effect and consent was refused. (Ref. P/ADA/TB/15, July 9, 1987.)

Waste land notices

10.52 Waste land notice—land not causing injury—notice legally bad

A waste land notice alleged that land with a building thereon was in a ruinous or dilapidated condition and required the demolition of the derelict building and clearance of rubble from the site (this despite the fact that the appellant had carried out works to restore the building). The planning authority submitted that as the renovation work was carried out without planning permission, they were entitled to proceed with the waste land notice as if the unauthorised work had not been done. In their view, the amenity of the land was seriously injured by the derelict building. However, the planning authority accepted that when the waste land notice was served, the building was not derelict and did not seriously injure the amenity of any land. The reporter took the view that the only reason for a planning authority serving a waste land notice was that the amenity of land had been seriously injured. The notice here made no such statement and the reporter considered the omission to be so serious as to make the waste land notice a nullity. The reporter considered that even if he was wrong on that point there was no factual basis for the service of the waste land notice and he therefore quashed it. (Ref. P/PPA/SS/101, February 17, 1984.)

10.53 Waste land notice—land not visible from outside

This was an appeal against a waste land notice served in respect of the curtilage of buildings. A corrugated iron fence surrounded the buildings. From outside the fence few glimpses could be obtained of the buildings and the ground could not be seen at all. However, the fact that this area could now be seen only by someone passing over in an aircraft or by standing upon a long ladder seemed to be immaterial to the true interpretation of section 63 of the 1972 Act. The reporter therefore considered the amenity of the land to be seriously injured by the condition of the site and the curtilage of the dilapidated buildings on the appeal site. (Ref. P/WEN/GA/1 and 2, March 30, 1982.)

10.54 Waste land notice—notice under section 63—whether land "derelict or waste" land

A notice under section 63 of the 1972 Act required the removal of motor vehicles, parts thereof, caravan chassis and other associated debris and the maintenance of the land in a neat and tidy condition. The appellants submitted that the notice was not competent because the land was not "derelict, waste or other" land; in this connection they referred to *Lawrie* v. *Edinburgh Corporation*, 1953 S.L.T. (Sh. Ct.) 17, in which it was held that mere untidiness did not, in the circumstances of the case, justify service of a notice under section 63. Here the appellants argued that the land might be untidy or unsightly. That was not, however, the right test to apply; it was not what section 63 was intended to deal with. Nor, they argued, had it been established that any amenity was prejudiced or suffered injury because of the condition of the land; no land outside the boundaries of the appeal site was affected. The appeal site consisted of private land with no possibility of enjoyment by persons other than the appellants. The reporter concluded that the fact that the land was private, not open to public access and comparatively secluded was not relevant to the issues under consideration. (Refs. P/ENA/LC/9 and 12–16; P/WEN/LC/2 and 5–9, November 16, 1979.)

10.55 Waste land notice—requirements

The reporter took the view that a ruinous former office building did not do serious harm to the amenity of any land other than the land itself. The Secretary of State upheld the notice saying: "The view is taken that having regard to the provisions of section 63(1) of the 1972 Act, the term 'the amenity of land' in the first paragraph of the waste land notice includes the amenity of the land of the appeal site." The appeal therefore failed on the ground that there was injury to the amenity of the land itself. (Ref. P/WEN/SJ/1, August 26, 1980.)

10.56   Waste land notice—boundary wall—site to be kept tidy

A waste land notice was served in respect of the land surrounding an inn. Two of the four requirements of the notice were complied with. The notice also required that the land should be maintained in a neat and tidy condition. The reporter considered such a requirement to be inappropriate in a waste land notice. The notice could only require the carrying out of specified steps within a specified period. The notice also required the repair of all boundary walls. The reporter considered that this requirement was lacking in specification as to what steps were required to be taken. It could be construed as the making good of sections of wall then existing or could mean that missing sections of the wall should be rebuilt. The appeal was therefore sustained. (Ref. P/WEN/LC/18, September 17, 1987.)

10.57   Waste land notice—multiple ownership—dumping and weed growth

An appeal was lodged against a waste land notice served by the planning authority. The Secretary of State noted the appellant's claim that the waste land notice was defective but took the view that the fact that the notice related to land which was owned by more than one person did not render the notice invalid. The Secretary of State considered that uncontrolled weed growth, especially of the varieties that made seed of the wind-borne type, was harmful to the visual amenity of the whole appeal site and it harmed the amenity of other land nearby by the spreading of weed growth. The dumping of refuse, whether in bags or not, was unsightly and also harmed the amenity of the appeal site. The planning authority were correct when they averred it was for the landowner to clear up the dumped material and for the landowner to pursue those who dumped it. It was also the responsibility of the landowner for his own protection to prevent new dumping. The dumping of refuse and the uncontrolled growth of vegetation were matters that could properly be the subject of a waste land notice. (Ref. P/WEN/LC/23, April 14, 1987.)

10.58   Waste land notice—detriment to amenity—requirements

A waste land notice was served in respect of alleged injury to the amenity of an area of ground, surrounded by houses, by reason of its derelict and neglected condition. The appellants argued that the matters alleged did not constitute a serious injury to amenity. The appeal site was made up of two plots of ground with a combined area of about 1.41 acres. Much of the land was overgrown with scrub, bushes and weeds. Demolition rubble and waste materials had been fairly extensively tipped on the site.

The appellants explained that the materials complained of consisted of bottoming for roads, footpaths and services in connection with a planning permission for residential development. The material had been on the site for 20 years. The site was now so overgrown that it was difficult to distinguish between the deposited materials and the natural undulations of the site. The appellants therefore claimed there was no injury to amenity.

The planning authority pointed out that the most recent planning permission in respect of the site was for the proposed erection of houses in 1964. That planning permission was said to have lapsed and therefore there was no valid planning permission with which the bottoming could be associated.

It was clear to the reporter that much of the disputed material was unconnected with any planning permission, whether valid or not. There were no noxious smells or excessive pollution and it was unfortunate that the appellants, as owners of the site, had to be held responsible for any "pirate" tipping that might have taken place. Nevertheless, the reporter was satisfied that there had been unauthorised tipping on quite a substantial scale and though the injury to visual amenity might not be great in absolute terms, he considered that as regards a site in an established residential area, it was sufficiently serious to produce a situation which could not be ignored. The reporter considered some remedial action was necessary but in his view removal of all the materials hardly seemed justified and might well create new problems. He considered it would be sufficient if the heaps of materials were graded so as to merge with the contours of the surrounding land, the areas so treated being covered with soil and sown with grass, all to the reasonable satisfaction of the planning authority's Director of Planning or, in the event of failure to agree, of the Secretary of State. The reporter further considered that speed of implementation was important in order that the remedial works could be carried out before the onset of winter. The waste land notice was therefore upheld subject to variation. (Ref. P/WEN/SN/2, October 30, 1984.)

10.59   Waste land notice—enforcement—abandonment of use

In effect, the reporter said, the enforcement notice in this case required the appellant to put the building in question into a state of disrepair. The planning authority argued that before the work to which the enforcement notice related was done, the building was in a derelict condition; that as the work complained of was undertaken without planning permission the planning authority were entitled to proceed with a waste land notice.

Nowhere in the waste land notice was it expressed that in the opinion of the planning authority the amenity of any land was seriously injured by the ruinous or dilapidated condition of the building. Since the fundamental reason for the exercise of powers under section 63 of the 1972 Act had to be a belief of that kind, the absence of such a declaration in the notice seemed to the reporter to be an omission so serious as to make the waste land notice a nullity. Even if he was wrong in that, the factual basis for service of the waste land notice was lacking.

There had been no abandonment of use of the building. Its use had, it was argued, continued sporadically—see *Fyson* v. *Buckinghamshire County Council* [1958] 1 W.L.R. 634. It was also argued by virtue of section 19(2)(*a*) of the 1972 Act that no development had occurred in that the external appearance had not been affected.

The reporter said that the sporadic use since the former owner retired was enough to dispel the notion of abandonment. The fact that the owner had at one time intended to convert the building to a house did not amount to abandonment. On the question of whether the works amounted to a breach of planning control, they did not amount to rebuilding though the repair work was large in relation to the size of the building.

The works did not materially affect the external appearance of the building. The building retained its former size and shape, the windows were similar to the former ones, and the door was where the previous door had been. The only changes were the colour of the roof covering, the use of brick in rebuilding the chimney-heads and of concrete blocks instead of stone in rebuilding part of one gable; these were all matters that could normally occur when the accrued dilapidations of an old building were finally tackled in a comprehensive scheme of repair. The application of some form of external rendering to an old stone wall in a building did not amount to work requiring planning permission. Such works might alter the external appearance of the building but not materially. (Refs. P/ENA/SP/16; P/WEN/SP/3, April 2, 1984.)

10.60　Waste land notice—contractor's yard

A waste land notice was served under section 63 of the 1972 Act in respect of a contractor's yard. It was alleged that amenity was seriously injured by reason of the condition of the land, namely the existence of derelict vehicles or vehicles under repair in the open air; the existence of scrap metal, tyres and oil drums in the open air; the existence of two bulk oil or paraffin storage tanks in a prominent position on the public roadside; and the existence of builder's materials, sand, stone, etc. in the open air.

Appeal was made on the grounds that (1) there was no serious injury to amenity and (2) the steps required by the notice to be taken exceeded what was necessary to remedy any serious injury to amenity.

The Secretary of State agreed that the planning authority were right to be concerned about the condition of the premises but the point at issue in the appeal was whether the authority were justified in serving a section 63 notice; was the amenity of land being seriously injured by the derelict, waste or neglected condition of the land? From the evidence, no part of the land could be considered to be in a derelict or waste condition and the notice could not be upheld in those respects. The Secretary of State did, however, conclude that part of the land was *neglected* by reason of the fact that scrap vehicles, tyres and vehicle parts were strewn about. The Minister concluded that the amenity of that land was thereby seriously injured and he decided to uphold the waste land notice to the extent of removing these materials. It was, however, considered that the requirement in the notice to remove the materials to a bulk refuse disposal site to be approved by the planning authority went beyond what was necessary to remedy the injury to amenity and that the appellants should be allowed to remove the materials and dispose of them as they wished. (Ref. P/WEN/HH/5, December 23, 1980.)

10.61 Waste land notice—applicability of section 63—scrap vehicles

A waste land notice required the appellants to remove from an area of land all scrap and damaged motor vehicles and parts thereof as were not immediately under repair and to maintain the said area of ground in a neat and tidy condition.

The reporter accepted that the amenity of the land was seriously injured by reason of the dumping thereon of scrap and damaged motor vehicles. However, there remained for consideration the question discussed in *Lawrie* v. *Edinburgh Corporation*, 1953 S.L.T. (Sh.Ct.) 17, namely whether in terms of section 63 of the 1972 Act, the land in question might properly be regarded as "derelict, waste, neglected or other land." Following that judgment, the reporter said that the land formed part of the operational land of a garage business, and that he did not consider that the land in question could reasonably be regarded as "derelict, waste, neglected or other land" for the purpose of section 63.

For the council, the reporter's attention was drawn to *obiter dicta* in Sheriff Middleton's judgment, in which he speculated that waste land enforcement action might conceivably be invoked with success in the event that, for instance, scrap material was allowed to accumulate on land. That comment appeared superficially apt in relation to the present case. But, firstly, Sheriff Middleton went no further than to indicate that action might conceivably be successful and, secondly, "scrap material" was difficult if not impossible to define with precision in relation to this garage business, bearing in mind that one man's scrap could be another man's essential and otherwise unavailable spare part, and that was the reason for retaining material on site.

The Secretary of State considered the arguments submitted for the parties and the reporter's remarks as to the applicability of section 63 in this case. In the Secretary of State's view a section 63 notice was appropriate if any land was in a derelict, waste, neglected or other condition and if the condition of that land was causing serious injury to the amenity of any land, irrespective of any question as to the lawfulness of any use of land. It was accepted that the type of business in which the appellant was engaged involved the accommodation of vehicles in various states of disrepair and at various stages of dismantling and that what would be regarded as neglect of land in some types of commercial use was the unavoidable result of the appellant's type of business. However, the Secretary of State considered that there was neglect of the land used by the appellant to the extent that cars which were no longer of any use to the appellant's business or to his customers and were now simply waste or scrap material had been allowed to accumulate and he considered that neglect to be the cause of serious injury to the amenity of the land adjoining the land occupied by the appellant.

He proposed therefore to uphold the notice but to vary its terms to exclude from the removal requirement any wrecked cars containing useful spare parts, cars awaiting or under repair and those on the site in connection with insurance assessment. (Refs. P/ENA/HF/19 and 20; P/WEN/HF/1, December 14, 1979.)

10.62 Waste land notice—partially-built garage

The Secretary of State declared that the service and appropriateness of a waste land notice under section 63 of the Town and Country Planning (Scotland) Act 1972 were not dependent on there having been a breach of planning control. He considered that the determining issue was whether the amenity of any land was seriously injured by reason of the ruinous or dilapidated condition of a building or the condition of land, for example by being derelict, waste or neglected.

The site inspection report described the appeal site as being occupied by an incomplete and roofless building with walls of concrete blocks which had been built to a height of about 11 feet and included metal windows in the longer sides. There was no flooring, merely uneven ground, inside the building. A crude shed occupied one corner. At the time of inspection the building also contained a quantity of timber, fishing creels and two open boats. The report drew attention to a trailer which was observed on land outside the building but apart from this there was no "clutter" about the site, although the open land was infested with weeds. The report also mentioned that the site lay in an area much of which was unused vacant land. From the report it was considered that the building, while incomplete, was not dilapidated or ruinous. The surrounding area was not cluttered. Given the vacant and unused state of much of the surrounding area, it was not considered that the state of the site was seriously injurious to the amenity of any land. (Refs. P/WEN/HH/2 and 3, May 15, 1979.)

10.63 Waste land notice—injury to amenity

A waste land notice was served in respect of a building. The reporter expressed some doubt as to whether the injury done to the amenity of the appeal site itself was relevant. He said:

> "In my opinion the ruinous former office building does not do serious harm to the amenity of any land other than the appeal site itself. If the harm done to the appeal site itself is relevant—neither principal party at the inquiry submitted that it was—the appropriate remedy might be either to repair the building or to demolish it; it would be right to give the appellant the choice."

With regard to the land within the appeal site the reporter said that "quantities of rubbish and waste material . . . do no harm to the amenity of any other land, but in my opinion do serious injury to the amenity of the appeal site itself. This injury cannot be perceived or experienced except from within the site."

The Secretary of State upheld the notice, stating that:

> "The view is taken that having regard to the provisions of section 63(1) of the 1972 Act the term 'the amenity of land' in the first paragraph of the waste land notice includes the

amenity of the land of the appeal site. Therefore in determining this appeal the Secretary of State has to consider whether there is injury to that land."

The appeal made on the ground that the matters alleged did not constitute serious injury to amenity therefore failed. The notice was amended to require that the appellant "repair or demolish" the building within one year. It was a requirement of the original notice that a stob and wire fence be erected in order to prevent dumping of material; that requirement was held to exceed what was necessary to remedy the injury to amenity. (Ref. P/WEN/SJ/1, August 26, 1980.)

Caravans

10.64 Caravan—stationing—works

A caravan stationed on land was in breach of planning control. An enforcement notice was served. The notice referred only to works of clearing and levelling the site and did not refer to the making of a material change of use. The works in question appeared to involve only the removal of turf and the laying of a bed of stones. The caravan was not supplied with water, electricity or drainage services. In the reporter's view the works were so slight as to be described as "*de minimis*"—too trifling to be concerned with. (Refs. P/PPA/SA 99 and 101; P/ENA/SA/44, July 4, 1985.)

10.65 Caravan—allotments—vandalism and theft

Planning permission was granted for the siting of a caravan on allotments subject to a condition that the caravan should not be used for residential purposes. The appellant stated that gardening was his only occupation and it was necessary to live on the site to deter vandalism and theft. The reporter refused the appeal; firm control over the siting of caravans should be maintained. He suggested that a more substantial security fence might serve the desired purposes. (Ref. P/PPA/LD/67, January 28, 1983.)

10.66 Caravan—enforcement notice—ambiguity

An appeal had been lodged against an enforcement notice relating to a caravan within the appellant's front garden. The notice required that "the caravan shall not project beyond the adjacent garage." The reporter found this condition so ambiguous that he could not tell whether or not it had been breached. He therefore quashed it. (Ref. P/ENA/LA/58, February 22, 1983.)

SECTION 11

EXPENSES

See Young and Rowan-Robinson, *Scottish Planning Law and Procedure*, pp. 514–516.

Section 267(7) of the Town and Country Planning (Scotland) Act 1972 empowers the Secretary of State to make an order as to the expenses of the parties to a public local inquiry. Section 267A of the 1972 Act enables the Secretary of State to make an award of expenses in relation to proceedings which do not give rise to an inquiry, in particular in cases determined by written submissions. In planning proceedings the parties are normally expected to meet their own expenses and expenses are only awarded on grounds of unreasonable behaviour. SDD Circular No. 6/1990, dated March 22, 1990, explains the conditions which require to be met before an award of expenses will be made. The circular also sets out examples of some of the situations in which an award of expenses may be made either against a planning authority or against an appellant or other party.

APPEAL DECISIONS

11.1 Expenses—planning authority's actions—outline and detailed applications

The planning authority treated an application as a full application when in fact it referred to a previous grant of planning permission. In the view of the Secretary of State the planning authority had acted unreasonably in treating the application as a fresh one. However, the appellant and his agents had contributed to their own costs by delays in producing drawings, with a poorly-designed building, by providing insufficient information on the design and layout of the site and the means of access thereto, and in requesting two postponements of the second public inquiry. The Secretary of State therefore decided that an award of expenses against the planning authority had to be made in respect of the expenses incurred by the appellant in the first inquiry only. (Ref. P/PPA/GA/52, July 5, 1983.)

11.2 Expenses—unreasonable refusal of planning permission

A public inquiry was held concerning a petrol station. At the close of the inquiry counsel for the appellants asked for an award of expenses on the ground that the district council had not put forward any substantial evidence to support the three reasons stated for the refusal of planning permission.

The reporter said that it had not been suggested that the council had acted frivolously or vexatiously. Thus the claim for an award of expenses presumed that the council had acted unreasonably in refusing to grant planning permission. The reporter agreed with the council's solicitor that the council was entitled to disagree with the views of the Director of Planning and the Highway Authority without it following that the council had acted unreasonably.

The reporter also agreed with counsel for the appellants that very little worthwhile evidence had been put forward at the inquiry to support the decision to refuse planning permission. At the time of the planning decision, the Director of Planning was satisfied that there would be no adverse effect on amenity. The full details of the landscape scheme were not known but the committee could have asked him to obtain such information before making a final decision on the application. In the event, it was shown at the inquiry that the development had been carefully designed to blend with the existing buildings and to be screened from its surroundings. The council's concern about amenity was totally unjustified.

On the question of need, the reporter accepted that this might have been a relevant line of argument if the development had been contrary to an established planning policy. Developers often claimed a special justification when seeking an exception to such a policy. In the present case the district council did not argue that the development was contrary to any policy. The discussion of need was pursued by a third party objector on the basis that the petrol station could harm the provision of petrol supplies in the rural area. This line of argument did not reflect the objections received by the district council prior to the determination of the application.

Finally, on the question of traffic, the council's witness conceded that the council had approved major developments that had or would increase the amount of traffic using the road in question, *i.e.* the western edge housing, the superstore to which the petrol station would be attached, and the new football stadium and auction mart complexes. In relation to these developments the reporter accepted that the amount of extra traffic likely to be brought into the area by the petrol station would be trivial. The council produced no evidence on traffic. Concern was expressed that the petrol station might attract customers from the bypass road but this argument was inconsistent with the Director of Planning's recommendation that a condition could be imposed to preclude any petrol sign being visible from the bypass and with the council's decision to approve a sign for the superstore deliberately sited for maximum visibility from the bypass.

The reporter's overall conclusions were that the second of the reasons for the refusal of planning permission was irrelevant in this case; and that in the context of the other planning decisions that had been made and the design of the scheme itself, the evidence put forward in support of the first and third reasons for refusal was ill-considered and untenable. While the reporter respected the council's right to form an independent view on the application, the reporter considered that the evidence presented in this case was so weak that it had to be considered perverse and unreasonable. The reporter therefore recommended that an award of expenses in favour of the appellants be made against the district council.

The Secretary of State accepted the reporter's views. (Ref. P/PPA/TC/246, March 31, 1989.)

11.3 Expenses—preparation for inquiry

An inquiry had been held into an appeal against the decision of the planning authority to refuse outline permission for the erection of three sheltered housing units. The appellants sought an award of certain expenses incurred in connection with their preparation for the inquiry. The basis of the applicants' case was that article 16(4) of the Town and Country Planning (General Development) (Scotland) Order 1981 required that "the planning authority shall submit to the Secretary of State and to the appellant not later than two months from the date when the Secretary of State notifies them of the appeal, a statement of their observations on the appeal." Further, in accordance with rule 2(1) of the Town and Country Planning (Inquiries Procedure) (Scotland) Rules 1980, where this has not already been done, not later than 28 days before the date of the inquiry, the planning authority shall serve a copy of the written statement of any observations which the authority propose to put forward at the inquiry together with copies of all representations received by them in relation to the appeal.

The appellants had not received the planning authority's statement until Friday, September 30, 1988, three days before the inquiry, and had received no copies of representations. On receipt of that statement the appellants had been surprised by the traffic matters which had been raised for the first time and by the countryside policies which had been referred to. These were not included in the reasons for refusal and the appellants had not therefore been prepared for them. The appellants restricted their claim for expenses to those occasioned by the late receipt of the authority's statement; these involved their planning consultant working over the weekend in preparation for the inquiry on the following Monday.

The planning authority responded that the delay had been caused by changes of staff, illness of senior staff, the lack of a formal report from the Director of Planning and a recent spate of public inquiries which had increased their workload. The countryside policies were in the appendix to the local plan and were therefore included in the first reason for refusal. The council did not consider that an award of expenses was justified.

The reporter agreed with the appellants that they had had no warning of traffic matters being raised by the district council, though they were rehearsed in the representations from local residents. Evidently their letters were not forwarded to the appellants with the statement of observations but they had received copies of these on June 2, 1988, despatched from the Scottish Office Inquiry Reporters' Unit. Nevertheless, the appellants would have been unaware that the council were preparing to incorporate traffic matters within their evidence.

The reporter considered that references to the appendix to the local plan, as inherent in the first reason for refusal, were too obscure for the appellants to expect direct evidence to be led on countryside matters. The local plan contained a great deal of other material which could also be raised on this pretext if this argument were to be considered as justifiable. There was no doubt that the council's statement was late. The reporter's copy had not arrived by the time he set off for the inquiry. Accordingly, he considered that the appellants' claim for an award for expenses merely to cover the additional work by their planning consultant over the weekend, in order to enable him to incorporate into his evidence answers to the new matters raised in the council's statement, was reasonable.

The Secretary of State agreed with the reporter. (Ref. P/PPA/CC/192, March 23, 1989.)

11.4 Expenses—planning authority's actions

At the close of a public inquiry the appellants submitted a claim for an award of expenses against the planning authority. The officials of the council had recommended that the planning application be approved. However no member of the planning committee had seen fit to appear at the inquiry to explain why the committee had departed from the officials' recommendation. The appellants considered that the planning authority had acted vexatiously and frivolously. It was unreasonable, the appellant argued, that he had been put to the expense of a public local inquiry to obtain planning permission. The council argued that the council members had the right to reach a different conclusion from that recommended by their officials. It was the appellants who had requested a public inquiry and to that extent they had contributed to the expense of the action.

The reporter said that the important issue in relation to this claim was whether the council's refusal of outline planning permission, and their defence of that decision at the public inquiry, was unreasonable. On the question of access to the appeal premises, the council's second reason for refusal, the council and the highway authority had acted in the mistaken belief that the appeal premises and two other houses were served by a private drive. It was the highway authority's policy that such an arrangement could serve two houses but not three. In fact, the appeal premises had their own access. The facts relating to the access were repeatedly deployed by the appellants during the consideration of their planning application, yet the council's statement of observations (which was only sent to the parties one week before the inquiry) did not reflect these facts and the reporter found that their grudging concession of the point at the public inquiry was perverse.

As regards other aspects of the decision, the first reason for refusal of outline planning permission stated that "the area is not allocated for development" in the local plan. The reporter found no substance in the argument that the normal presumption in favour of development was suspended because the land was not allocated for development in a local plan. He rejected the argument that one of the local plan policies was intended to ensure that infill developments were in some way linked to the treatment of vacant and derelict land. It was neither supported by policy nor reasoned justification contained in the plan. The reporter therefore found the council's refusal of outline planning permission on this ground to be unreasonable and the council's defence on this ground was also perverse.

Although the reporter did not support the terms of the council's decision, he did not find reasons to suggest that the matter should never have come to inquiry.

On balance the reporter found that of the four grounds for refusal of outline planning permission, two could not reasonably be sustained at the public inquiry. To that extent the council's actions had been unreasonable and their conduct had been such as to cause unnecessary trouble and expense to the appellant. The reporter recommended that the claim for an award of expenses should be sustained but only to the extent that the council be required to meet 50 per cent. of the appellant's expenses. (Ref. P/PPA/CC/188, March 23, 1989.)

11.5 Expenses—intimation of withdrawal

At the close of a public inquiry a claim for expenses was made on behalf of the City of Aberdeen District Council against the appellants. In a letter dated January 12, 1988 the appellants' agent confirmed that the suggested inquiry date of May 11, 1988 was suitable to his clients. On May 10, a telephone call was made to the Scottish Office Inquiry Reporters' Unit intimating the appellants' intention to withdraw the appeal. The view was taken in the Unit that because of the lateness of the intimation and the fact that it was unlikely that the large number of third parties, who had expressed their desire to be heard at the inquiry, could be contacted, the inquiry should be opened and appropriate motions put there.

The appellants' agents had changed in the period leading up to the inquiry but the reporter could not accept that the inept way in which the appellants' business arrangements had been handled prior to the public inquiry provided any justification whatsoever for the unreasonable behaviour which had undoubtedly occurred. Intimation of the intention to withdraw the appeal took place at such a late stage that the council was by then fully committed to its preparations. In these circumstances the reporter considered that an award of expenses was merited for the council's work in preparation for the inquiry up to and including the point when the inquiry opened.

At the inquiry itself the appellants' agent opened by stating that he had only recently been engaged to appear and his clients' instructions were that the appeal should be dismissed. He stated that he had no intention of cross-examining witnesses and confirmed that he was not using the term "dismiss" to mean that his client was seeking a postponement. In response to further questions put by the reporter he confirmed that his clients' case should rest on the grounds of appeal already lodged and in respect of which he did not intend to elaborate. He then went on to say it was his clients' intention to withdraw the appeal but a letter to that effect had not yet been sent. The two courses of action put forward by the appellants' agent were clearly incompatible. Despite a series of questions put by the reporter to clarify the position he still continued to request that the appeal be dismissed. In consequence the reporter decided that he had no option but to hear the evidence and statements of the council and third parties and to make a site inspection. No evidence was led on behalf of the appellants, no cross-examination took place, and no closing submission was made.

The expenses incurred over the few hours that the inquiry was in session were likely to be small in relation to the whole. Had the appellants' agent simply stated that the appeal was withdrawn, then the inquiry would have closed without further ado after hearing any motions regarding the council's application for award of costs. The fact that it became necessary to hear evidence and to undertake a site inspection had to be wholly attributed to the confused statements made by the appellants' agent. In the reporter's opinion an award was merited for expenses incurred by the council for the period that the inquiry was in session. The reporter's recommendations were accepted by the Secretary of State. (Ref. P/PPA/GA/403, February 16, 1989.)

11.6 Expenses—award in favour of appellant

A public inquiry was adjourned at the request of the appellant as soon as it opened. Next day the appellant withdrew his appeal. He claimed expenses.

In considering whether an award of expenses might be made on grounds of unreasonable behaviour the main criterion is whether one party has been put to unnecessary and unreasonable expense (a) because the matter should never have come to inquiry or (b) because although the appeal and inquiry could not reasonably have been avoided, the other party conducted their side of the procedure in such a way as to cause unnecessary trouble and expense.

In this case the planning authority's observations were served on the appellant 11 days before the date of the inquiry instead of the 21 days required to accord with rule 4(5) of the Town and Country Planning (Inquiries Procedure) (Scotland) Rules 1964. The appellant submitted that his request for an adjournment was caused by the late service of the observations. He argued that expenses should be awarded against the planning authority for the wasted day's hearing. The Secretary of State took the view that if the observations had been submitted timeously the appeal might well have been withdrawn before the inquiry, which would have obviated the expense of the appellant and his solicitor appearing. The Secretary of State therefore decided to make an award. (Ref. P/PPA/GA/40, September 28, 1978.)

11.7   Expenses—successive appeals

A public inquiry was held into an appeal against a refusal of planning permission to erect a replacement mast to support an amateur radio aerial. Towards the end of the inquiry the solicitor for the planning authority asked that expenses attributable to the costs of the inquiry be awarded to the council against the appellant.

In the case of the present mast, four appeals against refusals of planning permission—which appeals had been conjoined—had been dismissed by a reporter on September 24, 1985. The current appeal proposal was identical to three of those four appeal proposals. There had been no change in the planning circumstances since September 24, 1985. The planning authority argued that by submitting numerous identical applications the appellant had acted frivolously, irresponsibly and vexatiously and the costs of the inquiry should be awarded against him. The appellant denied that his actions could be so described. His current proposal was for a trial period of one year only and was therefore substantially different from all previous applications.

The reporter said that as the three appeals by the appellant for proposed masts were virtually identical to the current proposal and were dismissed on September 24, 1985, the appellant must have realised that he was unlikely to obtain planning permission for the present mast unless there had been a change in planning circumstances in the intervening period. Nevertheless, in May 1986, that is less than nine months later, he proceeded to erect the current appeal development. Then on March 9, 1987, when the unauthorised mast had been in position for almost one year, he had applied for planning permission for a trial period of one year. In the reporter's opinion these two actions—the erection of an unauthorised development and the subsequent delay in seeking planning permission for it—amounted to frivolous, unreasonable and irresponsible behaviour, and demonstrated a cavalier attitude towards town and country planning legislation. Furthermore, if his intention to seek planning permission for a trial period of one year had been a serious one, taking into account the dismissal of three appeals for identical developments and the continuing objections of local residents, the reporter considered that the appellant should have removed the mast within 12 months of its erection in May, 1986, or at least within 12 months of seeking planning permission on March 9, 1987. The reporter could only conclude that the trial period of one year was included as a ploy in an attempt (1) to overcome the refusal of planning permission by the planning authority for earlier proposals and the decision to dismiss the three previously-mentioned appeals for proposals virtually identical to the appeal development, and (2) to obtain planning permission for a period of more than one year by stealth. An award of expenses was made by the Secretary of State. (Ref. P/PPA/GA/398, November 18, 1988.)

11.8 Expenses—withdrawal of appeal

The regional planning authority and a firm of consultants requested an award of expenses in relation to work done in preparation for an inquiry due to be held on May 3, 1988. They sought expenses from the date of the formal intimation of the inquiry, February 17. The appellants' agents had intimated withdrawal of the appeal on April 26. A pre-inquiry meeting, aimed at clarifying the relevant issues and procedure, had been held on March 14.

The essence of the claim by the regional council and the consultants was that by persisting in the appeal until seven days before the date fixed for the inquiry, the appellants had acted unreasonably, having regard to the history of postponement and obvious lack of preparation on their part.

The reporter found himself bound to agree that the appellants' behaviour was unreasonable. The reporter's letters of February 17 and March 14 and 24 recorded increasing impatience at the inactivity shown by the appellants and gave ample encouragement to them to consider if they were still in a position to pursue the appeal at inquiry. By intimating the withdrawal only 10 days after the date on which productions required to be lodged, the other parties were already substantially committed to preparation for the inquiry. The reporter considered they deserved an award of expenses in respect of the abortive work in preparation for the inquiry. He therefore recommended an award in respect of the expenses incurred between the procedure meeting and the date of withdrawal. (Ref. P/PPA/SL/421, November 17, 1988.)

11.9 Expenses—withdrawal of appeal

This was an application by the planning authority that they be awarded expenses with respect to a public inquiry due to start on May 17, 1988, into an appeal against the authority's refusal to grant planning permission for opencast coal mining. The appeal was withdrawn on May 12, 1988, and the inquiry did not take place.

The authority stated that they had not received intimation that the appeal had been withdrawn until the late afternoon of May 12, *i.e.* two working days before the inquiry was due to commence. Preparation for the inquiry had involved a considerable amount of professional expertise and time on the part of both their own staff and independent professional experts. Considerable fees were incurred for the services of senior counsel who was to have presented the authority's case, not only in respect of preliminary consultations but also in compensation for the cancellation. The authority believed that the appellants had acted in an unreasonable manner, as regards both their lack of cooperation and preparation prior to the inquiry and their late withdrawal of the appeal without good reason or prior warning. The authority had forwarded a considerable number of productions 10 days in advance of the inquiry.

The appellants said that they were led to believe by British Coal that their application for a licence from British Coal would be successful and the appellants' solicitors did not learn that British Coal had changed their mind until receipt of a letter dated May 6. The appellants argued that they were justified in withdrawing their appeal when it became clear that a licence would not be granted. A licence was needed from British Coal before opencast working was possible. They should not be penalised because the appeal had to be withdrawn for reasons beyond their control.

The reporter considered that the subject matter of the inquiry was fairly complex and it was probable that the inquiry would have lasted for several days. The authority had paid fees for the services of senior counsel and had presumably allocated considerable staff time to preparation for the inquiry. The reporter had no doubt that the very late withdrawal of the appeal, together with the absence of productions in the preceding days would have caused major inconvenience to the authority. From the information before the reporter it was unclear whether the appellants were misled by British Coal or whether, as the authority alleged, they simply failed to undertake the necessary investigations in sufficient time. Either way, licensing procedures were technically separate from planning procedures and the reporter considered that British Coal's views on the suitability of the site for licensing had only limited relevance to the case. The reporter concluded that the appellants had inadequate justification for withdrawing the appeal at such a late stage and that they had acted unreasonably in not withdrawing the appeal until only a few days before the inquiry was due to start.

The Secretary of State agreed with the reporter's conclusion and ordered the payment of expenses. (Ref. P/PPA/LC/147, November 18, 1988.)

11.10 Expenses—adjournment

Claims for awards of expenses were made by the district council and the regional council at the end of a public inquiry into a deemed refusal of planning permission for alterations and change of use of a building to form motor vehicle sales premises and a workshop.

When the inquiry opened no representative of or witnesses for the appellant were in attendance. The appellant's solicitor arrived at the inquiry about half-an-hour late following a telephone call from the reporter. The solicitor explained that he had been given to understand by the appellant's planning consultant that the inquiry had been postponed. Neither the consultant nor the appellant himself was available to give evidence and there was therefore no way the inquiry could proceed on that date. The district council, represented by an advocate, a solicitor and a planning witness, and the regional council, represented by a solicitor and a traffic witness, accepted that the inquiry would have to be adjourned to a later date but requested reimbursement of the expenses of their abortive attendance.

The reporter considered that the question to be asked was whether the appellant's failure to appear was unreasonable. The appellant's planning consultant had tried to get the original inquiry date changed. He assumed that the district council had no objection to such a course of action. The appellant's solicitor accepted that the district and regional councils had been put to unnecessary expense but submitted that it was unfair that his client should be penalised because of the failure of the consultant to establish the position clearly.

The reporter said that the consultant had been wrong to assume that agreement to the postponement had been given. If it had been he should have contacted the Scottish Office Inquiry Reporters' Unit. The position would then have been checked. He considered that the planning consultant had acted unreasonably on both counts. He appreciated that the problem was not of the appellant's making but he was represented by the planning consultant. The question of liability for expenses would have to be sorted out between them.

The Secretary of State agreed with the reporter's views and made awards of expenses. (Ref. P/PPA/GA/400, November 10, 1988.)

11.11 Claim for expenses

A planning authority made a claim for an award of expenses against the appellants, a building society, in respect of a planning appeal which was withdrawn prior to the public inquiry into the appeal. The Secretary of State considered that the question was whether the planning authority had been put to unnecessary and unreasonable expense because, although the appeal and inquiry could not reasonably have been avoided, the appellants conducted their side of the procedure in such a way as to cause unnecessary trouble and expense. After consideration of all the evidence concerning the timing of the appellants' appeal in relation to the date arranged for the public local inquiry, the Secretary of State took the view that their behaviour could be regarded as unreasonable. He further considered that the planning authority should not have been expected to bear the expenses of their final preparations for the public local inquiry in circumstances where the appellants withdrew their appeal shortly before the public inquiry because, for their own reasons, the appellants decided they no longer wanted a major operating centre in the town in question. The Secretary of State therefore awarded expenses against the appellants in favour of the planning authority in respect of the unnecessary time and expense involved in preparing for the public inquiry. (Ref. P/PPA/SA/129, October 27, 1988.)

11.12 Expenses—unreasonable behaviour

At the end of an inquiry into an appeal against a refusal of planning permission for a change of use from a shop to an office the appellants' agent applied for an award of expenses incurred by his clients in connection with the appeal or, if that were not possible, at least in connection with the inquiry.

The grounds of the application were as follows:

(a) The appellants had requested that the appeal be determined by the written statements procedure; by requesting an inquiry the planning authority had put the appellants to unreasonable additional expense.

(b) The planning authority had acted unreasonably in refusing the appellants' application contrary to the recommendation of the Director of Planning.

(c) Three similar applications for the appeal premises had been refused since 1986 but the reasons were different in each case; this was a case of "moving the goalposts" and the appellants were unsure as to the correct planning position at any given point in time.

(d) The first reason for refusal—precedent—had been virtually abandoned by the planning authority.

(e) The second reason for refusal—prematurity—had not been supported by any substantial evidence; the authority's only witness had been the convener of the planning committee whose precognition had obviously been prepared by somebody else.

(f) The convener had referred to the Director of Planning's report on the application but the relevant part of that report (including the recommendation) had not been produced at the inquiry.

(g) The planning authority had approved a draft review of the relevant local plan which indicated that a proposal such as that advanced by the appellants would be viewed favourably; despite this, identical applications had been refused in 1987 and 1988.

For the planning authority the motion for expenses was opposed on the following grounds:

(a) Any party was entitled to request that an inquiry be held to determine a planning appeal and there was no justification for expenses being awarded for that reason.

(b) The authority were perfectly entitled not to accept the recommendation of the Director of Planning.

(c) Whatever reasons may have been given for the refusal of previous applications those decisions were irrelevant in the context of the present appeal.

(d) The precedent argument had not been abandoned.

(e) There had been sufficient substantial evidence from the convener of the planning committee on the question of prematurity to justify refusal.

(f) Although the whole of the Director of Planning's report on the application had not been produced, it was obvious what it contained and the appellants' agent could have asked a planning official to speak to it.

The reporter considered:

On ground (a) the council's response had to be supported. The council should not be penalised because they had exercised their legal right to have the appeal determined following a hearing.

On ground (b) merely not to accept the Director of Planning's recommendation did not of itself represent unreasonable behaviour. But in the light of the history of previous applications and recommendations, and of the changing policies of the local plan, he considered that on this occasion refusal was unreasonable.

On ground (c) the five reasons for refusal of the 1979 and 1980 applications were the same and included precedent and the belief that there was adequate scope for office uses in the town centre. The 1986 application was refused for the reason that the proposed change of use would be premature pending: (1) the implementation of a commercial development at Coatbridge; (2) the review of the Monklands District Plan. Different reasons were given for refusal of the 1987 and 1988 applications. On the last three refusals, precedent had once been used as a reason for refusal, local policy once, and prematurity three times (though the wording of the prematurity reason was different each time). The reporter accepted that situations changed and could result in amended wording of reasons for refusal but it was established that reasons required to be sound and clear-cut and that a high standard of behaviour should be expected from planning authorities. The reporter considered that a reading of the reasons for refusal, particularly of the three most recent applications, did not provide a clear picture of the planning position relating to these proposals and their wording represented unreasonable behaviour on behalf of the authority.

On ground (d), although the first reason for refusal was not actually abandoned at the inquiry, it was not supported by any substantial evidence and the reporter considered that this represented unreasonable behaviour by the authority.

On ground (e) the reporter had concluded in his decision letter that the council should have considered the likelihood of the premises being suitable for the displaced traders and of the traders actually wanting to move to them in much more detail than they did before determining the appellants' application. In view of the time that had elapsed since the redevelopment proposals had been approved, a more precise awareness of what premises might be required should have been obtained. To that extent, therefore, the reporter considered that the second reason for refusal was unreasonable.

On ground (f) the relevant part of the Director of Planning's report could have been produced if requested by the appellants' agent or the reporter. It was obvious that it contained a favourable recommendation, and the authority's witness—the planning convener—did not attempt to hide this. The reporter did not consider that the non-production of this part of the document by the authority constituted unreasonable behaviour.

On ground (g) the reporter said that the local plan did not feature as a reason for refusal but it was considered a material consideration by both the planning convener and counsel for the district council. To the effect that the council argued at the inquiry that the proposal offended against one of the policies in the adopted local plan when a review had been circulated in early 1988, effectively removing the presumption against the office use of the appeal premises, the reporter considered the council's behaviour was unreasonable. It did little for public confidence in the planning system for a document to be produced ostensibly representing current planning policy but with which the elected members were not in agreement.

For the above reasons the reporter recommended that the council should meet the appellants' expenses incurred in presenting their case at the inquiry. The wording of section 267 of the 1972 Act made it clear that the only expenses as to which the Secretary of State was empowered to make orders were those incurred in relation to a local inquiry and not in relation to an appeal generally. The Secretary of State accepted the reporter's recommendation. (Ref. P/PPA/SS/177, February 5, 1989.)

11.13 Expenses—adjournment of inquiry

At the end of a seven-day public inquiry into an appeal against a refusal of planning permission for the erection of a supermarket at Grangemouth the appellants made a claim for an award of expenses against Central Regional Council.

The regional council contended that the claim for expenses was misconceived because expenses can only be awarded to one of the parties involved in the inquiry. Section 267(7) of the 1972 Act empowers the Secretary of State to make an order as to expenses incurred by parties to a local inquiry. A request for an award of expenses was considered only where an inquiry into the merits of an appeal had taken place and the parties had appeared or been represented before the reporter. In this case the appellants did not attend the inquiry but were represented before the reporter. The Secretary of State therefore concluded that the claim for an award of expenses was competent.

Counsel for the appellants said that in terms of the White Paper "Lifting the Burden" the council should, *inter alia*, have encouraged the applicants to discuss their proposal with them before the submission of the planning application and to seek information about the technical requirements of the planning authority. After the refusal of planning permission the council should have encouraged inquiries by the applicants. In fact the council had totally ignored these requirements. The council had given no prior warning that the impact of the appeal proposal on the existing Grangemouth town centre would be critical. After the refusal of planning permission the council had refused to show to the appellants data upon which the council had based its estimates of impact. Despite numerous letters the data was not released by the council until January 12, 1988, about five months before the inquiry.

On May 5 the appellants had called a meeting with the council to discuss matters relating to the impending inquiry (due to start on June 14). The appellants wished (1) to reach agreement on the data which was to be submitted to the inquiry; (2) to establish whether an impact analysis would be submitted by the council; (3) to establish upon which policies the council would concentrate in presenting its case; and (4) to establish whether the council was mainly concerned about the proximity of the appeal site to the town centre of Grangemouth or about the impact of the appeal proposal upon that centre. The responsibility for calling such a meeting should have rested with the council.

The productions to be submitted by the council were eventually received by the appellants' consultants on June 11, 1988. Some of the productions contained such detailed statistics that it was impossible to understand them in the time available. In addition the council had attempted to introduce an additional production in the form of an appendix to a precognition during the opening session of the inquiry. Additional matters to which no reference had previously been made by the council, including references to alternative sites for the appeal proposal in Grangemouth and the claim that the Unit for Retail Planning Information supported the methods used by the council, were introduced by the council during the course of the inquiry.

If the costs of the whole inquiry were not awarded against the council, the costs attributable to the adjournment of the inquiry on June 14 until July 12 must clearly be awarded, said the appellants. That adjournment was necessary because of the late submission of several complicated productions by the council.

For the regional council it was argued that the claim for expenses was misconceived. The appellants had not attended the inquiry and had therefore been put to no expense. Expenses could not be awarded to the owners of the appeal site and premises, who had borne the expenses of the inquiry, because they were not the appellants. In dealing with the application for planning permission and the appeal, the council had not acted unreasonably, frivolously or vexatiously. The questions of adjacency and impact upon the existing town centre of Grangemouth were proper reasons for the refusal of planning permission and had always been in the forefront of the case for the council.

The council accepted that some of its productions had been submitted late. However, some of the appellants' productions had also been submitted less than 10 days before the opening of the inquiry. Furthermore, as the appellants' consultants had indicated in their letter of September 9, 1987 that they would carry out their own impact study, they should not have been surprised by the submission by the council of its own impact study. That study was merely a refinement of data given to the consultants in January 1988. For these reasons the council had opposed the adjournment requested by the appellants on June 14, 1988. If the appellants could not understand the contents of the council's late productions during the first morning of the inquiry, evidence could have been led on other matters, thus giving the appellants more time to study those documents. The council therefore opposed the award of expenses because the claim was incompetent and fundamentally misconceived.

The reporter concluded that although it might have been possible to have proceeded to hear other evidence on the opening morning of the inquiry, as consideration of the late productions occupied a considerable part of the council's case, he doubted whether the time taken to hear evidence on the other matters would have been sufficiently long to allow the appellants, or their advisers, to have understood the implications of the late productions. This opinion was supported by the difficulties encountered by their main planning witness in understanding the productions even with the assistance of officials of the regional council during adjournments on the opening morning of the inquiry.

In any case, the essential point was that some of the productions of the regional council were submitted only three days—and arguably only one working day—before the opening of the inquiry. In such circumstances, and taking into account the complicated nature of the statistical data, and the numerous adjustments which were applied to it, the reporter considered that the appellants were entitled to ask for an adjournment of the inquiry in order that they could read and understand the late productions. For these reasons the reporter was firmly of the opinion that the extra costs attributable to the adjournment of the inquiry during the afternoon of June 14, 1988, incurred by the appellants or their representatives should be awarded to the appellants or their representatives.

On the second issue the reporter could understand the frustration of the appellants' consultants in attempting to obtain information from the council or to meet specific officers of the council. Nevertheless, because of other commitments it was not always possible to meet the official of one's choice. Furthermore, it seemed clear to the reporter, from the reasons given for the refusal of planning permission, that the case presented by the regional council would involve the questions of adjacency to and the impact of the proposal upon the existing town centre of Grangemouth. In that event and bearing in mind that the applicants had already lodged an appeal against the refusal of planning permission it seemed unreasonable firstly for the appellants to obtain survey data from the council without supplying the council with similar types of information, and secondly for the council to agree to hold detailed discussions with the developers which might have developed into a small-scale inquiry.

Indeed, even when the council had provided the data in January 1988 the appellants' consultants did not use this, together with such additional information as they considered necessary, to calculate their own assessment of the impact of the appeal proposal upon existing shops. For these reasons the reporter saw no reason for awarding the expenses of the remainder of the inquiry against the council. The Secretary of State accepted the reporter's recommendations. (Ref. P/PPA/CB/142, May 10, 1989.)

11.14 Expenses—inquiry largely unnecessary

At the close of an inquiry Shetland Islands Council asked that expenses be awarded against the appellant. The reason was that the council considered that the appeal against disputed conditions was superfluous because the council had already issued a further planning permission for the part of the site remaining to be worked, containing revised conditions that had not been disputed. The only remaining issue was the restoration of the area that had already been worked.

In opposing this motion for expenses the appellant's agent stated that the day of evidence devoted to the discussion of the appealed conditions had revealed that there were still areas of dispute. These were the distance to be safeguarded on the north side of the burial ground, and the clarification of the standard of agricultural restoration that was expected.

The reporter said that it could be seen that the questions of after-use and after-care were interrelated. The Islands Council had already stated in their observations that the restoration of the land covered by the 1984 permission should be to a standard adequate to provide grazing for livestock, and that the 1987 aftercare details would be accepted in place of the 1984 requirements. Little further illumination of this matter was required at the public inquiry. The reporter considered that the clarification of the revised after-use and after-care details could have been achieved by an exchange of correspondence between the parties, rather than having to be rubber-stamped by an appeal decision.

Regarding the cemetery safeguarding area, there was some variation in the distance required by the Islands Council, but the appellant was prepared to accept whatever was necessary. The reporter considered that, thanks to that cooperative attitude, it was not necessary for the matter to come to inquiry to be resolved.

Regarding the depth of working and site drainage, the appellant was content to accept the 1987 conditions in place of the 1984 conditions. Accordingly it was not necessary to hear evidence on these matters at the public inquiry.

The reporter concluded that only one of the six matters discussed at the inquiry represented a continuing area of dispute between the council and the appellant. The other five matters were not the subject of continuing dispute, and did not require to be resolved at the inquiry. It was therefore largely unnecessary to hold an inquiry into these matters.

For these reasons the reporter recommended that Shetland Islands Council be reimbursed for two-thirds of their expenses. The Secretary of State accepted that recommendation. (Ref. P/PPA/Z/22, May 23, 1989.)

11.15 Expenses—public inquiry—circumstances of award

An application for expenses was submitted by the appellants. The Secretary of State said that the normal practice was for the parties to bear the expenses which they themselves incurred unless one party could be shown to have acted unreasonably, vexatiously or frivolously. In this case the reporter had criticised the planning authority's handling of consultations with the appellants. If the procedure amounted to maladministration a complaint could be made to the Commissioner for Local Administration. The Minister saw, however, no reason to regard the behaviour of the planning authority at the inquiry as falling within one of the categories justifying an award of expenses. (Ref. P/PPA/AL/183, December 12, 1976.)

11.16 Expenses—publicity—conduct of parties

It had been proposed to alter factory premises. Planning permission was refused because the process was likely to be detrimental to amenity through noise and fumes. The planning authority believed that stove-enamelling was proposed since that was shown on the submitted plan, though not mentioned in the application. It was agreed by both the appellants and the planning authority that the development should have been advertised as "bad neighbour" development under section 23 of the 1972 Act. A public inquiry was held but the Secretary of State took the view that both the application and the decision were defective and the appeal was therefore dismissed.

The appellants sought expenses in connection with the inquiry. They alleged that the planning authority had misled them in negotiations relating to the application. However, no evidence was produced to support the claim that the appellants' representatives had been misled. The Secretary of State accepted that the Council's handling of the application "fell short of what would normally be expected" in that doubts about the applicability of section 23 and about the exact nature of the proposal should have been resolved. On the other hand, the appellants omitted to produce the section 23 documents which they admitted at the inquiry were necessary. Also, the application form, as submitted, did not fully describe the proposed development, and the statement on the form that no change of use was involved was unfortunate, contrary to the submitted plans and, as it turned out, misleading in view of the council's *prima facie* treatment of the application. The decision letter stated: "In all the circumstances the view is taken that both parties contributed to the difficulties which have arisen and it is considered unfortunate that it required a public inquiry held at the appellants' own request, to clarify the position and to clear the way for a fresh application." Expenses were not therefore awarded. (Ref. P/PPA/SU/68, October 23, 1980.)

11.17 Expenses—decision on planning application

This was an application for expenses by the appellant against the planning authority. Having regard to the evidence submitted, the reporter considered whether the authority had acted unreasonably, vexatiously or frivolously. The reporter thought that the planning authority's decision on the application was, on the evidence and opinions before them, an unreasonable one bordering on the frivolous. However, the Secretary of State considered that there was no evidence that the authority's decision, albeit contrary to the views of their planning officer, of the regional council and of the river purification authority, had been taken for any reason other than a genuine concern for the amenity of the district. The Minister took the view that the district council were entitled to take the decision and that their natural concern about a potential increase in pollution and the effect of that pollution on the district's environment did not amount to unreasonable, vexatious or frivolous behaviour. The Secretary of State therefore decided that no award of expenses was justified. (Ref. P/PPA/TA/30, October 7, 1980.)

11.18 Expenses—Secretary of State—"call in"

The Secretary of State had "called in" for decision by himself an application for residential development on a site extending to 4.168 hectares. The Minister had called in the application because he considered that the proposal raised an issue of national importance in that it involved the development of an area of prime quality agricultural land. If the proposal were approved it might create a precedent for the development of other high quality agricultural land in the immediate vicinity. The reporter recommended that planning permission be granted and that recommendation was accepted by the Secretary of State.

At the close of the inquiry the appellants, the regional council and the district council all made application for an award of expenses against the Secretary of State on the grounds that he had acted unreasonably or frivolously in "calling in" the application and causing a public inquiry to be held and in giving less than thorough consideration to the question of whether a national issue was involved. This had led, in the view of the appellants and the council, to a waste of time and money for the parties concerned. The reporter pointed out that the National Planning Guidelines indicated that where development requiring more than 5 hectares of prime quality agricultural land was against the advice of the Department of Agriculture and Fisheries for Scotland, there was, *prima facie*, a conflict with national agricultural policy. The reporter also considered that it was not unreasonable for the Minister to take the view that a larger area than the 4.168 hectare site was threatened by this particular proposal. The reporter took the view that there were weaknesses in the Scottish Office case and its presentation. He said it was unfortunate that neither DAFS nor SDD was able or had seen fit to present to the inquiry a clear picture of the national position regarding agricultural land or how the application site related to that position. He had therefore found the available evidence inconclusive. However, the reporter did not consider that the weakness of the Scottish Office case or its presentation constituted unreasonable or frivolous action.

The Secretary of State was unable to accept that he had acted in any way unreasonably or frivolously and considered that only by holding an inquiry could he obtain all the information necessary to allow him to reach a reasoned decision on the application. He therefore saw no case for making an award of expenses. (Ref. P/PP/70/FB/4, May 14, 1980.)

11.19 Expenses—public inquiry

At the end of a public inquiry into a refusal of planning permission for the erection of four houses, the appellant made a claim for expenses. In his report the reporter noted that the appellant's solicitor had stated that his client had requested that the appeal be dealt with by written submissions, that there was little public interest in the appeal and that written submissions would have sufficed. The planning authority argued that they were fully entitled to opt for a public inquiry and that at no stage during the inquiry did they act unreasonably or vexatiously.

The Secretary of State's decision letter said that the normal practice in planning appeal inquiries was for the parties to bear the expenses which they themselves incurred unless one party could be shown to have acted unreasonably, vexatiously or frivolously. In considering if an award of expenses should be made on the ground of unreasonable behaviour, the main criterion was whether one party had been put to unnecessary or unreasonable expense (a) because the matter should never have come to inquiry or (b) because, although the inquiry could not reasonably have been avoided, the other party conducted his side of the procedure in such a way as to cause trouble and expense. The reporter recommended that there should be no award of expenses. The Secretary of State accepted the reporter's recommendation. (Ref. P/PPA/SH/109, September 1, 1988.)

INDEX